KOREAN SHOWDOWN

For Desrae

The University of Alabama Press
Tuscaloosa, Alabama 35487-0380
uapress.ua.edu

Typeface: Minion, Hiragino Kaku Gothic and Yu Gothic UI

Cover image: A gun crew of the 88th Field Artillery, ROK Army, fires a 155-mm
howitzer at Communist positions during action against the Chinese Communist
forces in the Shanghi Heights Area, west of Chorwon, 30 October 1952, Korea;
Signal Corps Photo #1-5219-14/FEC-52-32234 (Fisk), U.S. Army Center of
Military History
Cover design: Michele Myatt Quinn

Cataloging-in-Publication data is available from the Library of Congress.
ISBN: 978-0-8173-2073-7
E-ISBN: 978-0-8173-9329-8

‖ KOREAN ‖
SHOWDOWN

NATIONAL POLICY AND MILITARY
STRATEGY IN A LIMITED WAR,
1951–1952

BRYAN R. GIBBY

The University of Alabama Press   Tuscaloosa

CONTENTS

ILLUSTRATIONS

FIGURES

TABLES

PREFACE

THE KOREAN WAR has not yet ended. Only the fighting stopped; the confrontation continues. After two full years of acrimonious dialogue, the military commanders of the three major belligerents—the American Commander in Chief of the United States–led United Nations Command (a coalition of sixteen combatant nations along with the Republic of Korea), the Supreme Commander of the Korean People's Army of the Democratic People's Republic of Korea, and the Commander of the Chinese People's Volunteers—signed an armistice that froze the military line of contact as a boundary between the two Koreas.

The middle twelve months of the "acrimonious dialogue" that eventually terminated the conflict compose the "lost year" of a seemingly forgotten war. The only full fighting year, when both sides squared off for political leverage through military action, was 1952. Neither the United Nations Command (UNC) nor the Communist coalition of North Korea and the People's Republic of China (PRC) found a military solution to their negotiated deadlock. Yet, this important period of time is usually glossed over in favor of the drama of negotiations, the air war over MiG Alley, or the impact of propaganda warfare in the form of prisoner of war riots and germ warfare allegations. This work seeks to understand the burdens of the military men, generals to privates, who fought, argued, and did their best to accomplish their nation's political objectives with limited military means and authorities, and even though these efforts failed, they were essential trials for both sides to find eventually a workable solution to their antagonistic negotiated positions.

The Korean War's incomplete termination has been the source of great tension over the past six decades. Its destructiveness seared the psyche of the Asian nations most directly affected. For most Americans the unsatisfactory conflict remains captive somewhere between the triumph of an Allied unconditional victory in World War II and a Vietnam quagmire. This book is the story of how the Korean War came to occupy such an ambiguous position in the American collective memory. Because the war was *limited* both in scope and scale, political concerns tended to carry more weight in the policy and strategic decisions that informed the actual fighting in Korea. Indeed, the thesis of this work is that policy decisions on both sides caused the war to last much longer than was militarily justified and produced a lasting hostility between the two Koreas and a sense of bitterness among those who fought in the war. There is little triumphalism among Korean War veterans—they fought because their countries made them. Initial fervor and righteous feeling petered out in the stalemated battles of trench, patrol, and raid. It was a miserable war that defied the logic of straightforward application of military power.

The effort required to produce this book forced me to call on the assistance of many supporters, friends, and valued colleagues. I am especially indebted to the General Omar N. Bradley Foundation and Fellowship for a generous grant in 2012 that funded research trips to archives in Charleston, South Carolina; Washington, DC; and Carlisle, Pennsylvania. At these facilities I benefited from the patient expertise of Dwight Walsh (Citadel Archives and Museum), Eric S. Van Slander (National Archives and Records Administration), and Richard Baker (US Army Heritage and Education Center). James Tobias and Lauren "Alexis" Hammersen, librarians at the US Army Center of Military History went well beyond the call of duty to locate journal articles, historical reports, and other sources. Dr. William M. Donnelly, also of the US Army Center of Military History, shared his many insights into General James A. Van Fleet's war. Dr. Donnelly provided me with several valuable sources showing the inner workings of the Second Infantry Division fighting at Old Baldy in the summer of 1952. Additionally, along with Dr. Donald W. Boose Jr. (US Army War College), Dr. Donnelly read and commented on the entire manuscript. These two scholars' friendly critiques helped me correct errors of fact or interpretation. Any subsequent missteps remain my responsibility.

I am especially indebted to Anthony Sobieski and Norman Isler. Anthony is the author or editor of three Korean War books: *A Hill Called White Horse*, *Fire Mission!*, and *Fire for Effect*. He kindly granted permission for extended quotations from his works. He also read the entire manuscript and provided valuable criticism. Norman Isler served in the 430th Engineer Construction Battalion from 1952 to 1953. Norm's unit was one of the first to respond to the Koje-do riots in the summer of 1952. He generously shared his recollections and memorabilia, both official and personal, including beautiful color photographs from his tour of duty.

Dr. Allan R. Millett, Ambrose Professor of History and Director of the Eisenhower Center for American Studies, deserves special recognition as my former dissertation advisor and current mentor, colleague, and friend. His enthusiasm brought me into the Korean War, and his continuing support has kept me there. This work would not have been possible without his encouragement and productive criticism. Dr. Millett provided me with useful sources from his own collection of Korean War documents and, most valuably, shared a copy of "The Unforgotten Korean War," a monograph produced by the Office of Net Assessment, Office of the Secretary of Defense. This English-language history was written by a team of retired People's Liberation Army (PLA) officers and historians associated with the PLA Academy of Military Science in Beijing, and it contains a tremendous amount of operational detail and analysis of command decisions. This examination of "the other side" permits better analysis and evaluation of American, Korean, and Chinese strategy and tactics.

Professor Xiaobing Li, of the University of Central Oklahoma, graciously provided me with critical material from Chinese sources, along with translations. He also helped me to understand better the Chinese policy and military decision-making that led to the battles at White Horse Mountain and Shangganling in the fall of 1952. Dr. Jiyul Kim (Colonel, US Army, retired) performed a similar service with South Korean sources regarding the training state of the North Korean army prior to the conventional war. I am deeply indebted to their selfless collaboration and assistance.

Jeff Goldberg, cartographer for the Department of History at the United States Military Academy, West Point, New York, designed the peninsula maps for chapter 2. The Department of History has graciously permitted these maps to be published in this work.

Chapters 11 and 12 are revised versions of articles previously published respectively by the *Army History Bulletin* (US Army Center of Military History) and the *Journal of Chinese Military History* (Koninklijke Brill NV).

I am very grateful to the editorial staff at the University of Alabama Press: Dan Waterman, Jon Berry, Dawn Hall, and many others who plied their talent on my behalf. This work has benefited greatly from their professional advice and encouragement.

The views expressed in this work are my own and do not reflect those of the US government or the United States Military Academy. Errors of fact or interpretation remain my responsibility.

Finally, I acknowledge my most important debts to my wife and family. Desrae has patiently tolerated a two-decades-long attachment to the Korean War. She and our children Paul, Peter, and Parker accompanied me to the land of the morning calm when I was stationed in Korea from 1998 to 2000. Since then, even as our army life has taken us around the world, the family has grown to include Preston, Patricia, and Patterson. I can't imagine life without Desrae or my children—brave, intelligent, and loving.

NOTE ON TRANSLITERATION AND UNIT DESIGNATIONS

KOREAN PROPER NOUNS follow a simplified McCune-Reischauer system that omits diacritical marks and was used by American military and civilian officials during the Korean War. Personal names are rendered with the family name first. However, Syngman Rhee remains the exception based on historical usage.

Chinese names follow the modern Pinyin system: Mao Zedong instead of the Wade-Giles form Mao Tse-tung. However, Chiang Kai-shek is preferred over Jiang Jieshi.

All military unit designations are US unless otherwise noted or made clear through context.

INTRODUCTION

Operation Clam Up

THE 38TH PARALLEL (north) seemed a logical place to stop the fighting. So, shortly after the war's one-year anniversary, both sides entered into negotiations to establish a cease-fire agreement as a prelude to resolve the problem of Korean unification. The date was July 10, 1951.

It had been a tough fight for the four armies involved: two Korean, one Chinese, and one representing the United Nations (UN) led by the United States (US). However, the confident hopes of a quick military settlement were soon dashed. Both sides had unrealistic expectations of what they could demand of each other. Bound by "beliefs, values, education, historical consciousness, and mindset" that influenced their bargaining style and conditioned the initial results, both sides remained six months later as before: digging in, facing off, and trading shots across the width of the peninsula.[1] Negotiations had produced a stalemate, not a settlement. After a brief spell of sharp fighting between late August and early November 1951, both sides agreed on November 27, 1951, that the current line of contact would become the *actual* demarcation line if an armistice was agreed to within thirty days. Naturally, both sides became cautious and defensively oriented, soldiers leery of being the last man to die in Korea for ground that would be given up anyway.

But at the end of 1951, commanders and soldiers alike realized the cruel trick that had been played on them. No armistice was agreed to. The war would go on, but the Communists had used the de facto thirty-day cease-fire to good effect. They dug deep into the blasted hills, turning naturally strong terrain into a series of interconnected and nearly impregnable fortresses. They also worked hard to shore up their logistical position by stockpiling ammunition, resting and rotating units, and training for offensive action using new tactics. It was not going to be easy to restart the war.

Four days after the bogus truce expired, the American Eighth United States Army Korea (EUSAK, hereafter referred to as Eighth Army) came to life. At Lt. Gen. James A. Van Fleet's direction (Van Fleet was the third and longest-serving of Eighth Army's four wartime commanders), at one minute after midnight on January 1, every infantry, tank, and artillery gun opened up with a tremendous army-wide "Time on Target (TOT)," wishing the communist forces a not-so-happy New Year. Although the gunnery display may have lifted morale, cold soldiers soon had equally cold hopes.[2] Later in the month Van Fleet tried Operation Highboy, a coordinated air and artillery bombardment lasting four days. Heavy artillery and tanks fired directly at bunkers and other fortifications that were impervious to ordinary artillery and mortar fire. Van Fleet noted some progress in reducing enemy fortifications located on the steep mountain slopes, but the basic problem of prying the enemy out of the hills, or provoking new flexibility at the truce talks, remained unsolved. Despite these efforts and extensive patrols, the Communists rode out the storm as efforts to generate offensive momentum went nowhere.

The next experiment was perhaps the most intriguing of the war. Simplistically, it reflected the extreme lengths that Eighth Army staff and commanders were willing to go to find something, anything, to break the logjam along the front. Although uncomplicated, the plan known as Operation Clam Up was difficult to execute. It was designed to confuse the Communists and lead them to lower their guard and become vulnerable to US firepower. It had no chance for anything other than local success, but Van Fleet was desperate. Beginning on February 10 and lasting five days, Eighth Army dispatched no patrols, no artillery was fired, and no air attacks were permitted within twenty thousand yards of the front line.

This change of tactics was supposed to arouse the enemy's curiosity and lead him to unwisely expose his troops. The Chinese and North Koreans were not fooled, and they used the period to strengthen already strong defensive positions and bring up supplies. At the end of five days, it was back to the real war, and when the Eighth Army resumed full-scale patrolling at the end of the month, only a few prisoners were taken. The US army's official history laconically judged the success of Clam Up, stating, "The stratagem was not repeated."[3]

By the end of February 1952 both sides were better defended, more experienced, more hardened. Prospects for significant movements by either side seemed slim indeed. Little did either side know the spring, summer, and fall campaigns would be hard fought and disappointing to those desiring to bring the seemingly unending war in Korea to an end.[4]

ABBREVIATIONS

AA	Antiaircraft
APS	Air Pressure Strategy
CAM	Citadel Archives and Museum, Charleston, South Carolina
CB	Counterbattery
CEP	Circular Error Probability
CI	Civilian Internees
CMC	Central Military Commission
COMINT	Communications Intelligence
CPVF	Chinese People's Volunteer Forces
DMZ	Demilitarized Zone
EUSAK	Eighth United States Army Korea
FAG	Field Artillery Group
FEAF	Far East Air Forces
FEC	Far East Command
FO	Forward Observer
FRUS	*Foreign Relations of the United States*
GCMLA	George C. Marshall Library and Archives, Lexington, Virginia
GI	Government Issue (American soldier)
IG	Inspector General
JCS	Joint Chief/s of Staff
JOC	Joint Operations Center
KIA	Killed in Action
KIMH, *KW*	Korea Institute of Military History, *The Korean War*
KMAG	Korean Military Advisory Group
KPA	(North) Korean People's Army

KSC	Korean Service Corps
LLI	Low Level Intercept
MDL	Military Demarcation Line
MIA	Missing in Action
MLR	Main Line of Resistance
mm	millimeter
NARA II	National Archives and Records Administration, College Park, Maryland
NNSC	Neutral Nations Supervisory Commission
NSC	National Security Council
OP	Observation Post
OPLR	Outpost Line of Resistance
PG	Prisoner Guard
PLA	People's Liberation Army
PLAAF	People's Liberation Army Air Force
POW	Prisoner of War
PRC	People's Republic of China
RIP	Rail Interdiction Plan
ROK	Republic of (South) Korea
TACP	Tactical Air Control Party
TOT	Time on Target
TRP	Target Reference Point
UN	United Nations
UNC	United Nations Command
US	United States
USACMH	United States Army Center of Military History, Fort Leslie J. McNair, Washington, DC
USAF	United States Air Force
USAHEC	United States Army Heritage and Education Center, Carlisle, Pennsylvania
VT	Variable Time
WIA	Wounded in Action

KOREAN SHOWDOWN

1

THE LIMITED WAR PROBLEM

AFTER GENERAL MARK CLARK affixed his signature to the Korean War armistice on July 27, 1953, he reflected, "In carrying out the instructions of my government, I gained the unenviable distinction of being the first United States Army commander in history to sign an armistice without victory." His frustration was shared by others who felt that the war's conclusion did not signal an era of peace but rather a "heading of unfinished business."[1]

This story of the Korean War covers the period of the conflict when American army commanders "carrying out the instructions" of their government grappled with a complex confrontation that appeared immune to the traditional applications of force that had served the Allied forces well during the recently concluded global war against Germany, Italy, and Japan. Although the Korean conflict began in a conventional fashion with dramatic strategic movements down and up the peninsula, just twelve months later both sides had agreed to settle the war by negotiation instead of military victory. The first eighteen months (June 1950–December 1951) of the war were full of surprises, but the biggest were reserved for 1952.

The war's conduct caused major changes in US national security policy and military strategy, not least of which was a rearming for a Cold War against Soviet Communism that appeared indefinite and geographically unrestricted. It created a lasting though ambiguous impact on American defense force structure, doctrine, and sense of its utility in a world bifurcated between a capitalist "West" and Communist "East." Beyond the death and destruction of the war itself, Harry S. Truman's presidency was also shattered. Constraints the American government placed on itself to limit the war backfired in the battle for public opinion, leading a confused electorate to castigate Truman's conduct of the war, his prioritization of Western Europe over Asia, and his management of American strategy making. By 1952, he was the least popular president since Andrew Johnson.[2] Right or wrong, Truman has been held accountable for American surprise at the outbreak of the war and Communist Chinese intervention just as the war appeared to be won. He was also heavily criticized for firing Gen. Douglas MacArthur and blamed for the bloody and seemingly useless stalemate once the two sides settled down to negotiate an end to the war.

The real surprise over the North Korean invasion was not that it occurred but that the US government reversed its own policy of expecting the South Koreans to defend themselves. Instead, the Truman administration quickly formed a United Nations coalition to prosecute a war for South Korea—a war that endured several policy evolutions as to its political objectives, military strategy, and acceptable outcome. As one American commentator observed, "This was not a case of failing to understand the enemy. It was, instead, a case of failing to understand ourselves."[3] There were more surprises coming: the wild success of the Inchon amphibious invasion, the stunning Chinese intervention, and the interminable truce negotiations that began on July 10, 1951. Truman's so-called police action was a real war costly in terms of both men and material.[4]

The American president's controversial decision in February 1952 to take a hard and ideologically driven stance on prisoner of war (POW) repatriation, and not to repatriate forcibly communist POWs, as required by the Geneva Convention of 1949, made Korea a miserable war that appeared to grind on without end. Because POW repatriation was the final issue of substance blocking a truce agreement, this policy represented a true strategic bombshell that flummoxed military men from both sides who tried to end the conflict by both talking and fighting. Although employing the rhetoric of humanity, Truman had expanded his war aims (again) and stubbornly insisted that UN military strength impose American will on the Communists. In his memoirs, Truman reveals contradictory policy objectives as he sketches (and justifies) his own evolution as a wartime president intent on redressing what he perceived as a geopolitical moral imbalance. His war policy moved from the territorially oriented, and militarily limited, goal to reestablish and ensure the physical integrity of the Republic of Korea at a defensible line to a psychological and universal one, meant to drive a stake into the heart of international communism.[5]

In this context it is important to note that Truman made all policy choices outside traditional and wartime-tested processes. American congressional and military leaders were consulted, but ultimately the buck stopped with the president: intervention, expansion of the war north of the 38th parallel, negotiation to settle the war, and the demand for the Communists to accept voluntary repatriation of prisoners of war were all presidential directives to prosecute the war. This last decision, which was generally opposed by his military advisors, was not clearly articulated until seven months *after* negotiations to end the war had begun, and it was the crucial policy decision that suddenly and unexpectedly reset the ideological dimensions to the conflict and redefined the war's political object for *both sides*. Both sides struggled throughout 1952 with the strategic problem of determining the proper military objectives and applying adequate military means that could compel a satisfactory political settlement in this new kind of war.

The irony of peacemaking in Korea was that an armistice could have been agreed to as early as May 2, 1952. Perhaps even earlier than that; February or March were not inconceivable end points. Why then did the war take such a long time to settle? Or, more precisely, why did it take the two sides so long to get to their final respective positions on the repatriation of prisoners of war? This question formed the political basis for continued fighting until July 27, 1953. And finally, what military and political pressures did each side use to coerce the other, and why was neither side successful at imposing its will on its adversary?

These questions are examined here as they relate to the conduct of the war and negotiations through December 1952. The US military adapted to fight a long war in Korea—the secondary theater in the larger and even lengthier Cold War—limited by the expectation of a negotiated end to the fighting. Therefore, survivability, strategic sustainability, and coercive limited-objective operations displaced more traditional approaches of maneuver and firepower that had dominated the war's first year. For their part, the Communists in general, and the Chinese in particular, adapted to modern war conditions, successfully evolving from a light and mobile guerrilla-based army to one capable of fighting independently and in support of the Communists' negotiation objectives. These negotiations were a way to achieve an end, not an end in themselves, and the Chinese People's Volunteer Force's (CPVF) adopted strategies of persistence and military modernization to help them resist the Americans' coercive approach.[6]

The decision to settle the war through truce talks, without a clear battlefield victory, compelled both sides to fight a double war, one at the front and in the air, and one at the negotiation table. Further, these wars were interconnected as negotiation posturing and combat operations affected each other.[7] It was a cruel dilemma. Both sides would expend prodigious resources—bombs, bullets, shells, words, images, lives—to convince the other to give in on a variety of issues that seemed arcane to soldiers and civilians alike. Truman's tardy decision to reject forcible repatriation of Communist POWs, though lauded as a moral stand against Communist aggression, set an extremely high bar for peacemaking and did little to increase popular understanding for a war that seemed to be without end.[8]

For the Americans, decreasing domestic support increased the stakes and the risks of even minor tactical actions and produced a stasis on the battle-field that was both costly and indecisive. Beginning in the summer of 1952, Communist armies became much more active, compelling Eighth Army to fight territorially insignificant engagements for political, tactical, and psychological reasons. Politically, allowing the Communists to erode the UNC's outpost line strengthened their hand at negotiations. Tactically, the cumulative loss of outposts allowed the Communist armies to press Eighth Army's Main Line of Resistance (MLR) and give them an important advantage in the war of posts. Psychologically, Van Fleet feared that a failure to respond to Communist probes would completely cede the initiative to the enemy and undermine the will to win among his soldiers. American commanders could never be sure the Communists might not try one more major effort to win the war or change the military balance so fundamentally that the UNC negotiation position would be fatally compromised.[9] One thoughtful American regimental commander summed up the policy-strategy puzzle: "Without authority and ample resources to achieve [military] victory, Eighth Army could be kept tied down indefinitely in a war of attrition by the imaginative employment of the 1,200,000 Chinese in Korea and their 2,000 MiG-15 aircraft based on the Yalu [River]."[10]

From the Communist perspective, the truce talks prevented a military collapse and shifted the battle for Korea to the political arena—in their view, "negotiation was also fighting."[11] But this dimension of the conflict did not provide Mao Zedong and Kim Il-sung the opportunity for victory they craved because they could not possibly work out a truce without reference to the battlefield, as the two efforts were interrelated. In fact, the process of negotiation worked against the Communists, though the Americans would have disagreed. The Communist negotiators put up a good fight, and they scored some impressive propaganda victories to preserve their battlefield gains. They could even wrangle some concessions that produced tactical benefits for their troops in the field. But these victories were ephemeral, for the Communists could not leverage their military strength on the ground to compel the UNC to yield on the substantive issues of the final demarcation line, withdrawal of foreign troops, and the voluntary repatriation of prisoners of war, all of which were key political objectives for Mao and his revolutionary regime.[12]

Despite this failure at the war's political level, the Chinese intervention is remembered as a great victory for the CPVF, but very little is known about how the CPVF actually confronted the UNC to win that victory. Xiaobing Li documents Mao's decision to confront the United States in Korea as a brilliant gamble, for his army gained valuable experience in modern battle, much technologically advanced equipment such as artillery and jet aircraft from the Soviet Union, and tremendous stature by beating—then holding—the American army to a strategic draw.[13] Chinese operations seeking to annihilate UNC and Republic of Korea (ROK) forces evolved into a sophisticated strategy of persistence that substantially preserved China's military objectives and endowed Mao with immense national and international prestige. However, less is understood about Chinese and North Korean operations after the Fifth Campaign ended Mao's dream of a military victory.[14]

Forty years after the armistice agreement, a hint of Chinese historiography emerged from Yan Zu of the National Defense University in Beijing. Thanks to "brave and indomitable fighting spirit" of the soldiers and the "flexible strategies and tactics" of its commanders, the war "turned out to be the most splendid performance of China's military forces in all of her foreign wars during the past centuries."[15] After June 1951, fighting in Korea settled into a military impasse that contrasted with the dynamically mobile first year of the war. It was a different kind of war for Mao's guerrilla veterans. Mao and his field commander, Peng Dehuai, recognized that the CPVF had to find a way to neutralize UNC firepower and mobility. The result was a new tactical system to integrate artillery firepower with focused assaults against individual enemy positions, greater Soviet material support, and a significant logistics effort to ensure the CPVF long-term viability as a field force. Many historians delve into the gritty months of maneuver and battles of encirclement following the Chinese intervention in October 1950, but after July 1951 the primary focus tends to settle on the wandering progress of truce negotiations. It is rare to find a thorough analysis of military operations, a history that is almost lost. But there was still much fighting: Old Baldy, White Horse Mountain, Operations Counter and Creeper, the Autumn Counterattack Campaign, and Operation Showdown. Here is where the CPVF excelled. From the individual riflemen to the senior negotiators at Kaesong and Panmunjom, the Chinese led their own coalition to confront the UNC with a variety of supple tactics and adaptive operational approaches to counter their disadvantages in firepower and technology.[16]

The UNC air campaigns in support of the theater commander's military objectives are also typically shortchanged and treated in isolation. It is one matter to control the airspace over a battlefield; it is another to convert that control into military pressure that produces real effects on the ground. The Chinese reliance on positional war that evolved in the summer of 1951 helped it defy American ground pressure, but it opened another vulnerability. Because positional war ultimately regresses into a contest of logistics, the challenge for air superiority assumed greater importance once the two sides settled down into fortified MLR. Airpower became an increasingly important component in the UNC's attrition strategy by inflicting casualties and destroying military assets without exposing its ground combat forces to the enemy's attritional power.[17] Led by the American Far East Air Forces (comprising the US Fifth Air Force, Far East Bomber Command, and other numbered air forces that did not participate in the Korean War), UNC air forces launched several campaigns to choke off or impede the flow of Communist supplies from factories in Manchuria and the Soviet Union. However, Korea was a problematic case for interdiction, and conventional airpower's effectiveness as a coercive instrument supporting negotiated policy objectives proved elusive. After several months of strenuous effort, UNC airmen realized what quietly was known during World War II: interdiction harassed, hurt, and impeded the enemy, but it did not by itself generate critical results on the ground fighting. Crucially, the air force simply did not have the means. The United States could not (and under the demands of the greater confrontation with the Soviet Union in Europe would not) devote the numbers of aircraft, air crews, and ordnance (to include atomic bombs) required to cut the Communist armies off from their sources of supply. But that did not prevent the Americans from trying, and the story of the eighteen-month battle is spectacular in its own right.[18] That these efforts generally failed does not make them unimportant. To the contrary, as this book argues, these military operations were extremely important to the course and conduct of the war, eventually determining the shape of the final armistice agreement.

Therefore, 1952 was the critical year of the war. Both sides made major military and propaganda efforts to tilt the balance toward their respective strategic designs. During the first six months of the year, the UNC wiped out remnants of guerrilla units in southwestern Korea, accomplished POW screening (despite strenuous Communist objections) and crushed POW revolts at Koje Island, dramatically increased air pressure against North Korean infrastructure targets, and developed a more aggressive posture on the ground, seizing several additional outposts west of the Chorwon valley to include three hilltops (Hills 266, 255, and 395) that would later be immortalized respectively as Old Baldy, Porkchop, and White Horse. The Communists responded with their own verbal offensives to exploit the UNC's mastery of the skies, mishandling of the POW crisis, and the bombing of hydroelectric power stations along the Yalu River. While these propaganda efforts produced political problems for the UNC, they never translated into concrete military advantages for the Communists. It was this reality that provoked Mao (by mid-1952, Kim Il-sung's once vaunted army was a shell, still tenacious in defense but not very useful in offensive operations) to authorize a fall campaign to try to break the Americans' lock on the negotiation process, for the Communists were still losing at negotiations, along the front lines, and also in the air. Although the Chinese and North Koreans could and did stubbornly resist ground attacks and kill American and allied soldiers in uncomfortably large numbers, they could not inflict unsupportable casualties. More importantly, they could not prevent the Eighth Army from grinding forward, however slowly. Mao and Kim were willing to expend men. They were not willing to give up more ground. Until a tactical method and operational approach could be found that would allow the Communists to demonstrate military parity, a negotiated truce would never look like a victory.[19]

Under these conditions, the war was going to have to be won, or settled, on the ground. One of the heaviest of these trench battles, and the climactic contest for the year, took place from October 13 to November 25 at two small and seemingly insignificant features called "Triangle Hill" and "Sniper Ridge." Both were proximate to the strategically significant region known as the "Iron Triangle." The Chinese know this battle as "Shangganling," which shortly after the war was depicted in a famous Chinese film, *The Battle on Shangganling Mountain* (1956). American commanders planned Operation Showdown as a limited offensive to counter the Chinese limited-offensive campaign begun in mid-September. Throughout forty-five grueling days of battle the Chinese defenders endured constant air and artillery bombardment along with determined ground assaults by the Seventh Infantry Division and the ROK Second Division. The Chinese accepted the challenge and committed three divisions in a seesaw battle of attrition. It was the most concentrated bloodletting of the year, with US-ROK casualties topping eight thousand and the Chinese acknowledging nearly sixteen thousand killed, missing, and wounded. The CPVF claimed victory, which it was, but it did not change anything at the strategic level, and this was the battle's most important contribution to the war's outcome.

Therefore, although not on the scale of fighting seen in early 1951, the fall campaigns of 1952 were bloody enough, and they were also decisive, but not as the combatants would have wished. The Chinese army's demonstration of will and competence at last put the truce negotiations in a mutually acceptable context. Instead of breaking the military equilibrium, the Chinese offensive and American counteroffensive solidified it. Both sides saw clearly that military action alone without a substantial increase in military power would never produce a strategically decisive result. Victory, or even a settlement, would have to be found by other means.

In this context of multiple turning points and fragile military balances, Truman's decision to insist on voluntary repatriation should be seen as having profound consequences, for it was not intended to end or even shorten the war. On the contrary, the American policy to seek a settlement that guaranteed voluntary repatriation was sure to *extend* the war, as it did for a period of seventeen months. It committed the American military command in Asia to fight with limited means for an objective that had potentially existential implications in the larger conflict against Communism. It also underscored the vital condition of limited war. Policy objectives matter. Political decisions always have military significance. The story that follows is about how the American, Korean, and Chinese fighting forces dealt with those consequences and why it proved so difficult to reach a settlement that all sides could live with.

2

THE KOREAN WAR, JULY 1950–JUNE 1951

THE KOREAN WAR is frequently called a forgotten war for a reason. For most Americans, Korea is a misunderstood conflict, sandwiched between World War II and Vietnam. Allan R. Millett has gone so far as to say, "In terms of the collective memory of the American people, the Korean War is not just forgotten. It was not remembered in the first place."[1] The final two years of the war were exceptionally numbing. So much cost and effort produced not victory or surrender, but an armistice and a cease-fire. Sergeant First Class Fred E. Proft, an artillery observer, summed up the fighting man's frustration: "The peace talks were on again, off again, and from the news I got from home, it seemed the papers carried brief paragraphs about skirmishes on the front [line]. But those actions were taking lives." For many Americans drafted or recalled to active duty to fight in Korea, the war's end left a bitter taste to the experience resisting Communist encroachment. Therefore, many prefer not to remember it.[2]

Additionally, the war never conformed to a familiar pattern. It was "a strange mixture of old-fashioned military conflict and an ill-defined new concept of collective security . . . compounded with a large portion of psychological warfare . . . an outgrowth of the cold war."[3] Coming as soon as it did after total Allied victory in World War II, its causes and conduct baffled many contemporary observers, politicians, and generals. The conflict, which lasted more than three years and resulted in over 33,000 US fatalities, generates ambivalence or misunderstanding of what really was at stake and what the American intervention accomplished. It also obscured significant strategic decisions. This is unfortunate, for what Korea did was reintroduce Americans to war as it really is: a contradiction of choices to address unforeseen problems producing unanticipated consequences.

What Kind of War?

Almost immediately following the first reports from east Asia that Kim Il-sung's North Korean military forces had crossed the de facto boundary along the

38th parallel, US president Harry S. Truman, his closest advisors, and the Joint Chiefs of Staff (JCS) became enmeshed in the most difficult problems involved in waging war, namely, determining exactly what was wanted and (as precisely as possible) the level of commitment and military means to accomplish that result. In short, they had to determine a national military strategy, and they had to do it in a matter of days.

The nineteenth-century war philosopher Carl von Clausewitz anticipated the conundrum. He wrote, "No one starts a war—or rather, no one in his senses ought to do so—without first being clear in his mind what he intends to achieve by that war and how he intends to conduct it."[4] But as American political and military leaders soon discovered, the Korean War defied easy categorization and definition of war aims. Truman did not seek a congressional declaration of war, a stance that did not clarify over time the immensity of cost in dollars and lives and the sacrifice demanded of thousands of American servicemen. (By Truman's own recollection, he gathered congressional leaders to "inform them on the events and the decisions" already taken.[5]) During the war US objectives swung like a pendulum along with the fortunes of the American-led United Nations military coalition. At first, the objective was simply to repel aggression and restore the status quo ante bellum.[6] A very dismal summer, in which the survival of the ROK itself and the troops of General Douglas MacArthur's UNC (at this point almost entirely American or South Korean), placed that objective very much in doubt.[7]

MacArthur's risky but ultimately successful amphibious landing at Inchon in September 1950 suddenly turned the tables, and just as suddenly, Truman confronted the opportunity to discard a "police action" to repel aggression and adopt a stronger and more punitive objective—the elimination of North Korea as a Communist state. After brief deliberation, the logic of the tactical situation being persuasive, MacArthur was cut loose to go on to the Yalu River, the natural border between Korea and mainland China.[8]

MacArthur's military objective is best described as one of annihilation: the total overthrow of an opponent's means and will to resist. This existential threat to the North Korean regime was sufficiently threatening to Communist China that Mao Zedong was forced to react. "When the lips are gone, the teeth are cold," ran a Sung dynasty's strategic aphorism. Mao could not afford to allow Kim Il-sung's Korean People's Army (KPA) to be destroyed, thereby exposing China's most valuable strategic region, Manchuria, with its industry and communications links to the Soviet Union, to American military pressure.[9] The intervention by thousands of Chinese "volunteers" completely changed the character of the conflict. These were regular PLA soldiers assigned to fight in the Korean theater. The fiction was useful, as Mao too desired to limit his strategic liabilities.[10] Volunteers or not, the CPVF not only administered a humiliating defeat to MacArthur's forces, but suddenly the status quo ante bellum was looking very attractive again, especially as American and Korean divisions streamed past the 38th parallel, gave up Seoul for a second time, and thought seriously about an evacuation through Pusan.[11]

Furthermore, Mao's intervention completely overturned American policy and its associated assumptions that the war would limit itself. The US Departments of State and Defense temporized and provided contradictory advice and guidance to MacArthur's stunned headquarters in Japan. Washington had to consider how the Soviet Union, now also an atomic power, would view any expansion of the conflict. MacArthur reflexively demanded the resources (troops) and authorities (attack targets in Manchuria, blockade China's coast, unleash Chiang Kai-shek) to meet the challenge to the UNC's military objectives. Burton Kaufman summed up the military dilemma well: "He [MacArthur] was not to win the war in any conventional sense, but neither was he to allow the enemy to claim victory in Korea." As the UNC position became even more dire in December and early January 1951, MacArthur received further ambiguous orders to defend successive positions while "inflicting maximum damage subject to primary consideration of the safety of your troops and your basic mission of protecting Japan."[12]

The Chinese intervention did eventually generate a positive result once the crisis of defeat passed by the second week of January. It focused the mind of Washington's political and military castes to think through the problem of American policy in Asia and to focus on what was a realistic strategic outcome, given Truman's reluctance to engage in a military conflict that could potentially have unlimited consequences. After months of deliberation the result was a coherent but controversial statement of policy to resolve the Korean conflict, known as National Security Council memorandum 48/5 (NSC 48/5). Its premise stated that the United States should "continue as an ultimate objective to seek by political, as distinguished from military means, a solution of the Korean problem." At the end of May 1951, NSC 48/5 was operationalized by separate instructions from the JCS, who instructed MacArthur's successor in the Korean theater, General Matthew B. Ridgway, "to create conditions favorable to a settlement of the Korean conflict . . . under appropriate armistice arrangements."[13] In a stinging self-indictment, US army chief of staff Gen. J. Lawton Collins explained, "For the first time since he [the Commander in Chief, Far East] had assumed overall command he knew clearly his responsibilities and the limits of his authority."[14]

The JCS's instructions communicated a policy that Ridgway and his commanders could pursue with the military means at their disposal. However, this newly articulated responsibility and limits on military authority were likely not what military leaders expected. The strategic goals were negative:

defend the territory of the ROK, prevent escalation or expansion of the fighting, minimize American and allied casualties. As will be shown, it was not an easy or popular proposition. American commanders were comfortable judging success by ground gained and enemy killed. It was clear to tell when the Eighth Army was winning, which it was in the summer of 1951. Now the mission was to achieve results through the carefully calibrated application of military power to destroy Communist forces without provoking an increased effort in response. To economize his forces, Ridgway limited Eighth Army's attacks while relying on an intense air campaign to discourage further Communist resistance. Shrewd negotiations that limited concessions and maintained the prestige of the United States, and by extension the United Nations, provided the main effort to achieve Washington's policy objectives. This dual mission remained in effect as American air and ground commanders exerted all of their professional skills to coerce the Communists without risking a break or suspension in the truce talks.[15] Subsequent plans, nearly all rejected out of hand, to achieve a military victory or to establish a better defensive line along the Korean "waist" (running roughly from Pyongyang in the west to Wonsan in the east) all collided with Truman's decision to limit American military commitment in Korea and to avoid thousands of unnecessary casualties for a stalemate a hundred miles farther north of the current line of contact.[16]

Although military strategy tends to attract the most attention in wartime, how political leadership formulates and articulates war objectives strongly influences military strategy and its associated tactics. The interanimation between political objectives and the military means employed to realize those objectives is more than academic. It is an immutable interplay that characterizes and expresses the nature of war.[17] Truman's policy decisions, uncoupled as they were from military considerations, did more to shape the course of the war in its last two years than anything his generals advocated or accomplished. Indeed, President Truman was in reality calling the shots, forcing the Communists as well as his allies and military commanders to dance to his tune. It was a tune that rang through the Korean hills as the cacophonous symphony of artillery, aerial bombardment, machine gun fire, small arms, and hand grenades.

The First Twelve Months

At the time that American policy had determined the military objective to be a cease-fire armistice, the fighting in Korea had already experienced four major turning points.

War in Korea was a blend of local, national, and international influences.[18] Kim Il-sung and his partisans had been trying since 1947 to undermine

American attempts to establish a pro-US regime. Leftist subversion against the American-led postwar occupation government culminated in open re-bellions beginning on Cheju Island (Cheju-do) in April 1948 until the Yosu-Sunchon mutiny of October/November of the same year. What sedition could not accomplish from within, North Korean regular and border forces attempted along the 38th parallel, which gradually hardened into a de facto boundary. The border war in the summer of 1949 stressed the ROK and underscored its deficiencies in firepower and conventional warfare training.[19]

The real test followed that fall and winter, when ROK forces, advised and supported by American officers, launched a concerted campaign to obliter-ate Communist-sponsored guerrillas in the south. The campaign was a suc-cess, so much that North Korean cadres began to infiltrate in large numbers across the border to reinvigorate the resistance to Syngman Rhee's govern-ment, but this was a stopgap measure. Kim Il-sung was not interested in the slow strangulation of South Korea. He wanted a knockout blow, and by Feb-ruary 1950, the guerrilla effort was being discarded in favor of a lightning strike to shatter the South Koreans, seize the capital of Seoul, and present the world—really the Americans—with a fait accompli.[20]

Kim's KPA benefited from sustained Soviet military support, to include weaponry, equipment, and most importantly, advisors to educate and train the North Koreans in Soviet military principles, doctrine, and culture. The advisory mission began in September 1946 and gradually expanded until the summer of 1950 when 236 officers were organized to support KPA head-quarters, its combat divisions, and infantry brigades. In some cases, Soviet officers were assigned to regiment and even battalion levels to coordinate the reception of military equipment, training, and eventually combat opera-tions. Much of the KPA's arms, ammunition, and equipment was left behind by the Soviet Twenty-Fifth Army when it withdrew from its postwar occu-pation duties in 1947. Because Korean soldiers lacked experience and edu-cation in modern fighting methods, advisors established several schools to train and indoctrinate soldiers and leaders. An important contribution the Soviet advisors made was teaching combined arms fighting, which integrated infantry with artillery and armor units. The commander of the 105th Tank Brigade was a Soviet Korean, Yu Kyong-su, who was a veteran of the World War II Red army.[21]

The border clashes during the summer of 1949 accelerated the Soviet drive to prepare the KPA. Although grateful for the equipment, Kim's soldiers gained only a superficial knowledge of how to use it. Because most Soviet advisors were ignorant of Korean language, culture, way of thinking, and traditions, Soviet forms and methods tended to be mechanically laid on the KPA's orga-nization. Serious consequences would emerge once the KPA had outrun its initial objectives laid out in its invasion plan, and subordinate units had to improvise in the face of increasing resistance on the ground and from the air.[22]

Still, Kim had reason to be confident. He anticipated a weeklong campaign culminating in a decisive battle over Seoul and the Han River. Well-armed and trained, soldiers of the KPA believed they were invincible revolutionaries. Organized in ten infantry divisions (three of which contained substantial numbers of veterans from Mao Zedong's just concluded revolution in China) supported by one tank brigade and employing the doctrine and tactical style of their Soviet patrons, they were additionally confident in the operational plan designed by their Soviet advisors. Following the annihilation of South Korean forces, the remainder of the country would be occupied and "liberated." The Soviets had not provided the most modern tanks, self-propelled artillery, or towed artillery howitzers, but the KPA's superiority in military equipment was sufficient to give the blitzkrieg punch Kim Il-sung hoped would fracture the ROK army and destroy its will and capability to resist before the Americans could intervene in a meaningful way.[23]

This was the first turning point in the confrontation. South Korean forces were woefully underprepared to face a conventional invasion. The defenders had no tanks or modern antitank weapons, and their artillery consisted of surplus airborne howitzers, with reduced accuracy and range compared to their KPA counterparts. Beyond equipment disparities, the ROK army lacked coherent defenses in depth with adequate reserves to fight a mechanized enemy. They fought, but the outcome was never in doubt. When the North Korean conventional attack threatened to overwhelm Syngman Rhee's army in a matter of days, it provoked active American military intervention.[24] President Truman's decision to commit American military power in South Korea turned a fraternal bloodletting into an international conflict, with great strategic implications for the United States and its allies vis-à-vis the Soviet Union, even, some would say, putting Armageddon in the balance.[25] At the request of the Truman administration, the United Nations on June 27, 1950, authorized military force and called on member nations "to furnish such assistance to the Republic of Korea as may be necessary to restore international peace and security in the area."[26] Truman promptly ordered US air and naval forces to provide immediate support, and less than eight hours later, aircraft from the Far East Air Forces (FEAF—rhymes with "leaf"), based in Japan, were flying combat missions over the ROK.[27] Of greater significance was the political tint to this unilateral action, as it set the tone that would color American military strategy in Korea.

The Americans' new war in Asia remained conventional, with air, naval, and then ground forces entering the Korean theater to blunt the North Korean juggernaut, but their forces in the Far East were unprepared for a large-scale battle for Korea.[28] Even after the commitment of American airpower, the mainstay of resistance remained the shattered ROK army, which was being hastily reformed as stragglers crossed over the south bank of the Han River. For six days the KPA was kept north of this obstacle, stymied as much by the need to reconsolidate and resupply its assaulting elements following the fall of Seoul as by stubborn South Korean defenders. Then, it was on to Taejon, the next major city midway between Taegu and Seoul.[29] The hasty commitment of American ground troops did not begin to make an impact until late July, when elements of three US divisions (in order of arrival, Twenty-Fourth Infantry, Twenty-Fifth Infantry, First Cavalry) were on the ground.[30] Even then, North Korean troops had too much momentum. By the end of July, the American divisions, organized along with several reconstituted Korean divisions as the American Eighth Army, were holding on by their fingernails to a porous defense line known as the Pusan Perimeter. There was no more room to retreat. Ferocious battles during the month of August eventually brought the North Korean drive to a halt and pinned the KPA in place, enabling American aircraft to exert their destructive power in the World War II tradition. Air interdiction (the attack of enemy lines of communication and his means of movement, transportation, and supply) helped to disrupt the KPA's offensive momentum and bought time for the ground forces to establish more effective defenses along the Perimeter and set the stage for a dramatic and decisive turn of events.[31]

General Douglas MacArthur's surprise landing at Inchon cut the KPA off from its main logistics corridor and trapped it between Eighth Army and X Corps. The gamble paid off: the North Koreans were taken by complete surprise, and with the vast majority of their frontline forces tied down far to the south, there was little they could do to avoid disaster. As Eighth Army broke out of the Perimeter, ROK First Division commander, Paik Sun-yup saw "the enemy that had fought with such ferocity now vanished like a fog under a burning sun."[32]

In just two weeks the tables were turned completely. After hard fighting the South Korean capital was liberated, and the X Corps anvil was firmly in place to shatter the retreating North Koreans pursued by the Eighth Army. Kim Il-sung's army ceased to exist as an organized force. Scattered resistance did little to delay the victorious American and Korean divisions, by now leavened with small United Nations contingents (with more on the way), from capturing Pyongyang in the west and the port of Wonsan in the east, and then driving forward to the Yalu and Tumen Rivers. MacArthur's triumphal sweep north of the 38th parallel gave the impression that nothing could stop the complete dissolution of Kim's Communist regime.[33]

Unfortunately for the advancing UNC troops, Mao Zedong watched the un-

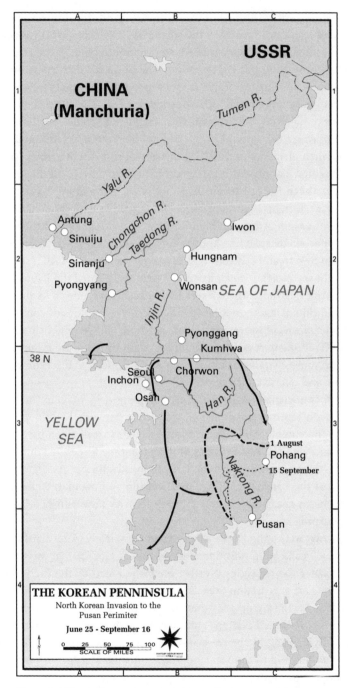

Figure 2.1 North Korean invasion—Pusan Perimeter, 1950. Source:
Jeff Goldberg, Department of History, United States Military Academy.

folding drama with trepidation. As chairman of the Military Affairs Committee (later renamed the Central Military Commission, or CMC), Mao wielded extraordinary influence in matters of strategy, force allocation, tactics, and even logistics. His personal preference drove much of the momentum behind the CPVF's initial advance into Korea and its first encounters with MacArthur's forces in the final weeks of 1950.[34]

Shortly after American military forces began operations against the KPA in July, Josef Stalin rushed to assure Mao of Soviet support and assistance as a way to prod the Chinese to enter the conflict.[35] But Stalin played coy throughout the summer, promising air support for Chinese ground forces while never letting on that he did not really mean to commit Soviet airpower but to provide training, aircraft, air defense guns, and advisors. Friction over this fundamental misunderstanding only got hotter after Inchon and the consequent collapse of KPA resistance south of the 38th parallel. As late as October 1, Stalin urged Mao to commit immediately "five to six divisions toward the 38th parallel" to enable the KPA to reorganize their forces behind a protective shield of Chinese volunteers. The promise of Soviet air support remained undefined.[36]

Mao formally appointed Peng Dehuai, a trustworthy, experienced, and competent veteran of China's multiple civil wars, war against Japan, and Mao's revolution, on October 5 to command the *Renmin Zhiyuanjun*—Chinese People's Volunteers. Peng was a well-regarded military figure with long experience both in Chiang Kai-shek's Guomindong (Nationalist Party) and Mao's Red Armies. As one of the PLA's most dedicated and experienced generals, he was a natural choice to command the CPVF. In Korea he directed all major campaigns, made or approved all operational decisions, communicated daily with Mao, and worked with Kim Il-sung and the KPA. It is hard to conceive of a better theater commander to rescue the KPA from destruction and defend China's border.[37]

Mao made his strategic intentions clear through third party intermediaries: no non-Korean forces could cross the 38th parallel. It was bad enough that Truman neutralized the Taiwan Strait with the US Seventh Fleet, ostensibly to keep Chiang in check, but in reality, thwarting Mao's planned invasion to finish off the Guomindong that summer. The unchecked advance of UNC troops north of the 38th parallel induced strategic panic in Beijing. Although acknowledging China's material and military weakness in a confrontation with the United States, the PRC's leadership saw little alternative to mobilizing the nation to "resist America and assist Korea."[38] While MacArthur actively minimized the Chinese threat, suggesting that any intervention would result in an immense slaughter, the endgame for Korea now became a political problem, with "manifold and delicate nuances," as chairman of the JCS

General Omar N. Bradley remembered the situation.[39] What objective should American policy pursue? MacArthur's view was clear and compelling: American airpower was not only decisive but also supreme; naval power was unchallenged. China's only trump card to play was manpower, and there was no intelligence that MacArthur was willing to acknowledge that would counsel caution.[40]

Assuming the war was as good as won, MacArthur directed Lt. Gen. Walton H. Walker, commanding Eighth Army, to continue the pursuit north along the western corridor, through Pyongyang to the Chongchon River and thence to Sinuiju on the Yalu River. Perhaps in another effort to reap a final measure of glory, he enjoined the X Corps commander, Maj. Gen. Edward "Ned" Almond, to mount another amphibious attack, this time against Korea's *eastern* coast, at Wonsan. Although the idea of a second amphibious démarche may have had some strategic merit, the potential reward was undermined by practical obstacles. The First Marine Division had to be out-loaded through Inchon, its priority dictating that no supplies or reinforcements for Walker would make the short journey from that port northward. The Seventh Infantry Division, again with MacArthur's priority, countermarched *south* toward Pusan, clogging up that vital road artery and port facility. Meanwhile, Walker's troops struggled to cross the Han River and maintain contact with the retreating KPA.

MacArthur's shoestring forces and breezy orders directing Almond and Walker to pursue divergent lines of operations (generally northwest and northeast) failed to destroy the KPA. What appeared to concern MacArthur little was that he had two elements, one field army and one amphibious corps, separated by hundreds of miles of mountainous wasteland, a hopelessly complicated logistics situation, and air support divided and deprived of its greatest operational feature, flexibility to mass against specific targets. The intelligence picture was likewise murky as MacArthur's command had its attention and resources divided to support two major efforts that not only diverged from each other but also failed to focus MacArthur's pursuit against any strategically important objectives.[41]

At this time, in mid-October, Mao's volunteers were already streaming across the Yalu River under cover of darkness where they remained invisible from American aerial reconnaissance. Even in the age before satellite surveillance, the infiltration of six armies, comprising eighteen infantry divisions and three artillery divisions along with support troops—in all 300,000 men—was a major coup. Mao had achieved one of the rarest feats in war, strategic surprise.[42]

Mao's generals recognized their technological inferiority compared to the Americans, but Mao had long believed the human factor in war was supreme and would always overpower an enemy possessing higher-quality weaponry or employing more advanced techniques or tactics.[43] His PLA volunteers had extensive combat experience in mobile warfare, and they maintained high morale and personal motivation. Mao was confident in his soldiers' superior ideological commitment to press the attack and to exploit their superior mobility to pressure the enemy's front, flanks, and rear. Although technologically weak, the CPVF could still successfully defend China's interests in Korea. American commanders who may have dismissed the Chinese peasant as a ragtag soldier quickly gained a high respect for his fighting qualities and endurance. Gen. Matthew B. Ridgway, who commanded the Eighth Army in 1951, said it simply: "Chinese made [sic] an excellent soldier."[44] Maintaining political cohesion amongst the Chinese volunteers in Korea became a significant pillar in the Communists' strategy of persistence against UNC firepower and gave them the political power to resist the UNC's coercive tactics in the air and on the ground.[45]

The CPVF division that deployed to Korea was slightly larger than, but organized in a similar fashion as, the KPA infantry division. It contained three infantry regiments but lacked an artillery regiment. In its place, the Chinese substituted a 75/76 mm pack howitzer battalion (9–12 tubes) and a 120 mm mortar battalion (up to 12 tubes). Each infantry regiment possessed a few Japanese or Chinese 70 mm howitzers for short-range direct fire. Battalions and companies were completely reliant on mortars and occasionally on captured man-portable rocket launchers (the American "bazooka" anti-tank rocket) for close-range fire support. The Chinese division, therefore, was much less capable in a firepower contest. It had to rely on the army or army group artillery to make up the difference, but even these higher echelons possessed smaller calibers and fewer guns than would be found in an American unit of similar size.[46]

These lightly armed and equipped Chinese peasant soldiers delivered a sharp response to MacArthur's divided forces. The initial blow, known as the First Campaign (October 25–November 5, 1950), landed in western Korea against the Eighth Army. It was meant as a defensive deployment, a blocking and delaying action, to keep UN troops away from the Yalu River and provide the Chinese with a buffer in which to deploy additional forces as they became available. On October 25, Chinese troops struck the ROK Sixth and Eighth Divisions, completely shattering their forward momentum. The ROK First Division, committed as a stopgap, fared little better, and one regiment from the First Cavalry Division, rushing toward Unsan, was cut off and badly cut up on November 1. The Chinese veterans then disappeared into the gloomy Korean landscape, almost as imperceptibly as they had materialized a week prior. Interrogation of the few Chinese prisoners confirmed their identity, strength, origin, and motivation. Walker ordered his forces to pause, but MacArthur and his staff continued to discount the threat of Chinese intervention. Korean commander Paik Sun-yup believed the Americans "continued to fool themselves because the Chinese had yet to challenge a U.S. Army division directly."[47] This hubris would cost the Americans dearly, as the American command in Tokyo and administration in Washington had, and ignored, the rare chance to reevaluate its Korea policy without significant military pressure.

During this initial campaign the Chinese infantry displayed characteristic tactics they would employ successfully over the next six months. They marched at night and lay still during the day, thus spoofing the Americans' aerial reconnaissance apparatus that MacArthur relied on for early warning. Operating at night permitted the Chinese to move long distances through difficult terrain and infiltrate into advantageous positions without detection. Fifteen to twenty miles a night was not unusual. Attacks developed quickly, exploiting surprise and shock, relying on the "three fierce actions"—fierce fire, fierce assault, and fierce pursuit. Automatic weapons and hand grenades passed for fire support to enable infantry squads and platoons to maneuver against defenders and wipe them out in close combat. The typical outcome was the Chinese took their objective; these were assault troops.[48]

It was mobile warfare at its finest. As the stricken ROKs and then Americans, recoiled, the CPVF commanders ordered the advance to continue, thus turning an urgent withdrawal into a rout. Although the CPVF managed to wipe out several ROK and US battalions, Peng was not ready to commit fully. Despite Mao's urgent demands, Peng's volunteers had to go into battle without the air support that the Soviets had promised. Peng rightly worried about his troops' exposure to UNC airpower, and after ten days of running battle his troops were exhausted; the Thirty-Eighth, Thirty-Ninth, and Fortieth Armies had suffered significant casualties, and American air and artillery were making their weight felt, "developing an unacceptable power of destruction in daylight."[49] Peng, whose motto was, "Be prepared, no disaster," ordered his forces back, waiting and "showing ourselves to be weak, increasing the arrogance of the enemy . . . luring him deep into our areas."[50] This may be what happened, but it is more likely that Peng still anticipated the supplies, weaponry, and air support that Mao said Stalin had promised before Peng was willing to launch a full-bore counteroffensive.

General Bradley called the next sixty days—the months of November and December—as "among the most trying of my professional career."[51] Indeed, probably all American military and political leaders were flummoxed by the CPVF's Second Campaign and MacArthur's unsteady reaction to it. The storm broke the day after MacArthur's much anticipated "Home by Christmas" advance, November 25. The addition of Peng's Ninth Army Group against the X Corps brought another 150,000 men to confront MacArthur. This major offensive provoked near panic in Washington; in Tokyo the panic was real. For a short while, it looked as if the whole UNC might fall into the Chinese bag.[52] In eastern Korea, US marines chiseled yet another stile for their pantheon of valor; army troops of the Seventh Infantry Division fared less well in the public eye, though their suffering and fierce fighting to escape entrapment was no less noble. Navy and marine aviators provided support with an around-the-clock aerial blanket ready to pounce and chew up any Chinese formations that followed too close to the retreating Americans.[53] Almond's X Corps evacuated Hamhung and Hungnam harbors from December 17 to 24, blowing up thousands of tons of equipment and ammunition just as the last troop ships made good their escape. The result of Chinese intervention in the west, however, was a disastrous retreat. The collapse of Eighth Army's eastern flank, the ROK II Corps, and the rough handling of the Second Infantry Division in the gauntlet at Kunu-ri, produced irreversible momentum for what was supposed to be an orderly withdrawal to a line stretching from Pyongyang to Wonsan.[54] CPVF pressure convinced Walker to evacuate Pyongyang on December 8, and his retreating forces did not stop until early January when they finally outran the foot-bound Chinese, who had launched a third campaign and captured Seoul for a second time just four days after the New Year (1951).

The Chinese intervention completely changed the strategic calculus for the American-led United Nations coalition. Bradley lamented MacArthur's apparent defeatism and prophecies of doom. MacArthur "seemed to be saying that [he] was throwing in the towel without the slightest effort to put up a fight," Bradley recalled.[55] Not only did it appear the Americans were out of military options to achieve unification, but also the survival of the UNC in Korea was in doubt. Therefore, the final turning point before the initiation of negotiations in July 1951 was truly remarkable. The turnaround of Eighth Army to a confident and nearly irresistible instrument was the work of Lt. Gen. Matthew B. Ridgway. It is rare in war that the fortunes of an entire army can hinge on one man. In December 1950 that man was General Walker, the bulldog on the peninsula. He had kept American and Korean divisions in the fight during the darkest days, and although he made some quirky pronouncements—his "Stand or Die" order being the most celebrated—and some questionable tactical decisions early in the war, he was a fighter. It was his professional misfortune not to be part of MacArthur's circle, and he did not enjoy much confidence from his superior. On December 23, Walker died in a traffic accident when his jeep collided with a South Korean truck. The JCS had already decided to send Ridgway to Korea should anything happen

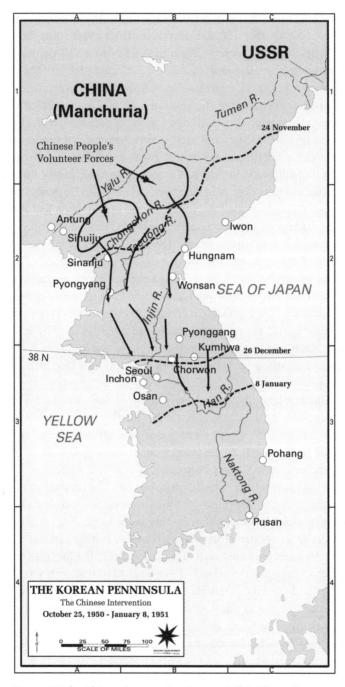

Figure 2.2 The Chinese intervention. Source: Jeff Goldberg, Department of History, United States Military Academy.

to Walker, and within twenty-four hours, the future Eighth Army commander was on his way to the Far East.[56]

Ridgway's appointment was fortuitous. If Walker merited a kinder fate, Eighth Army certainly deserved the man Washington sent to replace him. Ridgway's pedigree and exploits as a paratrooper commander in Sicily, Italy, France, Holland, Belgium, and Germany are well known. His time in command of Eighth Army was brief—just four months—but what he wrought in those few precious weeks was just short of a military miracle. There is no shortage of genuine admirers for this Soldier's soldier, a man who carried a hand grenade on his battle harness "just in case" and who tolerated no defeatism in *his* army. Announcing by radio message his assumption of command, with the adjunction, "You will have my utmost, I shall expect yours," Ridgway immediately impressed on his staff that his fight was not in the rear amid the tents, clutter, and radio masts of an army headquarters, but at the front.[57] He immediately relocated his tactical headquarters (christened "Tempest") forward and spent his days personally inspecting units, their situations, and above all, their leaders. He delivered one message: Eighth Army was going to attack, but it would do so smartly, relying on "good planning, well-timed execution, close cooperation among units and above all old-fashioned coordination of infantry, artillery, and air power."[58] The impression he made was nearly universal on his Eighth Army. Ridgway was the tonic Eighth Army needed.[59]

Ridgway's genius was twofold. He first realized that Eighth Army suffered from defeatism, and that to survive tactically the army would have to demonstrate aggressiveness and resiliency. He had to revitalize its morale and fighting spirit. He appealed to his army's martial pride and fighting professionalism, reminding the individual soldier of why he was fighting and how he could win. Simultaneously, he reassured and encouraged his military and political superiors. Whereas MacArthur publicly contemplated an inevitable evacuation from Korea, Ridgway confidently stated that he could hold Korea for at least two to three months. General J. Lawton Collins, army chief of staff, later remembered, "Responsible authorities in Washington were no longer pessimistic about our being driven out of Korea and, though it was realized that rough times were still ahead of us, no longer was there much talk of evacuation. General Ridgway alone was responsible for this dramatic change."[60] Second, he recognized that encirclement battles of annihilation were too hard, too costly, and too unpredictable. He planned to keep Eighth Army active and "warmed by the sun of victory" through a series of short and limited offensive thrusts. In his mind, the only thing that counted was to kill as many communist soldiers as possible while preserving UNC and ROK troops.[61]

Figure 2.3 General Matthew B. Ridgway at the front. Source: US army photo.

Once Peng's Third Campaign (December 31, 1950–January 8, 1951) had shot its bolt, Ridgway resolved to attack with a coordinated advance to gain contact with the enemy, wear down his forces, and push him back to the Han River. There the Eighth Army would pause and consider the next phase to punish the CPVF and drive it farther north. This was his operational objective, and the tactical means stood in strong contrast to MacArthur's instructions the previous November to rush pell-mell to the Yalu River. All attacks were contingent on American strength being applied against Chinese and North Korean weakness to ensure objectives taken did not incur needless losses. Battalions, regiments, divisions, and even corps were expected to move in mutual support to prevent enemy infiltration, provide overlapping artillery firepower, and increase the pressure on the communist logistics and support system.[62] Lt. Col. Harold K. Johnson, a future army chief of staff, recalled that "forward units were holding hands all the way across the front to ensure that the attack progressed at about the same rate."[63] Ridgway instructed his corps commanders to observe fundamentals: leaders at the front familiar with their men, the enemy situation, and the terrain; properly constituted reserves capable to plug a hole or exploit a gap; officers promoting unit identity and the motivation to fight. Additionally, he encouraged all leaders to advance with "tenacity, and determination to accomplish fully every mission assigned."[64]

Ridgway also had an important operational change to make. On February

8, he instructed his corps commanders to focus on the "destruction of enemy forces and preservation of our own. Terrain for its own sake is immaterial." He knew Eighth Army could not compete in a manpower struggle for ground, so he determined only to fight for specific terrain that exposed the enemy to devastating firepower from the air and ground. Maneuver would be closely controlled to ensure the Communists no longer could exploit gaps, robbing Peng's troops of their most potent capability: mobility. From this point forward, Chinese attacks would, with a few notable exceptions, strike surfaces, not gaps, along the Eighth Army lines. Presciently, Ridgway foretold the real benefit of smart fighting: "We can provide a strong backbone for American diplomacy."[65]

Ridgway's attacks, sequenced expertly to avoid exposing UNC troops to a surprise counterthrust, proved the Chinese were no supermen and that their advanced elements were worn out, exhausted, sick, and in no condition to resist the onslaught of artillery fire, unhindered air support, and mobility that Ridgway was about to unleash. A hastily assembled force launched the Fourth Campaign in mid-February 1951 but failed to stem Ridgway's broad advance. Follow-on operations inflicted tremendous casualties on the Communist armies attempting to hold their newly won ground while subsisting at the end of their meager logistics lifeline.[66] American casualties (January 22–March 31, 1951) fell to a daily rate of fewer than one hundred killed, wounded, and missing, while the KPA and CPVF's rates shot up to nearly one thousand soldiers estimated lost each day, on average.[67]

The UNC line advanced more or less continuously from mid-February through March, confirming Eighth Army's fundamental superiorities. By mid-March it was clear that the CPVF's general offensive potential was limited in both scope and duration. After the CPVF's Fourth Campaign petered out, Ridgway was confident that Eighth Army would soon carry the battle back to recapture Seoul and then across the 38th parallel.[68] Eighth Army benefited from prodigious supply and rolling stocks that ensured no unit ran out of fuel, food, or ammunition. Deployed National Guard truck and ordnance repair companies greatly enhanced Eighth Army's resilience and flexibility, not to mention its sustained combat power.[69] Air to ground coordination continued to improve and, when combined with the Americans' artillery, inflicted a devastating blow to any concentrated Chinese or North Korean units.[70] And even more help was on the way. Truman's mobilization orders the previous summer began to bear fruit with the arrival and in-country training of corps level artillery battalions—the 155 mm towed and self-propelled howitzers, and longer ranging 155 mm guns and heavy 8-inch howitzers that American doctrine called for to support a field army. Ten artillery battalions came from the National Guard, and another battalion of 8-inch howitzers was activated from the Army Reserve. Ridgway urged Collins to expedite the deployment of these units called up in the late summer of 1950, rapidly formed, equipped, and filled with recalled or volunteer reservists, new enlistees, and some regular army officers and noncommissioned officers. He would see to their training in Korea. Their arrival at the front in early spring 1951 helped tip the scales of firepower decisively in Ridgway's favor just in time for the Communists' first phase Spring Campaign (April 22–30).[71]

In March, Operation Ripper swept through Seoul, Chunchon, and right up to the 38th parallel.[72] Ridgway called this operation, with its surprise crossing of the Han River and the following turning movement that compelled the Chinese to attack at a severe disadvantage or face destruction, "the most successful single action fought by troops under my command during either World War II in Europe, or in Korea."[73] Eighth Army suffered few casualties, recaptured Seoul, and proved convincingly that Ridgway's fire and maneuver operational approach was working both to gain ground and kill Communists.

Ridgway's success in Korea as the Eighth Army commander cannot be overstated. He made the army successful. With his military bearing, fighting ethos, and intellect, his influence was felt up and down the chain of command. His personal leadership "breathed humanity into that operation," and when he visited fighting men at the front, which was often, the common infantryman knew their commander was looking out for them.[74] According to Harold K. Johnson, "There were a lot of checks made by General Ridgway in person . . . to hold conferences with division commanders and their principal subordinates and to visit subordinate units."[75] Ridgway was also not shy about ensuring his soldiers had the very best leadership. He urged Collins to insist that all general officers in combat commands "attain the highest standards for our military traditions . . . let's be ruthless with our general officers if they fail to measure up."[76] The entire general officer leadership of the IX Corps was replaced as were a handful of other division commanders who failed to show sufficient drive or tactical acumen.[77]

Furthermore, Ridgway was trusted by the JCS, the national security team, and President Truman. Five days after MacArthur spoke to newsmen in Korea about the "theoretical stalemate" about to drop on the Korean theater, thanks to "endless bloodshed . . . to enforce international banditry or blackmail or both,"[78] Ridgway gave his own press conference: "We didn't set out to conquer China. . . . We have demonstrated the superiority on the battlefield of our men. If China fails to throw us into the sea, that is a defeat for her of incalculable proportions. If China fails to drive us from Korea, she will have failed monumentally." Here was a general who spoke of winning in Korea a "tremendous victory for the United Nations" even if the final battle lines settled on the 38th parallel. It was a breath of fresh air, and another peg in the board of waning patience with MacArthur in Washington.[79]

Eighth Army continued to push forward, launching powerful attacks and punishing Chinese and North Korean forces unlucky enough to be in the way. Although Ridgway had taken significant territorial objectives, the victory was incomplete as Chinese and North Korean troops reverted to mobile defensive tactics, withdrawing when pressed and thus avoiding destruction—Ridgway's actual objective. Ridgway's troops now found few opportunities to annihilate large enemy formations. Although materially weak, the Chinese armies never reached a crisis in manpower, and their willingness to expend men as bullets had to be respected. In April, disquieting signs appeared as Chinese resistance stiffened, and intelligence assessments saw the telltale signs of a fifth Chinese campaign. The American command remained confident; the Chinese had limitations, notably, their lack of staying power against a well-led, mobile army with firepower supremacy.

A curious outcome of Ridgway's counteroffensive during the winter and spring of 1951 was a debate over the 38th parallel's military significance. According to ROK general Paik Sun-yup, Ridgway declared the parallel irrelevant as a military feature, but he did speak in great detail about Line Kansas (later known as Kansas-Wyoming). A control measure drawn on the map, Line Kansas ran west to east, generally six to twelve miles north of the parallel (except in the far west, where Line Kansas was south of the prewar boundary). Ridgway desired identifiable and defensible terrain to position his forces, and he wanted some method to place tactical limits on the advancing forces and to ensure continuity of the front in the face of an expected Chinese offensive. Line Kansas fulfilled both of these needs, and it became the UNC's major military objective to defend and hold all territory south of this line.

Once the UNC ground forces occupied Line Kansas, the next step was to drive forward in the center of the peninsula to another control measure, Line Wyoming. This line would take American forces into a geographic feature known as the "Iron Triangle," which was bounded by Pyonggang at the northern apex, Chorwon at the southwestern apex, and Kumhwa at the southeastern apex. Communist rail and road movement north of Line Kansas along an east–west axis moved through the Iron Triangle, and the CPVF maintained significant logistics and staging bases in the region around Pyonggang. Control of the Iron Triangle conferred significant operational advantages in logistics and intelligence early warning. As the UNC would discover, both impulses of the Chinese Fifth Campaign would derive their power from within the Iron Triangle. Control or at least denial of the Iron Triangle region to the Communists thus became another major military concern for the UNC.[80]

By April 11, President Truman had had enough of MacArthur's public statements at variance with administration policy. The general's relief for insubordination stunned the Far East Command, but Ridgway's elevation to replace the majestic MacArthur soothed everyone's nerves. He would not challenge Washington, even though he often disagreed *militarily* with Truman's strategic policy goals. Tactically, he was far more involved than his predecessor, issuing restrictive guidance to his replacement, Lt. Gen. James A. Van Fleet, regarding troop disposition, major operations, and casualty avoidance. He also frowned on any actions that required "frontal assaults, reckless advances, or last-ditch defenses."[81] To Rutherford Poats he emphasized, "We are not interested in real estate. Our mission is solely the destruction of hostile forces and the conservation of our own."[82] Eighth Army's continuous advance toward the Iron Triangle was partially to induce Peng to strike prematurely and expose his troops to American firepower and maneuver.

Van Fleet replaced Ridgway on April 14. He presented an immediate contrast to the suave and polished paratrooper. Van Fleet was earthy, blunt, "a football coach in uniform."[83] But he too was a fighter. An infantry regimental commander at D-day, he was among the few senior army commanders eligible to wear the prestigious combat infantryman's badge. He gained rank rapidly in the campaigns across Normandy and northern France, becoming a division and then corps commander. His most recent overseas assignment was in Greece, where he helped crush a communist insurgency by building and training the Greek army. He displayed an uncanny sense of the battlefield's tempo, and he possessed all the qualities of a great captain—cool under pressure, aggressive, and a fertile mind determined to win.[84]

Before Eighth Army could make its next thrust toward Line Wyoming, Peng's volunteers struck back in their Fifth Campaign on April 22, but the Eighth Army was prepared. Van Fleet was ready to accept some nighttime enemy penetrations, but he strongly discouraged withdrawals during darkness as "such action usually results in major losses, loss of control, less coordinated fire power, difficulty identifying terrain and of distinguishing between friend and foe."[85] Eighth Army forces were expected to counterattack during daylight with tank-infantry teams, artillery, and air support to liquidate infiltrators, restore positions, and punish the enemy at every opportunity. With one notable exception—the collapse of the ROK Sixth Division—Van Fleet's plan blunted the Chinese drive and inflicted heavy losses, causing Peng to call off the offensive before achieving any of his desired objectives, namely, the capture of Seoul and the destruction of UNC divisions.[86]

The CPVF's mobile operations against a solidly anchored linear defense that was stubbornly defended and backed by powerful and mobile reserve forces was no longer the path to victory. Still under pressure to defeat the

Eighth Army, Peng shifted the weight of his forces east to confront the weaker line of ROK divisions in the X Corps, ROK III Corps, and ROK I Corps sectors. Perhaps he hoped that a breakthrough in this area, where the more rugged terrain and the less well-equipped ROK divisions would reduce the UNC's relative advantages in airpower, transportation, and artillery support, could collapse Eighth Army's eastern flank and open a deep operational level envelopment of Van Fleet's line in western Korea. If that could not be achieved, the annihilation of nearly half the ROK army certainly would change the tactical balance and give the initiative back to the Chinese.[87]

Van Fleet welcomed the Chinese move. He did not fear a deep penetration in east-central Korea: "We'll let them alone. There's nothing down there. Their soldiers will starve, or surrender," he remembered telling his staff as the Chinese attacked.[88] Just as importantly, the communist forces came into the open again, and though ROK army units did not fare well, the American and other UNC troops held fast and gave Van Fleet the best opportunity to inflict a decisive defeat on Peng's field army. "May is the month in which to defeat him," Van Fleet told his corps commanders. "We can do it better in this area than in any other. If we don't beat him now we will have more and more unfavorable weather for some months—less air—less mobility. Now is the time to destroy him . . . and do it north of the Han [River]." Van Fleet urged his subordinates to retain the defensive initiative: solid positions, firepower, keeping units intact, and avoiding isolation. Each corps was directed to prepare a regimental combat team to launch counterattacks.[89]

On May 16 four Chinese armies and two KPA corps swept through the mountains south of the Hwachon Reservoir, stampeded a succession of ROK divisions, and opened a gaping hole in Van Fleet's line. Paik Sun-yup's ROK I Corps held barely in the east and the Second Infantry Division anchored the western shoulder. It was here that Van Fleet's philosophy of stalwart defense plus artillery firepower proved its worth against Peng's desperate veterans. It was the birth of the "Van Fleet load," the authorization, even expectation, that American artillerymen would shoot all the shells they could physically load into their smoking guns.[90] Maj. Gen. Clark L. Ruffner, commanding the Second Infantry Division, informed Van Fleet, "We're killing Chinese faster than we can count them." American guns and bombs broke the back of the CPVF, and American forces were for the first time since October 1950 bringing in a significant haul of prisoners and captured material.[91] Again, Van Fleet had anticipated the outcome. The allies "launched a counterattack in the main area of battle and instead of being outflanked by the Reds who had poured down the mountains and roads east for as much as fifty miles, we pinched them off and disposed of them at leisure."[92]

Sensing that the Chinese were off balance, Van Fleet ordered an immediate counteroffensive to begin May 20. Acknowledging that the CPVF could not defeat the Eighth Army with a single blow, Peng ordered the troops that had penetrated deeply into Eighth Army's lines to retreat. The undeniable scale of loss was staggering. Not only were CPVF casualties immense, but also the loss of valuable weaponry and supplies was irreplaceable in the short term. Peng disguised the magnitude of the defeat with euphemisms such as "our armies advanced too far," were "confronted with supply problems," and consequently "the men were exhausted."[93] Whole units disintegrated, resulting in nearly twenty thousand Chinese taken prisoner. The 180th Division was nearly annihilated ("because of oversights," according to Marshal Peng), four thousand survivors ended up in UNC POW cages. It was one of the PLA in Korea's worst military setbacks.[94] Peng's troops had impaled themselves on the American defenses and consequently lost the initiative and their strategic momentum.[95]

Within a week, I Corps units, led by the newly organized Canadian Brigade, had advanced thirty miles toward the Iron Triangle. Van Fleet quickly issued orders for all of Eighth Army to return to Line Wyoming, not only to secure valuable terrain (the Hwachon Reservoir and the road networks east of Seoul) but also to annihilate Peng's troops before they could find sanctuary in their prepared defenses.[96] Prisoner interrogations confirmed casualties were high, morale low, and Chinese troops at the end of a long and failing supply line. American firepower and complete control of the air spelled doom and destruction for the hapless Chinese. One marine officer, Lieutenant Walter Murphy, remembered, "It was a massacre, truly."[97] In Van Fleet's view, Eighth Army was on the cusp of the battle that would trap and destroy the best units of Peng's volunteers south of the Soyang River. After his retirement in 1953, he wrote, "Those days are the ones most vivid in my memory—great days when all the Eighth Army, and we thought America too, were inspired to win. In those days in Korea, we reached the heights."[98]

Van Fleet's rapid advance had shocked the Chinese, but increasing poor weather gradually slowed Eighth Army's momentum and gave time for the Chinese to recover.[99] On May 28, a desperate Van Fleet urged Ridgway to approve an audacious thrust across Line Kansas coupled with an amphibious landing on Korea's east coast to encircle and destroy Chinese and North Korean forces in eastern Korea and envelop the major Chinese logistics hub in the Iron Triangle. China may have had inexhaustible reserves of manpower, but Peng needed veterans, not fodder, if he hoped to hold on in Korea. Van Fleet was confident that he would not only annihilate Peng Dehuai's and Kim Il-sung's remaining field forces, but also place UNC lines as far north as the "waist" of Korea (roughly from Pyongyang to Wonsan). Van Fleet's intention was strictly force-oriented, but his emphasis on a Pyongyang-Wonsan line may have inadvertently caused Ridgway and the Joint Chiefs to worry more about a repeat of China's initial intervention with UN forces operating so far from their supply and support bases. Van Fleet was confident enough that the destruction of so many Chinese divisions would compel a settlement that he told Ridgway, "the potentiality of enemy defeat should override any objections."[100]

Ridgway shied away from such grandiose plans promising victory. They smacked too much of MacArthur, and he remembered how the JCS and the White House reacted when MacArthur's bellicose rhetoric torpedoed Truman's first tentative attempt to promote a cease-fire. He knew Truman's temperament and his eagerness to wrap up the war in Korea.[101] The new theater commander was also solidifying his own thoughts that would shape and guide American military strategy for the next twelve months. Late in April he drafted instructions for each of the American operational commands serving in the Far East: Eighth Army, Far East Air Forces, and Far East Naval Forces. The instructions to each commander began with identical strategic premises and then followed with operational instructions, constraints, and restrictions. Both Van Fleet and FEAF commander Lt. Gen. George E. Stratemeyer were to base their operations on the assumption that CPVF and KPA forces determined to destroy or drive Eighth Army into the sea. Soviet intervention could not be ruled out. Additionally, no further reinforcements could be expected in theater, though ground and air units already deployed ought to be filled up to their authorized strength. The course of the ground war could not yet be determined. Van Fleet could be directed to fall back to a defensive line to hold indefinitely; just as likely, Eighth Army could be ordered to withdraw entirely from the Korean peninsula. But, until "competent authority" issued such instructions, Eighth Army's mission remained "to repel aggression against the Republic of Korea . . . [to] maintain intact all your major units, [to] retain the initiative while inflicting maximum losses on the enemy personnel and material." In his own script, Ridgway added that no operations in force beyond Line Kansas could take place without his approval.[102]

With these instructions, Ridgway was taking charge of the war in a way that MacArthur had not. In a postwar interview, Ridgway claimed, "I had the highest confidence in General Van Fleet and I gave him the freest reins," a statement he appeared to contradict almost immediately, underscoring the unique tension the new UNC commander endured in this kind of war: "I did keep a rein on the major operations . . . General Van Fleet might conduct."[103] Whereas MacArthur interfered in Eighth Army operations to increase his own prestige and to pressure the Joint Chiefs, Ridgway was determined that he would direct military operations toward a political objective that was at the time unstated, but of which Ridgway could not have been entirely ignorant. On May 30, he transmitted to Washington a thorough report of Van Fleet's current endeavor to regain Line Kansas-Wyoming while pursuing the beaten Chinese divisions. Significantly, he did not relay Van Fleet's own proposal to pursue beyond Line Kansas-Wyoming but he did include a political assessment, which was a virtual regurgitation of the NSC 48/5 memorandum of May 17, 1951, reflecting the primary goal of US policy to seek a political solution in Korea. He stated, "The enemy has suffered a severe major defeat. Within the past few days there has been a rapidly increasing deterioration of the Chinese forces . . . Eighth Army [is] at near full strength with morale excellent . . . inflicting maximum casualties on a defeated and retiring enemy. I therefore believe that for the next 60 days the United States government should be able to count with reasonable assurance upon a military situation in Korea offering optimum advantages in support of its diplomatic negotiations."[104] This was an astonishing, though understandable, position for the new senior military commander in the Far East to take. MacArthur had gotten in trouble and ultimately fired precisely for advocating a political policy action. Ridgway was more astute, though, and saw an opportunity to frame the problem the way Washington wanted to see it. He could also be satisfied that his recommendations to Washington corresponded with the instructions he was already enforcing with his subordinates.

Whatever his motive, the next day Ridgway got the instructions he wanted from the JCS. As the commander in chief of the Far East Command (FEC), Ridgway was directed to support UN operations in Korea, defend Formosa (Taiwan) and the Pescadores (Penghu) Islands from the Communist Chinese, prevent Chiang Kai-shek from using the same island bases for attacks on mainland China, and in the event of Soviet attack on the FEC, assume as his "basic and overriding mission" the defense of Japan. As the commander in chief of the United Nations Command, Ridgway was charged with inflicting maximum personnel and equipment losses on North Korean and Chinese forces "operating within the geographic boundaries of Korea and [its] waters." Above all, he was to create conditions favorable to a settlement that would terminate hostilities, establish the authority of the ROK over all Korea south of an undetermined line ("in no case south of the 38th parallel"), provide for the withdrawal of non-Korean forces from the peninsula, and permit the building of sufficient ROK military power to maintain any armistice achieved.[105]

This was a curious turnabout for the Americans' strategy in Korea. By June 2 the UNC surged over the 38th parallel and reoccupied its positions lost during the April offensive, but the JCS had just instructed Ridgway only to maintain the military conditions that Eighth Army had won, as any further deterioration of Chinese military power might make a negotiated settlement less, not more, likely. In other words, the JCS seemed to tell Ridgway, "Good enough—don't do anything to make the Chinese want to fight back." Significantly, Ridgway's orders also appeared to formalize as national policy the ideals of attrition as practiced by the Eighth Army, to maximize communist casualties while minimizing those of the United States and the United Nations contingents in Korea.[106] The JCS also included the injunction to obtain prior approval before launching any general advance beyond Line Kansas-Wyoming, the exception being for "necessary" or "desirable" tactical operations in the enemy's rear area to harass or maintain contact with the communist armies. Bringing military force to bear to destroy an enemy's capability to wage war and to defeat his will to resist is often a tall order; to bring *only enough* strength to ensure military equilibrium, however, is a task of an altogether different magnitude. This was Ridgway's conundrum, though he probably assumed that in a sixty-day time frame, the strategic dilemma would resolve itself through intensive and good-faith negotiation. Van Fleet was beside himself with frustration.[107]

With the opportunity to launch a general offensive to encircle, destroy, or otherwise disable Communist China's war machine in Korea eclipsed by the war's new political direction, Van Fleet did convince Ridgway to sanction a limited attack to secure the UNC position along Line Kansas-Wyoming. He ordered Operation Piledriver to drive the I Corps toward Pyonggang, the railway nexus at the northern apex of the Iron Triangle. Simultaneously, the IX Corps was to drive north from the Hwachon Reservoir toward Samyang-ni and Kumsong, while the X and ROK I Corps cleaned out the region from the "Punchbowl," a circular volcanic valley northeast of the Hwachon Reservoir, to Kojin-ni on the east coast. The three corps would then establish another line, called the Outpost Line of Resistance (OPLR), to act as a shield for Line Kansas-Wyoming, which was now designated the Main Line of Resistance (MLR). However, even if wildly successful, Operation Piledriver promised limited results. The Chinese and North Korean defenders were sure to demonstrate their resiliency and tenacity when given even the briefest respite. From a military viewpoint, the critical flaw was not in its objective, or even its limited nature, but rather its prescribed scope. By focusing Eighth Army offensive thrusts to essentially four obvious targets in the eastern half of the country, Van Fleet greatly simplified Peng's operational problem by allowing him to economize in the west while concentrating force in the more easily defended terrain of central and eastern Korea.[108]

The attack was scheduled to kick off on June 3, but heavy rains in the last two days of May ensured slow going along the three major roads American troops needed to penetrate the Triangle's southern base. Lt. Gen. Frank L. "Shrimp" Milburn ordered three of his I Corps divisions to strike at the base

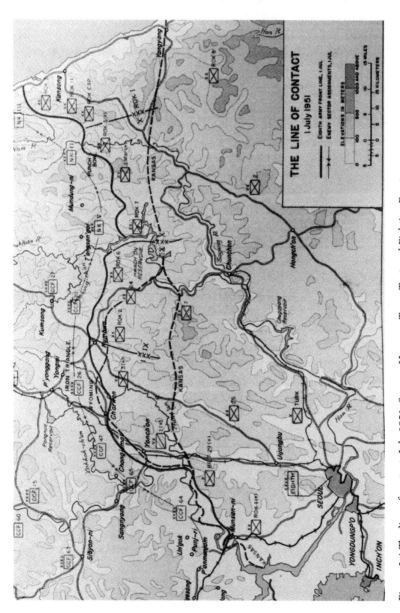

Figure 2.4 The line of contact, July 1951. Source: Hermes, *Truce Tent and Fighting Front*.

of the Iron Triangle from Chorwon to Kumhwa, while Lt. Gen. William M. Hoge's IX Corps aimed three divisions to push out from Line Wyoming toward the Hwachon Reservoir. Once the attack kicked off, Chinese resistance was stiffer than expected, and the weather again turned foul, limiting close air support and observation. After five days the US troops finally broke through, and tank-infantry teams tentatively occupied Pyonggang on June 13. Farther east, IX Corps made similar gains, slow but steady, toward Kumsong, and the X Corps reached the lower lip of the Punchbowl.[109]

Despite this successful advance, Eighth Army could go no farther. By mid-June, all three US corps realized that the Chinese and North Koreans held the higher ground in strength, and further gains were to be had only in exchange for heavy casualties. The Americans withdrew from Pyonggang, and a week later Van Fleet reported to Ridgway that Eighth Army was secure on the MLR. Line Wyoming formed a large salient thrusting north in the center of Line Kansas to neutralize the towns of Chorwon and Kumhwa, the base towns of the Iron Triangle. But the high ground running along the base of the Triangle remained in Communist hands. Van Fleet realized his fears had come to pass. Although severely beaten following their May offensive, after only three weeks the Communists had regained their equilibrium and were in the mood to fight.[110] The great vision of a decisive pursuit was over. As one tired veteran knew, "There was no way the Chinese were going to give up [those] hill[s] without some serious . . . fighting."[111]

But Van Fleet constantly worried an enemy buildup for a future offensive was ongoing. His concern caused Eighth Army to push its OPLR farther north in the name of "securing" the previous OPLR. Despite the suspension of Van Fleet's offensive drive, there could be no true stalemate on the front, for one side's OPLR was destined eventually to collide with the other's. The Chinese were going to fight for the Iron Triangle just as Van Fleet was determined to hold Kansas-Wyoming. This tactical imperative to control the ground between the respective MLRs defined the structure for ground combat through the next eighteen months. Perhaps the greatest lost lesson for the Americans was the simple observation of an artillery officer, who realized the Chinese were determined to hold their position: "We didn't know how badly they wanted it."[112]

3

THE NEW WAR, JULY–OCTOBER 1951

SIX MONTHS OF campaigning winnowed the CPVF's ranks by nearly one-third, and air attacks had decimated Peng's meager truck transportation sufficiently that clothing, food, and ammunition were in critically short supply.[1] The Chinese had invested a great deal in the war in Korea, and their battlefield success against the UNC was making Mao's China a regional power. Mao could not help but let the heady early campaigns reinforce his own high opinion of himself as a strategist. In the CPVF's first four campaigns, the Chinese successfully employed a tactical method featuring mobile operations, bold assaults emphasizing the role of spirit over American technology, and a willingness to endure casualties.[2] The CPVF would recover before the lines stabilized and negotiations for an armistice began, but it was a near-run thing. The lessons of logistical preparedness and protection from American firepower were learned and would influence how Peng and his generals adapted to the new conditions of battle obtained the following year. But Peng's failure to drive the Eighth Army back to Pusan with a military victory in Korea convinced Chinese political and military leaders the war was going to be protracted. A strategy of annihilation yielded to a longer-term strategy of persistence to allow the CPVF to resist UNC firepower and strategic pressure while still increasing the Communists' experience in modern warfare and the buildup of equipment and supplies.[3]

Peng agreed with this strategic direction, recognizing the CPVF "needed to find a way to consolidate our positions" and adopt new tactics to emphasize survivability while maintaining a credible offensive capability. "Mouths should not open too wide" when fighting the Americans. Chinese tactical objectives would become more manageable and the fighting momentum more sustainable.[4] In a conference with his subordinate commanders held from June 6 to 9, he directed as the best way forward "an active positional defense" that would hold a solid line of resistance. Meanwhile, Chinese troops were instructed in new tactics to counterattack and retrieve lost positions, as it was recognized any loss of terrain now carried political consequences. At the same time, the CPVF accepted reinforcements from China without releasing its veteran units. The additional artillery these new formations brought with them would do much to help equalize the tactical contests that would occur in the summer of 1952.[5]

Before Mao could wax exuberantly about his revitalized ground forces, the war in Korea was to endure another metamorphosis. Prior to Eighth Army's turnaround under Ridgway, President Truman made two fundamental policy decisions that directly affected American strategy in Korea. First, the UNC would not voluntarily abandon Korea, the ROK army, or the ROK government. They would have to be forced off the peninsula through superior military strength. By the same token, the UNC would abandon its political goal to unite the two Koreas under ROK sovereignty. Instead, an armistice based on the status quo would be the objective, and the 38th parallel was considered an acceptable condition. This decision, taken when UN forces were far from the 38th parallel, was going to come back to haunt the future negotiations. The Chinese, for their part, in an equally unfortunate statement, came out strongly against the 38th parallel as a basis for a settlement, claiming that it had been "obliterated forever." The Chinese were right—the prewar parallel boundary could not be a militarily secure line, but it would take months of hard fighting to make that point stick.[6]

Talking While Fighting

Air force Lt. Col. A. J. Kinney, marine Lt. Col. James C. Murray, and ROK Lt. Col. Soo Young-lee circled Korea's ancient capital city of Kaesong just after 0900 on July 8, 1951. The two American helicopters carrying the small liaison team finally landed near a large white "W" laid out in the center of an open area in the north-central part of the town. Kinney immediately noticed the presence of a large number of communist soldiers lining the edge of the makeshift landing zone. No Korean civilians were visible.

Two lieutenants, one from the CPVF and the other from the KPA, approached Kinney's group as they stepped out of the helicopters. One, identified as Lieutenant Lin, indicated they were the escort for the UNC team to the meeting place. Six American jeeps stood by to transport the group. All the jeep drivers were Chinese. After a short drive to Kwang Mun Dong, Kinney met his counterpart, KPA Colonel Chang. The Communists were in no hurry "to get down to business."

Finally, at 0947, the two teams began the first of what would be hundreds of liaison sessions. With a short break for lunch, talks went on until 1600 hours, when the Americans headed back to their helicopters. Ten minutes later, Kinney and his team were safely back at their base camp at Munsan-ni.

Throughout the day Kinney observed that the Communists' behavior had been polite and correct, but he could not shake the feeling that the UNC delegation was actually under the enemy's control at Kaesong, "under close observation of armed guards." It was a small but prescient reflection as the Communists had been keen to ensure they controlled the locality. Negotiations at Kaesong for a truce would not proceed in a direct manner. For that matter, the UNC was soon to learn that any bargaining under the enemy's guns was bound to be problematic. The stage was now set for a new, separate, and no less dangerous campaign that both sides hoped would bring the Korean War to a favorable conclusion.[7]

Neither side saw negotiations as merely a nonviolent means to an end, but rather they were a forum to win a war that could not be won by fighting. The truce talks could be seen as a separate event in the war's drama, almost with its own logic and outcomes. In reality, the talks' progress (a squishy term as "progress" meant different things to the Americans, Chinese, and Koreans) was firmly linked to battlefield results. Both sides played the game to their best advantage, alternating between posturing, hectoring, demanding, and sulking—and both sides were ready to substitute bullets and shells when words did not convey the right message. It was a confrontation in a different domain, with episodic conflict influencing the negotiating stance of both parties. Many western-oriented histories—particularly by those directly involved—tend to give the Communists high marks for their acumen at Kaesong and (at the subsequent site of) Panmunjom.[8] Chief UNC delegate Vice Admiral C. Turner Joy established this narrative early. Shortly after the war he observed, "Communists neither blunder into conferences nor rush pell-mell to engage in negotiation. *First, they carefully set the stage* [original emphasis]."[9] There was truth to Joy's analysis. We know now that Zhou Enlai, Mao's foreign minister, ran the negotiations through his personal representative Li Kenong, who exercised his position as negotiations "commander" for the Communist side. As Mao's confidence in Peng slipped, the latter spent increasingly more time focused on the administration of the army—weaponry, logistics, medical services, and living conditions. Day-to-day tactics fell more on a committee of CPVF senior officers led by Deng Hua, CPVF deputy commander, and Xie Fang, CPVF chief of staff. Both men also served as delegates at Kaesong and Panmunjom and were thus in a better position to link negotiations to tactics and operations. Deng had a low opinion of American fighting qualities, believing "their infantry is weak. Their men are afraid to die and will neither press home a bold attack nor defend to the death." The ROK army, likewise, was underappreciated. These attitudes go a long way to explaining the Communists' initial bargaining position and obstinacy at Kaesong. This combination of political and military decision-making so close to the point of negotiations allowed a greater suppleness and coherence to Chinese talking and fighting.[10]

The Americans could be equally obstinate and dismissive of their opposite numbers. American armed forces had never faced the prospect of negotiations dictated by military stalemate. This generally successful tradition of armed politics failed to develop within the Americans' military culture a recognition of the virtues of diplomacy and compromise.[11] Rather, Admiral Joy, along with his colleagues, assumed a polarity to the conflict: UNC armed forces versus the Communists' armed forces. Since the UNC dominated the air and sea, and held its own on land, it made perfect sense for the American delegates to presume that they had the Communists on the ropes. However, what Joy and his superiors were not prepared for was the Communists' reliance on rhetorical intimidation and trenchant propaganda. He characterized the Communist negotiation style as insisting that two plus two was six, and only after exhaustive haggling and much bombastic browbeating, finally conceding that it made five. Only much later did Joy take stock of the new reality of limited war as he reflected that the Communists in Korea "shrewdly combin[ed] force and negotiation."[12] Even so, these are curious assertions, as the Americans likewise pursued a positive strategy of coercive pressure, and it would be wrong to assume that Chinese and North Korean delegates by themselves set a new course for the war through tough talk and stubborn demands to produce an enduring stalemate characterized by a contest over sterile terrain objectives. The reality is that the Americans, who continued to dominate the UNC coalition, assumed an aggressive stance from the beginning and achieved virtually all of their substantive aims, whereas the Communists had to settle, at best, for their minimal positions.

The negotiations, which were long, complex, repetitive, and plagued with distrust, can be divided into three unequal phases. The first, July 10 through the end of August, was a false start as both sides went in with hopeless optimism. The Communists thought to regain the 38th parallel and the removal of all foreign (meaning Western) forces, while the UNC planned for a quick military settlement followed by an unspecified political conference to resolve issues such as borders and the status of foreign forces. Both sides were disappointed by the real difficulties in coming to a settlement that would uniformly satisfy everyone's policy and strategic objectives. The Chinese in particular were playing for time. If the status quo ante bellum could not be restored, then Mao needed breathing room to prepare for a sixth offensive campaign. Kim Il-sung wanted to stop the bombing of North Korean cities, which were practically defenseless against UNC air attacks. Serious negotiations stalled as both sides realized they were not prepared to compromise on their significant strategic objectives. Ambiguous security "incidents" gave excuse to break off the talks just as Eighth Army began a limited and costly offensive in east-central Korea.[13]

The second phase convened at a more neutral site at Panmunjom, about five miles south of Kaesong. The Communists dropped their demands for the 38th parallel, and the Americans showed some flexibility with the final military demarcation line (MDL) being the current line of contact without any air or naval premiums. In mid-November UNC negotiators agreed to this formula for establishing the MDL if within thirty days all other outstanding issues were resolved. This curious play went into effect from November 27 to December 27, but it turned out to be a mistake as the Communist forces used the de facto armistice to dig fortifications, resupply their worn-out units, and prepare for the resumption of hostilities. When final agreements were not forthcoming, the UNC realized that the cost to resume effective pressure on the ground had become much higher. The soft truce was extended into 1952, mainly at Washington's insistence, so great was Truman's desire to settle the war. Progress continued to be languid, but many remained confident that the two sides were narrowing the issues sufficiently that an armistice was nearly accomplished.

The third phase began in February 1952 when President Truman made a policy decision on the disposition of POWs that bound the UNC to pursue a strategic objective for which it did not possess adequate military means. Contrary to accepted international agreements and his own military's advice, the president determined that no prisoner would be forcibly returned to Communist China or North Korea. The policy became known as voluntary repatriation (or nonforcible repatriation), and the UNC's unexpected adherence to this policy completely ossified the talks at Panmunjom and left both sides at a loss of what to do. Although the question of POW repatriation struck at both Korean regimes, it was felt most acutely by the People's Republic of China (PRC). Any semblance of "defection" was potentially a mortal blow against Mao's legitimacy. At this point, neither side could back down from their respective positions without significant loss of prestige and credibility.[14] Both sides had agreed early that armistice talks would focus on purely military questions, but in this third phase the argument was strictly political, which explains why the phase lasted so long and cost so many lives. Terrain was nothing; casualties were regrettable; bargaining position, propaganda, and perceived posture at Panmunjom were everything. A hill won or lost was only valuable insofar as it increased the military costs and political pain for the other side. And so it went: for much of 1952, the only talking done was from the barrel of a gun.

The False Start, July–August 1951

Ideas for a negotiated settlement and reestablishment of the territorial status quo ante were born early in the conflict. As American and ROK forces were barely hanging on to their shrinking chunk of the peninsula around Pusan, Canada's secretary of state for external affairs, Lester B. Pearson, articulated a hopeful basis to settle the fighting in a way that would "remove the possibility of a repetition" of aggression, while "commend[ing] itself to the inhabitants of Korea . . . command[ing] support from Asian opinion, and . . . recogniz[ing] the progress which has already been made under the auspices of the United Nations in establishing an independent government in Korea."[15] This was a tall order and one that did not lend itself to military efforts limited in scope and intensity. Pearson's advocacy for such a peace never diminished, and in many ways his major points did find themselves being addressed in some fashion once the two sides met to establish a cease-fire. A few months later, at the height of the Chinese intervention crisis, Dean Acheson also realized a negotiated settlement would only be possible when "we have the capability to stabilize the front somewhere in the peninsula and to engage a large number of Communist forces [successfully] for a long time."[16] Fruitful negotiations would have to be underwritten by effective fighting.

At about the same time, the assistant secretary of state for Far Eastern Affairs, Dean Rusk, advocated a framework to salvage the American policy objective in Korea while punishing the Chinese. A crucial aspect was to pursue military action and seek a cease-fire in the vicinity of the 38th parallel. Attrition, if unable to keep the Chinese away from the 38th parallel, would at least "make [a settlement] in the interest of the Chinese Communists to accept . . . by making it so costly for them that they could not afford not to accept."[17] Acheson agreed that increasingly heavy military losses would likely compel Beijing (and by extension Moscow) to accept the status quo ante, though he was unsure of the wisdom of recrossing the 38th parallel.[18] While Washington wrestled with policy options, Ridgway's campaign from January through April 1951 supported this strategic logic by inflicting casualties while preserving his own forces to create conditions for a negotiated settlement. By mid-April, just as Peng launched his Fifth Campaign, the Eighth Army had substantially regained the 38th parallel and was in a good position to withstand a general assault while imposing heavy casualties again on Peng's attacking forces.[19]

The conclusion of Peng's Fifth Campaign and Van Fleet's counterattack at last put Ridgway's orders deriving from NSC 48/5 into the right political and strategic context. The Chinese for their part needed to feel sufficiently secure in their military position without being provoked to increase their own

efforts. The JCS certainly hoped to bring the Korean conflict to a quick finish. Although the shooting war was in Asia, General Bradley and the other
members of the Joint Chiefs had always kept their vision for a future war
with the Soviet Union in Europe. When a diplomatic revolution appeared to
be in the offing, the administration seized the opportunity. That revolution
appeared to materialize when the Soviet Union's representative to the United
Nations, Yakov Malik, intimated that his country might be prepared to support a settlement of the Korean War by influencing North Korea and Communist China. By mid-June it was obvious that Mao's armies were not going to drive the UNC into the sea; to the contrary, without some mechanism
to relieve the military pressure, the CPVF faced destruction.[20] Between June
13 and 14, Stalin prevailed on Kim Il-sung and Gao Gang, Mao's representative in Moscow, to accept Soviet military advisors, additional training and
aircraft for the Chinese air force, and modern weapons to outfit up to sixteen divisions as a guarantee for any political settlement that left unfinished
business on the peninsula.[21]

On June 23, 1951, Malik delivered a radio broadcast that rambled on in
his style about the aggressions of the capitalist West, when he dropped an unexpected bombshell revealing, "The Soviet peoples further believe that the
most acute problem of the present day—the problem of armed conflict in
Korea—could also be settled. . . . [A]s a first step discussions should be started
between the belligerents for a cease-fire." He also implied that the 38th parallel should be the point of military settlement. However, two days later, the
Soviet foreign minister, Andrei Gromyko, privately suggested that any armistice settlement should deal strictly with military matters, avoiding political
or territorial questions. This stance suggested that the 38th parallel was not
necessarily a solid position from the Soviet viewpoint, even if the North Koreans vocally asserted that it was.[22] Two days later Radio Beijing broadcast an
editorial statement that the Chinese people fully supported the Soviet's public initiative. Excitement in the West began to mount and the pressure was
now on the American president to respond.[23]

Accepting the Soviet position to be as binding as possible, Truman authorized the JCS to direct Ridgway to broadcast on June 30, "I am informed that
you wish a meeting to discuss [an] armistice providing for the cessation of
hostilities and all acts of armed force in Korea, with adequate guarantee for
the maintenance of such armistice. Upon receipt of word that such a meeting is desired, I shall be prepared to name my representative. I would also at
that time suggest a date at which he could meet with your representative. I
propose that such a meeting could take place aboard a Danish hospital ship
in Wonsan harbor."[24] Ridgway's words were carefully chosen, full of conditional tenses, avoiding direct responsibility, and giving no hint that either

side would be liable for the success or failure of any cease-fire talks. The fact that the Communists responded the next day, July 1, appeared to bode well for a rapid commencement of negotiations. In fact, it was too rapid, and the Americans were going to be unprepared for the opening of a "second front" that enabled the Communists to attempt to gain at the truce talks what Chinese armies failed to deliver on the battlefield.

Significantly, the Communists' reply offered a change of venue. Instead of Wonsan harbor, where the Communists knew they would be in UNC-controlled waters, they offered to meet Ridgway's representatives in Kaesong, the historical Korean capital, then unoccupied but close to the Communists' influence. From their perspective, Kaesong had the additional advantage of straddling the 38th parallel, a not so subtle indicator of their military goals. More importantly, Kaesong's location could provide the opportunity to block any further Eighth Army advances in the western half of the peninsula, which was flatter, more accessible to vehicular traffic, and more difficult to defend.[25] In the rush to begin talks, the UNC failed to take these conditions under serious consideration, and because allied patrols suggested little enemy activity at Kaesong, Ridgway decided it was a sufficiently neutral site, and he agreed to the Communists' proposal.

Rutherford Poats, an American journalist present for much of the negotiations, later recalled, "Here trouble and disillusionment started."[26] It had been three weeks since the end of Operation Piledriver, and the front had achieved a degree of stability that benefited the Communists more than Eighth Army; they were no longer under the pressure of imminent collapse. Additionally, the opening moves at Kaesong illustrated how negotiations, though perhaps sincere, were in reality another form of confrontation. Col. Chai Chengwen later reflected that "the truce talks could not be separated for even one second from the situation on the battleground."[27] A later observer suggested the negotiations were "a depressing spectacle . . . from the beginning they were marked by a propensity for prolonged and unproductive disputation that was without precedent in the history of diplomatic affairs."[28] It was a fitting companion to a military contest that also was without precedent.

Secretary of State Dean Acheson was cautiously optimistic, but even he figured the chances for an early armistice were "at least fifty-fifty."[29] American and other allied newsmen held similar confidence that the war in Korea would come to an end, perhaps within six weeks.[30] Characteristically, Mao was also supportive of negotiations as he saw an opportunity to use the talks to open a new political front to occupy the enemy while the Communist armies regrouped, rearmed, and prepared to renew (potentially) the offensive in August. But the option of renewing the offensive would be necessary only if the UNC did not agree to a restoration of the 38th parallel and the allocation of "a neutral zone" between North and South Korea, in reality a de-militarized zone (DMZ). Significantly, Mao was willing to forego for the time being the political issues of Taiwan and PRC membership in the UN.[31] He also expressed (misplaced) confidence in the military situation that "it would take ten to fourteen days to prepare and go through the negotiations." Traveling to Kaesong, Chinese delegates brought only summer-weight clothing.[32]

The Communist delegation comprised three officers from the KPA and two from the CPVF. Lt. Gen. Nam Il was the chief delegate and the KPA's chief of staff. Supporting him were Maj. Gen. Lee Sang-cho and Maj. Gen. Chang Pyong-san. Representing the CPVF were Deng Hua and Xie Fang. They were all longtime Communists who had survived Japanese invasion, occupation, and civil war. Nam Il had served in the Soviet army during World War II. The UNC contingent was headed by Vice Admiral C. Turner Joy. His associates included army Maj. Gen. Henry I. Hodes, air force Maj. Gen. Laurence C. Craigie, Rear Admiral Arleigh A. Burke, and ROK Maj. Gen. Paik Sun-yup. Unlike their counterparts, the UNC delegates were all combat commanders. None was a staff or "political officer," nor did any have experience with political work, intelligence operations, or propaganda warfare. And despite Ridgway's desire, the US Department of State declined to send anyone who might unbalance the military nature of the discussion. It was a mistake the Communists did not make.[33]

Kaesong may have lain in "no-man's-land" at the time of Ridgway's truce talk invitation, but by the time liaison officers gathered, Chinese and North Korean troops had moved forward to occupy the town and its environs. The Communists clearly controlled the site and the surrounding area when Kinney and his fellow officers arrived to be met by surly soldiers. Because the UNC team would have to pass through Communist lines, it was determined that they would wear white armbands and be met by an escort and some photographers and "newsmen." These additions to what was merely a coordination meeting caused severe frictions as the Communists quickly capitalized on the appearance that the UNC was suing for peace.[34] Because the Communists controlled the site, they also controlled the seating: their delegates sat on the north (victorious) side of an oblong table, while the UNC sat on the south (defeated) side. Nam Il towered over Joy, as the two officers' chairs had been modified to give Nam the height advantage. A controversy over newsmen also highlighted the subtle play for advantage the Communists made. Eventually, it was worked out, but the Communists clearly had scored the first all-important victories in the initial skirmishes at Kaesong.[35]

The night before the first meeting of delegates convened, Commander Li Kenong gathered the Korean and Chinese negotiators for a strategic planning session. Li articulated three principles as first steps to solve the Korea problem. There had to be an immediate cease-fire, mutual withdrawal of military forces from the 38th parallel (creating a de facto demilitarized zone but also requiring the UNC to give up ground it had seized north of the parallel during the previous months' operations), and foreign forces had to leave Korea. Based on public statements Li did not believe the first two points would be contentious, and this was the Communists' opening bargaining position. Additional guidance Li presented was to be always in favor of "peace" as their actions were displayed before the world. This might be dismissed as mere propaganda, but the Communists took the idea seriously that their strategic audience was world opinion. Therefore, it was important to "avoid being tied up with minor problems," what the Americans would call "details." Finally, the negotiators had to remember they were fighting a "political battle" as important as the frontline soldiers fighting the "military one."[36] Diplomacy was an extension of war, and Sunzi (Sun Tzu) advised, "All war is deception." The Chinese, at least, could be counted on to speak carefully and to apply the flexible methods of guerrilla strategy to the talks.[37] Peng, for his part, had cautioned Xie prior to his departure, "Don't let the enemy get anything from the negotiating table that they couldn't get on the battlefield."[38]

Truman articulated his intent that the UNC's "principal military interest in this armistice lies in a cessation of hostilities in Korea, an assurance against the resumption of fighting, and the protection of the security of United Nations forces." Ridgway also had to avoid engaging the United States "in a negotiating position as to make retreat to our minimum terms impossible."[39] Because the armistice talks were intended to cover only military matters, and avoid politically binding agreements, Ridgway ordered that military operations had to continue until an armistice was obtained. He also felt compelled to remind the JCS that Line Kansas was for him a sine qua non for a sustainable defensive posture. The JCS agreed, but they also directed Ridgway not to do anything that might impede the opening of truce talks. They accepted that any final demarcation line had to be on defensible terrain, and to achieve that line Ridgway was authorized to propose a demarcation line north of Eighth Army's battle positions "for purposes of negotiation."[40]

A peculiar precedent was now set. Although Ridgway, as the theater commander, was responsible for obtaining the best possible terms for a military cease-fire, he would be taking his cues, and at times his actual positions, from policy makers in Washington who had the technical means to communicate directly to Tokyo and transmit instructions to the delegates staged at Munsan-ni in rapid form. The Communists did not enjoy the same level of communications, but they too labored under political control, often recessing the talks for days at a time to receive authoritative direction from Pyongyang and Beijing. From the beginning, political considerations dictated the stance and the pace of the military negotiations.[41]

It took more than two weeks, between July 10 and July 26, for the two sides to agree to define and guarantee the security of a neutral zone around the conference site, the mutual equality of the respective delegations' activities, and a five-point agenda, the first point of which was to establish an agenda. Every statement was translated into English, Korean, and Chinese. Vice Admiral Joy delivered the first keynote speech on July 10. Joy was the commander of US Naval Forces, Far East. He had a distinguished wartime career as a commander of fleet cruisers in action against Japan during World War II. His first remarks at Kaesong underscored the UNC's viewpoint that armistice talks would be restricted to military matters in Korea only, that the UNC would continue military operations until a cease-fire was agreed to, and that the cease-fire would establish conditions to prevent the recurrence of hostilities. The North Koreans, supported by CPVF Maj. Gen. Xie Fang (Joy called him "markedly the mental superior among the Communist delegation" and the real power on the Communist side of the room), opened with the more ambitious position, attempting to establish Li's three principle conditions as fundamental to the structure of the negotiations. Nam Il countered that both sides should order the respective forces to cease operations, the 38th parallel be restored as the de facto boundary between North and South Korea, and all foreign forces be removed from Korea. The repatriation or exchange of prisoners was part of the restoration of the status quo ante bellum.[42]

The Americans quickly parried and took the lead to define the agenda and to limit the focus of talks to the technical military details. As the Communists assumed talks would revolve around vague agreements, they were unprepared and reluctant to dive into particulars, which is exactly what the Americans wanted to do. Whereas Nam proposed three issues, Joy countered with eight that articulated the nuts and bolts of an armistice agreement—not just the "what" but also the "how."[43]

However the two sides came together to negotiate meaningful terms, the armistice had to accomplish three essential tasks. First, it had to settle the military situation in situ. This meant more than merely establishing a cease-fire. Both sides had to be satisfied that the tactical situation was tolerable and would not encourage further military activity.[44] Second, each side needed to have a plausible claim to victory or success, however defined. Each country involved in the negotiations would define and redefine its own war aims throughout the period of negotiations. Each country would also undertake military action in an attempt to influence its opponents' war aims or definitions of victory. Finally, the armistice would have to ensure the survival of two Koreas, for neither the Chinese nor the Americans were going to agree to any proposal that jeopardized their Korean client's survivability.

The Chinese probably were sincere in wanting to settle that July, provided their stated demands in Korea were met. Although Mao signaled his willingness to forego demands regarding PRC entry into the United Nations and the immediate resolution of Taiwan's independence, he remained wedded to the 38th parallel as the final demarcation line.[45] However, as already outlined, the demand to appoint as agenda items the reestablishment of the 38th parallel along with the withdrawal of foreign forces from Korea as the links to a peaceful settlement was fanciful. Chinese forces were not strong enough to drive forward to the 38th parallel in central and eastern Korea. Terrain, UNC air supremacy, and the Eighth Army's moral recovery made further military progress improbable. The removal of foreign forces was equally problematic, as the Chinese clearly failed to eject the UNC forcibly, why would western forces voluntarily abandon South Korea? The military situation at the time did not support either of these positions, but that did not stop the Communists from making the play—they had nothing to lose and much to gain. It was a long shot, but in the end a naive demand.[46]

The procedural difficulty of settling on an agenda should not be underestimated. After only two days the talks nearly broke down for breaches of protocol that were minor on the surface but communicated portentous bargaining in the future. Reflecting on those first few weeks at Kaesong, Gen. J. Lawton Collins remarked, "Haggling over agenda is not an idle Communist exercise."[47] Although Joy's intent to establish an agenda was to delimit clearly the military topics pertaining to a cease-fire to be discussed, the Communist negotiators would continue to inject their broad demands as issues assumed to be resolved. Joy recorded this early discussion, which captured the logic of peacemaking and the difficulties of two alien cultures attempting to settle a war that was itself militarily inconclusive:

ADMIRAL JOY: When I use the term "agenda," I am referring to a group of items which are general questions . . . you, however, are in fact talking about one line [the 38th parallel] when . . . there are many [possible] lines.

NAM IL: We have showed you our line. What are the possible lines for you?

ADMIRAL JOY: We do not suggest any line yet because that is getting into the substance of that item of the [unsettled] agenda.

NAM IL: As for a line, we proposed a concrete line [the 38th parallel] . . . You do not agree?

ADMIRAL JOY: We will agree to place on the agenda an item calling for the establishment of some demilitarized zone . . .

NAM IL: We cannot consider the 38th parallel line as an imaginary line. The [line] had existed and the war broke out right on that line. Therefore, it is the principle that the question of the cease fire must be concluded also on the 38th parallel line. Therefore, this must be on the agenda.[48]

After two and a half weeks and ten plenary sessions, the American-driven proposal became, with minor modifications, the five-point agenda for the remaining months of truce talks:

1. Settle on an agenda

2. Fix a demilitarized zone as a basic condition for a cease-fire

3. Establish concrete arrangements for a cease-fire and armistice that would insure against a resumption of hostilities:

  a. Military armistice commission, including its composition, authority, and functions

  b. Military observer teams, including composition, authority, and functions

4. Arrange for the disposition and exchange of prisoners

5. Recommendation to governments of countries concerned on both sides for a political conference to settle the Korean problem.

The last point was a compromise (Collins called it a "face-saving device") catchall for the political issues that the Communists had hoped to set as actual agenda items. Whereas they equated peace with the removal of foreign UNC forces, the Americans saw the inverse. Once peace was established through a concrete and enduring armistice, then their forces would withdraw. It was a political question, and in getting his way, Admiral Joy was demonstrating the strength of the UNC's position. That strength, however, was transitory and susceptible to manipulation.[49]

The prime example of this manipulation is that although Joy scored a significant victory by setting the terms of the agenda, the Communists determined that the agenda items would be resolved sequentially. Therefore, by placing the establishment of the demilitarized zone second, the UNC was now in a position to agree to a cease-fire line before settling the composition, authorities, and mechanism for the armistice itself. Joy later acknowledged they had "opened for the Communists a road to a de facto cease-fire prior to agreement on other substantive questions. . . . This allowed the Communists a sorely needed breathing spell in which to dig in and stabilize their battle line."[50] Given the amount of time it would take to settle this one point, and the military strength the Communists would enhance during that time, the UNC's victory over the agenda proved to be a hollow one, and a great disappointment for the thousands of American soldiers and marines who anticipated a settlement by early fall at the latest.[51]

Because the Communists controlled Kaesong and the road leading from Munsan, where the UNC negotiators staged, they could and did restrict movement and security. The haggles over liaison officers and delegates traveling under a flag of truce, the ubiquitous presence of armed Communist soldiers, and the refusal to permit entry to the UNC's news personnel provoked Admiral Joy's unbending protest.[52] Paik Sun-yup recognized that "we could not escape the intimidation one feels when entering an armed enemy camp."[53] Political posturing through words and passive-aggressive actions could be war by other means. The UNC had to regain its equilibrium before meaningful talks could resume. General Ridgway's stern demands for truly neutral and equal treatment of both delegations got talks going again, but five days later. Joy recognized "that a great multitude of these maneuvers can add up to a propaganda total of effective magnitude."[54] It was to be a long and laborious education for all involved.

Serious negotiations on agenda item two began on July 26, when Nam Il re-presented the Communists' demand to establish the cease-fire line as the 38th parallel, even though they had consented to leave it off the agenda. Nam and his delegates offered a reasoned argument that contained a significant *political* concession—the 38th parallel had been an internationally recognized boundary, which implied recognition of the Republic of Korea. By extension, a return to the parallel would also imply mutual recognition of two regimes on the peninsula that ought to have been a firm basis for a permanent settlement: two Korean states sharing one peninsula. Given the military situation, it is probable that even Kim Il-sung would have reluctantly agreed.[55]

However, Syngman Rhee, president of the ROK, was dead set against any negotiations for a truce, and he orchestrated demonstrations and lobbied intensely against "secret negotiations" while demanding "complete disarmament of the [Communist] aggressors" and a military advance to the Tuman and Yalu Rivers. Separately, Rhee wrote Ridgway to chide the Americans for being duped into accepting "a settlement which settles nothing." He urged Ridgway to take a hard stand, press the Communist negotiators, and prepare to fight to victory. Otherwise, the ROK government demanded the removal of all Chinese troops from Korea before any armistice was settled. Only then would the "permanent security of Korea" be guaranteed.[56] Ridgway naturally discarded Rhee's advocacy, when the UNC had neither the will nor the means to impose such conditions on North Korea supported by China. But Rhee was going to demonstrate over the next two years the ability of the weaker ally to play the spoiler. It was not to be the last time that the UNC position was sorely tried by the Korean government.

At Kaesong, Joy countered Nam Il's politically charged solution with a strict reading of the military map. He proposed the militarily defined line of contact between the two forces as the line of final demarcation and demilitarization. He then suggested, probably as much for ROK consumption as for the Communists, that the final demarcation line be drawn twenty miles north of the line of contact, arguing that UNC air and naval superiority, though abstracted on the ground, justified additional terrain compensation. Nam Il could not conceal his shock or outrage, and he rejected the demand as "arrogant and absurd," but he had no military means to dispute Joy's position.[57]

As the Americans recognized much later, their implicit military viewpoint discarded the 38th parallel as insignificant. It had not occurred to them that the Communists would never be led to assume agreement on an item that was very much in the UNC's favor. Dean Acheson believed the Chinese's dismay derived from the recognition that the UNC was "demanding a new line . . . not only more militarily significant but involving considerable loss of prestige for them."[58] Not to mention that the Americans and other United Nations leaders had previously made several public statements regarding the suitability of the 38th parallel as a demarcation line. For example, Acheson informed the US Senate on June 7 that the United Nations forces in Korea would agree to an armistice based solidly on the 38th parallel, clearly signifying a willingness to return the military situation to the political state of June 1950.[59]

The changing military situation made these proposals unrealistic. Eighth Army troops were across the 38th parallel along much of the stretch of the peninsula. The conference immediately deadlocked over the issue as each side's rhetoric appealed to historical precedent. (Joy argued that Japan had been subdued by American air and sea power without any need for soldiers to step foot on Japanese soil; Nam Il replied that Japan had been conquered by the brave resistance of the Chinese, Korean, and other Asian peoples.) On August 10, Joy flatly stated that the UNC considered the matter closed and that discussion should turn toward the mechanics of establishing a demilitarized zone. Nam Il said nothing, replying with an icy stare that lasted two hours and eleven minutes. The following day, Nam returned to the issue, declaring, "As our proposal of making the 38th parallel the military demarcation line and our proposal of establishing a demilitarized zone is fair, reasonable, and proper, we will continue to insist upon it."[60]

William H. Vatcher observed, "They were not 'fighting men,'" but the senior communist delegates were masters of propaganda and political conflict.[61]

The war of words was on in earnest from this point, and negotiations quickly degenerated into personal insults. Nam called Joy "neurotic or muddle-headed," while Joy retorted, "presumed military men" would acknowledge that "bluster and bombast . . . cannot affect the facts of any military situation."[62] The Americans' impatience is understandable. Both Ridgway and Joy were accomplished soldiers who led the ground and naval forces of the first rank western power. Ridgway had helped to collapse the Nazi empire while Joy had fought to choke the Japanese one. As one analyst observed, "The level of Chinese military competence was assumed by outsiders to be little above the level of what it always had been—not a very high one."[63] And yet, here the Communists were, sitting as equals with the Americans at the conference table. What had Nam Il and his Korean comrades done to free the world, let alone his own country, from imperialist tyranny? Or Mao's Red Army for that matter? From the perspective of American flag officers, their communist counterparts had played exceedingly minor roles, and now they were the ones making insolent demands when they lacked the military power to back up those demands.[64]

Across the table, the North Korean and Chinese delegates felt they had earned status in fighting the world's preeminent military power to a standstill, after having inflicted a severe defeat and pushed the UNC forces south of the 38th parallel. What is more, although the Communists fought against a United Nations coalition, when they sat to negotiate an armistice, they were arguing against the United States as equals. This turn of events had to have been heady stuff. Nam Il often exploded in verbal attacks "bitter in nature claiming we were arrogant, etc. [He] used many vulgar adjectives" to deflect the military logic of Joy's claim. Having gained a victory in fighting, Nam was not about to lose on the field of rhetoric. Since the line of contact had moved repeatedly back and forth over the 38th parallel, it only made military sense that the war should end there. With a strong verbal jab, Nam accused the UNC of arrogance and intent to extend the war. Joy responded by lecturing Nam and his colleagues on the proper decorum of officers "whose military organizations are respected throughout the world."[65]

Yet the Americans were not the only ones blinded by faith in their own ethnocentrism. For the Communists, this was a chance to strike a crushing blow against decades of Western imperialist humiliation. The Chinese in particular felt they were upholding (or being upheld by) centuries of pride in their own race and culture, which observed boundaries and frontiers as sacrosanct. The loss of the 38th parallel was going to be a bitter pill to force down, although Mao's negotiators were pessimistic about being able to push the Eighth Army back off of Line Kansas and recommended a reconsideration regarding the 38th parallel as a strategic war aim.[66]

Ridgway wanted his government to take a strong stand and allow him to suspend the talks as a means to pressure the Communists into settling this most fundamental military matter of a cease-fire. Washington disagreed, emphasizing that in this political confrontation, it was important that the Communists be seen as the uncompromising party. Ridgway had early urged the UNC negotiators to work in good faith, understanding the necessity of not pinning the Communists to a hopeless position. But now, Ridgway sang a different tune. As early as July 16, he had been warned that "the concessions which have been made and the events that have transpired in connection with the negotiations have provided Russia and the Communist countries in the Far East with propaganda material, which can do incalculable harm to the cause of the free world."[67] In early August he cabled to Washington:

> Communists . . . understand only what they want to understand . . . [they] consider courtesy as concession and concession as weakness . . . [they] are uninhibited in repudiating their own solemn obligations . . . [they] view such obligations solely as means for attaining their ends. To sit down with these men and deal with them as with representatives of an enlightened and civilized people is to deride one's own dignity and to invite the disaster their treachery will inevitably bring upon us.
>
> I propose to direct the UNC delegation to govern its utterances accordingly and while remaining . . . scrupulously factual and properly temperate in word and deed, to employ such language and methods as these treacherous savages cannot fail to understand, and understanding, respect.[68]

The fundamental problem was that both sides staked out positions that unintentionally had committed their respective governments' prestige. It also did not help that the UNC sent only military commanders, men who were going to be knowledgeable about and speak to military issues in detail. The Communists, on the other hand, despite wearing military uniforms, were largely political creatures reluctant to be pinned down to detailed agreements. Every statement they made had political implications, which necessarily meant they were cautious and deliberate, prepared to defend every statement they made.[69] These differences drove frustration at the negotiations as much as the tactical situation on the ground did.

Despite his misgivings, Ridgway ordered Joy to continue discussions. For the rest of August, the opposing delegates groped toward a compromise whereby the Communists appeared, by August 22, to have accepted the UNC's proposal (minus any air or sea premium) on the military line of contact. However, the next day, the Communists unilaterally suspended the talks, alleging deliberate UNC violations of the neutral zone around Kaesong. The talks would remain recessed until October 25.[70]

Alleged violations of the zone around Kaesong, called "incidents" by the Communists, were another way the Communists attempted to pressure the UNC. Control over the area around Kaesong facilitated the Communists' efforts. Joy learned through experience that incidents were "calculated to provide advantage for their negotiating efforts or for their basic propaganda objective, or for both . . . they are plotted and triggered" at appropriate times to apply political pressure, divert attention from unpleasant lines of argument, or to make a military statement intending to intimidate or alter the UNC's posture.[71]

The first incident occurred in early August in response to Ridgway's rebuke of the Chinese armed presence threatening the UNC delegates at the initial meetings between liaison officers. This posture confronted the Communists with a significant challenge, and they quickly backed down. They had misplayed their hand publicly; subtlety was required. On August 4, the UNC delegate convoy halted as a company of heavily armed Chinese soldiers trooped across the road and through the conference area, in direct violation of their previous agreements to neutralize the site. Nam called the troops "military police." Joy understood what it was—a blatant attempt to intimidate the UNC delegation by reminding them of the CPVF's military control of Kaesong. Once again, it was a play to put the UNC in the position of supplicants and the Communists as victors. Again, Ridgway reacted strongly, suspending the talks until the Communists agreed to an actual demilitarization of Kaesong. Five days passed before the UNC was "requested" to return "as soon as possible." Still Ridgway demanded more concrete assurances of neutrality and equity at Kaesong. The reply was sufficiently compliant that the talks resumed, but in an atmosphere of distrust and hostility, and "with all the speed of a stiff concrete mix."[72]

The exposé of this incident did not put to bed the opportunity for other incidents. Two weeks after the first violation of neutrality, the Communists demonstrated they had learned their lesson. From now on the Communists ensured the UNC was the party violating Kaesong's neutrality. On August 19, Communist liaison officers alleged that unidentified UNC troops had fired on a Communist "security patrol" in the neutral zone. A few days later, Colonel Chang, another liaison officer, hauled Col. A. J. Kinney into the rain to view "evidence" and answer charges that a UNC aircraft had intentionally bombed Kaesong. Kinney, an air force pilot himself, recognized the put-up job and refused to make any admissions. Chang then surprisingly announced the immediate and indefinite suspension of further talks.[73]

Joy saw through the charade. No lowly colonel would have assumed responsibility of terminating the conference without specific authority. The talks had been going very badly for the Communists. They had made no headway against Joy's argument for the military line of contact as the minimum basis for the final demarcation line. Further, the Eighth Army was on the move again, putting pressure on North Korean forces in east-central Korea. The alleged UNC violations appeared to be unsophisticated pretexts to justify suspending negotiations while painting the UNC as the responsible party. This particular tactic did not play out very well, but it did reveal the sensitivity that the Americans felt regarding world opinion and the maintenance of a coherent UN coalition. This knowledge would be exploited the following year in the grandest incident of them all, the Koje-do riots.[74]

Fighting the War of Posts

American and UNC soldiers found some relief as the lines stabilized in the early summer of 1951. A British Commonwealth engineer remembered during the early days of armistice anticipation: "Guns apart, the war was in a thoroughly phony state. The peace talks had been on, then off, [then] on again and there had been no infantry contact near us for many weeks."[75] As days dragged on into weeks and months, the GIs realized they were stuck on the MLR for the long duration. Ridgway was concerned about troop morale, knowing that these battle-hardened veterans would have a hard time understanding their enforced idleness. He cautioned Van Fleet to take "every possible step . . . which judgement and common sense dictate . . . to completely eliminate the type of thinking" that produced expressions such as "war-weary troops," "let's get the boys back home," and (probably the worst to Ridgway's ears) "a cowardly surrender."[76] It was important that officers used their inherent authorities to educate and motivate their soldiers to stay ready and vigilant, but they found it hard to inspire aggressive attitudes and risk taking when every man knew further losses might be in vain. As the trench lines and command bunkers and rear support areas sprang up so did the road signs. One of the most popular was "CAUTION: This is the MLR. The Reds direct traffic beyond this point." If a new GI needed any further encouragement to tread with caution, he got it as soon as he stepped into a forward trench or bunker and endured the increasingly voluminous Chinese shelling, which tended to strike in volume in time for breakfast or when GIs were otherwise indisposed and unable to reach shelter.[77]

The stability of Line Kansas, coupled with the reluctance to risk casualties for ground that would be surrendered with any armistice, deprived the UNC of its most potent pressure tool, which was the credible threat of offensive action. To keep his own troops sharp and maintain pressure on the Communists, Van Fleet devised new tactical imperatives for Eighth Army to extend the defensive zone forward. Outposts, patrol bases, and other forward positions consisting anywhere from a squad to a company-size element were to provide intelligence about the enemy, disrupt his offensive moves, and act as a jump-off point for any friendly attacks, raids, or patrols—hopefully with one or two enemy soldiers in tow as prisoners. Sometimes the pressure to report positive results from a raid or patrol (especially if no POWs were taken) compelled units to fabricate enemy casualties, reported as "estimates" of enemy killed and wounded. Van Fleet's patience soon ran out, and in June 1952 he directed every division to use "ambush patrols" to capture an enemy soldier once every three days. If a corps commander foresaw a lengthy dry spell, Van Fleet authorized reinforced company-size raids, so long as "paramount consideration be given to holding friendly casualties to a minimum and further that they are supported adequately by all types of fire."[78]

These operations were not mere window dressing. Van Fleet wanted his army to maintain its combat efficiency, a task that became increasingly difficult the longer Eighth Army remained in static positions and veteran soldiers and leaders rotated out of Korea. He also understood the critical importance of intelligence and tactical initiative. Patrols and raids that penetrated the enemy's security zone helped identify defensive positions, artillery emplacements, and opposing units. An aggressive posture also prevented surprise attacks, but Chinese and North Korean soldiers proved to be the most reluctant prisoners, and even when captured and sped to the rear alive they rarely revealed information of greater than immediate tactical value. Eighth Army units also tended to suffer disproportionate casualties when patrolling, and "the results obtained were not in keeping with the hazards involved" because raiding units often had to move "more deeply into enemy territory than was feasible with this size force [at costs] incongruous with the resulting information."[79]

Eighth Army patrols fell into two categories: reconnaissance and combat. The reconnaissance patrol's mission was intelligence: determine enemy location, strength, and intentions. These patrols were almost always run during daylight hours and consisted of small four- to five-man teams. These teams worked their way into no-man's-land to a concealed spot where they could safely observe the opposing lines. They located potential ambush sites and confirmed activity such as construction of new positions, occupation of older positions, and logistics buildups that might indicate potential for a future attack. As a rule, they did not seek contact with opposing troops. The combat patrol was entirely of a different character. Combat patrols were expected to make contact with the enemy, inflict casualties, and secure a prisoner. A patrol could also be assigned the task of raiding the opposing OPLR. As such, these patrols were larger, usually platoon strength (thirty to forty soldiers), reinforced with light machine guns and forward observers to call for artillery. Although a patrol sounded less dangerous than an outright attack, reality often blurred any distinction between the names.[80]

Patrolling was hard, requiring detailed planning, realistic rehearsals, and effective procedures standard to all subordinate units. An infantry battalion's S-2 (intelligence) officer was usually responsible for identifying "knowledge gaps" and for planning, rehearsing, and debriefing patrols.[81] Lt. Col. Ellis B. Richie, commanding the 180th Infantry Regiment just west of Chorwon, published several patrol directives, each adding to a patrol's requirements based on unit experience. Directive Number 8, published May 24, 1952, outlined planning procedures for patrols and outposts, requiring personal leader reconnaissance, acknowledgment of the division's and regiment's operational control measures, liaison, fire support planning, presence of an artillery forward observer for night patrols, communication plans, mission briefs to the battalion's operations and intelligence officers, patrol objectives disseminated to every soldier, actions on contact, clearance of minefields, and rehearsals followed by reports and debriefings.

Richie emphasized rehearsals and debriefings, underscoring the value commanders placed on the successful completion of a patrol. He directed, "Except in extreme operational emergencies, each patrol will participate in a rehearsal over similar terrain prior to the conduct of the patrol . . . will be supervised on the ground by the battalion commander . . . followed by a critique." Once a patrol finished its mission and accounted for all its personnel and equipment, "Patrols will be debriefed under the direct supervision of the battalion commander, executive [officer], S-2, or S-3. A detailed report will be forwarded [to the regiment's headquarters] . . . within one hour after debriefing." These were not "check the block" kinds of tasks. Richie appreciated the value of fresh combat information that could be converted into intelligence to minimize surprise, and he was willing to expend the extra effort— not to mention the extra risk of a meaningful patrol—to maximize his unit's mastery of no-mans'-land along with the enemy's capabilities and intentions.[82]

An infantryman from the Forty-Fifth Infantry Division captured the tension well between the patrol's mission and personal vulnerability: "We had to learn the ways of a patrol type of war. In order for a patrol to be credited with making enemy contact you had to exchange small arms fire. It wasn't sufficient to get close enough to his positions to see him and direct mortar and artillery fire on him, it had to be small arms."[83] This requirement put a lot of pressure on young officers and noncoms. Making small arms contact required getting a lot closer to the enemy than many considered prudent. A patrol wandering close to enemy lines was likely to find itself quickly outnumbered and outgunned. Because patrols were so demanding and dangerous, units usually required a day or two of advance preparation, reconnaissance, drawing of special equipment or weaponry, integration of new or attached soldiers, test firing of weapons, briefings, and rehearsals. All of these activities, though essential to increase a patrol's success and survivability (for most soldiers, these were synonymous objectives), simply increased tension and anxiety. At last, the patrol left the friendly wire and ventured into no-man's-land.[84]

From a static position on the MLR, patrols inevitably become predictable, and their small size (between ten and thirty soldiers) made them vulnerable to counterambush. A patrol that got into trouble could also become bait to lure out larger numbers of troops into an unanticipated engagement. This condition made the OPLR a vital element of a unit's defensive security and offensive potential. An outpost could be anywhere from two hundred to one thousand meters in front of the MLR. In extreme cases, Eighth Army soldiers could be posted as much as two kilometers into no-man's-land. (Not everyone became as enamored with outposts as the Americans. Commonwealth troops thought outposts were "an invitation to disaster" and preferred to maintain a robust MLR instead.)[85] Most were defended by platoons (thirty to forty soldiers); more significant outposts would be occupied by a company (three platoons plus a headquarters). US army organizational changes by the summer of 1952 added significant firepower to the infantry squad and platoons in the form of additional automatic rifles and .30 caliber machine guns. These additions, along with recoilless rifles and 60 mm mortars not only augmented the outpost's firepower, they also increased survivability and effectiveness of the outpost.[86] From these outposts the infantrymen would sleep during the day and watch for the Chinese at night. If a unit were particularly aggressive, or if orders came down as they frequently did demanding a prisoner, a squad or platoon would gear up for a long night to move into an ambush position or to conduct a raid on the opposite line or outpost. A relief rotation came about every four to five days. Soldiers joked that going back to the front line was the only way to catch a break in Korea.[87]

The American infantryman found much to learn about survivability in Korea. Chinese and North Korean soldiers were deadly enough, but as the war went on, both adversaries learned better techniques to employ their increasingly large inventories of artillery and mortars. Ordinary soldiers now found themselves pressed into service as field engineers building bunkers and dugouts strong enough to withstand their own weight as well as the shock impulse of an explosive shell or recoilless rifle round. They dug miles of trenches connecting sleeping bunkers with fighting positions and medical stations.

Artillery observation posts connected to a company or battery headquarters with field-phone wire dug in sufficiently deep not to be cut during an artillery barrage. The life of an outpost or MLR strongpoint depended on these details being known and enforced by the unit's leadership.[88]

A typical company strongpoint on the MLR or as an outpost comprised three platoons on line, with the company headquarters posted behind the topographical crest of the hill (beyond direct observation from the enemy occupying the next terrain feature). On a good position, platoons sited their crew-served weapons, rocket launchers, and small arms to cover avenues of approach, usually along the natural terrain features on the forward slopes. Antipersonnel mines, trip wires, and concertina wire attempted to channelize attackers into kill zones and deny large areas that the unit commander had no chance to cover himself with his limited manpower. Along with the mines and wire, up to ten thousand sandbags were the normal tools to give the MLR strongpoint or outpost as much early warning as possible and to enhance survivability.[89] As an added measure of security and insurance against feared but misnamed "horde attacks," soldiers half-buried fifty-five-gallon barrels filled with a flammable napalm mixture along the fence perimeter. A burst of machine gun tracer bullets or an improvised white phosphorus grenade detonator sufficed to spray hundreds of jellied gasoline fireballs to immolate nearby attackers. All these obstacles, explosives, mines, and rifle and machine gun fire from bunkers "made the place a death trap for the enemy when he decided to attack."[90]

Ideally, bunker construction supported all-around defense, with machine guns and automatic rifles placed to provide interlocking fields of fire, so that any one bunker could be "covered" by at least two, or even better, three rapid-fire weapons. This was an important tactical consideration, as the rough ground rarely yielded natural fields of fire, requiring machine guns to fire straight ahead rather than diagonally across the unit's frontage. Automatic rifles, more portable, but still hard-hitting weapons with ranges comparable to light machine guns, proved useful and flexible.[91] Stout overhead cover from logs and iron ties protected soldiers from enemy artillery and friendly variable time (VT) fuse artillery, which produced deadly airbursts. A good bunker constructed and manned on Hill 200 by the Forty-Fifth Infantry Division in the Chorwon valley had one layer of logs, two layers of sandbags, and about one foot of earth as overhead protection. The roof of the bunker was constructed to be almost flush with the slope of the hill. A small entrance at the side of the bunker led into a room that served as living quarters. A narrow trench then led to the main trench, known as the communication trench, which led in turn to every other fighting bunker and the company command post[92] (figure 3.1).

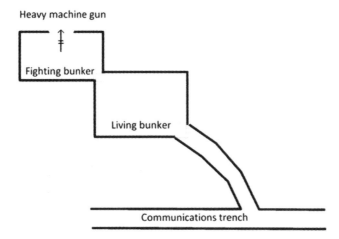

Figure 3.1 Bunker and trench diagram.

American soldiers were eligible for rotation home after accumulating thirty-six points. Eighth Army allocated points based on a man's proximity to the enemy on a monthly basis. Service in a combat unit along the MLR garnered the most points, four per month. Assignments at regiment, division, or army earned a soldier progressively fewer points. For the combat soldier attempting to accumulate his four points per month, basic existence was tedious.[93] A unit's position could always be improved, and soldiers spent most of their free time enhancing their defenses. Holes were dug deeper, fields of fire were cleared ever further, more wire and booby traps were demanded, and overhead cover was always inadequate. The bunkers protected soldiers from shrapnel and bullets, but only the most stoutly constructed and maintained ones withstood the blast of a direct hit from artillery or heavy mortars. Therefore, especially dangerous were positions of "the 'hotdog stand' or 'sandbag castle' variety—built up instead of dug down." It took active leadership to get soldiers to dig in for their own protection.[94]

In a well-disciplined unit, these priorities of work came second nature, but it became more difficult to motivate the men to attack the never-ending list of chores required to maintain the outpost. The work always fell on the infantrymen, who rarely had the tools and enough construction material to labor by day while preparing to fight at night.[95] By 1952 the bizarre nature of the seemingly on again, off again war was taxing to the utmost. Death could come at any time. One veteran assessed that "the real problems on the hill came about not because of major fights, or so it [seemed] to me. The main problem was Chinese mortar fire . . . that could hit you at any time. I remember on certain hills you just could not get out of your bunker without drawing fire."[96] Even the simple task of relieving oneself carried extreme risks, as outposts were almost always under enemy observation and guns.[97]

Hot food was a rarity and, along with water, ammunition, and nearly every type of supply support, had to be carried by human porters, the Korean Service Corps (KSC). These civilian conscripts of the ROK army were the essential support for positional warfare in Korea. The KSCs were generally loyal, diligent, and uncommonly brave for men who bore heavy burdens on their backs up and down hills, under fire, and in the worst environmental conditions imaginable for an unarmed man to find himself.[98] A single battalion could have one hundred or more "*yobos*" in support at any one time. Lt. Gen. John W. "Iron Mike" O'Daniel urged his division and regimental commanders to "take care of them as we do our own troops." They frequently assisted in digging trench lines and clearing roads of suspected mines, in addition to their portage responsibilities. Many a wounded GI owed his salvation to the KSC stretcher bearers ("Every time a shell landed anywhere, they dropped me and *that* hurt!").[99] Casualties among the KSC were considered serious incidents. O'Daniel believed American commanders had a moral obligation to conserve and preserve their Korean porters.[100] Despite the many obstacles and inhuman difficulties, Eighth Army men were among the best fed and best supported of any army ever fielded prior to the twenty-first century. Many an outpost's soldiers owed their endurance and very survival to these hardy and unselfish men.[101]

Defense of an outpost relied on equipment and technology: napalm, artillery, mines, tanks, intelligence collection and analysis, and logistics. American defensive doctrine emphasized obstacles integrated with direct and indirect fire weapons to inflict enough casualties on an attacker that should the attacker manage to penetrate the position, he could easily be thrown back by a sharp counterattack. In this type of battle, the premium was on experienced infantry leadership that could intuitively feel when the moment had come to shoot final protective fires, call for supporting air bombardment, and to launch the reserve force into the breach.[102] Such experience came dearly and was still no guarantee for success. Gerard Corr relates a story told by a noncommissioned officer serving in Korea: "He described a Chinese attack that came in over a ridge down a steep gully, and up on to his hill position. 'As [the Chinese] came over the ridge our artillery caught them and prevented their effective withdrawal. Down in the gully our mortars rained death on them and the American planes flew up and down the gully frying them with napalm. As they came up our hill they were caught in our concentrated machine gun cross-fire.' Despite the beating, the Chinese 'took our position.'"[103] The Americans and their allies faced the daunting task of holding a position the Communists had determined to take.

Perhaps the most psychologically valuable and, in some respects, the signature weapon of American destructive power—whether from ground-based improvised bombs to tactical airpower flying in support of troops in contact or against interdiction target—was napalm. A jellied-gasoline explosive mixture contained in a 90- or 100-gallon-barrel bomb, napalm was extremely effective against point targets such as dug-in personnel, artillery guns, trenches, and field fortifications. Explosive bombs caused considerable harm only when achieving a direct hit; napalm's destructiveness was altogether more fearsome. A napalm strike "vaporized, melted, warped, or reduced to ash" its target. Even a near miss inflicted serious damage on structures and humans alike. According to Robert M. Neer, an American airman named Richard E. Smith was one of the few servicemen in Japan who remembered how to mix powdered napalm with gasoline to produce the first batches that were loaded into jettisonable fuel tanks. Hand grenades made improvised ignitors. Napalm-armed planes preceded American ground troops to Korea by forty-eight hours.[104] On an average day in 1951, including both interdiction and close support demands, napalm expenditures were as follows: 45,000 gallons for the air force, 10,000 for the navy, 4–5,000 for the marines. According to Col. Donald D. Bode, an Eighth Army chemical officer, the tactical value of napalm was "indicated by the great number of requests for its use."[105] A single plane, dropping two 110-gallon napalm bombs, created a fifty-yard-square inferno of effective blast and fire and up to 15,000 square feet of ground was likely to continue to burn long after the plane peeled away from the target. A late 1952 napalm strike dropped more than 5,000 gallons on a troop concentration southeast of Wonsan, destroying wide swaths of the target area and wiping out numerous caches of supplies, railroad track, and local bridge traffic.[106]

To help defend the MLR or an important outpost, napalm packed in 55-gallon barrels (known as "fougasse bombs") was placed on top of a small explosive charge that when detonated hurled the barrel ten to twenty feet into the air before a secondary explosive ignited and spewed flammable gel thirty yards or more in all directions. Eighth Army's chief chemical officer, Maj. Gen. Egbert F. Bullene, gave napalm credit for stopping "a number of bloody massed attacks" and celebrated both its utility and destructiveness: "Suddenly geysers of flame erupted along the defense line, a flame so hot the American soldiers ducked to shield their faces. In just a few seconds, the flames billowed out, merged into a solid wall along the perimeter and engulfed the Reds. The shooting halted abruptly. . . . The Chinese do not like to attack a position that has liquid fire."[107]

Such destructive potential, however, was tentative. Without reliable communications within a defensive position, or more importantly with the outside world of air and artillery firepower, an infantry platoon or company was in a tight spot. The company's artillery forward observer (FO) team, consisting of an officer, a sergeant, and an enlisted radio/telephone operator, usually co-located with the commander, but the team often did have a specialized bunker forward to allow artillery fire to be called anywhere in the valley separating the two sides or on all enemy positions that could affect the MLR or its outposts. Soldiers quickly recognized that the FO, with his EE8 field phone or radio, would often be their sole link to outside support and that he commanded tremendous firepower that would often be the margin between life and death during an attack. Smart commanders and platoon leaders learned to let the FO fight as much of the battle as he could, and they allowed him tremendous leeway to determine the course of a tactical engagement.[108]

The FO's work on the MLR or OPLR began long before an enemy attack was expected. Along with the company commander and platoon leaders, the FO identified likely places where enemy troops would congregate—known as assault positions—prior to jumping off to the attack, "dead" ground that was unobservable from the military crest of the friendly positions, the "final protective line" where enemy infantry could be expected to be immobilized on concertina wire or other obstacles just outside the main defenses. These areas, called "concentrations," were numbered, labeled on a map, and distributed to platoons and to the FO's parent field artillery battalion. This technique allowed anyone to identify a concentration, call it up to the FO (wherever he was), and request artillery fire on that known target. The FO had to be fast as well as accurate when calling in defensive fires close to friendly lines. A good FO could bring down a wall of steel to support his position in less than sixty seconds. One FO sergeant, Danny O'Keefe from the Fifty-Seventh Field Artillery Battalion, recalled how this worked in practice. Supporting the Second Infantry Division in the fall of 1951 he directed a fire concentration at a formation of Chinese soldiers: "It was like throwing a perfect strike in a bowling game. Through the glasses you could see the enemy bodies blown into the air and down the sides of the ridgeline. It was magnificent, it was terrible."[109] As a result of actions like this, Americans, and later Koreans, got used to getting responsive artillery in large quantities that often was effective from the very first volleys.

In addition to artillery firepower, the ground infantry soldier made copious use of antipersonnel mines. Mines were most effective when emplaced in belts that soldiers could observe and engage with direct fire weapons. On occasion, though, unit leaders were tempted to use mines in lieu of troops, or as hasty obstructions. In these cases, enemy troops often simply helped themselves to free munitions. But when used properly, meaning units laid sufficient mines on likely dismounted avenues of approach, recorded and marked their minefields (and ensured these records were passed along to subsequent units), used darkness to conceal the emplacement and daily maintenance, and most importantly, maintained observation and the ability to fire on any troops in the mined area, the results could be spectacular. In some cases, the results were so lopsided that a handful of American or ROK casualties were answered by hundreds of the enemy killed or wounded.[110]

Despite the difficult terrain in central Korea, tanks were rediscovered as useful supporting weapons for their protection, firepower, and communications. Experience showed that the tank was a versatile weapon endowed with mobility, protection from small arms and shell fragments, and a powerful gun.[111] When tankers and foot soldiers developed habitual relationships, the two worked well together, leveraging their strengths while minimizing vulnerabilities. It was especially important for tank commanders to trust their infantry comrades sufficiently that they could fight with their turret hatch in the open position. This was the only way a tank commander could reliably observe his assigned sector and direct precision fire. Gordon E. Tucker, First Platoon Leader, C Company, Seventh Cavalry Regiment, used the tanks accompanying his daytime foot patrol to fire at a number of Chinese bunkers covering his route of march. "Those tankers were really sharpshooting," he said. "Every time they'd fire those big guns [76 mm] they'd smack one of those [Chinese] positions and send logs and dirt flying in all directions." Tucker reported more than twelve bunkers dispatched in this manner, which enabled the patrol to accomplish its assigned mission.[112]

After months of positional fighting, some ingenious soldiers mounted powerful searchlights on their tanks and rolled forward of the MLR to support infantry raids, patrols, and counterattacks at night. Occasionally, a couple of tanks were permanently positioned on the OPLR, as the Forty-Fifth Infantry Division did to defend Outpost Eerie in the summer of 1952. Some tankers found themselves tangling with infantry in close-in fights. A unit commendation was awarded to a tank platoon for defensive actions on Hill 854: "Hostile troops swarmed over the vehicles firing inside through vision apertures. Disregarding all thoughts of personal safety, the tank crews [isolated from infantry support] held their ground and tenaciously remained on the hill throughout the night . . . inflicting heavy casualties on the enemy."[113] Because the Chinese in particular lacked effective antitank weapons, if tanks had a protected area from which to draw maintenance, fuel, and additional ammunition, supported infantry could be sure to have a nearly continuous presence of moveable steel pillboxes providing cannon and machine gun fire support that could reach out and be effective at distances up to 1,500 meters. It was an advantage the Communist armies never adequately countered.[114]

Another area where stalemated conditions benefited the Americans was in the arcane arena of communications intelligence (COMINT). The Americans had proven themselves adept at signals intercept, interpretation, and exploitation—the summation of enemy plans, capabilities, intentions rendered into plain English and given to a fighting commander or policy maker—during World War II. Intelligence coups such as the dramatic and decisive Battle of Midway in 1942 encouraged American commanders (many of whom later fought in Korea) to expect COMINT to produce miracles. The war in Korea, though, was an intelligence vacuum for much of the first twelve months of fighting. Just as COMINT procedures penetrated KPA networks in time to support the climactic struggle for the Pusan Perimeter, Inchon, and MacArthur's pursuit to the Yalu River, the Chinese intervention overwhelmed the limited analytical capability focused in the theater. Only gradually, with greater linguist availability, understanding about North Korean and Chinese orders of battle, and the arrival of additional units and equipment, were opportunities for effective exploitation realized.[115] COMINT support became more reliable as the line stabilized in mid-1951, and by 1952 it played an increasingly effective and critical role in the stalemated war. Advanced warning of impending attacks often was derived through analysis of communications associated with CPVF artillery preparations. In fact, COMINT analysts could reconstruct much of the enemy's order of battle through traffic analysis, a process that suggests who talks to whom, when, and from what locations. In May 1952, Chinese plain-text messages allowed analysts to identify a significant number of CPVF divisions and regiments facing Eighth Army along the length of the MLR.[116]

Another technique pioneered during the war allowed intelligence analysts to estimate "back azimuths" toward the origin of the enemy radio signal, usually a headquarters or artillery position. If two or more azimuths were obtained on the same signal from laterally dispersed units, the Americans could assess with some precision the originating location. Intelligence analysts at the corps headquarters maintained files recording individual targets, such as artillery emplacements, suspected headquarters locations, or supply dumps, along with a ten-digit map grid location. Other cards listed all known and suspected targets in any 1,000-meter grid square.[117] Using these data to correlate the azimuth checks, another asset, such as aerial reconnaissance or an infantry patrol, would be cued to confirm enemy activity. If the assessed location were an already known enemy position, or if other information sources corroborated the signals plot, the intelligence would then be transmitted to a friendly artillery or air unit for an immediate attack mission.[118]

A perishable skill of intelligence collection and analysis that underwent a renaissance was aerial photo reconnaissance and interpretation. An air force's effectiveness is heavily dependent on fresh intelligence. Whereas ground forces can perform reconnaissance while engaged with the enemy, aircraft are unable to multitask. Without speedy, accurate, and as-complete-as-possible knowledge of the enemy's situation and target systems, warplanes are flying on hope, and any damage inflicted is usually incidental. When the Korean War broke out, much of the American air force's analytical capability had atrophied. Three aerial reconnaissance squadrons eventually were stationed in Japan, along with one photographic technical squadron, though the latter squadron was seriously understrength in both materials and manpower. Air superiority enabled air photographers to cover almost any area desired, but the shortage of trained photo-interpreters was especially serious.[119]

Eighth Army was equally reliant on photo reconnaissance, with nearly 70 percent of all photography missions flown in Korea dedicated to Eighth Army requests. Especially as the static ground situation limited or reduced many other sources of intelligence information, most of the ground commanders' confirmed intelligence was obtained through photo interpretation. The Fifth Air Force's Forty-Fifth Tactical Reconnaissance Squadron's contribution to this aspect of the ground war is greatly underappreciated. The Forty-Fifth flew specific missions forward of the army's MLR, snapping change detection photographs to capture evidence of movement and newly constructed facilities or troop emplacements.[120] Corps and division headquarters, with their associated artillery units, showed increasing interest in the 1/25,000 scale photo map—a photograph with superimposed map gridlines—that provided good information about road networks while doubling as an improvised firing chart. It did not, however, provide timely information about enemy artillery emplacements and so was of limited value to identify targets for immediate attention.[121] The Communists' increasingly expert camouflage forced photo interpreters to rely on terrain and other nonmilitary indicators, assumptions, and knowledge of the tactical situation to locate enemy installations and defensive positions. Pilots also flew hazardous missions to obtain vital evidence of Communist movement at night, though equipment limitations made this effort an inefficient use of the already stretched fleet of night-capable tactical aircraft.[122]

To meet the demand for strategic targeting information, the Strategic Air Command dispatched additional assets to augment FEAF's Bomber Command's Thirty-First Reconnaissance Squadron, which became the Ninety-First Strategic Reconnaissance Group, flying the RB-29, a converted Superfortress. The RB-29 provided detailed and extensive photo reconnaissance of North Korean airfields, bridges, rail yards, and suspected troop concentrations, artillery parks, and logistics movement. Other missions included mapping, bomb damage assessment, SHORAN computations (radio triangulation to pinpoint targets and guide aircraft at night), and leaflet drops. As soon as any reconnaissance aircraft landed, its precious cargo was rushed to photo de-velopers, who produced, washed, and dried thousands of prints. These then went to trained interpreters, who conducted three phases of evaluation. The first phase was for immediate-action information, post-strike assessments, and identification of targets worthy of immediate strike. The second phase looked at accounting measures, such as number of buildings, amount of traf-fic in marshalling yards or shipping in a harbor or river, and the presence of aircraft at airfields. The third phase got down into detail on these individual targets, identifying and counting the number of antiaircraft guns, assessing serviceability of bridges and roadways, and developing other intelligence re-ports to support future targeting and assessments.[123]

The war of posts increased already hard demands on logistics—the re-quirements to move, supply, and maintain fighting forces. Logistics were Eighth Army's ace-in-the-hole advantage to even out the long odds American and Korean troops faced in terms of manpower. Highway transportation had al-ways been critical to both defensive and offensive operations. Unfortunately for the road-bound Americans and their UNC allies, Korea's already limited road infrastructure suffered immensely through overuse, air attack, and ne-glect. Ground transportation through the mountainous regions was especially problematic, as "roads" on a map were often little more than unimproved trails, narrow and restricted to one-way traffic. American division- and corps-level transportation officers had to improvise and make use of native expe-dients to deliver the tons of food, small arms ammunition, fuel, and artillery shells that Eighth Army consumed every day. Under the pressure of battle, of-ficers were not averse to outright confiscation of truck assets, wherever they could be found. Commanders directed ordnance companies to keep roving maintenance patrols on the road twenty-four hours a day, and light aircraft were pressed into service to spot and report disabled or broken-down ve-hicles. Whenever possible, repairs were executed on the spot, and the truck, with its precious cargo, was then sent on its way.[124]

Working back from the regimental and division rear areas, railroad trans-portation was vital for the bulk movement of replacement troops, heavy equip-ment, and ammunition. Fighting in August and September 1950 resulted in vast destruction of rail lines, bridges, and communications facilities south of the 38th parallel. Railroad soldiers were also overtaxed, often responsible for five to six times more track than doctrine suggested. To manage and miti-gate the inherent dangers of railroading—magnified by the fortunes of war—experienced Koreans were vital to success. More than one senior transport officer testified to the "ingenuity of the Koreans as they put freight cars back onto the rails with little or no [heavy] equipment."[125] Given the reliance on material to fight China's manpower, transportation soldiers shouldered their share of the load in fighting in Korea. Without the investment in doctrine, equipment, and above all, necessity as the mother of improvisation, it is questionable if Van Fleet and his commanders could have stood toe to toe to the Communists, who had no compunction against expending men against fire and steel when the situation warranted it.

The King of Battle

Whatever differences Ridgway and Van Fleet may have had regarding strategic direction, they both agreed on one thing: send a shell to save a soldier. From December 1951 through August 1952, UNC and Korean gunners fired a monthly average of 741,400 rounds of all calibers. Never during this nine-month period were more than one million shells fired at the enemy. (During this same time period, Communist shelling was assessed at 345,000—less than half of the monthly average for the UN and ROK forces.) But the pace of shelling picked up in response to enemy activity. When the Chinese began their Autumn Counterattack Campaign (September 1952), the UNC responded with nearly a million (932,600) shells. To support the battles at White Horse Mountain, Triangle Hill, and Sniper Ridge (October–November 1952), the monthly average soared to 1,303,900 shells fired. The rate of fire in the IX Corps area topped 110 rounds per gun per day for 105 mm howitzers and 82 rounds per gun per day for 155 mm howitzers—twice the Department of the Army's authorized daily combat ration of artillery munitions. The totals dipped a bit in December to just over 850,000, but from January 1953 until the armistice no fewer than one million shells were fired per month.[126]

Lt. Col. Homer P. Harris, senior quartermaster officer for the Second Infantry Division, observed, "Korea is a paradise for the artilleryman, but not for the quartermaster."[127] Nowhere was the war of logistics more visible than in feeding Van Fleet's guns, the king of battle. During the defensive Battle of the Soyang River and the pursuit that followed, which included Operation Piledriver (May 10–June 7, 1951), the X and IX Corps exceeded all previous artillery ammunition expenditures, establishing "a wall of steel" to halt the Communist drive. Some witnesses recorded guns and howitzers firing up to five times the authorized daily rate.[128] Captain Lawrence Daly, from the Fifteenth Field Artillery Battalion, described shooting what eventually became known as the "Van Fleet rate of fire" or the Van Fleet load: "In a matter of four or five minutes . . . 120 rounds had been 'unloaded, unpacked, uncrated, put in the pieces, and fired. We fired every damn thing but the tubes at them [the attacking Chinese] that night." During the twenty-four-hour period during 16 and 17 May [1951], his battery of six howitzers fired a total of 2,760 shells—nearly a tenfold increase over the standard day of fire ration.[129]

Van Fleet's belief "in the transcending value of firepower" produced a dra-

TABLE 3.1. THE VAN FLEET LOAD OR DAY OF FIRE

	Van Fleet day of fire	Army day of fire
105 mm howitzer	300	55
155 mm howitzer	250	40
155 mm gun	200	50
8-inch howitzer	200	50

Source: Mossman, *Ebb and Flow*, 442n8.

matic spike in demand following the Spring Campaigns that taxed American logistics to the limit.[130] The army's logistics system surged to satisfy the prodigious hunger of American howitzers, mortars, machine guns, and rifles. In a two-month period (August 19–October 18, 1951) following the beginning of negotiation talks at Kaesong, 158,303 tons of ammunition were delivered to the three US corps. It took 39,527 two-and-one-half-ton trucks (each overloaded 100 percent) to deliver 3,092 shells to each 105 mm howitzer, 2,579 to each 155 mm howitzer, 1,830 to each 155 mm gun, and 1,631 to each 8-inch howitzer. By contrast, in the same time frame the fighting infantry soldier received only 546 bullets for his M1 rifle.[131] To handle the increased demand for ready shells, each corps established its own forward ammunition supply points as an intermediate stage between the division points that were "unable to sustain continued heavy replenishment withdrawals" and the corps-level ammunition dumps that were typically four to eight hours distant by truck transport.[132]

The difference between a Van Fleet day of fire and the army's doctrinal day of fire was dramatic (table 3.1). To be sure, limitations on daily rates of fire were imposed at various times during the war, but the amount of shelling still far outpaced doctrinal norms and logistical quotas. Artillerymen in the Forty-Fifth Infantry Division speculated that "greater numbers of rounds were fired daily [in Korea] than had been fired weekly in Europe."[133] They may have exaggerated, but the impression clearly favored Korea as the artilleryman's war.

Field artillery therefore was the mainstay of the American army's punch and tactical effectiveness. The Time on Target (TOT) procedures perfected during World War II were awesome achievements of technical skill coupled with industrial production. The introduction of the VT fuse in December 1944 only added to the fearsome destructive potential on call to support American infantry. VT shells contained small transmitters fitted into the nose of an artillery shell. When a radio signal reflected from the ground indicated a predetermined height of between 10 and 30 meters, the fuse detonated the shell. Such airbursts spread lethal fragments over a wide area. When fired as a TOT, a barrage of VT shells was sure to annihilate even the most determined attackers.[134]

The deployment of US Army Reserve and National Guard artillery battalions in the spring of 1951 brought Eighth Army's fire support arm to its maximum strength. Additional artillery units would only be added in 1952 as the ROK army increased its own fire support capabilities. By October 1951, there were fifty-seven complete artillery battalions in the UNC order of battle. A year later, there were eighty-two. However, this accretion of firepower was more apparent than real, as Korean battalions had to undergo a lengthy apprenticeship under American command and control before they were released to fire missions in support of Korean or UNC troops. It wasn't until January 1953, when ninety-five artillery battalions were on line, that the number of tubes was commensurate with an American field army's firepower demands.[135]

While direct support to troops was a crucial fire support task, a second and equally important mission for artillery was "counterbattery" (CB): the identification, observation, and effective fire to destroy (unlikely), neutralize (hopefully), or suppress (most likely) opposing guns. A successful CB mission would at a minimum require enemy artillery to cease-fire and relocate ("displace") to another location, resulting in reduced fire over the space of several hours. Eighth Army's most effective asset to identify likely artillery locations for CB was the First Field Artillery Observation Battalion, which detailed to each US corps one battery with two sections, one for visual ("flash") and the other for aural ("sound") observation. Flash was considered the most reliable means to find targets, but both flash and sound techniques were employed to support CB fire and determine its effectiveness. Flash sections also had visual scopes, allowing them to call for and adjust normal fire missions as forward observers.[136]

A second technique to locate enemy artillery was known as the "shell report." Shell reporting was a hazardous undertaking, requiring an officer or senior noncom to dash out to a newly blasted crater to measure its depth, diameter, and estimate a back azimuth along the probable line of impact. These characteristics, combined with a quick terrain analysis, would suggest a potential enemy artillery position. The key was to compile the data accurately and report it quickly, before the firing piece could be moved. Despite constant reminders to regiments and battalions "to render timely, complete and accurate shell reports," experience was conclusive that "shell reporting in general leaves much to be desired."[137] The failure of Eighth Army artillery to affect meaningful Communist artillery fire support was an important factor shaping the battlefield.[138]

Experience had taught the Americans to divide tasks among their artillery assets to take advantage of each caliber's characteristics—range, rate of
fire, weight of shell, and relative responsiveness. In many cases, these qualities were exclusive. For example, a heavy piece (8-inch or 240 mm) was adequate to crush a fortified position, but its slow rate of fire made it less useful to stop an infantry attack compared to the lighter and (shell for shell) less
lethal 105 mm howitzer. However, when it came to defensive fires, where
rapid volleys counted more than the weight of the shell, the 105 mm howitzer proved its worth again and again, accounting for nearly 70 percent of all
artillery shells fired.

The medium 155 mm howitzer was considered the most versatile indirect
fire weapon. Its rate of fire was marginally less than a 105 mm, but it had
greater range, and because of its larger burst radius was useful in a counterbattery role. Its most fearsome contribution to the Korean battlefield was in
combination with the VT fuse. VT fusing turned each 96-pound shell into a
giant airbursting shotgun, instantly lethal to any exposed personnel. A common technique was for American (or Korean) troops to hunker down in
defensive bunkers while calling repeated volleys of VT 155 mm. Airbursts
would not harm the defenders, but they practically swept clean any enemy
troops standing in the impact area. Less useful was the 155 mm gun, affec-
tionately known as the "Long Tom," which had a longer range (twelve miles)
than its howitzer cousin but was correspondingly less accurate. For the purpose of bunker busting, close was not good enough. However, the use of VT
fuses made these guns useful for interdiction and harassment of known or
suspected supply depots, road junctions, staging areas, artillery parks, and
headquarters facilities.[139]

To achieve the accuracy and range necessary to engage hardened point
targets beyond the reach of division howitzers, and for sheer crushing force
to destroy underground facilities, the 8-inch howitzer, flinging a powerful
and heavy projectile in a steep parabolic arc, was without peer for the pinpoint capability required. Private First Class Herman G. Nelson recalled the
first time he saw an 8-inch howitzer fire in Korea. "When we fired our guns,
everyone knew it for miles around. They had a range of around twenty miles
and fired a shell eight inches in diameter and about thirty inches long. The
concussion . . . was so powerful . . . they would blow down pup tents two
hundred yards away."[140]

First Lieutenant Howard Maki, Thirty-Seventh Field Artillery Battalion,
employed this weapon to great effect, requesting rounds fired sequentially
from a single howitzer, which reduced dispersion to a very predictable and
precise pattern. Once the target was "zeroed in" with point-detonating rounds,
he ordered subsequent shells "to be fired with time-delay fuses. The delay was

TABLE 3.2. ARTILLERY EXPENDITURES BY CALIBER,
OCTOBER 1, 1951–JULY 27, 1953

Caliber	Range (yds.)	Subtotal	Percent of total (rounded)	Average monthly expenditure
105 mm How	12,200	17,506,428	70	795,644
25 Pdr*	13,400	1,300,231	6	100,017
155 mm How	16,350	4,748,155	19	215,825
155 mm Gun	25,700	568,725	2	25,851
8-inch How	18,500	741,916	3	33,722
Total		24,865,455	100	1,171,059

Source: Eighth Army, The Employment and Effectiveness of Artillery, 44, USAHEC.
*The 25 Pdr was the British artillery piece comparable to the US 105 mm.

not long, perhaps 0.5 seconds, but it was enough for the 196-pound projectile, loaded with high-explosives, to penetrate the thickly constructed bunkers and destroy them along with the occupants and their weapons." Another FO recalled that after only three rounds he hit a Chinese bunker, "actually [seeing] the round go through the window opening. We loved the eight inch [howitzer] because it is the most accurate artillery piece ever designed." Despite the utility and demand for 8-inch support, it was relatively scarce and accounted for a small minority of total artillery ammunition fired during the war (table 3.2).[141]

In addition to the traditionally recognized forms of artillery used in Korea, the humble mortar proved a versatile support to infantry soldiers. These simple weapons, essentially capped tubes launching explosive projectiles in a high arc, were highly accurate, responsive, and rapid firing. Each US corps typically had one chemical mortar battalion, 4.2-inch (107 mm) attached to its own artillery or supporting Korean guns. These larger pieces, as opposed to those supporting infantry companies (60 mm) and battalions (81 mm), rarely got a break, often displacing to where any threat emerged. Their mobility, relatively shorter logistics tail (compared to a comparable 105 mm howitzer battalion), and flexible punch made the chemical mortar the corps commander's "hip-pocket" artillery in a pinch.[142]

The inauguration of truce talks at Kaesong changed the character of the war in many ways that disadvantaged the Eighth Army. However, these disadvantages were not fatal to Eighth Army's military objectives in support of President Truman's political aims to fight the war in Korea without escalation and to achieve an honorable cease-fire. Van Fleet's forces still maintained significant tactical capabilities to defend its MLR. As will be shown in the following chapters, the Americans also retained the initiative in the air and on the ground during the last six months of 1951 to influence the Communists to concede on critical agenda items. The degree to which the Americans would be successful depended on how the CPVF and the KPA adapted their own tactical techniques and developed new capabilities to fight a modern war.

4

THE WAR IN THE AIR

FROM THE BEGINNING of the Korean War, airpower played a key and at times decisive role in maintaining United Nations military power on the peninsula. American airmen in Korea believed in the theory of strategic attack both to destroy war-making potential and the enemy's will to continue fighting. This doctrine was the product of the interwar Air Corps Tactical School that trained a generation of airmen to think of airpower as indivisible, and hence inherently strategic in effects.[1] Despite this doctrinal prejudice and the post-1945 strategic emphasis on atomic bombs, there remained a high degree of experience in conventional or "tactical" operations from World War II. Although equipment and airframe shortages caused air force chief of staff General Hoyt S. Vandenberg to call the FEAF "a shoestring air force,"[2] this experience quickly made itself felt as US and UNC airmen quickly dominated the skies, flying nearly 700,000 sorties compared to the fewer than 100,000 flown by North Korean, Chinese, and Soviet pilots. This domination cannot be neglected, nor its significance downplayed, as it often is, when compared to the drama of the war of movement during the war's first twelve months and the ennui of stalemate that followed. UNC airmen quickly achieved air superiority and therefore shielded UNC ground forces from air attack while devastating exposed communist forces who lacked any appreciable air cover. While airpower could not by itself produce victory, it often provided Eighth Army with a crucial combat margin to offset communist manpower advantages, thereby keeping the ground forces in the field long after the statistics should have suggested otherwise.[3]

Lt. Gen. George E. Stratemeyer, commanding MacArthur's air force, was no stranger to Asia, having served as the senior air commander in the World War II China-Burma-India theater of operations. On May 31, 1950, Stratemeyer's FEAF had a total of 1,172 combat aircraft, spread across three numbered air forces (Fifth—Japan, Thirteenth—Philippines, Twentieth—Okinawa and Guam). Because FEAF had responsibilities for the defense of Japan and

Okinawa, the Philippine Islands, and the Marianas, only 657 aircraft were available for service in Korea one month later.[4] FEAF's immediate striking power was invested in a handful of B-29 "Superfortress" bombers (now classified as medium bombers), twenty-two B-26 "Invader" light bombers (designed for interdiction, that is, attacking targets beyond the line of contact with friendly troops), and fewer than one hundred F-80 "Shooting Star" jet fighters and F-82 "Twin Mustang" all-weather fighter-interceptors that would be pressed into unanticipated roles as ground attack and interdiction aircraft. What the South Korean and American defenders needed above all were aircraft that could drop bombs, fire rockets, and shoot up North Korean tanks, artillery, and attacking infantry. The high-performance characteristics that made jets the weapon of choice for fighter pilots were exactly the opposite of what close support and low-flying interdiction missions demanded. Accordingly, in July 1950, FEAF agreed to convert six F-80 squadrons to F-51 "Mustangs," piston-engined aircraft that helped plug the immediate gap in close air support and loiter time useful for armed reconnaissance missions behind Communist lines.[5]

Regardless of what they flew, American pilots, many of whom were seasoned in the great air battles of World War II, proved superior to the Communist air forces. FEAF's tactical arm, the Fifth Air Force, won air superiority by mid-July, when the North Korean air force had been driven from the sky. Lt. Gen. Otto P. Weyland claimed after the war, "The most significant fact of the entire [North Korean] phase is that the enemy air force was completely destroyed, leaving our air bases and ground forces free from air attack, our extensive logistics and communications completely secure, and the bulk of our air force free to attack the advancing army at will."[6] The question then became, how could that advantage best be put to use?

The fighter-bomber was a fighter plane capable of a ground attack role, and it became the jack-of-all-trades aircraft. The fighter-bomber pilot "received the most comprehensive lesson of all" airmen flying in Korea.[7] More than any other flyer, he had to master the topography of the country, becoming intimately familiar with coastlines, lakes, rivers, railroads, bridges, gorges, and mountain trails. Not only did accuracy demand such knowledge; the pilot's survivability depended on it. It was a grueling type of fighting, zooming and twisting at high speeds and low altitudes. There was little margin for error on small, elusive, and defended targets.[8] Fighter pilots had little training flying at jet speeds to provide close support to ground troops, but the F-80 Shooting Star proved to be an accurate gun platform, and with an experienced and steady pilot at the controls, it was converted into a satisfactory dive-bomber. Pilots appreciated its ruggedness and versatile weaponry: six nose-mounted .50-caliber machine guns, ten five-inch rockets, and two napalm tanks or two 500-pound or 1,000-pound bombs. Its higher speed increased chances for surprise, but loiter time over Korea was limited to forty-five minutes to an hour. By October 1, 1950, the Forty-Ninth Fighter-Bomber Group had relocated its planes to Taegu, which greatly enhanced Fifth Air Force's contribution to the air-to-ground war. The F-80 was durable, easily maintained, and became the ubiquitous workhorse for Fifth Air Force's interdiction and close support missions for most of the war.[9]

Although the F-80 possessed many desirable characteristics, the piston-engine, propeller-driven, F-51 Mustang fighters flying from Taegu proved their value, flying low and slow, to attack vehicles, artillery, and ground troops. The Mustangs were in such high demand that flight operations at Taegu dispatched flights of two planes rather than the customary four. As soon as a flight landed, ground crew quickly refueled and rearmed the pair with .50-caliber belts (1,880 rounds total), six 5-inch rockets, and two 500-pound bombs. A fresh pilot might be tossed into the cockpit before the planes roared down the pierced-steel planking that converted a muddy rice paddy to a tactical airfield.[10] The Fairchild Republic F-84E Thunderjet, which arrived in Korea after the Chinese intervention and flew its first missions from Taegu on December 6, 1950, was more suited to ground attack thanks to its superior gun sight system. Its typical combat load of eight rockets and six .50-caliber machine guns could be increased with a jet-assisted takeoff rocket to twelve rockets and two 500-pound bombs.[11] All three aircraft played key roles during FEAF's various interdiction and air pressure campaigns later in the war.[12]

General Stratemeyer, whose war diary exhibits a near pathological obsession with the air force's public image and sensitivity over FEAF's capabilities to perform close air support just as well as the navy and marine corps, wanted to do more; the air force *needed* to do more.[13] Vandenburg agreed. Strategic Air Command rapidly transferred additional bombers to the Far East, acknowledging that "a primary consideration in making these additional [bomber] groups available is the vital necessity of destruction of North Korean objectives *north* of the 38th parallel [emphasis added]."[14] Stratemeyer eagerly and immediately declared that battlefield interdiction was, after close air support, the paramount priority. However, three weeks later Stratemeyer complained to air force headquarters in Washington, DC, "[The] effectiveness of FEAF interdiction plan is hampered by close and general support requirements necessarily imposed by CINCFE [Commander in Chief, Far East—MacArthur]."[15] In other words, although close air support was MacArthur's priority for FEAF's effort to support the theater commander, it just was not the air force's priority for winning the war.

In case there was any doubt as to what the air force leadership had in mind, Maj. Gen. Emmett "Rosie" O'Donnell Jr., an experienced bomber commander in the Pacific, informed MacArthur in July 1950 he intended to lay waste to North Korea's industrial and urban centers, as World War II experience had demonstrated that airpower applied against tanks, bridges, and airfields was useless. In the airman's view, the path to victory lay not in providing close support or even interdiction bombardment, but in the heavy city-centric efforts that defined the strategic air campaigns against Germany and Japan. FEAF's Bomber Command leaders itched to start a strategic campaign to wipe out North Korea's industry and means to support war, such as they were. On July 13, B-29s flew the first strategic strikes of the war, targeting ports and harbors, railways, oil and lubricant factories and storage, weapons arsenals, and raw materials. But not until August was Bomber Command able to devote comprehensive efforts to wipe out North Korea's infrastructure. By FEAF's stated objectives, the campaign was a success. Within six weeks, all eighteen targets nominated had been severely damaged or destroyed. By September 15, Stratemeyer acknowledged that practically all important industrial targets had been neutralized. There was nothing left for the Superforts to hit (table 4.1).[16]

The attitude that airpower provided the means for low risk, precise results, and above all *a decision*, would reemerge to beguile every Far East commander in the years ahead. Lt. Gen. Otto P. Weyland, who assumed command of FEAF in July 1951, was the commander of the XIX Tactical Air Command supporting George Patton's Third Army in World War II. Patton allegedly referred to him as "the best damn general in the Air Corps."[17] He understood the tactical employment of airpower and firmly believed that between close support for ground forces and strategic attack far from the battlefield lay an opportunity to employ airpower in an operationally significant way to support the UNC's overall objectives. As negotiations at Kaesong failed to make concrete progress, a frustrated Ridgway recognized he could not use significant ground power to coerce concessions without giving the Communists a propaganda coup and the excuse to break off talks. Weyland used his capital to influence Ridgway to expect the FEAF to provide military leverage at low cost and risk. For his part, Ridgway was open to the idea that airpower could substitute for a general ground offensive and provide effective military pressure against the Communists.[18]

Just a few weeks after truce talks began, Ridgway informed the JCS of his intent to order an all-out airstrike on Pyongyang to be executed by 140 medium and light bombers and 230 fighter-bomber aircraft. He justified the strike against the North Korean capital to target the buildup of supplies and personnel as a reminder that the price of continued hostilities was high. The raid, executed on July 30 in unfavorable weather conditions, "failed to achieve our best potential results," Ridgway later pointed out to Weyland. There were also significant civilian casualties, which appeared to outweigh the military benefit of the strike.[19] Along with expanded "strategic" attacks against hitherto restricted North Korean targets, this air blitz did not, however, produce the desired results at the armistice negotiations.[20] The intense attacks appeared

TABLE 4.1. FAR EAST AIR FORCES SORTIES, BY TYPE, JUNE–SEPTEMBER 1950

Period	Sortie type			
	Close Air	Interdiction	Strategic	Other
June 25–30	408	59	0	100
July 1–31	4,635	1,023	56	1,827
August 1–31	7,397	2,963	539	4,582
September 1–30	5,969	3,818	158	5,382

Source: The Employment of Strategic Bombers in a Tactical Role, 1941–1951, USAF Historical Study 88, Maxwell Air Force Base, 1954, 134.

to only harden the Communists' resolve and may have been a factor behind the promotion of "incidents" as a way to retaliate. Nam Il attempted to parlay the destructive attack into propaganda advantage, accusing the UNC of holding its present positions only because of "your strategic air effort of indiscriminate bombing . . . of our peaceful civilians and cities and villages."[21]

In August 1951 Ridgway determined to try something different. Airpower would be unleashed against the enemy's logistical lifelines—his road and rail networks—to starve the enemy's guns of ammunition and men of food. The air force defined aerial interdiction as the use of airpower "to prevent or hinder . . . enemy use of an area or route,"[22] the purpose of which was to attack the unengaged potential of an enemy military force, that is, to "prevent men, equipment, and supplies from reaching a place of combat when the enemy needs them and in the quantities he requires."[23] Aerial interdiction had a generally positive record in American operations both in the Pacific and European theaters of operations. MacArthur's army and naval air forces effectively isolated strongpoints such as Rabaul and Truk, allowing allied forces to bypass these island fortresses and strike at more vulnerable points.

It was the European model, though, that held the greatest allure for a successful independent air campaign. General Carl "Tooey" Spaatz, one of the fathers of the USAF's postwar independence, asserted that the correct use of airpower was not tied to the ground battle in close air support, but in air superiority (destruction of enemy airpower wherever it was found—in the air or on the ground or in its logistics and supporting infrastructure) and interdiction, getting at the enemy before he could reach the battlefield. This was the primary lesson tactical airmen derived from North Africa, and which they continued to apply during the continental campaigns against Italy and Germany.[24]

Air force doctrine following World War II anticipated that air attack against vital centers producing war material would have decisive influence on the course of any modern conflict: "Success in war will depend more than ever before on the industrial capacity and efficiency of the protagonists, therefore, destruction of the enemy's industrial capacity will contribute most toward reduction of his ability to wage war."[25] Since North Korea's industrial base was already fairly wiped out by 1951, and communist manufacturing centers in Manchuria and the Soviet Union were off limits, the next best option was to attack war material en route to the front lines. This was the doctrinal basis for the various interdiction campaigns FEAF waged in 1951–52.

Ridgway hoped to realize these promises, even as the empirical evidence in Korea was ambiguous. Interdiction operations were already in effect and had played a role to blunt the KPA and CPVF's major offensives.[26] FEAF desired any way to begin shifting the air effort away from close air support—so necessary to offset the communist manpower advantage during the Fifth Campaign—to a new strategy that engaged enemy MiGs closer to the Yalu River, attacked airfields in North Korea capable of handling jet fighters, and choked off their main supply lines. General Vandenberg, to the chagrin of the army's ground commanders in Korea, had declared, "Airplanes are inefficient weapons for killing individual soldiers," and the best way the air force could support the army was to "knock out the mortar before it is made. The next best is to knock it out while it is in the convoy on the way to the front." He left unstated the obvious conclusion, that once the mortar was in place, dug in, and deployed in action, it was not so fun or easy to find and destroy with airpower.[27]

Therefore, what FEAF proposed in the summer of 1951 was something different: a concerted campaign, separate from the army, to pressure the Communists by disrupting transportation networks enough to bring supply shortages to a crisis point. Weyland and his planners saw the mission "to maintain maximum pressure on the enemy in North Korea, and thus to create a situation conducive to a favorable armistice." Because rail lines appeared vulnerable to attack—track and rolling stock were hard to conceal and location of major rail facilities were known—the most enthusiastic believers expected air action to starve the front-line troops of the means to wage war. While ground forces held the communist armies in check, airpower would assume the offensive burden to compel an armistice agreement.[28] It was an ambitious project, and it would also be a costly endeavor. Over half of FEAF's aerial losses would be from interdiction missions.[29]

Korea appeared to present an ideal situation for an interdiction solution (figure 4.1).[30] The extensive range of mountains that split the peninsula along a north–south axis also separated the rail network into two discrete units. Only two lines connected the western coastal network to its counterpart along the more constricted eastern coast. Roads in Korea were extensive but poor

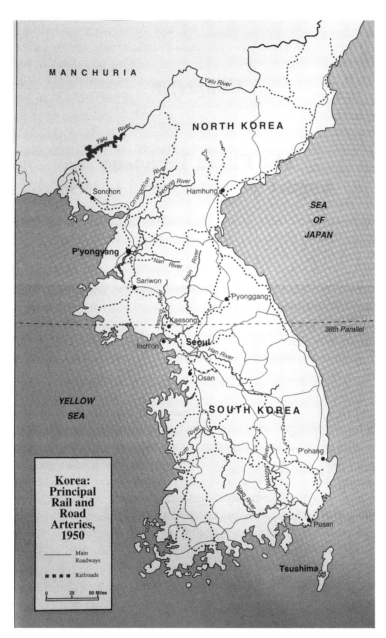

Figure 4.1 Korea road and rail network. Source: Mark, *Aerial Interdiction in Three Wars*, 266.

in quality. The hard-surface, all-weather road capable of carrying significant military traffic was largely nonexistent. This condition made rail transport appear the most important and dependable, and therefore vulnerable, method of military transportation.[31] Despite these characteristics, airmen found interdiction to be a tantalizingly elusive means to influence the UNC's strategic position in Korea. Over time the Communists recognized their weak position and took active measures to reduce their vulnerabilities to air attack, stockpile what supplies did reach the front, and husband carefully their resources to permit limited and specifically calculated attacks in strength supported by artillery. During the height of FEAF's interdiction campaign, the Communists made a significant effort to challenge UNC air superiority by introducing the Chinese air force into the battle zone. The effort failed to neutralize American superiority, but the disruption to the interdiction plan was enough to ensure its failure as a strategic blow, which seriously undermined Ridgway's military strategy in the fall of 1951.[32]

FEAF tried three different interdiction plans in 1951. The first, known as Interdiction Campaign No. 4, was in direct response to the Chinese intervention and in support of the late winter ground fighting in early 1951. It specified 173 targets spread across eleven zones. The most important zones, A–C, encompassed the area of Sinuiju-Sinanju-Pyongyang. The rail lines and road network in these zones comprised the main logistics channel for western Korea and carried the bulk of enemy supplies. Pilots knew the area by the more poetic name, "Flak Alley," which over time increasingly lived up to its moniker.[33]

Campaign No. 4 marked the first time FEAF coordinated its attack on North Korea's transportation backbone. B-29 bombers received the highest priority targets, attacking and destroying forty-eight of sixty rail bridges, including all the key bridges over the Yalu River, excepting the Sinuiju-Antung bridge. They also closed down twenty-seven of thirty-nine marshaling yards. Fighter-bombers focused on highways and railroad lines, paying special attention to chokepoints such as bridges and tunnels. Missions to attack trucks, locomotives, and rolling stock were known as "armed reconnaissance," a term that briefed well but confused army commanders with unfulfilled expectations.[34] These sweeps of four planes flew at low levels, between 50 and 1,500 feet above the ground. Upon identifying a target, bombs and rockets were used to disrupt the enemy's convoy or formation. The real killing was accomplished by strafing. Each plane usually could get two to three good strafing passes per mission.[35] Attacking tunnels and bridges required "steel nerves and expert flying" to place a bomb effectively and still have enough time to pull up and away from the looming mountainside or enemy ground fire. Troop concentrations also received attention, taking up about 10 percent of interdiction sorties flown. By March 1951, it appeared that Campaign No. 4 was successful. Eighth Army had regained its equilibrium and was pushing the Communist armies back north (figure 4.2).[36]

However, the technique of targeting by zones proved flawed. Pressure in one zone simply displaced traffic into other less pressured ones. The lack of broad damage across multiple zones eased the demands on limited repair and construction crews, which reduced the amount of time any particular rail line was out of service. American pilots learned the truth about road and rail interdiction: anything bombed by man can be fixed by man. Working mostly at night, North Korean and Chinese rear area troops and gang-pressed civilians managed to cut additional bypasses, fill in holes, and use improvised materials to replace destroyed bridge spans or support damaged ones. Even when the Americans returned at night to drop napalm and delayed-action fragmentation bombs to dissuade work crews, the North Koreans stoically accepted their losses and continued their repair work. These efforts substantially reduced the strategic effect the series of tactically successful strikes during the campaign promised.[37]

More alarming, the cost in bomber aircraft was rising due to increased opposition from secretly introduced Soviet MiG-15 jet fighter-interceptors.[38] B-29 sorties in February, March, and April 1951 met increasingly aggressive resistance over northeast Korea, known as "MiG Alley." One B-29 (out of twenty-three) was lost on April 7 during a raid on the bridge at Sinuiju, where 184 two-thousand-pound bombs failed to drop the span, giving rise to its nickname the "rubber bridge." However, April 12 was even worse, when seventy-eighty MiGs swarmed around a formation of forty-two Superforts attempting to drop the rubber bridge, downing three and severely damaging seven.[39] General Stratemeyer, shocked at the losses and the ineffectiveness of fighter escorts to intercept the MiGs, put Sinuiju off limits to further daytime attacks.[40] Later in the month, the air force chief of staff informed Stratemeyer that SAC could not support a daily sortie rate greater than twelve B-29s. From that point forward, the Superforts were primarily directed against rail marshaling yards and supply centers—the more difficult point targets such as bridges and individual rail lines were turned over to the tactical aircraft of the Fifth Air Force.[41]

In any event, the rail network and its supporting infrastructure proved to be too resilient. The central and western lines, as opposed to the line that ran along the eastern coast, were well inland, double-tracked, and often serviced by a good number of transverse lines, permitting relatively easy bypass of disrupted sectors.[42] A destroyed set of railroad bridges at Sinanju (between Sinuiju and Pyongyang) gave the Americans evidence of the Koreans' ingenuity. Photo reconnaissance found traffic fully operational, using "the bypass

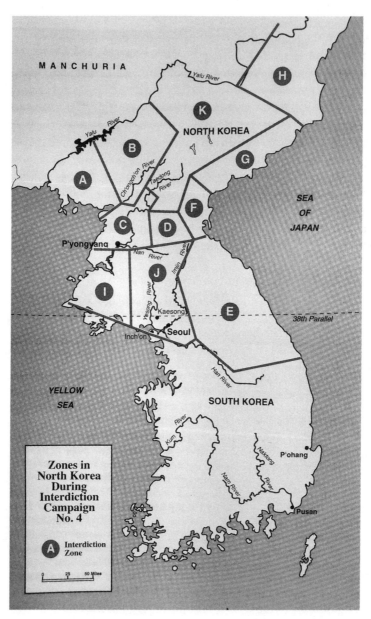

Figure 4.2 North Korea interdiction zones, 1951. Source: Mark, *Aerial Interdiction in Three Wars*, 296.

to the bypass to the bypass."[43] After the war, Van Fleet, reflecting on this phase of the air campaign, placed the results within this context: "We won the battle to knock out the bridge[s], but we lost the objective, which was to knock out the traffic."[44] Additionally, ground commanders objected to the "diversion" of valuable fighter-bomber and attack aircraft from close support missions. The fact that over 50 percent of Fifth Air Force sorties flown in May (in response to the CPVF's Spring Campaign) were dedicated to close support simply highlighted the constraints on the Far East theater's airpower. In addition to supporting the ground battle, FEAF intensified its counter-airfield efforts while continuing "round-the-clock" attacks on built-up supply areas and on road and rail traffic. There simply were not enough airframes to do all that air planners and ground commanders wanted done.[45]

Following the collapse of the CPVF's May offensive, Interdiction Campaign No. 4 evolved into a new effort to sever the Communists' lines of communication. Fifth Air Force's commander, Maj. Gen. Edward J. Timberlake,[46] attempted to split the difference between close support and operational interdiction focused on rail logistics. He ordered the execution of an operation he dubbed Strangle. Consciously borrowing the cover term from the 1944 Italian interdiction campaign of the same name, Timberlake hoped to garner support for an air offensive to paralyze road transportation between railheads north of the 39th parallel and the front. Significantly, Strangle's priority target focus was against trucks (when they could be found), bridges (a standard target for any interdiction), and the roads themselves. The heavy emphasis on roadway disruption included a mix of cratering attacks, delayed action bombs that functioned as mines, and other disruptive obstacles like metal tetrahedrons, four-pronged spiked metal objects designed to puncture holes in tires. An "interdiction belt" was established, sixty miles deep, and subdivided into eight zones. The various air forces in theater were assigned to destroy every truck and bridge along seven major highway routes in the interdiction belt. Fifth Air Force assumed responsibility for the three westernmost zones, Navy Task Force 77 was assigned the central two zones, and marine corps aviators took the three easternmost ones.[47]

The success of daytime interdiction forced the Communists to move only at night, which in turn forced Fifth Air Force planners to shift their attack patterns. The B-26 Invader became the primary attack plane for four types of "night-intruder" missions during Strangle: road reconnaissance, rail reconnaissance, road block, and bomber stream. Road and rail reconnaissance missions were similar in that attacking B-26s simply followed a designated route searching for targets. Trains were most frequently located during moonlit nights, whereas trucks were more vulnerable when total darkness forced them to use their lights. Road block tactics consisted of cratering a choke point or other high-traffic stretch of roadway, waiting for traffic to pile up, and then attacking the stalled convoys with delay-fuse bombs, rockets, and strafing runs. Bomber streams were effective against towns and known supply dumps or troop assembly areas. A pathfinder aircraft flew ahead of the main bomber force to locate the target and mark it with incendiary bombs. Once the target area was well lit, the pathfinder aircraft then circled the area directing successive B-26s to drop their payloads on the ever-expanding fire.[48]

Although all USAF aircraft played some role in the interdiction campaigns, the B-26 was the indispensable workhorse. One historian called it "the best piston-engine light bomber ever built."[49] The Invader certainly was durable, with long range and versatile armament. Although FEAF overall lacked the right equipment and tactics "to seek out, see, and attack" targets at night, the B-26 indicated its potential early in the air campaign.[50] It proved an accurate and devastating platform against stationary logistics targets. The Invader's "B" variant's standard armament was a massive battery of fourteen .50 caliber machine guns concentrated in the wings and solid nose; some night-flying B-26s, the "C" variant, traded eight machine guns for a glass nose with a more accurate bombsight. A combination of bombs, rockets, and napalm rounded out its destructive payload.[51]

Two B-26 wings, the 3rd and the 452nd, flew some of the most harrowing and risky missions of the interdiction campaigns and amassed an impressive record in Korea, flying altogether more than 53,000 sorties to claim 39,000 vehicles, 4,000 rail cars, 406 locomotives, 168 bridges, and 7 aircraft destroyed.[52] But the Invader had its limitations as well. It was large and slow, and its low-flying altitude also made it vulnerable to ground fire, which became more effective in 1952 as Soviet-made guns proliferated along the most heavily targeted road and rail lines in North Korea. Its greatest handicap, though, was to point up the Achilles' heel of FEAF's interdiction strategy. At the time when the Communists' greatest window of vulnerability was at night, the B-26 was "a most imperfect instrument" for nighttime interdiction. It possessed no radar altimeter, short-range navigation radar, or blind-bombing radar. It was also an ungainly aircraft, lacking the fine handling characteristics needed for low-level, nighttime flying through Korea's mountains and valleys. Despite the loss of many Invader crews (fifty-six aircraft failed to return) due to enemy action or the hazards of nighttime low-level flight, there was no supply crisis for Communist forces at the front.[53]

This iteration of Operation Strangle (June–July 1951) not only targeted the road network but also continued to strike supply depots, airfields, rail transport, troop concentrations, and vehicular traffic. Although rail facilities, lines, and resources were still bombed, the operational restrictions in terms of geographic zones placed the bulk of UNC airpower much closer to the front lines, leaving the most lucrative rail targets relatively unmolested during the critical period from May through July.[54] From General Timberlake's perspective, this decision was likely not all that controversial. UNC aircraft had already inflicted serious damage on North Korean rail infrastructure and equipment in the first year of the war: every major marshaling yard south of the Yalu (excepting Rashin, located only seventeen miles from the Soviet–North Korea border) was wrecked; four of five rail bridges into Manchuria were down or undergoing constant major repairs to facilitate even limited traffic; thousands of rail line cuts needed to be repaired; and 893 locomotives and 14,200 rail cars were claimed destroyed or damaged. To support Van Fleet's Piledriver offensive, it made sense to focus attacks closer to the front.[55]

But gradually the reduction of American ground action combined with a buildup of Soviet-supplied anti-aircraft guns along supply routes produced diminishing returns.[56] For armies that appeared on the verge of collapse in late May, both the CPVF and KPA demonstrated remarkable resiliency and morale. Even though the number of truck sightings and corresponding claims of kills increased dramatically, indicating the Communists were making major efforts to resupply their forces, evidence on the ground did not suggest logistical shortfalls significant enough to alter the ground tactical situation. Eighth Army intelligence even worried the communist armies were building capacity to restart offensive operations as early as September.[57] Simply put, too many supplies were allowed to enter Strangle's too restrictive interdiction zone to expect a crippling level of attrition. Strangle continued through July and into early August, but it was clear that it had failed to isolate the battlefield sufficiently to starve the communist armies enough to cause their collapse.[58]

Analysis of Strangle's failure to affect Communist supply operations in a strategically meaningful way was captured by Eighth Army and Fifth Air Force intelligence assessments of the CPVF's logistical system. An army–air force study in September 1951 determined that a Chinese or North Korean division of ten thousand men required only forty-eight tons of supplies per day, which compared favorably to a US division requiring five hundred tons per day. Communist soldiers had "small basic needs," and their logistical network exploited all forms of transportation—mechanical, animal, and human—to deliver "combat-essential supplies only." No matter how much damage was inflicted on roads, there was always enough capacity in the transportation network to sustain vehicular traffic moving south. "By far the most outstanding feature of the enemy logistical achievement" was not his overall capacity but his "ability to shift and reorganize . . . according to the dictates of the military situation." The study also noted "record breaking vehicle sightings" (4,623) from September 5–6, indicating the Communists had enough fuel and trucks for the major logistical effort necessary to counter Eighth Army's limited offensives. Furthermore, prisoner of war reports, captured documents, agent observations, and other intelligence sources depicted a system that though rudimentary from a Western standpoint, was still effective and highly resilient. A "shallow" interdiction campaign focused on tactical support to Eighth Army could not choke off enough supplies to cause a collapse in the Communists' fighting power.[59]

Therefore, FEAF analysts logically concluded that the key to interdiction success was the "strategic" railroad system originating at the Yalu and Tumen Rivers (respectively the boundaries with the PRC and Soviet Russia) and its rigid control system that appeared less flexible to adjust resources to needs. It was felt that if the railroad infrastructure itself could be rendered unusable, the Chinese would have to rely on inefficient and presumably more vulnerable truck transportation over longer distances to feed the front lines. Planners considered three ways to attack this system: destroying rail cars and locomotives, attacking bridges, and attacks on the rail lines themselves. The first two options were deemed impractical or inefficient. The emphasis, therefore, was on rail-cutting, "to destroy the enemy's rail system to where its rail traffic was as near zero" as possible. The campaign was expected to take ninety days.[60]

On August 18, 1951, the same day Eighth Army began its campaign of limited objective attacks, allied air forces began this more comprehensive effort, which FEAF officers continued to refer to as "Strangle," though its official name was the Rail Interdiction Plan (RIP). As suggested, the emphasis broadened from road to rail targets, but the area of aerial battle also expanded to include all of North Korea between the Yalu River and the line of contact. Strangle (RIP)'s purpose was "to interfere with and disrupt the enemy's lines of communication to such an extent that he will be unable to contain a determined offensive . . . or be unable to mount a sustained offensive himself."[61] Navy carrier-based planes assumed responsibility for the east coast lines while Fifth Air Force fighter-bombers swarmed over central and western North Korea, attacking extended lengths of main railway lines hoping to effect multiple "cuts" on a single line that would eventually exhaust the supply of replacement tracks. B-29 bombers attacked key bridge and marshaling areas at Pyongyang, Sinanju, Sunchon, and Songchon in an attempt to trap rolling stock for follow-on fighter-bomber strikes. Though the medium bombers deliberately shied away from Yalu River bridges, Rashin was bombed on August 25.[62]

Soon the effects began to tell as the Communists were surprised by the scale and scope of the aerial assault. Also, renewed ground fighting increased demand for military supplies, forcing both rail and road transport into the open. Along the critical double-track line from Sariwon through Pyongyang to Sinanju and Sinuiju on the border with China, American fighter-bombers destroyed enough track to shut down between 50 and 70 percent of its capacity. Between Pyongyang and Sinanju the rate of interdiction resulted in a 90 percent reduction of double-track usage. Even to keep this amount of track open required the harvest of 117 miles of track between Sinuiju and Sariwon; marshaling yards and smaller spur lines were also cannibalized for replacement track.[63] Simultaneously, truck traffic spiked upward, as expected. B-26 pilots, now flying the "C" model variant with a glass nose in lieu of additional machine guns, reported fantastic kill scores: from 750 trucks claimed destroyed in July to 1,935 in August. Even after strict rules on what constituted a vehicle "kill" were established, the night intruders went on to report the destruction of seemingly every truck in east Asia—6,761 in October, 4,571 in November, and 4,290 in December. Either the claims were fanciful or the Soviets really were willing and able to contribute a never-ending stream of vehicles to keep Chinese and North Korean soldiers in the field.[64]

The one-two punch by ground and air forces was having a serious effect, but Ridgway was impatient for strategic results. On August 30, he told his top airman that Strangle was not producing adequate pressure. He believed FEAF could get better results by concentrating fighter-bomber efforts on interdicting enemy supply lines from the Yalu River southward, especially against the rail line from Antung to Pyongyang. As if this were Weyland's first air war, Ridgway emphasized "the mission in each case of cutting [rails] and keeping them cut" and including medium bombers (the B-29s) "whenever practicable."[65]

Weyland did not need the lecture; he knew how to blow up railroads. The problem was one of supply and demand. By September and then into October, Fifth Air Force and naval Task Force 77 aircraft were destroying track faster than the Communists could rebuild it, potentially threatening the viability of Communist defenses at the time that Eighth Army was grinding forward. Prisoner interrogations in August admitted to a "critical ammunition situation" such that KPA gunners could only fire unobserved missions with pinpoint intelligence. Artillery company and battalion commanders criticized their men "for extravagance with ammunition." In comparison, American artillery had unquestioned superiority and did not suffer any appreciable degradation in support of the infantry attacks grinding forward across the front.[66] But the Americans gradually recognized that localized and limited objective attacks would never stress the communist logistics system sufficiently to threaten collapse across the front.

While Communist supplies appeared to be surging south, Ridgway worried that he might have made a colossal mistake in agreeing to the Communists' demands to settle the demarcation line first and "neutralizing" (making off-limits) Kaesong and its surrounding areas. In an unsent message to the

JCS, Ridgway believed he was operating in "a situation very different from that existing at the time my present policy instructions were formulated and dispatched." He noted that the armistice situation had not changed at all, but that the military situation had evolved dramatically. He acknowledged that despite the rail interdiction campaign, "soundly planned and well executed," and Van Fleet's punishing ground attacks, Chinese and North Korean forces had had seventy-five days to rebuild their units, replenish stocks, and recover from their "extremely heavy personnel losses [in April and May]." Under these conditions, the UNC commander worried that an armistice, calling off air and ground pressure, "would then permit the buildup in a relatively brief period . . . of the full offensive potential of all their forces in Korea." His intelligence analysis suggested the Communists were deliberately exploiting the talks to conceal their preparations for future operations. "His offensive potential [is] unquestionably greater than it was on 22 May," he concluded.[67] Aware that his implied criticisms put him at variance with US policy and would likely confuse the Joint Chiefs, Ridgway decided not to send the message.[68]

Ridgway's natural optimism continued to sink during the fall months. In response to FEAF's new effort, Soviet air forces became more active, contesting FEAF's presence in MiG Alley between the Yalu and Chongchon Rivers. The tentative Soviet air intervention in the fall of 1950 had failed to seriously challenge UNC control over North Korean airspace, but that began to change in the summer of 1951 with the deployment of more experienced pilots flying more advanced MiG-15s. Coincident with the inauguration of Strangle (RIP), American pilots reported much larger formations of MiGs "bouncing over" the Yalu River, making life much more hazardous for the straight-winged F-80 and F-84 fighter-bombers. By September 1951 the Chinese and Soviet forces fielded an estimated 525 MiG-15s. As many as ninety MiGs would overwhelm B-29 formations and their puny escort of F-86 Sabres or F-84 Thunderjets. FEAF urgently requested additional F-86s to increase fighter coverage, a request that went unfulfilled until December 1951 when Sabre numbers more than doubled (43 to 108). The result was fewer missions into the lucrative zone north of Pyongyang and south of the Chongchon River.[69]

Despite the increased air threat, FEAF reported that rail traffic ceased after October 2 between Pyongyang and Sariwon, which was one of four focused target segments. By October 25, mere days after Chinese and North Korean negotiators agreed to meet their UNC counterparts at Panmunjom to settle on the demarcation line, rail movement between Sinanju and Sukchon, part of the Sinanju-Pyongyang target segment, also ceased. Air attacks also intensified on the Kunru-ri–Sonchon and the Kunru-ri–Huichon corridors. By November the situation was even more dire with nearly all railroad connections to Manchuria rendered unusable, and most rail traffic that did make it into North Korea was forced to off-load onto trucks for movement south of the Chongchon River.[70]

But the surge in airframes and air crews was not sustainable, and apparent progress at Panmunjom toward a settlement that encouraged "active defense" (that is, no deliberate offensive action) on the ground inevitably granted the Communists another respite. The proliferation of MiGs, greater concentrations of air defense guns, and mass mobilization of manpower to repair rail and road cuts certainly played their roles to limit Strangle (RIP)'s effectiveness. During this same time period, American aircraft losses over North Korea spiked. October was a critical month and demonstrated the degree to which air interdiction was affecting Communist staying and fighting power in Korea. Desperate to blunt FEAF's thrusts along the Yalu River, the People's Liberation Army Air Force (PLAAF) at last entered the fray in strength. Flying from airfields around Antung, PLAAF MiG-15 jets contested American air superiority over the Yalu bridges and marshaling yards of northwest Korea. The battle for MiG Alley, the region lying within a 100-mile radius of Antung and where some of the most lucrative transportation targets were located (figure 4.3), intensified during these crucial fall months. Whereas MiG sightings from June through August numbered in the 300s, 1,177 were observed in September; the number of enemy jets observed coming up to challenge American planes surged to 2,573 in October; 2,326 in November; and over 4,000 in December.[71]

An additional limitation to Strangle (RIP)'s effectiveness emerged as FEAF intelligence identified several jet-capable airfields under construction in MiG Alley. On September 27, 1951, FEAF reconnaissance discovered three all-weather airstrips, each seven thousand feet long and studded with revetments for protected aircraft parking and anti-aircraft guns. Air commanders recognized the potential threat to expand MiG Alley and contest UNC air superiority much farther south, and they immediately diverted substantial assets, namely, B-29 bombers and F-86 escorts, away from rail and bridge targets to destroy the airfields. Because Fifth Air Force had so few Sabre jets relative to MiGs, some F-84 squadrons were retasked to fly as escorts—a role for which they were patently unsuited, as events would soon demonstrate. Of course, every sortie devoted to bombing a still (for now) unusable airfield was an aircraft not flying against interdiction targets. Furthermore, the battle for airfields resulted in some of the heaviest casualties UN airmen endured during the entire war. Although FEAF Bomber Command attempted nighttime strikes, the results were disappointing and failed to halt progress. Every day seemingly brought the threat of a supersized MiG Alley closer and closer. Lt. Gen. Joseph W. Kelly, Bomber Command's recently arrived leader, finally opted for daytime missions.

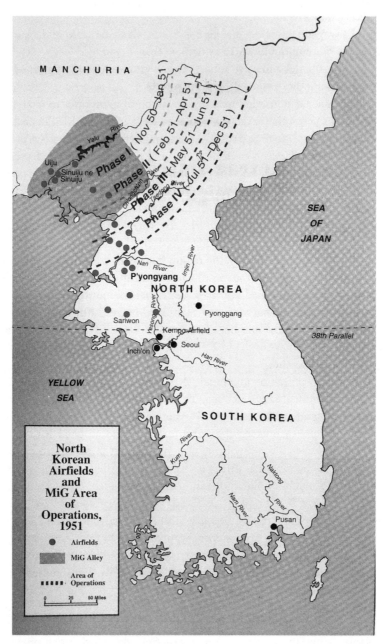

MANCHURIA

Phase I (Nov 50 – Jan 51)
Phase II (Feb 51 – Apr 51)
Phase III (May 51 – Jun 51)
Phase IV (Jul 51 – Dec 51)

Yalu River

Uiju
Sinuiju ne
Sinuiju

Ch'ongch'on River

SEA
OF
JAPAN

Taedong River

Nan River

Imjin River

P'yongyang

NORTH KOREA

Pyonggang

Sariwon

Yesong River

Kempo Airfield

Inch'on

Seoul

38th Parallel

Han River

YELLOW
SEA

SOUTH KOREA

Kum River

Naktong River

Nam River

Pusan

North Korean Airfields and MiG Area of Operations, 1951

● Airfields

　 MiG Alley

∎∎∎∎∎ Area of Operations

0　25　50 Miles

Figure 4.3 North Korean airfields and MiG Alley. Source: Mark, *Aerial Interdiction in Three Wars*, 288.

The third week of October was the deadliest for the B-29 missions. Bomber Command losses from July 1950 through September 1951 were limited to six B-29s lost to MiG fighters. A daytime airfield mission over Taechon on October 22 cost one Superfort, but the next day was far worse. Known as "Black Tuesday," the mission over Namsi cost FEAF Bomber Command eight B-29 bombers, three shot down and five more severely damaged—all in a twenty-minute period. Fifty-five crewmen were killed or missing. The F-86s flying high escort were held in check by dozens of Chinese- and Korean-flown MiGs, while the F-84s, responsible for close-in defense, were completely outclassed and helplessly watched the faster and more nimble MiGs flown by Soviet airmen tear apart the lumbering Superforts.[72] B-29 crewmen stoically watched the swirling MiGs bear down on them, "clos[ing] to fifty feet before unleashing withering barrages of 23-mm and 37-mm cannon shells." Indeed, the bomber crews referred to a MiG's guns as "horizontal flak."[73] Two days later, the Soviets again took to the sky to cut up another B-29 formation over Sunchon. Once again, the MiG pilots skillfully evaded the F-86 cover jets and pounded the bombers with cannon fire. Another Superfort went down in flames. Later that afternoon, FEAF acknowledged the loss of three Sabres. It had been an unfair fight. The F-86 had many good qualities and advantages over the MiG: cockpit visibility, advanced radar gun sight, six heavy machine guns capable of buzzing a wing or tail completely off within seconds, and hydraulic controls. However, the MiG was lighter and smaller with an engine similar to the Sabre, therefore it held the advantage with speed, climbing ability, and an altitude ceiling that fuel-starved Sabres could not reach and then fight with any semblance of parity. American pilots complained that the F-86 had to get close and achieve multiple hits to destroy a MiG, while the heavy weight of metal thrown by the MiG's cannons nearly guaranteed a kill if a solid hit was scored.[74]

The week of Black Tuesday's casualties constituted 45.5 percent of all B-29 combat losses since the beginning of the war. The era of daylight bomber raids against the northwesternmost targets came to an end thanks to Soviet air intervention. Future medium bomber attacks took place only at night with the aid of radar navigational guidance, known as SHORAN. SHORAN missions had been flown previously with indifferent results. Now a matter of necessity, bomber crewmen gained additional experience and proficiency attacking targets at night with no further loss to MiGs. But decreased pressure allowed the Communists to make enough progress to declare airfields south of the Yalu River at Namsi, Taechon, and Saamcham as "partly serviceable," and they remained that way for the rest of the war. The Chinese did add two jet-capable fields by Antung, in Manchuria, which increased their defensive capacity just as Strangle (RIP) was reaching its climactic stage at the end of

1951. The potential that Communist air bases would proliferate before and after an armistice greatly concerned General Ridgway and influenced his desired stance on negotiations.[75]

Although the Communists' efforts to sustain the air contest south of MiG Alley failed, their pilots did at last begin to limit the effectiveness of rail interdiction in this vital region, and they bought time to establish effective supply and transportation networks that would never again be seriously threatened by airpower.[76] Fifth Air Force attempted to keep Communist jets bottled up north of the Chongchon River through intensive "fighter sweeps" through MiG Alley and "fighter screens" established closer to the Yalu River that interposed the F-86s between the MiGs and the fighter-bombers making interdiction attacks.[77] But even if the American jets avoided MiGs, they were not yet home free. From October 1951 through January 1952, 111 aircraft were lost to ground fire. As a result of higher densities of ground fire, fighter-bomber aircraft increasingly were dedicated to suppress ground defenses, which further reduced the available sorties to strike rails and roads. The conscription of local civilian labor and the dedication of uniformed road and rail construction units soon managed to match the airmen, "cut for cut." In some cases, a rail cut could be repaired and supporting locomotives within eight hours.[78] Other prodigious efforts established multiple alternate bridge crossings and redundant rail lines along the crucial Sinuiju–Pyongyang corridor. By December 23, FEAF had to admit that the Communists had "broken our railroad blockade of Pyongyang and . . . won . . . the use of all key rail arteries."[79]

Strangle (RIP) officially continued until February 1952, but Fifth Air Force's heart was not in it. The UNC's reliance on airpower alone to strike a decisive blow turned out to be a mirage. Despite its failure to choke the Communists' logistical system, air force leaders argued that Strangle (RIP) had achieved a "fair measure of success" and had been "sort of a prophylactic measure" against an anticipated sixth Chinese campaign in the late summer of 1951. General Weyland regretted the choice of cover terms for the Rail Interdiction Program, but if the intent was only "to deny the enemy the capability to launch and sustain a general offensive," then Operation Strangle (RIP) could be considered "an unqualified success."[80] The RIP's last month, February 1952, produced 2,470 rail cuts, destroyed or damaged 55 locomotives and 700 rail cars, knocked out 80 bridges, and destroyed 2,365 trucks.[81] There was also some evidence that FEAF's F-86s were gaining the upper hand in the air-to-air battle as well, with some squadrons claiming a 25–1 kill ratio over the MiG-15s.[82] This reported rate of attrition, if approximating actual results on the ground and in the air, was impressive, but no one could say for certain that it had lasting military—that is strategic—effects. The Communists had not attempted a sixth major offensive and had been unable to resist completely Van Fleet's limited attacks across the peninsula. Furthermore, the Communists eventually agreed to relocate truce talks to Panmunjom, a more neutral site. Progress toward establishing a cease-fire condition that substantially conformed to UNC demands appeared to be approaching realization.[83]

But the apparent progress masked a more serious strategic problem regarding airpower as a coercive tool. The basic fact remained that Chinese airpower and US political limitations on the strategic bombing force in theater (coupled with the self-generated restrictions regarding the number of B-29 sorties permitted to fly into MiG Alley and Van Fleet's constrained offensive posture) gave the Communists a logistics sanctuary south of the Yalu River that soon brought the overall situation into a disappointing and expensive equilibrium. Unknown to the American commanders in the air or on the ground, the Chinese were simultaneously investing, with Soviet help, tremendous resources in transportation, security for their lines of communication, and above all manpower to repair bridges, roadbeds, and rail lines.[84] Aerial interdiction alone could not deprive the Communists of a "long-term capability to launch limited attacks, or even more, to deny him the capability to conduct an obstinate defense."[85] It was this latter condition that gave Korea's stalemate its bitter taste. For all its effort (16,000 rail cuts, 200 locomotives destroyed and 240 damaged, 210 bridges knocked out of use, and 775 more damaged), the UNC could not compel the Communists to give in at Panmunjom. They demonstrated tremendous resilience tactically and strategically, and they seemed capable of adjusting operations and logistics to keep pace with the UNC and frustrate attempts to gain insurmountable leverage at the bargaining table.[86]

Unfortunately, Strangle was bound to disappoint. The Communists' primitive needs as a light infantry army, and plentiful manpower and materials, all inhibited Strangle from living up to its name. Compounding these disadvantages, American airmen failed to coordinate effectively Strangle's efforts across all the services to include navy and marine corps aircraft until later in the war when Operation Saturate superseded Strangle (RIP). The only way to deny permanently a resource from the air is to keep bombing it, permanently. This FEAF simply could not do. Finally, the efforts of the air force were not synchronized with those of the army, and both services relearned the lesson that investment in interdiction without significant ground pressure pays poor dividends.[87]

Ironically, interdiction had gained an unlikely convert. General Ridgway, on January 4, 1952, reported to the JCS that Strangle (RIP) had adversely affected Communist supply operations, forced the diversion of thousands of troops who otherwise might have been committed to a late summer offensive, and destroyed or damaged thousands of trucks, locomotives, and other vehicles, imposing an increased demand on Russian and Chinese production facilities. The bottom line, from his perspective, was that even if Strangle (RIP) had not produced strategic results, to discontinue or even reduce interdiction over North Korea would in all likelihood result in the accumulation of enough supplies to permit the Chinese to explore their own offensive options. Ridgway was not willing to run that risk, and he was reluctant to order a resumption of large-scale ground operations that might result in empty territorial gains to be returned at the conclusion of a real cease-fire. Not yet able to escalate the conflict by attacking "strategic" targets along the Yalu, Ridgway was willing to settle for more interdiction—if it could be done better.[88]

After much analysis of Strangle (RIP)'s outcome, airmen determined some key findings. Rail cuts during the summer and fall of 1951 were widely scattered and were not maintained with follow-up strikes at night, in bad weather, or even in subsequent days. In other words, once hit, air planners simply scratched that particular target off the attack schedule and moved on. These single rail cuts were easily repaired even if heavy machinery were not available. In a similar vein, road cratering attacks had little effect at blocking traffic. Road cuts were generally filled, bypassed, or repaired with even less effort. Intelligence analysts concluded, "It is a fallacy to assume there is an area target for traffic interdiction . . . the only [valid] target is the pinpoint destruction of road and rail lines proper, bridges and rolling stock." What was needed was a targeting system that would saturate a specified zone with day and night attacks over a sustained period of time to discourage or disrupt repair and compel significant diversion or exposure of transportation assets to destruction.[89]

A Fifth Air Force targeting study issued February 25, 1952, recommended a new approach to interdiction: twenty-four hours of continuous attack "with sufficient concentration of effort . . . to mutilate, and if possible, destroy selected stretches" of rail lines. Daytime attacks by F-80 and F-84 fighter-bombers would hit the same segment of track, with no more than eight hours between attacks. At night, B-26 Invaders would follow to drop bombs at irregular intervals on the target area to increase the level of damage and potentially catch repair crews and their vital machinery at work. An additional task for the B-26s would be to expand their radius of action hunting vehicular and rail traffic attempting to bypass or shelter in the targeted area.[90]

The cessation of Eighth Army's offensive momentum in late November followed by deadlocked negotiations in early 1952 gave airmen the opportunity to attempt a more comprehensive and hopefully decisive campaign, called Operation Saturate. A very important difference to the Saturate operation was that the efforts of all air units involved would be centrally controlled through the Fifth Air Force's Joint Operation Center (JOC). At last all air assets were centrally assigned and coordinated. If weather, enemy ground fire, or other factors dictated a change in targets, the JOC would direct all available aircraft to a new target area.[91] On March 3, Fifth Air Force fighter-bombers started attacks along four axes: Kunu-ri to Huichon, Sunchon to Samdong-ni, Sinanju to Mamsi-dong, Pyongyang to Namchonjom (through Sariwon). Over the following twelve days, these tactical aircraft attempted three hundred sorties to drop six hundred bombs per rail segment per day. B-26s then joined the campaign on March 15, increasing the pressure through round-the-clock operations. Aircraft also attacked other stationary targets. The most intense napalm attack of the war occurred on March 11, when more than 250 F-80 sorties laid waste to a four-mile-square depot at Sinmak. Blown-out factories and facilities can be repaired, but those struck by a mixture of explosives and incendiaries are utterly ruined. This attack, which dropped nearly 33,000 gallons of jellied gasoline, incinerated thousands of tons of supplies.[92] However, as in previous efforts, initially promising results soon turned to disappointment as weather, increased Communist ground fire, and air crew exhaustion prevented Saturate from maintaining operationally significant rail interdiction.[93]

In Saturate's first month, FEAF flew 24,690 effective sorties and claimed 37 MiGs shot down and 55 locomotives destroyed or damaged, along with 1,765 trucks, 595 rail cars, 1,600 supply buildings, 45 warehouses, 90 bridges, and 11 tunnels destroyed. Road and rail attacks resulted in, respectively, 95 and 2,700 cuts.[94] Variations of the Saturate plan continued to be employed throughout the war against a wider area of targets, but the results were correspondingly less impressive. JOC-controlled attacks became more efficient but losses to flak increased. Refinements were made to B-29 and B-26 sorties, but the outcome was the same. Despite the airmen's best efforts—and there is no doubt their courage and skill inflicted grievous damage on Communist logistics and their ability to fight in the spring of 1952—it became apparent that the most interdiction could sustain, with all available flying units including naval and marine corps assets, was six enduring cuts. Analysts assessed that several times more cuts would have been required to deny the Communists operational use of the North Korean railway network.[95]

May 1952 was Saturate's climax. FEAF generated 30,234 interdiction sorties, the highest of any month to date, to achieve 2,579 rail cuts, knock out 34 rail bridges, and destroy 527 rail cars and 52 locomotives. Two missions of note tested Saturate's assumptions. On May 8, 227 fighter-bombers attacked a supply storage depot at Suan-Myon, destroying 228 buildings with their material and 81 trucks and other vehicles, while a three-day strike (May 22–24) against a storage and manufacturing center at Kiyang-ni obliterated 506 buildings. The Communist logistics system was hurt, but it never did come close to collapse.[96] Despite these fantastic losses, Chinese and North Korean divisions continued to fight on the ground; in fact, beginning in May, CPVF

TABLE 4.2. UNITED STATES AIR FORCE COMBAT AIRCRAFT STRENGTH
IN KOREAN THEATER OF OPERATIONS, MAY 1951–JUNE 1952

Type	May	June	July	Aug	Sep	Oct	Nov	Dec	Jan	Feb	Mar	Apr	May	June
F-51	130	117	121	110	120	110	88	77	72	68	57	53	45	52
F-80	156	144	125	118	112	108	84	76	68	73	84	80	83	89
F-84	82	93	120	132	142	128	125	139	116	101	87	85	97	108
F-86	50	41	40	35	45	43	95	108	127	136	132	125	138	136
B-26	115	111	112	110	104	101	99	105	105	105	108	106	111	105
B-29	92	94	96	99	95	85	91	94	92	96	104	105	97	88

Source: Command Reference Book–General Headquarters, Far East Air Forces, June 1951–July 1952, Record Group 407, NARA II.

divisions became much more active, responding to Eighth Army moves. By midsummer, they would be launching multiple regimental-size assaults against Van Fleet's OPLR.

FEAF terminated Saturate in June. The UNC simply did not have enough aircraft to maintain the kind of constant suppression and bombardment potential necessary to disrupt communist logistics in a strategically meaningful way (table 4.2). This is not to say that the air force's interdiction was of only marginal value. During the eighteen months that UNC air forces prosecuted their interdiction campaigns, FEAF dedicated 126,702 sorties (including Bomber Command and Fifth Air Force); carrier-based naval and marine corps aviators added another 20,567 sorties, and ground-based marine air contributed 25,266. Task Force 95, the UN's sea combat command, fired over 230,000 shells at interdiction targets.[97] Allied pilots claimed the destruction of 34,211 vehicles, 276 locomotives, and 3,820 rail cars. Over 19,000 rail cuts were made.[98] These results compelled the diversion of significant Communist assets to defend, repair, or replace transportation equipment and infrastructure in support of their forward armies. The destruction and delayed delivery of thousands of tons of military supplies helped to restrain Communist capabilities, but they did not destroy either their will or ability to fight. That these armies were no longer under serious pressure or threat of annihilation was not the airman's fault. It was the result of policy and national strategic objectives.

The lack of active combat on the ground reduced the demands for ammunition, fuel, food, and weaponry at the front to a level that even a trickle of supplies could support. Communist artillery totals continued to increase throughout 1952, even surging during the midst of Saturate. Ridgway worried that communist forces in Korea had increased their logistical stockpiles, endowing them with greater offensive potential than at any time since July 1951. The merits of interdiction versus close air support were hotly debated (and continue to be), but the army chief of staff Gen. J. Lawton Collins summed up the dilemma well. It would be impossible to expect aerial bombardment alone to prevent completely forward movement of an enemy's supply and reinforcements in a region where ample manpower was available to be employed in countering such a campaign.[99]

This did not mean the air forces were quitting the fight. In April FEAF planners were hard at work to determine how airpower could not only increase the tactical and logistics stress against ground forces but also bring significant strategic pressure against the Communists' policy of delay and dissimulation at Panmunjom. It would take a change of command along with a Communist propaganda blitz that threatened the UNC's moral stand on prisoner repatriation to allow FEAF to take the gloves off in their efforts to coerce a settlement.

5

THE COMMUNIST ARMIES REFORM,
SUMMER 1951–SPRING 1952

To be relevant strategically, the Chinese and North Koreans needed to adapt to survive tactically. The Communist armies, and the CPVF especially, made the greatest progress in the twelve-month period following the Fifth Campaign toward competing with the UNC forces on an equitable plane. The reform of the Communist armies in the summer and fall of 1951 was a most unwelcome development for the Eighth Army and for Ridgway's conception of an attrition-based coercive strategy.

The KPA's attack doctrine, inherited from the Soviet experience in World War II, was generally inflexible, meaning that subordinate units were not authorized or expected to adjust plans to accommodate unexpected terrain, enemy defenses, or other factors. Alternate or secondary missions were not assigned. An assaulting unit was expected to drive forward and seize its objective; worn out units were pushed aside to make way for fresh forces.[1] When the KPA enjoyed armor and artillery superiority, this doctrine produced substantial success. By August 1950, however, lengthening lines of communication, stiffening American and ROK resistance, UNC air superiority, and attrition combined to sap the KPA's offensive momentum until it was fixed in place at the Naktong River. The American-led amphibious assault at Inchon, the capture of Seoul, and Eighth Army's pursuit north to the 38th parallel essentially destroyed this Soviet-model offensive army. The CPVF intervention took the pressure off of the KPA, the remnants of which concentrated in the vicinity of Kanggye along the Yalu River. Although reconstituted during the winter of 1950/51, the KPA assumed by necessity a defensive stance, for which it was well suited and equipped. It remained the runt of the Communist coalition, but it never did lose its reputation for tenacious and ferocious fighting. Ridgway thought "the North Koreans displayed a disregard for human life . . . [and a] fanatical spirit in [battle] exceeding the Chinese."[2] They would live up to their reputation during the intense fighting in the late summer of 1951.

By January 1951, Kim Il-sung's army consisted of fourteen divisions organized into three army corps with 75,000 men. Two more corps were undergoing reorganization, retraining, and reequipping. Hastily raised, these new formations were clearly inferior in quality, training, and experience. Stalin reflected that the KPA "increased the number of divisions and forgot about quality."[3] Kim agreed with Soviet proposals to reduce the number of divisions being formed, which helped to avoid complete dilution of the KPA's leadership. When Peng launched his Fifth Campaign in April 1951, the KPA had 340,000 soldiers, of which 150,000 were front-line troops. The remainder were organized to support the war in the rear against UNC air interdiction as anti-aircraft and railroad repair units. Koreans were also responsible for coastal defense, a task they took very seriously for the remainder of the war, devoting thousands of men and miles of fortifications to prevent another amphibious assault behind the lines of contact.[4]

Artillery was a critical element of the KPA's defensive tactics for the remainder of the war. KPA artillery generally was limited to direct fire (a technique where the gun crew observes their own targets) or indirect fire (a technique where an independent observer calls for fire and adjusts the gun crew's aim) against preplanned targets, usually a defensive position overrun by Eighth Army troops. When negotiations began at Kaesong, each KPA division had one artillery regiment, consisting of three battalions, each battalion possessing three companies: two of 76 mm guns or mountain howitzers, and one of 122 mm howitzers. A full-strength company had four tubes.[5] The Americans conceded that Soviet artillery in the hands of the KPA was skillfully employed. Their largest piece was the M1931/37 122 mm gun, weighing 15,692 pounds and firing a 47-pound shell 22,747 yards. More common were the M1938 122 mm howitzers (12,904-yard range) and the rapid firing M1942 76.2 mm division gun (14,545-yard range). Both pieces provided excellent tactical support to attacking and defending infantry, were relatively mobile, and had high rates of fire.[6]

The KPA infantry soldier lost none of his tenacious fighting skill now that he was defending sacred homeland soil. KPA divisions participated in Peng's Third, Fourth, and Fifth Campaigns, but their offensive potential was limited. Soviet advisors assessed most KPA units effective at the regimental level, but deficient at battles requiring division-level coordination. An additional handicap was tension between the KPA and the CPVF. A Sino-Korean joint command existed on paper, but Peng and his staff called the shots. Friction between the two armies gave the Eighth Army a small margin for leverage as attacks against the KPA belatedly attracted Chinese support, but when Van Fleet pummeled the CPVF, the Koreans were incapable of rendering any meaningful support.[7]

In the summer of 1951 most of the front line Kim's new divisions held was in the east, where the rough and canalized terrain was more advantageous for defensive operations. KPA soldiers discovered a fondness for the spade and dug elaborate defensive works that complemented the already difficult terrain. They also employed camouflage effectively to conceal fighting bunkers and artillery positions. For his guns, overhead cover was strong enough that a direct hit was insufficient to declare a position destroyed. Often a weapon fired from a bunker or embrasure that had twice previously been reported as "destroyed."[8] The KPA was therefore well established on the eastern side of the peninsula when Van Fleet decided to open a limited objective attack to eliminate Communist possession of the Punchbowl region in the late summer of 1951.

The Chinese forces also reinvented themselves in response to the Fifth Campaign's failure to win the war. The CPVF command digested four significant lessons from their most recent offensive: ensure attacking troops gain some experience before entering battle; support infantry with sufficient artillery and motorized transport; prioritize the logistics battle; and develop professional command staffs for intelligence, communications, and planning.[9] The CPVF was outgrowing its guerrilla heritage to fight a modern war. But for Peng Dehuai's immediate concern, the question boiled down to, how could the CPVF hold its existing line without suffering unbearable casualties to American firepower? Therefore, the potential to settle the conflict, or at least to earn a breathing spell, by negotiation came none too soon, and the Chinese quickly seized on the reduced threat of destruction to revise their military strategy and develop new doctrines for attack and defense.[10]

CPVF commanders quickly realized that their field forces, steeped in a guerrilla tradition that emphasized maneuver and surprise over a reliance on firepower in defense of positions, were at a severe disadvantage in the restricted terrain of central Korea that was dominated by UNC airpower and Eighth Army's mobility and firepower. Mao, to his strategic credit, also recognized the need to accept a protracted war of attrition that would reduce the CPVF's vulnerabilities to American firepower and maneuver while maximizing its strengths in "stealth, field fortifications, camouflage, night operations, concentrated artillery and mortar barrages of short duration but upon very precise targets, and combat patrolling and raiding."[11] It was a strategy for the weak, but Peng and his skillful subordinates would play this weak hand well with nerve, grit, and the lives of brave and capable Chinese soldiers.

It took nearly a year to solve the survivability problem. The answer was to dig down into the earth, constructing a complex network of tunnels, bunkers, firing places, and fortified command posts. Like their KPA counterparts, the Chinese did their share of digging, exploiting their manpower to move a tremendous amount of earth and burrowing deep underground to avoid observation and the Americans' firepower. Each Chinese outpost, and even their MLR, consisted of an elaborate network of linked tunnels, such that troops and supplies could enter unseen into hidden entrances on the northern slopes and walk through the mountain to their front-line openings and bunkered embrasures. These fortifications were usually immune to artillery fire, excepting a direct hit. Recoilless rifles and the flat trajectory of a tank main gun proved to be the only direct fire weapons capable of dislodging Chinese defenders. Otherwise, it took an 8-inch heavy howitzer to do the job.[12] Snipers, machine gun teams, even 76 mm field guns could fire from manmade keyhole caves and then quickly withdraw when UNC aircraft or counterbattery fire arrived. As an example of the durability of these improvised fortifications, one forward observer, Sergeant First Class Fred E. Proft, called on the USS *Iowa*'s tremendous 16-inch guns to silence one such nuisance. The incoming shells seemed to be long delayed when suddenly "they came roaring in like a freight train. [We] worked that fortification over good, but would you believe, about thirty minutes after the shelling stopped, we could see some enemy soldiers come out of their caves . . . like they were drunk! I didn't think anyone could survive such a pounding."[13] American commanders with experience fighting the Germans evaluated Chinese defenses as often superior to those encountered in western Europe during the last war.[14]

These tunnel-based complexes not only protected Chinese (and North Korean) troops from bombardment and UNC ground attacks, they also enabled effective counterattack bases right in front of enemy forces. If a Chinese position were lost, even a forward outpost, they often could quickly organize a counterattack, up to company size, within thirty minutes. Unaware that they faced a third dimension in the struggle to control hills, tired and disorganized American and Korean infantrymen often found themselves fighting unexpected close-range battles just when they thought an objective was secured. In this way, Mao and Kim Il-sung aligned their tactical methods to their strategic and policy objectives. They protected their own forces without sacrificing their offensive potential. The Communists could fight the war of words at Kaesong and Panmunjom, confident that their armies would not suffer any significant reversals without exacting a correspondingly painful price from the UNC.[15]

When the war settled to competing patrols attempting to dominate the ground between the lines, the Chinese devised tactics adapted to both the natural terrain and the cover and concealment man could improvise. Canadian troops patrolling near Chorwon in July 1951 experienced "the Chinese practice of permitting us to closely approach their positions before opening fire . . . this allows him to do either of two things: one, withdraw after inflicting maximum casualties in the first contact, or two, reinforce his position having determined the point of our attack." The consequences of this style of fighting mitigated to some extent Eighth Army's firepower advantages while enabling a small number of soldiers to hold and contest "a great deal of ground." It was an efficient way of fighting a war of patrols.[16]

However, Chinese commanders knew that in the give-and-take of negotiations to stand permanently on the defensive would not achieve anything strategically significant. The CPVF needed to learn to attack and survive, and the command was confident that they could plan and fight in a manner such that the Chinese soldier "will not, therefore, throw away his life profitlessly in a pointless battle joined on badly chosen terrain for an inferior cause. But if the time comes when he can sell it at a price worth dying for, he [will] sell. And that, to him, is the measure of valor."[17] For the next two years, Peng and his subordinates demonstrated that quality of their army. If they could not destroy large enemy formations, they would mobilize what meager resources they possessed to fight a new kind of battle in Korea to inflict a thousand cuts and make the UNC bleed for every day the war continued.[18]

During the CPVF's most successful offensives, infantry units preferred to get close through nighttime movement and infiltration. Their march discipline was excellent, and their ability to find and exploit a vulnerability was uncanny. Defending UNC troops often got their first inkling they were under attack when they were hit by a shower of grenades and charging Chinese soldiers firing automatic weapons. Rather than "human waves," companies and platoons echeloned in depth kept continuous pressure on an objective until it was overrun.[19] After the disastrous Fifth Campaign, the CPVF commanders refined their small unit tactics with improved techniques for command and control to work in tandem with mortars, artillery, and other supporting arms to produce a new synthesis of offensive fighting that came to be known as *lingqiao niupitang* (eating sticky candy bit by bit).

Shortly after the conclusion of the Fifth Campaign, Mao unveiled his ideas for this new tactical system to Peng Dehuai and asked for his observations. Mao's new vision focused massed manpower and fire support against discrete enemy units to fight a deliberate attritional battle before attempting to advance on to the next objective—much as one eats *niupitang*, breaking off pieces to consume the whole after prolonged biting and chewing. In the fall of 1951, the new tactical system was put to the test, but it really did not demonstrate its potential until the following year. Mao was so encouraged by the results of these battles, in particular around Kumhwa in 1952, he wrote his field commanders, "If we continue to employ such methods of fighting, we will surely bring our enemies to their knees and force them to come to terms so as to end the war in Korea."[20]

When Peng addressed his senior commanders to explain *niupitang*'s application in Korea, he stressed the *niupitang* battle as a deliberate affair, carefully planned in a location where defensive patrolling, raids, and counterattacks had demonstrated or uncovered a weakness in Eighth Army's defenses. Peng expected his commanders and unit staffs to devote careful attention to coordinate artillery, anti-aircraft, and anti-tank weapons with infantry fire and assaults to wrestle for any lost positions and to ensure the "disposition of a large number of reserves so as to ensure that the longer we fight, the stronger we will be."[21] Further, Peng urged his troops to relearn under Korean conditions "a complete set of tactics for taking strong fortifications . . . [such as] digging trenches towards the enemy's fortifications, and then approaching under cover to make sudden attacks; tunnel operations, that is secretly digging trenches to and under the enemy's blockhouses, then blowing them up with explosives and following up with fierce attacks . . . [and] concentrating manpower and firepower to effect a breakthrough and to cut up the enemy forces."[22]

Niupitang tactics scaled back Mao's ambitions to destroy "another ten thousand" American or Korean troops with each offensive strike. Tactical objectives were redefined to stress the capture and use of terrain and prepared positions to inflict maximum casualties on the enemy over battles of annihilation of large units. Whereas previous CPVF attacks focused on enemy regiments and divisions, Peng trained his subordinates to look for opportunities to attack platoons and companies, akin to breaking fingers rather than limbs. He called it "see-saw battle" and envisioned short, sharp attacks that rarely massed more than a battalion of infantry at a time against a single UNC position. Repeated nighttime forays to dominate no-man's-land were crucial in building momentum to attack a target with larger and larger infantry teams backed by artillery and strong reserves to ensure continuous pressure against the enemy.[23] Once taken, fresh Chinese troops would reinforce the objective and prepare to receive any counterattack, which would also be met with concentrated artillery and mortar fire. Victorious troops would then consolidate and surge on to the next objective and repeat the process.[24] In this manner Peng expected to "overcome the US with a 'sea of men'" and avoid concentrations vulnerable "to the US 'sea of fire' [air and artillery]."[25]

Although dressed in apparently new strategic garb, the reality of Mao's idea harkened back to China's own military tradition of back-and-forth conflict: "The wooden mallet strikes the chisel—the chisel splits the wood" is an appropriate metaphor illustrating the contextual setting for *niupitang*. Whether chisel or wood, the winner depends on which is doing the striking.[26] To Peng's relief, Mao now urged patience and deliberation when attacking the Americans. Peng was grateful for Mao's enlightened approach, as it played to one of the CPVF's inherent strengths, which was to capitalize on tactical patience and allow the passage of time to set the right circumstances for battle that would have the best strategic effects.[27] More urgently, Peng knew his troops needed time to recover losses, prepare field fortifications, and integrate greater numbers of artillery and mortars to carry out this new approach.[28]

Chinese artillery techniques remained primitive by American standards until well into 1952. The Americans believed Chinese doctrine assigned mortars to destroy personnel, while artillery engaged fortifications. This assessment made for neat categorizing but was in practice not all that telling. More significantly, Eighth Army intelligence reporting showed that CPVF fire support typically was generated from single pieces or platoons of two to three guns firing on a preplanned target.[29] It was still rare in 1951 that Chinese artillery showed the capability to mass artillery from multiple firing positions. Rates of fire fluctuated wildly during a campaign; by May 1951, acute shortage of ammunition severely limited the effectiveness of his fire support, and the tactical results showed how unreliable this arm was for the Chinese.[30]

The ability to maintain themselves logistically in the face of the greatest sustained interdiction effort ever attempted was a phenomenal achievement and contributed signicantly to the CPVF's strategic relevance. Ridgway grasped, but could not fully exploit, the essential weakness of Chinese operations: the CPVF had serious problems arming, equipping, feeding, and sustaining their soldiers in continuous combat. The Chinese volunteer was human and could not be expected to endure indefinitely the inevitable ravages of exhaustion and attrition. Once negotiations began and Eighth Army relaxed its offensive stance, Chinese armies were never again threatened with logistical collapse. Further, they maintained to the end of the war an uncanny ability to mask the massing of troops and supplies prior to any major attack. Still, they were not invisible, and good patrolling, aggressive intelligence gathering, and attentive analysis could and often did give the American and Korean forces some kind of advanced notice.[31]

By the fall of 1951, Peng's infantry made overwhelming an outpost its specialty, and his soldiers learned to accomplish that objective in a short amount of time, "then departed with their prisoners, leaving the small patch of ground invitingly empty again."[32] In early November, Peng's version of active defense won its first success when eleven companies from the Forty-Seventh Army attacked three company-size positions defended by First Cavalry Division soldiers. The attackers, led by special "penetration units," wrested their objectives, defended against American counterattacks, and then withdrew.[33] They returned the following night to smash the unprepared defenders and retain control of the hilltops.[34] Both Peng and Mao were satisfied; the former could fight active defense indefinitely, while the latter got his beloved protracted war to wring political prestige if not outright victory from the Americans.

The commencement of truce talks afforded Peng's volunteers the time and space they needed to reorganize, establish a firm defensive line out of contact with Eighth Army, and begin the transition from "surface defensive positions" to underground fortifications and a tunnel system to shelter and conceal CPVF logistics, command posts, and troop movements.[35] But Peng was also confident that "toughness and tenacity in combat" combined with "close coordination of the artillery, antitank, antiaircraft, and infantry firepower" would make the Chinese competitive against the Americans. "The longer we fight, the stronger we will be" was more than an aphorism. It was the philosophical essence of the CPVF's modern fighting doctrine that carried it through the difficult campaigns of 1952.[36]

Elbowing Forward—The Punchbowl: Bloody and Heartbreak Ridges

Coincident with the beginning of truce talks, July 10, the JCS relayed to Ridgway Truman's approval to remove any tactical restrictions on Eighth Army's operations to secure a defensible cease-fire line. Ridgway and Van Fleet recognized that the time had passed for decisive gains at an acceptable cost, but they both recognized that Line Kansas-Wyoming represented the best defensive terrain, and therefore, it was important to push enemy lines as far north of it as could be done economically. By August 1, Van Fleet considered Line Kansas "almost impregnable" and strong enough to resist any offensive comparable to the Fifth Campaign. He also reported that Eighth Army's offensive patrolling had consolidated gains made in June, and that Line Wyoming had become a de facto MLR. Therefore, it was important to fortify and secure the outpost terrain to protect it just as Eighth Army had done for Line Kansas. From this point forward, Van Fleet's offensive posture was limited to actions to inflict casualties, seize prominent terrain that would keep Chinese and North Korean forces away from the MLR (Line Kansas-Wyoming), and keep the army's edge offensively sharp. It was a difficult and bloody undertaking.[37]

At the same time, the Chinese and North Koreans were playing for the best possible outcome, a return to the 38th parallel. If the UNC refused, then they too needed to have a military option to enforce their demand. An indefinite pause was counterproductive. The Chinese in particular appeared to take advantage of the truce talks to rebuild their shattered armies and resupply and reorganize their ground and air forces. In fact, Mao was hopeful that a new offensive might be possible by September. In the meantime, the CPVF "adopted a strategy of defensive operations, conducting protracted warfare on advantageous terrain until the ratio of military forces of the enemy and our forces would be in our favor." The Chinese hoped this realignment of "ratios" would either lead directly to victory in the field or evolve into a situation at Kaesong "in which the enemies . . . would give up and withdraw by themselves."[38]

American aerial reconnaissance, patrol reports, and intelligence analysis began in August to paint a gloomy picture regarding the Communists' capabilities. Intentions remained opaque, but across the front the Communists were constructing strong field fortifications, laying minefields, and building up supplies. Chinese and North Korean artillery became more active in July, and several instances are recorded of Eighth Army artillery having to displace after receiving accurate indirect fire.[39] Additional Chinese armies were either identified or assessed as being in positions that could support a defensive attitude or provide impetus to a sudden offensive thrust. Eighth Army G-2 reported the Communists possessed "an alarming capability" to sustain a seventy-two-division offensive for up to seven days or a forty-five-division one for nine to eleven days.[40]

The fresh CPVF Twelfth and Forty-Second Armies near Pyonggang, the northern apex of the Iron Triangle, were symptomatic of Eighth Army's dilemma. The road network from Pyonggang permitted either army, each with three full-strength divisions (30,000 men), to move west or east. Forward movement in either direction would reinforce already strong reserves capable of sustaining a series of limited attacks that could evolve into a general offensive. Van Fleet's intelligence declared, "The enemy is presently considered capable of offensive action at any time. He [sic] has accumulated a logistic base greater than that preceding previous offensives, his depleted units have been rehabilitated and reequipped, new units have been identified in Korea . . . all exceed the base from which he launched preceding offensives."[41] Van Fleet and his corps commanders also worried that the increase in communist shelling indicated "an improvement in the enemy ammunition supply situation."[42] Eighth Army was rapidly losing its relative advantages gained over the previous two months.

In July 1951 Van Fleet and his staff began work on an ambitious offensive plan, named Overwhelming, that he hoped would win Ridgway's favor should negotiations fail to produce a quick settlement. As its name suggests, Overwhelming involved a massive offensive move: a ground-amphibious attack (the allure of a second Inchon was ever present in the minds of American commanders, and the amphibious "end-run" would feature in every strategically offensive plan proposed until 1953) that aimed at battering the Communist forces so severely, and pushing them back to a line running from Pyongyang to Wonsan, where peace could be dictated rather than bargained for. Van Fleet acknowledged that the fundamental strategic conditions would have to change for Overwhelming to live up to its promise, namely, the Chinese armies would have suffered some deterioration of power in Korea, begun a unilateral withdrawal from contact, or the Eighth Army would have received substantial reinforcements and a change of mission for a strategic offensive. None of these conditions was likely.[43]

But Van Fleet was not one to wait around. One area that attracted his attention was in east-central Korea, a geographic location known as the Punchbowl (figure 5.1). Located northeast of the Hwachon Reservoir, the Punchbowl was a circular valley about four and a half miles in diameter and five miles north of Line Kansas. The valley itself possessed little intrinsic strategic value, but it was ringed by high ridges that formed a salient protruding south and offered the Communists unimpeded observation of UNC supply lines and positions defending Line Kansas. This situation—the MLR and its supply lifelines on lower ground dominated by Communist-held positions farther north—would become a common refrain for the next two years, and it was a difficult temptation to resist just going after the next piece of high ground. Van Fleet determined to clear the Punchbowl because of its military value, and on July 21 he gave the task to draw up plans to seize the western rim of Punchbowl to the X Corps, now commanded by Maj. Gen. Clovis E. Byers. The ROK I Corps was given a similar mission to seize the eastern rim.[44]

Paik Sun-yup's ROK I Corps began its attack on August 18 against the eastern rim, his troops prying out the elements of three KPA divisions in a bitter contest for "J-Ridge." Paik's troops attacked day after day, but they failed to secure their gains with fresh troops to withstand the inevitable counterattacks. When Van Fleet toured the Koreans' headquarters he pointed out the tactical error, which was corrected in subsequent attacks. He also requested Paik's recall from the stalled negotiations at Kaesong so the corps could have its reliable commander at the head. After eleven days of intense fighting, the ROK troops finally owned the southeast corner, which alleviated some pressure in the Soyang Valley and permitted the ROK artillery to observe and fire on KPA units on the north side of the Punchbowl (figure 5.2).[45]

Paik recognized the problem then coalescing across the front. The Communists took stock of their positions, much like the Americans had, and determined their own line of resistance, and they simultaneously reinforced and fortified advanced areas, such as the Punchbowl, to resist any further UNC encroachment. The KPA brought in six divisions to defend the region, and Paik's two divisions, the ROK Capital and Eleventh Divisions, had a tough fight up steep mountain slopes dominated by KPA mortars and machine guns. Only after Paik convinced Van Fleet to direct American artillery to support the Eleventh Division's advance did the South Korean troops finally establish themselves on the high ground overlooking the Punchbowl from the east.[46]

Simultaneously, the Second Infantry Division began a month-long struggle

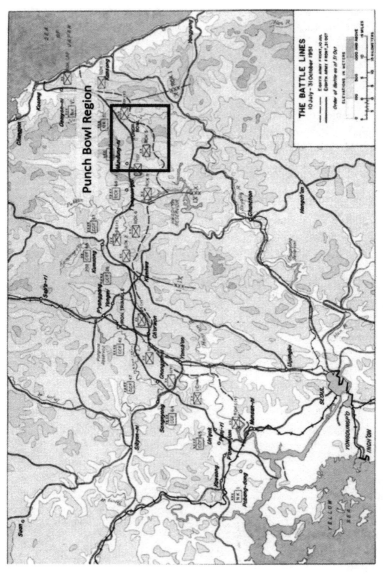

Figure 5.1 Situation map, fall 1951. Source: Hermes, *Truce Tent and Fighting Front.*

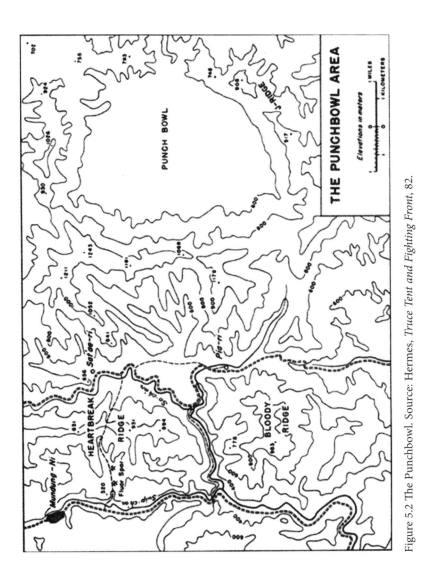

Figure 5.2 The Punchbowl. Source: Hermes, *Truce Tent and Fighting Front*, 82.

to seize "Bloody Ridge" (known in Korean as Suribong) along the Punch-bowl's southwestern rim. Van Fleet wanted to show that ROK troops "had come of age," but Byers took this intent too far, directing "command to be U.S., maneuver and movement to be ROK forces."[47] Korean troops from the ROK Fifth Division were attached to the Second Infantry Division and re-ceived orders on August 16 to seize the ridgeline consisting of four hilltops, known as Hills 731, 983, 940, and 773. The terrain sloped steeply southward, giving a significant advantage to the North Korean defenders, who devoted two regiments from two divisions to its defense.[48] KPA efforts to strengthen Bloody Ridge and the surrounding high ground had begun in early July. After nearly six weeks the fortified works consisted not only of artillery dugouts and shelters but also elaborate bunkers and protected assembly areas on the north side of Bloody Ridge. An American marine who fought in the Punch-bowl region, Lt. Frederick J. Brower, noted the North Koreans put up a for-midable defense. They "had been retrained and armed with new Russian weapons [and] unlike the Chinese, they had lots of shells."[49] A captured KPA document highlighted the commitment to defend their lines to the end: "We are to defend and further fortify the present positions of our battalion; there-fore, we must not yield a single inch of ground or allow even one enemy sol-dier to penetrate. At the same time, in order to inflict a large number of ca-sualties, we must be on the alert in the front lines so that we may seize upon suitable opportunities for aggressive small unit action."[50] KPA defenders on Bloody Ridge rarely surrendered, even when surrounded. They continued to fight on until completely subdued or destroyed by UNC firepower.

Maj. Gen. Clark L. "Nick" Ruffner, a 1924 Virginia Military Institute gradu-ate in the cavalry branch, had commanded the Second Infantry Division dur-ing some of its most distinguished encounters in the war where the division relied on air and artillery firepower to destroy attacking Chinese infantry.[51] This time, the tables were turned and Ruffner's troops would be the ones charging defensive positions and exposed to artillery firepower. Concerned about relying on ROK troops, Ruffner's plan committed immense firepower to soften up the KPA defenses: seven artillery battalions, close air support sor-ties, and shells from US warships in the East Sea. He also ordered his Thirty-Eighth Infantry Regiment to support the ROKs with fire, block any counter-attacks that bled through the ROK lines, and continue the attack if the ROKs were successful.[52]

The opening bombardment began on August 15 and lasted until 0630 on August 18, when the Koreans started their attack. To the Korean troops anx-iously waiting the signal to move out, it appeared that the Americans were trying "to kill the hill itself, piece by piece."[53] Unfortunately, as the ROK in-fantry would soon discover, conventional weaponry had not been invented that could blast a determined enemy from his fortifications. The only way to reduce and secure the ridge would be bunker by bunker, rifle and grenade fighting at close ranges. By the afternoon, ROK troops had seized Hills 710 and 731, two intermediate points leading up to Hill 983. Resistance soon intensified as the ROKs hit minefields and 82 mm mortar rounds fell on the tired Koreans, who stopped to dig in and find protection from shell fragments.[54] The KPA mortars proved the most severe trial for the advancing ROK troops. Emplaced on the reverse slope (ten yards or so from the crest on the side opposite the advancing troops), the tubes enjoyed protection from direct fire weapons and any observation that could call for effective artillery or air strikes. At the same time, the KPA's forward observers often were within speaking distance of the mortar crew, and by placing themselves on the "gun-target axis," made computations for deflection (left to right adjustments) unnecessary when calculating firing data.[55]

For six days the ROK soldiers pressed on, attacking one bunker after the next, before finally overrunning Hill 983. But the cost was high, especially among the platoon leaders, whose life expectancy was measured in hours if not minutes. In the enlisted men's macabre vernacular, they were "commodity" or "consumptive" lieutenants, an inexact translation from Korean (*somo jangyo*) that reflected a mixture of the English terms "expendable" and "naive." It was considered bad luck to be positioned next to a commodity lieutenant on Bloody Ridge.[56]

Frustrated by the slow progress and high casualties, Van Fleet ordered X Corps to loosen restrictions on artillery rates of fire, telling his troops to expend artillery liberally "to kill the enemy and to extricate UN forces or prevent their capture or destruction."[57] The increased fire support, however, was insufficient to repel a strong counterattack by the Second Regiment, Twelfth KPA Division, on August 26 that drove the ROKs steadily back from Hills 983, 940, and 771.[58] The disappointing ROK performance was felt keenly by both Van Fleet and President Syngman Rhee, who had agreed to come to Bloody Ridge and decorate his soldiers in commemoration of the victory. The visit never occurred, and Brig. Gen. Haydon L. Boatner, Ruffner's assistant division commander, felt that the ROK troops tried bravely but suffered heavy casualties because the division, corps, and army leadership had underestimated the North Koreans' defensive strength and will to fight for Bloody Ridge. Too much was expected, too soon, from the South Koreans.[59]

General Ruffner then committed the Ninth Infantry Regiment, commanded by Col. John M. Lynch, to retake the ridge. Unfortunately, the Ninth Infantry was not a good choice, as it had responsibility to secure the MLR and could send only one battalion forward in a "piece-meal frontal attack" that was doomed to fail in the face of heavy fire. Boatner was disgusted by the regiment's failure to regain the lost ground. He recalled, "The 9th [Infantry] thought they could take Bloody Ridge easily. They under-estimated the enemy and over-estimated their own strength." He also felt that Eighth Army in general had adopted an attitude that "the war was over." Officers and men "let up, dug in on the Kansas Line, and when battle was renewed," they advanced reluctantly and without the winning spirit the Americans had displayed so effectively just three months earlier. One of Boatner's most trenchant observations about the Ninth Infantry's combat effectiveness centered on the effects the Far East Command's rotation policy caused. Because President Truman refused to hold noncareer personnel on active duty for the war's duration, battle-experienced veterans began to leave Korea.[60] In the case of the Second Division, the division commander, one regimental commander, and three battalion commanders all rotated out during the battle. Boatner himself only arrived the day Bloody Ridge started. In his opinion, "many extra casualties resulted in the final stages of assaults on enemy bunkers and pill boxes" due to inexperienced leadership, immature teamwork, and the neglect of basic combat skills that proved effective confronting similar fortifications in the late Pacific campaigns of World War II. Boatner immediately noticed the Ninth Infantry troops failed to employ their flame throwers in the battle—no one knew how to use them effectively in the close fighting that required exquisite teamwork at the squad level. Artillery battalions supporting the division also felt the loss of experienced officers and warrant officers, which negatively affected their support to the attacking infantry. At Bloody Ridge, the Second Infantry Division was the first major unit to experience these conditions that would affect all subsequent American operations in Korea.[61]

Van Fleet, recognizing the impasse at Kaesong where negotiations had just broken off, determined to widen the X Corps's offensive to drive the KPA farther back from the Hwachon Reservoir. He directed Byers to commit additional troops from the reserve ROK Fifth and US First Marine Divisions to expand the battle zone on the west and north sides of the Punchbowl. More artillery was called in and the IX Corps laterally transferred its reserve stocks of ammunition to X Corps.[62] Ruffner's other two American regiments, the Thirty-Eighth and Twenty-Third Infantry, simultaneously advanced along the flank ridges and hills to cut off KPA reinforcements and isolate the defenders on Hill 983. Even then the desperate fighting ground on, as the defenders continued to pour fresh troops into the fight, despite having "suffered staggering losses."[63] Eventually the full weight of three American regiments shifted the balance. American soldiers relearned old lessons about attacking fortified positions: organizing platoons into assault, support, and reserve squads; directing close air support; and employing flamethrowers, demolitions, and recoilless rifles at point-blank range in a struggle to the death. Finally, Hill 983 fell into a deep silence on September 5, when Brig. Gen. Thomas DeShazo, Ruffner's immediate replacement, declared Bloody Ridge secure.[64]

Boatner called Bloody Ridge "the poorest [battle] tactically of any I have ever participated in."[65] Frontal attacks without proper fire support and maneuver techniques against strong fortifications and artillery cost Eighth Army dearly: 326 killed, 2,032 wounded, and 414 missing. Most of the missing were likely dead, consumed in the hellish bombardments from both sides, their shattered remains unidentifiable among the detritus of the battle. The Americans had failed to suppress the KPA artillery, which devoted nearly all its fire to support local counterattacks, increasing the casualty rate among the exposed American and Korean soldiers. Most of their guns were emplaced at the military crest of the hill in stoutly constructed bunkers that gave the crew protected direct-fire capabilities and reduced the technical expertise needed for defensive fire and support to infantry counterattacks. Infantry fortifications had similar protection and were difficult to spot from the ground or the air, and even when spotted, on average eight bombs were required to knock out one bunker.[66] The Americans had also failed to isolate Bloody Ridge from KPA reinforcements and resupply. The struggles for Bloody Ridge and later Heartbreak Ridge illustrated one of the principal flaws behind Van Fleet's strategy of limited objective attacks. The communists were rarely placed in positions of relative disadvantage, and they had little difficulty repulsing frontal assaults, no matter how well supported by artillery or close air support (figure 5.3).

North Korean losses were assessed as topping 15,000, surely an exaggeration, but the scale of casualties helps to define the brutality of the combat that was limited in scope, scale, and time. Attack on a fortified position is always difficult, and Bloody Ridge was already a naturally strong position. Col. Hwang Yup, commander of the ROK Thirty-Sixth Regiment, remembered that "in spite of the supporting fire of the US artillery, many of the enemy's fortified bunkers were not destroyed, and we were obligated to rely on human bombs. We suffered more than 1,000 casualties in this battle because of the mine field and close combat. We had to conduct bitter close combat in spite of the fierce friendly bombardment that left hardly any trees or grass on the ground. The gruesome battle continued, and the valley was filled with human blood."[67] Colonel Hwang recognized the new norm for the Korean battlefield. The Communists had had two months to recover their equilibrium and build up their defenses organized around strong terrain features. Their supporting artillery was dispersed and well camouflaged. It was going to take much more than bombs and shells to pry the Communists out.[68]

Meanwhile, X Corps pressed its attack against the northern rim of the Punchbowl. On August 31, Byers hurled the First Marine Division (with the

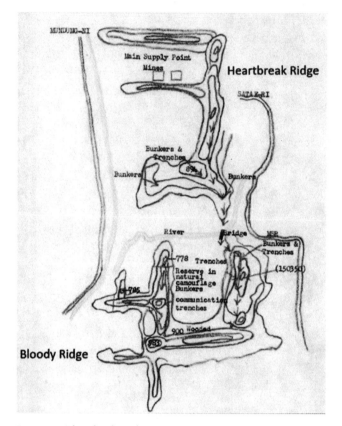

Figure 5.3 The Bloody Ridge–Heartbreak Ridge complex. Note
that the KPA depot at Mundang-ni was untouched, which allowed
KPA troops to resupply their fighting forces. Source: Heartbreak
Ridge, USACMH.

ROK Marine regiment attached) forward. After three days the marines got
their part of the Punchbowl under control. Encouraged by this initial success, Van Fleet told Byers to keep going with the marines' final objective as far
north as the northwesterly leg of the Soyang River. The marines jumped off
again on September 11 and fought their way up and down the ridges against
mutually supporting positions. They endured some of the heaviest mortar
and artillery barrages of the war as the KPA refused to withdraw under the
tremendous pressure brought to bear by American and ROK marines, air,
and artillery bombardment. When the marines did capture an important objective, Hill 749, KPA counterattacks arrived before reinforcements and resupply could make the marine position secure. The North Koreans yielded
only after repeated assaults and counterattacks against overwhelming fire-

power had worn their forces down and substantial air attack interdicted their own supply of men and shells.[69]

Hoping to capitalize on the North Koreans' withdrawal from Bloody Ridge, Van Fleet ordered DeShazo's tired Second Infantry Division to set out once more to seize the final dominant ridge in the Punchbowl region remaining in North Korean hands. "One of the most formidable positions on the entire battle front,"[70] the ridge itself was a north–south mountain mass, consisting of three main peaks. The southern terminus was Hill 894, which covered the approaches from Bloody Ridge; 1,300 meters to the north was the highest peak, Hill 931; and 2,100 meters farther at the northern end was a needle-like summit, Hill 851. Climbing hand over hand, infantrymen carrying recoilless rifle and mortar rounds along with their own ammunition and equipment threw themselves repeatedly at these enemy strongpoints, only to be pushed off by desperate counterattacks. It was common for these positions to change hands several times in a day. Correspondents quickly dubbed the place "Heartbreak Ridge."[71]

Van Fleet engaged in a contest of wills as he flung his infantrymen at Heartbreak Ridge. Although the Americans used somewhat better infantry-artillery tactics, the North Korean defenders had eight days to prepare bunkers, trench lines, and gun positions, which completely dominated the ground below. Again, underestimating the extent of opposition—two North Korean divisions, the Sixth and Twelfth from the KPA's V Corps, were dug in on Heartbreak Ridge and its surrounding areas, with mortar and artillery arrayed in the flanking valleys to pummel the attackers—DeShazo ordered the Twenty-Third Infantry Regiment, commanded by Col. James Y. Adams, to attack frontally and without any supporting attacks from the Ninth or Thirty-Eighth Infantry Regiments. The plan was for Adams's regiment to advance from the east and penetrate the KPA lines between Hills 851 and 931. A battalion would then peel off to the north to secure Hill 851, while a second veered south to strike Hill 931 and then Hill 894.[72]

DeShazo served in World War I as an artillery corporal. He then graduated from West Point in 1926, commissioned as a lieutenant in the field artillery branch. His World War II experience was with armored artillery, commanding the Sixth Armored Field Artillery Group in North Africa, Italy, and southern France. Following the war, he served at the Artillery School, Fort Sill, Oklahoma; Ankara, Turkey, as the senior artillery officer for the American Military Mission to Turkey; and the Pentagon as Chief of the Policy Planning Branch. In September 1950, DeShazo became the IX Corps artillery officer. He held this position until March 1951, when he assumed command of the Second Division Artillery, which fought the Battle of the Soyang River in May 1951, breaking the momentum of the CPVF's final campaign of the year.[73] His experience in fighting the Chinese in the Fifth Campaign may have clouded his judgment when it came to overcoming fanatical KPA troops. Oliver Le Mire, the deputy commander of the French Battalion, attached to the Twenty-Third Infantry, observed, "The North Koreans only give up terrain foot by foot—they are decidedly tougher than the Chinese."[74]

DeShazo's faith in artillery caused him to envision American firepower as the solution to the problem of Heartbreak Ridge. One battalion of 105 mm howitzers was in direct support to the Twenty-Third Infantry, while three more battalions (one of 105 mm and two of 155 mm) were in general support to the division. A battery of 8-inch howitzers provided heavy counterbattery and bunker-busting support. Even with this impressive array of fire support, to call his plan ambitious would sell short DeShazo's confidence.[75] The approaches were high and steep; straight up was the only way to go forward. This kind of fight was extremely tough on platoons and squads, who struggled to maintain cohesion and forward momentum over the rough ground, narrow ridges, and steep slopes. A Canadian observer pointed out, "This Korean fighting is hard on [squad] commanders who must lead in order to keep control. . . . Here he must lead and be the pivot on which his [squad] moves. This calls for leadership of the highest order."[76] Not to mention nearly suicidal courage.

Adams's Twenty-Third Infantry moved out against Heartbreak Ridge after a short forty-five-minute bombardment, but once the soldiers hit the web of spurs extending eastward, their momentum collapsed. Despite the shelling, little actual destruction occurred, and because of the steep slopes and narrow ridgetops, the Americans found it difficult to generate enough small arms fire to suppress the multitude of bunkers and trench lines. Most attacking squads found their fire reduced to the lead man (who was not in a good position to survive for long) and the automatic rifleman, known as the BAR gunner. The BAR was both powerful and accurate, an effective weapon to suppress bunkers. It also tended to be the weapon most likely to galvanize the infantry squad to move forward. One observer noted that where the BAR goes, men move and fire.[77] But the North Korean defenders, sheltered in their log and earth bunkers, remained mostly unfazed by American artillery, and they continued to emerge from their protective shelters to pour withering fire downslope, driving the attackers to the ground. All day the GIs vainly sought protection from the unyielding rocky soil. According to Lt. Ralph Hockley, a forward observer attached to the Twenty-Third Infantry, the Americans "could count on a firefight of some kind every night."[78] Then the mortars and artillery fire began to fall. Corporal Benjamin Judd, a squad leader in F Company, endured "shells [falling] over the entire company. There was no place they were not falling, and there was no place to take cover. We sat like ducks in a hailstorm of fire."[79]

DeShazo and his staff realized the attacking force was in the worst imaginable position: under the observation and guns of the enemy, incapable of advancing, and unable to withdraw. Piecemealed battalion-size frontal assaults could not overcome the defenders with enough strength to establish a firm defense against the inevitable counterattack. Not only was the enemy deeply entrenched, the western valley of Mundung-ni was firmly in the KPA's control, and it was from here that the Koreans introduced reinforcements and supplies without effective interference from American artillery or airpower.[80] Colonel Lynch suggested on September 19 to expand the division's attack westward. He wanted to send a battalion from his Ninth Infantry across the Mundung-ni valley to seize high ground that would threaten the North Koreans' route of supply and troop support. DeShazo demurred, claiming that the corps commander had assigned the division's priority effort to seize Hill 931.[81]

As if to punctuate the division's terrible situation, that same evening Company L, Third Battalion, had finally flushed the enemy out of their fortifications on Hill 851. They were then hit by a large KPA attack, probably battalion strength, with substantial reinforcements that overran the company, effectively wiping it out. Two days later another assault was made against Hill 931. It was also driven back with heavy losses. On September 23, five more attempts were made against Hill 931. GIs reported that the defenders were throwing "what appeared to be 'sacksful of hand grenades.'" At last, a handful of men from Company A plying bayonets and flinging hand grenades reached the narrow top, where they saw "so many enemy dead that the bodies were stacked several feet high."[82] The GIs discovered that to take a bunker or clear a trench required killing every single defending North Korean inside of it. Despite the company commander's determination, the dozen or so exhausted Americans withdrew in the face of a nighttime counterattack.[83]

As the standoff solidified, the division welcomed a new commander, Maj. Gen. Robert N. Young. Young was an ROTC graduate of the University of Maryland in 1922 and a former instructor at the army's Infantry School at Fort Benning, Georgia. He served as assistant commander of the Third Infantry Division in the last months of the European campaign of World War II, and he was awarded the Silver Star, Purple Heart, and Bronze Star medals for gallantry in action. His experience and fresh perspective allowed him to understand the tactical problems his division faced and grasp a workable solution.[84] The division G-2, Lt. Col. Albert W. Aykroyd, informed the new commander that the ridge line dominated the two valleys to the west and the east, and that through these same valleys the KPA brought reinforcements and supplies to keep the battle going. On the ridge itself, the Koreans' bunkers resisted all bombardment. The enemy would have to be "blasted, burned, bayoneted and finally dragged out of his bunkers."[85] Adams's regiment had already lost more than 950 soldiers killed, wounded, and missing. With such a difficult tactical problem, Young resolved to take a step back and plan a division-level attack, and he considered using his three infantry regiments to assault the three main points of the KPA defense—the ridgeline and the two valleys—simultaneously.[86]

To solidify his plan, he spent the next few days flying over the division zone in an L-19 plane, studying the ground from every angle. Although conventional wisdom suggested that the terrain would only support limited armored forces, Young's personal reconnaissance, along with a briefing he received from the French Battalion commander, Lt. Col. Ralph Monclar, and Colonel Adams, convinced him that a well-planned armored thrust west of Heartbreak Ridge combined with a division attack across the Mundung-ni valley just might give his troops the crucial element of surprise needed to overthrow the defenders.[87] His engineer battalion commander, Lt. Col. Robert W. Love, reported that although it would take a major engineering effort, a passable route to support tanks could be carved from the valley floor.[88]

Young dubbed his plan Operation Touchdown. It was a combined-arms attack against all the terrain features that protected Heartbreak Ridge and facilitated the North Koreans' supply and troop movements. Colonel Lynch's Ninth Infantry drew the task to seize the series of hills on the division's southwestern flank to tie down enemy reserves and draw away some of his artillery strength. The Thirty-Eighth Infantry, commanded by Col. Frank T. Mildren, was to attack across and up the west side of Mundung-ni valley to control the high ground overlooking the KPA's line of communication and outflank the KPA's support zone. Adams's Twenty-Third Infantry with the attached French Battalion would assault Heartbreak's two main peaks, but in a phased attack that kept roughly parallel to the Thirty-Eighth Infantry's advance. The crux of the operation was an engineer-armor-infantry thrust up to Mundung-ni to seize the hamlet and complete the isolation of Heartbreak Ridge. Young set the start time of the attack at 2100 hours on October 5.[89]

Love's engineers set to work immediately, grading and smoothing one of the most heavily mined and cratered roads the Americans had seen in Korea. In many places not enough of the road remained to work, so the engineers created bypasses into the rocky stream along the roadside. At the same time, the infantry battalion commanders were busy developing detailed fire plans, reorganizing their companies, training with recoilless rifles and flame throwers, and rehearsing drills to assault bunkers.[90] Operation Touchdown commenced with an artillery barrage of high explosives punctuated with close air support. Although the KPA continued to fight back, it was a different kind of battle. Both the Ninth and Thirty-Eighth Infantry Regiments moved out to pressure the North Koreans as the division's shift to a nighttime attack with greater fire support suppressed Korean mortars and tied up his reserves. By 0300 hours, American infantry were occupying Hill 931 in strength, beating off several uncoordinated counterattacks. By daylight, Adams had his own Third Battalion and the French Battalion firmly holding the center of Heart-break Ridge. Work continued on the Mundung-ni road with the infantry advance providing cover to the engineers.[91]

On October 10, Love's engineers opened the eight-mile-long road to Mundung-ni. It was a fantastic and unprecedented achievement. The unexpected appearance of Lt. Col. Joseph Jarvis's sixty-eight Sherman tanks from the Seventy-Second Tank Battalion loaded with high-explosive shells and carrying extra ammunition for a battalion of the Thirty-Eighth Infantry providing close-in defense and support against antitank squads broke the KPA's ability and will to resist.[92] The loss of Mundung-ni sealed the fate of the last of Heartbreak Ridge's defenders, even as advance elements of the CPVF 204th Division intervened to bolster the faltering North Koreans. The resulting confusion of introducing new troops into the battle area only benefited the Americans.[93] Boatner, enthusiastic about the fine display of combined-arms teamwork, called the maneuver "the best I have ever seen in combat units."[94] By the evening of October 13, French and American infantrymen closed in with fixed bayonets to eject the diehards out of their trenches and smashed pillboxes. The prisoners taken, as well as the dead strewn about, proved that Chinese infantry had entered the battle, but too late. Colonel Adams then radioed the news to General Young: the ridge was firmly in the Twenty-Third Infantry's hands. After more than a month of continuous fighting, the Second Infantry Division, reinforced with the French Battalion, at last seized and cleared the remaining holdout ring of the Punchbowl.[95]

General Young later characterized his division's two-month struggle in the Punchbowl as "a fiasco." Senior commanders and staff of the Second Infantry Division demonstrated ossified tactical methods to commit troops in a frontal attack within a narrow zone, where they were easy targets for North Korean machine guns, grenades, and mortars. An American assessment at the end of September revealed the Communists' fighting power in this kind of war: "The enemy defended his fortified positions tenaciously and fanatically against the assault of his MLR by friendly forces. He has resisted until his units have been decimated and are no longer effective. It has been necessary to dig the enemy out of bunkers with flame throwers and grenades. Commanders who served in the Pacific during World War II report that the fighting in this sector for the past month has been as fierce as any observed during that war."[96] The Americans gained ground only after the entire division launched a coordinated attack. Artillery preparation and suppression of enemy mortars was crucial as Young credited KPA mortars with causing 85 percent of American casualties between September 13 and 27. An American FO attached to the French recalled his bitter feelings at not being able to call fire missions against unobserved KPA mortars and guns. Because artillery fire rarely destroyed a fighting bunker, perhaps if the Americans had concentrated more artillery on the western side of the ridge, where most of the KPA's artillery was, their casualties would have been reduced and the defenses overcome sooner. Not until the division's command and staff planned a division-level attack that relied on both firepower *and* maneuver could the Americans bring both sides of Heartbreak Ridge under effective attack, while penetrating with powerful armor-infantry forces deep into the rear of the North Korean defensive system.[97]

Bloody and Heartbreak Ridges laid out a new tactical template that Eighth Army would confront over and over again for the remainder of 1951 through November 1952, when further limited objective attacks were prohibited. On the disputed ground the fighting was hellish with unheard-of concentrations of artillery from both sides pounding single hilltops to pieces. Because the focus of the battle was so restricted, units were committed piecemeal. Division- and even regimental-size actions became much rarer, which in practice meant that battalions and companies were quickly chewed up, withdrawn, and replaced by more cannon fodder. Ironically, a few miles to either side of the disputed ground, the guns were quiet, the two sides content with patrolling and some shelling. This limited style of fighting was anathema to American doctrine, and it defied common sense to fail to engage the enemy across his front and force him to commit reserves and supporting artillery against multiple threats simultaneously. The strategic fact was that an expanded offensive would inevitably lead to expanded casualty lists. It was a Faustian bargain that Van Fleet and his Eighth Army had to live with.

Elbowing Forward—Operations Commando and Nomadic

A less dramatic but equally important operation took place on the western side of the peninsula, just as the fight for the Punchbowl was reaching its bloody conclusion. Realizing that an armistice was not imminent and that UNC troops faced the probability of another winter on the line, Van Fleet regarded the Seoul-Chorwon-Kumhwa railroad as a key operational objective for a limited, single corps attack. The Chinese MLR and outposts either straddled the rail line or overlooked it, complicating logistics support to the IX Corps and some elements of the I Corps. Because Korean rail carried 98 percent of Eighth Army's supply requirements, securing the rail line was no impulsive task. Given the breakdown of negotiations, Van Fleet needed to secure his logistical lines to prepare the Wyoming Line to resist any potential Chinese offensive.[98]

Additionally, because Van Fleet could not organize an army-wide offensive, he instructed his subordinate commanders to be offensively minded and seek ways to apply pressure by "patrolling, reconnaissance-in-force, and brief limited-objective attacks . . . to harass, unbalance, and destroy the enemy."[99] He wanted plans to continue the campaign of limited objective attacks to probe deeply into the communist lines to deter or preempt any offensive buildup, and to prevent his well-trained Eighth Army from stagnating in a "sit-down war."[100]

The I Corps commander, Maj. Gen. John W. "Iron Mike" O'Daniel, already chafed under the enforced idleness provoked by the talks at Kaesong. "It is a must to think in terms of successful operations," the aggressive O'Daniel counseled his gathered subordinate commanders in early September, and he reminded them to keep their soldiers "offensively minded" by continually enforcing discipline, aggressive patrolling to capture prisoners, and physical conditioning.[101] A veteran of Italy's rugged mountain campaigning, he identified many deficiencies with the corps's outposts and MLR. He reminded division and regimental commanders to follow the basics of defensive fighting: proper siting and checking of automatic and support weapons, clear fields of fire, protective and defensive obstacles and wire, observation posts, and rehearsals integrating artillery and reserves to counterattack against any penetration or to reinforce a threatened position.[102]

The I Corps staff made preparations to advance to a new line called "Jamestown," which would allow the corps to strengthen its defensive position by screening the Yonchon-Chorwon valley from Chinese observation and artillery interdiction and permit the rehabilitation and full employment of the Seoul-Chorwon-Kumhwa railroad. A successful advance would not only relieve logistical pressure but also give O'Daniel a chance to get at the enemy. On September 29 Van Fleet finally gave O'Daniel the nod to conduct his own limited attack, Operation Commando, in early October, with a less ambitious advance to push the Chinese back six miles along a forty-mile front. Although the plan did not promise a decision, it would place the Eighth Army's center and western flank in a stronger and more secure position for the winter.[103]

The naturally difficult terrain—wooded razorback ridges, the crests of which were rarely over fifty feet in width—combined with complex fortifications, limited tactical options. Attacking troops would have to drive straight forward, overcoming one fortified knoll after another, clearing bunkers, trench lines, mortar pits, and tunnels that gave the defending Chinese plenty of cover from artillery and air strikes and concealment from all but the closest observers on the ground. The Chinese sighted their weapons well; machine guns covered each successive position. They emplaced mortars on the topmost peaks, "in small arms defilade." The loss of flexibility to fire in all directions was more than compensated by survivability as "only a direct hit in the opening could destroy the emplacement." And they had plentiful stocks of grenades, ammunition, and mortar shells. It was not going to be an easy advance.[104]

Unknown to the Americans, the Chinese were prepared to employ their new defensive philosophy and tactics, which had begun to evolve since June. Instead of a traditional fluid defense, CPVF troops now sought to defend ground and extract high casualties from the UNC. Yang Dezhi, commander of the Nineteenth Army Group and Peng's deputy for combat operations, understood the new conditions of fixed defenses, and he encouraged his subordinate commanders to think broadly about defensive fighting. "The concept of defense should not be understood as merely clinging to a fixed position," he urged. Defenses needed to be organized not only to preserve ground but also to preserve forces. Chinese troops dug quickly and expertly: bunker walls were double tiered with logs bound with cable to prevent a close hit from collapsing one or more sides; roofs were typically four to eight feet thick, often with a slight overhang protecting the firing embrasure from plunging fire and shrapnel; all bunkers were shellproof up to 8-inch artillery; concealment was sufficient that "the trained observer cannot pick up a specific target or see any significant activity" until the moment the bunker occupants opened fire. Fortifications like these would prove their value during the I Corps's upcoming offensive.[105]

As a preliminary move, the Fifteenth Infantry Regiment, Third Infantry Division, fought a desperate four-day battle beginning on September 28 to seize Hill 487 and Hill 477. Although not completely successful, the American advance pushed the CPVF away from the railway embankments at the north end of the corps's line and gave O'Daniel's forces additional room to maneuver. The corps attack with four divisions began October 3, and in some places UNC or Korean troops gained up to four miles of ground without much resistance, though Commonwealth troops did have a prolonged fight to wrest Hill 355, known as Little Gibraltar, from determined Chinese defenders, who were reluctant to abandon the "good deep defences they had dug themselves for winter." British and Australian infantry relied on napalm strikes and the bayonet to secure this critical piece of ground.[106]

The First Cavalry Division, on the other hand, had a tougher fight on its hands when it collided with the CPVF's Forty-Seventh Army west of the Third Infantry Division's zone, in a region dominated by Hills 287, 272, and 346. These hills protected a ridgeline (designated Objective Coursen) that masked a significant supply base at Sangnyong-ni. Fighting here was as stiff as that seen at the Punchbowl—mutually supporting bunkers, plenty of machine guns, and heavy concentrations of artillery and mortar fire made the going slow and bloody. Two Chinese regiments defended the ridgeline and its forward hilltops. When ejected from a position, the Chinese expended manpower freely in furious counterattacks to retake lost ground. On the first day, the Seventh Cavalry Regiment was hit hard by two separate company-size counterattacks, supported by nearly one thousand artillery shells, that stalled its advance. The Forty-Seventh Army poured in reinforcements so that the Americans faced a total of four regiments arrayed in depth. Chinese artillery support increased each day, bombarding the Americans in their hasty positions and supporting numerous counterattacks. Three separate counterattacks, "well supported by artillery fire," battered the Eighth Cavalry Regiment beginning at 0100 hours on October 9 and holding up the troopers' advance until the afternoon.[107]

By the morning of October 10, O'Daniel declared the operation successfully concluded, with the exception of Objective Coursen, which was still in Chinese hands. The First Cavalry Division remained locked in this close battle with elements of the Forty-Seventh Army, even as the rest of the corps reached its assigned sectors on the Jamestown Line. Hill 346 was a particularly difficult position, with good observation and fields of fire. Fifth Air Force fighter-bombers flew in so close that the American infantry watched napalm canisters seemingly float in the air above them before exploding on the hill, while hot brass casings from strafing runs fell on the troops below. One notable Chinese attack originating from this area on October 12 overran two cavalry companies in a massive "banzai charge" preceded by the heaviest shelling of the month.[108]

O'Daniel made daily visits to each of his divisions, and he worried about the cavalry's lack of progress. "Progressive and inventive military thinking" was required, he complained as much to himself as to his subordinates, to deal with the bunkers and well-concealed fighting positions. Direct hits were "a 1-in-1000 accident," and the stubborn occupants proved resilient enough to resist effectively (figure 5.4).[109] Finally, during the night of October 17–18, the Chinese infantry withdrew from Hills 272 and 346, allowing the cavalry troopers to secure their portion of Line Jamestown on October 18. Corps and division artillery had fired 672,566 shells of all calibers from September 29 to October 18. Surviving soldiers marveled that artillery rarely destroyed bunkers directly. It was an infantry assault at close quarters that carried any position. For the I Corps commander, whose motto was, "Sharpen the bayonet!," it must have been a sobering scene. O'Daniel ordered his troops to dig in and hold their newly won positions. The importance of the corps's advance can-

Figure 5.4 Chinese fighting bunker encountered during Operation Commando with capacity for four men. Note how little damage was sustained despite American air and artillery firepower. Source: US army photo, USACMH.

not be overlooked, particularly in light of the serious fighting that occurred along this MLR the following year. Line Jamestown, which generally followed the southern track of the Yokkok River, at last secured the Chorwon-Seoul rail and road network feeding UNC troops at the southwest and southeast apexes of the Iron Triangle.[110]

Operation Commando gained a tactical advantage over the CPVF, giving Eighth Army substantial real estate through attrition of Chinese defenders, but as in the X Corps sector, the advance was not without its costs. The American, Korean, and Commonwealth troops found many of their firepower advantages nullified by terrain and fortifications. Air support was unsatisfactory both in timing and scale as infantry forces found it nearly impossible to exploit artillery, napalm, or bombing. Attacking battalions were unable to isolate their objectives, necessitating wasteful frontal assaults with small elements dangerously exposed to the enemy's fire.[111] It had been a bitter struggle and a costly month for the corps: 4,466 casualties (636 killed, 3,637 wounded, 193 missing), of which 2,966—60 percent—were from the First Cavalry Division. By comparison, the Third Infantry Division suffered 562 battle losses for the entire month of October.[112] The I Corps G-2 estimates placed Chinese losses at just under 25,000 men—a severe mauling of the CPVF's Forty-Seventh and Sixty-Fourth Armies.[113]

While Commando was ongoing, Van Fleet visited IX Corps headquarters and found its commander, Lt. Gen. William M. Hoge, also eager to push his troops forward toward Kumsong to improve his own defensive line. The corps planned Operation Nomadic to attack with three divisions to Line Nomad, 10–15,000 meters forward of Line Wyoming. Line Nomad would give the corps a more secure defensive line for the winter as well as improved logistics and artillery support by clearing out the Chinese from high ground overlooking the Kumsong River valley. The town of Kumsong was also an important logistics center that could support a Chinese attack south toward Kumhwa, and Hoge wanted to disrupt the CPVF's supply buildup as much as he wanted to keep pressure on the Chinese and prevent their defensive scheme from becoming too strong to overcome. Van Fleet gave his approval and the attack began on October 13.[114]

As found in the I and X Corps zones, the Chinese opposite the IX Corps had used their armistice respite well, constructing well-organized strong points with fortifications providing overhead cover for both machine guns and defending riflemen. Mortars, dug in on the reverse slopes, were camouflaged and plentiful. Some mines and antitank obstacles were identified on the few major roads leading into the enemy positions. However, the Chinese forces here were less prepared to resist the corps advance. The Twenty-Fourth Infantry Division, flanked by the ROK Second (west) and Sixth (east) Divisions ground forward, beating off half-hearted counterattacks and successfully erasing the bulge south of Kumsong. As in the I and X Corps attacks, allied UNC troops also played a strong role. From October 13 to 22, the Colombian Battalion, attached to the Twenty-First Infantry Regiment, captured Hills 561 and 552, both heavily defended. As the American and Korean divisions overcame stubborn defenses, they noted that enemy counterattacks were poorly organized, haphazard, and generally ineffective at stopping the advance. Sensing that the enemy's depth was not well organized, Hoge planned on October 16 to exploit their disarray by pressing the attack an additional 3,000 meters to Line Polar, which was secured five days later. As the infantry consolidated their new positions, the Twenty-Fourth Infantry Division dispatched tank-infantry teams even farther north. For the next week these armored patrols ranged unimpeded through the Chinese rear area, shooting up bunkers, killing or capturing hundreds of soldiers, and destroying valuable supplies.[115]

The corps established itself on commanding heights just two miles south of Kumsong by October 23, reversing the salient that had pinched the corps's main supply route through Kumhwa. Line Polar also brought the Eighth

Army up against the eastern shoulder of the Osong mountain complex, linch-pin in the Chinese defense of the Iron Triangle's southeastern apex.[116] At the end of the operation Hoge was satisfied with the results and noted that the CPVF's Twentieth Army Group's future offensive potential had been set back significantly. Its Sixty-Seventh Army was wrecked and the Sixty-Eighth Army was barely hanging on, with two divisions committed at Kumsong and a third fighting at Heartbreak Ridge.[117] The IX Corps claimed to have killed 43,562 and wounded 14,087 Chinese soldiers. These were overestimated figures. But, a good measure of the weakness of the Chinese position was the capture of 1,232 prisoners for the loss of less than five thousand allied total casualties.[118] Van Fleet also heaped praise on the ROK divisions that bore the brunt of the corps's casualties. Their "exemplary manner . . . to overcome not only tena-cious enemy resistance but also to repulse his numerous and heavy counter-attacks" validated his faith in the ROK's evolving combat capabilities.[119]

Despite these losses, Peng was sufficiently impressed by the Nineteenth Army Group's tenacious resistance against Commando, especially when com-pared to the performance of the Sixty-Seventh and Sixty-Eighth Armies op-posite IX Corps.[120] Although the Americans seized Line Jamestown and pushed their MLR dangerously close to the Iron Triangle, Peng saw the potential that such defensive battles had to turn the attrition calculus against the UNC. "This is an expression of the combined excellent characteristics of our revolu-tionary army's political and combat capabilities, creating extremely favorable conditions for protracted warfare," he reported, and he directed all subordi-nate commands to immediately prepare for extended "positional warfare."[121] *Niupitang* tactics seemingly fit very well with the strategic adjustment to po-sitional warfare, which meant preparation for a protracted conflict where re-silience, aggressive limited attacks, coupled with increased modern fighting power and secure logistics, played to the Chinese strengths. It would take time for the Chinese to mature this offensive-defensive amalgam. Fortunately for the Communist armies in Korea, outside influences were about to gift that time.

Van Fleet's limited objectives offensive from August through October in-volving three American and one ROK corps had been costly (some estimates putting the price for the advance at 60,000 ROK, American, and UNC killed and wounded). Throughout the month of August, which saw most of the Eighth Army static, the American fatality rate was 9.9 men per day. In Sep-tember, as the battles for Bloody Ridge, Heartbreak Ridge, and the Punch-bowl reached their climax, American soldiers and marines were dying at a rate of 36.7 per day. In early October Eighth Army endured a fatality rate of 51.5 soldiers and marines per day. In fact, the first two weeks of October were as lethal to the US army divisions as the entire month of September (5,635 total casualties compared to 5,725).[122] But this level of attrition, when balanced with the losses inflicted on the communist forces and combined with the territory seized, had also provided strategic effects. Eighth Army's advance and the losses inflicted on the communist armies shocked the communist negotiators and broke the equilibrium that had led to the suspension of the talks. The Communists now agreed to restart talks at a more acceptable location as Eighth Army gained ground uniformly across the peninsula and gave the UNC a strong defensive position, one from which Ridgway's negotiators could work. Van Fleet's aggressive posture seemed to deliver the elusive dividend of bringing the Communists to terms: "Limited offensives had proven themselves profitable; this was the outlook for the future."[123] It was a sanguine assessment of a transitory nature.

Admiral Joy saw the effect of the UNC's blitz against the Communists on the ground and in the air. Previously recalcitrant negotiators became "most reasonable" at the conference table, and Joy's liaison officers appeared to achieve "marvels of negotiating skill." Joy remembered one of these days in late October and early November, when he sat in his tent at Munsan (near Panmunjom, the new venue for negotiations), listening to "the sound of our shells and bombs crunching against Communist positions." Col. Andrew J. Kinney said, "Those [explosions] are your most effective arguments." Both Joy and Ridgway knew the Chinese were very sensitive to loss of ground, and that they would clamor for talks as a means to stop the terrestrial hemorrhage at the front.[124]

However, these tactical triumphs were short-lived. While the UNC had gained valuable real estate, the communist armies remained just as threatening as before Van Fleet's limited objective attacks (figure 5.5). The costs for these operations may have shocked the Communists back to the truce tent, but the outsized numbers of killed and wounded for modest, even if important tactical gains, stunned the American public and the Truman administration. Effective pressure against the Communists could only come at a cost in lives that the Americans were unwilling to pay. The battles for the Punchbowl and along the Imjin, Pukhan, and Kumsong Rivers were the last offensive maneuver campaigns in the Korean War. It was the last time the UNC attempted to attack for the purpose of gaining ground beyond a limited area, or to do more than inflict casualties on the CPVF and KPA. The losses suffered during the entire campaign to clear the Punchbowl and to straighten out the outpost line ahead of Line Kansas had political consequences. How could the military expend so many lives at a time when the two sides were engaged in "peace" talks? It did not compute for the American public, but the political calculus was clear. Truman needed to preempt public demands for stronger military measures while bringing the Communists back to the

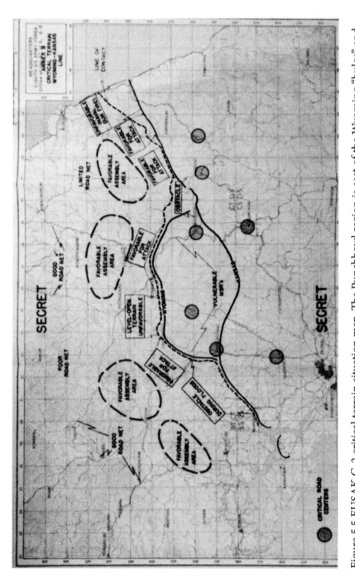

Figure 5.5 EUSAK G-2 critical terrain situation map. The Punchbowl region is east of the Wyoming "bulge" and circumscribed by dashed lines, indicating a favorable concentration area and attack zones for Communist troops. Operation Commando occurred on the opposite side of the bulge to push Chinese forces away from the western shoulder of Line Wyoming. Source: (Declassified) Eighth Army Command Report, G-2 Section, August 1951, NARA II.

table. The JCS already felt that Van Fleet "had more or less reached a line that seemed satisfactory for defense," and they instructed Ridgway to find a solution to the impasse at Panmunjom. He was directed to accept Communist proposals to freeze the current line of contact as a preliminary step to achieve an agreement. Because there was no desire to break off talks or to appear to be the side obstructing a cease-fire, Ridgway tied Van Fleet's hands operationally, directing no further offensive action without specific approval from Ridgway's headquarters in Tokyo.[125]

6

REOPENING THE NEGOTIATIONS

Settling the Demarcation Line and Active Defense

A NEW PHASE in the war was about to begin—the war of posts, patrols, raids, and small hilltop struggles. Any loss of terrain now carried political implications as the restart of truce talks would have to reflect the new current reality on the ground. For the UNC soldiers, the question was one of balance between maintaining troops' readiness and combat edge (Van Fleet's worry), and "the needless wasting of soldiers' lives" in battles over terrain that in all probability would be turned back over to the side that lost it or abandoned in a demilitarized zone. In their impatience to move the talks forward, American leaders too often succumbed to the temptation to invest significant military outcomes to minor tactical actions, believing that doing something was better than waiting for the Communists to launch their own offensive or limited attacks that would endanger Line Kansas.[1]

One of the issues Ridgway had to confront following the suspension of talks in August was the extent to which UNC offensive operations should be used as the primary instrument of American policy and strategy. Van Fleet and his staff developed a large number of plans involving South Korean, American, and other UNC forces, all intending to inflict casualties and seize terrain. Such military options were completely in line with Ridgway's attrition-focused military strategy, but the UNC commander was reluctant to approve operations that promised only more casualties without a military decision. For example, in early September he disapproved Operation Apache, an ambitious plan to make an "end run" up the east coast to encircle and destroy the three KPA corps opposite the ROK I and X Corps. Ridgway noted that UNC forces were enduring a monthly casualty rate of 5,550 killed, wounded, and missing "during a period characterized by only relatively minor friendly offensive ground operations." It was his opinion that Apache "would result in relatively heavy casualties," even beyond the four thousand estimated by

Van Fleet's staff. A similar fate awaited Van Fleet's Operation Wrangler. An offensive planned on the opposite side of the peninsula, Operation Cudgel, likewise did not find favor with Ridgway. Van Fleet's staff drew up Cudgel on September 19, a two-corps attack to clear out the Chinese from the high ground overlooking the Yonchon-Chorwon valley and push the line back some 20 kilometers. However, Cudgel was canceled just four days later when "the probable cost, when weighed against the advantages to be gained," was recognized as "too great." To keep Van Fleet and his staff's planning appetite in check, Ridgway pledged to give twenty days' notice if the current situation and "certain elements of my directives from the JCS" changed, warranting an expanded role for Eighth Army.[2]

In fact, Ridgway's fear was the specter of another surprise Chinese offensive for which American intelligence had predicted would begin in August or September. Ridgway preferred to hold his forces close and let the enemy come "out in the open where our full fire power can be brought to bear." Then, a powerful Eighth Army counterattack would "stand an excellent chance of inflicting another major severe defeat."[3] Only such an outcome would likely advance American objectives in the negotiations.

One problem with Ridgway's preferred solution was its reliance on Communist cooperation to engage in a contest where the UNC's "full fire power can be brought to bear." Peng had learned this lesson well, and he too preferred to fight defensively for the time being. A second problem—the primary problem—was political. The Joint Chiefs were eager for Ridgway to get a settlement in Korea so that Washington could turn to other pressing problems in the worldwide struggle against communism. They did not want him making any statements or having the UNC delegates assume positions that made a breakdown in talks likely. Already in early August the JCS had chastened Ridgway for making "a proposal completely out of line with his instructions." On August 10, he informed the JCS that unless otherwise directed, he intended Admiral Joy to deliver an ultimatum at Kaesong: either drop the demand to establish the final demarcation line at the 38th parallel and accept the UNC's proposal within seventy-two hours or "the UNC would consider the conference deliberately terminated by the Communists."[4] Within twenty-four hours both General Bradley and the full JCS, with Department of State concurrence, reiterated previous instructions: "It is basic to your present directives that you not break off armistice discussions without specific instructions to do so . . . also that you should not, without further instructions, recess talks indefinitely, to be reconvened on condition of Communist concession."[5] Any failure of negotiations had to be visibly the fault of the Communists and not because of any perceived inflexibility on the part of the UNC. This policy of flexible patience with the enemy continued throughout the resolution of the various "incidents" at Kaesong. Neither President Truman nor the JCS wanted Ridgway to turn Kaesong into a battlefield. Washington was in control of the UNC's negotiation strategy and would continue to impinge on Ridgway's operational authority and circumscribe his military options.[6]

The breakdown in the talks in late August and the renewed intensity of fighting across the front did nothing to soothe Ridgway's mood. After many back-and-forth exchanges it was clear that Washington's viewpoint was much different from the UNC commander's. Collins attempted to mollify the UNC commander, assuring Ridgway, "I am sure that at times you find it difficult to accept the point of view which we feel that we must take here in Washington with respect to the continuance of the [armistice] discussions. I do want you to know, however, that we thoroughly appreciate the difficult problems with which you have to struggle and that you have our unbounded confidence and support."[7] On September 26, Ridgway sent an "eyes only" cable to Collins, expressing his frustration in having to fight the enemy in Korea while constantly looking over his shoulder at his superiors who appeared to be overly anxious to appease the Communists' demands. "We have either watered down or abandoned, sooner or later, almost every position taken," Ridgway complained. "We appear to continue voluntarily to search for and to employ means for making further concessions." This conciliatory strategy failed to employ the "one language the Communists understand . . . and [to] conform our actions to our words." It was Ridgway's opinion that the UNC, and by extension the free world, stood at a crossroads. Should it fail to take a stiffer line militarily and diplomatically, then "we shall have voluntarily created insuperable difficulties which will ultimately make any honorable outcome to these discussions utterly impossible."[8]

Ridgway knew how to turn a phrase, and his declared pessimism prompted an immediate personal visit by General Bradley and Charles E. Bohlen, counselor of the State Department. Arriving on September 28, they spent three days with Ridgway and Joy to gain a better appreciation of the operational and policy dimensions of the war and to reconcile opinions on the best way forward. Bradley and Bohlen found the tactical situation much more favorable than previously believed in Washington. Bohlen concluded there was no real urgency for the UNC to gain an armistice. Eighth Army appeared to be holding fine and inflicting punishing blows on the recalcitrant Communists. Under these conditions, the UNC may even want to draw out the talks. Bradley opined, and Ridgway and Bohlen agreed, that talks needed to continue for public appearance, but that a true breakdown could raise the stakes politically by inciting the American public to demand greater military action to force a settlement. But Ridgway won his most immediate point: it was not required for him to return to Kaesong.[9]

Fortunately for Ridgway (and the JCS), the late summer attacks probably influenced the Communist negotiators to request a resumption of talks. At the height of the fighting for Heartbreak Ridge, and one day after I Corps's attack in Operation Commando, October 4, Ridgway offered to reopen talks at Songhyon-ni, a site more easily secured and genuinely neutral to both sides. Although the JCS informed Ridgway that a more neutral location was a "nonessential topic," Ridgway felt the military momentum was in his favor, and that the UNC needed to reestablish the high ground in the propaganda conflict. Kaesong's location had given the Communists several inherent advantages that they had used to great effect, and Ridgway recognized that the adverse conditions at Kaesong had contributed little to his mission of obtaining a cease-fire agreement. Ridgway was not going to give away any more unearned concessions.[10]

The JCS concern was misplaced. Force of arms gave Ridgway control over the negotiation location. Just three days later the Chinese and North Koreans proved willing to make concessions to gain relief at the front. Panmunjom was proposed, and the UNC quickly accepted after new security arrangements were established to prevent a reoccurrence of those events that proved so distracting at Kaesong.[11]

Liaison officers again met on October 22, and plenipotentiary talks resumed three days later. In just a three-week period the communist delegation not only agreed to relocate the talks to Panmunjom, but they also demonstrated a more willing attitude to settle agenda Item Two, the military demarcation line, substantially as the UNC had demanded. Even as demands for the 38th parallel were dropped, attempts to regain ground lost from Commando and Nomadic underscored the Chinese's acceptance of negotiations as a strategic maneuver, to be supported by tactical action on the ground. As the two sides sat down to agree on a demarcation line, the Communists felt the pressure to roll back the Eighth Army's gains. In the I Corps zone, Chinese infantry appeared in the aftermath of Commando to be preoccupied with constructing new entrenchments. Artillery fire on allied lines was relatively light, and Commonwealth patrols frequently operated as far forward as the CPVF's own outpost positions. It was the calm before the storm. Isolated fights took place with Chinese battalions increasing pressure on the MLR; artillery and mortar fire also picked up significantly during these probing attacks.[12]

Then, on November 4, proving "the reed only bends so that it may straighten again at an opportune moment," Peng's troops suddenly came alive with an artillery bombardment noted for its increased intensity and accuracy that struck I Corps's lines. It was a strong reaction to Commando, and the Chinese compelled the Commonwealth Division to fight tenaciously to defend its positions. Still, the weight of Chinese artillery and their advanced infantry tactics overran two important positions, Hill 217 and Hill 317. Hasty counterattacks were called off in the face of the stubborn resistance encountered. Four days later the CPVF launched similarly strong attacks against the Kumsong salient. The IX Corps retained its position, but it was clear that the Chinese would counterattack any further UNC advances.[13]

Peng's counterpunch alarmed Van Fleet, and he immediately requested Ridgway's permission on November 5 to respond with another limited offensive to a new line called Duluth, which cut a generous slice off the Iron Triangle. Van Fleet wanted to commit one US and one ROK division from IX Corps and another ROK division from I Corps to push the Chinese back from the Chorwon-Kumhwa railroad. Van Fleet was confident of success and that the American public would support the move. Ridgway temporized for three days as he weighed the costs. He queried Hoge, the IX Corps commander, who did not necessarily subscribe to Van Fleet's urgency, but noted the Chinese "were good on defense" and that any territorial gains were marginally important and probably not worth the casualties. That was good enough for Ridgway, who informed Van Fleet that the railroad was superfluous, and the Duluth Line would bring no advantage to Eighth Army.[14]

The jockeying for more convenient tactical positions along the MLR continued in anticipation of an agreement. Although it still took another thirty-three days of haggling to fix the demarcation line as the final line of contact between the two sides, with a four-kilometer "demilitarized zone" instead of a twenty-mile zone, the UNC managed to defeat the Communists' efforts to return to the 38th parallel, though they did give in to allow Kaesong, Korea's ancient capital, to remain behind Communist lines. Ridgway felt that Kaesong was a key to keeping the road to Seoul closed. The South Koreans certainly looked at Kaesong as a must have, but Washington was not in the mood for military geography lessons.

On November 15, the JCS again weighed in, warning Ridgway not to be too tough when it appeared a breakthrough was so near. From Washington's perspective, "combat expected during the next month [is] unlikely to materially alter [the] acceptability" of the line of contact as the final demarcation line. If the Communists were prepared to accept the current line of contact, that was good enough to establish a tactical truce for thirty days to hammer out agreements on the remaining agenda items. Ridgway responded vigorously against an early settlement of agenda Item Two, noting that the final demarcation line was a "point of extreme importance." He was confident the Communists would continue to concede to the UNC's demands if the pressure remained firm. He also speculated that the whole idea might be a charade to buy the Communist armies in the field time to recuperate from a hard summer and fall.[15]

Ridgway's instructions, however, went even further, indicating the tremendous domestic and foreign political opinions pressuring Truman to end the war, which was increasingly a hard sell at home with American casualties now exceeding one hundred thousand.[16] Gallup polling in October–November 1951 asked Americans whether they agreed with the statement, "The Korean war is an utterly 'useless war.'" A whopping 56 percent agreed. At the same time, 51 percent of surveyed Americans thought employing the atomic bomb in Korea would be appropriate—a reflection of growing frustration and ambivalence toward Truman's limited war policy objectives.[17] Leaders in Congress, the secretary of the army, and other prominent Americans voiced their apprehension over the "considerable adverse reaction in the public mind concerning the rather heavy casualties the 8th Army has been receiving recently." Intensive battles over hills that did not materially alter the strategic situation appeared wasteful, and operations named "Killer," "Meatgrinder," and "Ripper" sounded too violent and did not help to shore up support for a limited war that showed no signs of ending.[18]

Political pressure from other quarters to achieve a settlement likewise increased. America's allies worried about an escalation in Asia to fight "a peripheral engagement . . . which must not be allowed to drain [strength] from more important theaters."[19] By using the term "more important theaters," Canada, Great Britain, and France demonstrated their worry over American commitment to the defense of Europe, and they were understandably desirous to reduce Asian tensions in the face of increasingly aggressive Soviet propaganda and other political initiatives.[20] From their position, the JCS opined that in view of the substantial concessions the Chinese and North Koreans already made, such as dropping their demands for a return to the 38th parallel and the immediate withdrawal of foreign troops, the UNC should offer to freeze the current line of contact as the actual demarcation line, provided all other remaining items were settled within a thirty-day period. Any terrain lost during the combat freeze would be restored. Still assuming that an armistice was close to being finalized, the JCS urged Ridgway to end the impasse by insisting on a deadline, after which if no cease-fire were agreed to, the war would go on with either side eligible to modify their tactical position on the ground at the other's expense.

On November 17, Admiral Joy submitted the proposal to freeze the line of contact and to use it as the final demarcation line if all remaining items of the agenda were settled in a thirty-day period. Both the North Koreans and Chinese agreed after the possibility to extend the thirty-day truce was accepted. Many negotiators believed "the most important problem . . . is solved." Li Kenong concurred, telling his delegates, "We must seize this opportunity and make great effort for reaching the armistice agreement within this year."[21]

Li was bowing to military realities. Not only had Eighth Army pushed the line of contact northward since its August offensive began, but UNC airpower was also pinching Communist supply lines and wiping out any potential all-weather airfields. They obviously had no idea that the pressure was about to slacken; Li likely recognized the need to settle the tactical issues before the Americans launched another major offensive. "We should be firm with principles and flexible with tactics," he averred.[22] Finally, it was agreed that between November 27 and December 27 any ground taken or lost would be restored upon the conclusion of the armistice, when both sides would withdraw two kilometers from the line of contact. The clock to peace now had a "countdown" quality to it as soldiers quietly celebrated with "hopeful peace drinking." These weary troops had no idea that the Korean War was only at its halfway point.[23]

The drama, though, was not yet over. The task of drawing out the demarcation line on a large-scale map of Korea, post by post and mile by mile, was fraught with dispute, and Chinese probes encroaching on Eighth Army's OPLR threatened to undo any informal agreement as to the actual line of contact. Eventually, a line was drawn out, but no sooner was the task complete when Col. Chai Chengwen denounced as unacceptable the positions marked on a portion of the map he drew in, and to which the UNC officer, Col. James C. Murray, had agreed. Murray, a marine veteran of Pacific island campaigns from Guadalcanal to Okinawa who was tired of the interminable delays, slammed his fist on the table and burst out, "Why, you damned buffoon! You deny agreements you entered into not an hour ago—in fact one you yourself offered!" Chastened but not overwhelmed, Chai retreated and let the line stand. It would not be the last time that the Communist negotiators would appear to renege on deals already made.[24]

The Americans got their deal, but it was a fool's bargain. Ridgway had already on November 12 instructed Van Fleet to assume "active defense . . . along the general trace of your present forward positions . . . and, where required within the prescriptions of this directive, seize terrain best adapted for defense with your present resources, and organize and defend it." Ridgway's "active defense" directive instructed Van Fleet "to maintain a firm, unquestionable line of contact" at least two kilometers in advance of the OPLR, which would become the UNC's final withdrawal line when the armistice went into effect.[25] Operations intended to kill the enemy were no longer automatically sanctioned. Ridgway specifically limited offensive operations to patrols, local counterattacks, and attacks to recapture lost outpost positions. Defensive counterattacks to maintain an outpost line three to five thousand yards deep were permissible, but all such moves were further limited to no

Figure 6.1 Col. James C. Murray and Col. Chang Chun-san mark and initial the MDL. Source: US army photo, USACMH.

more than one division in any single operation. There would be no more attacks with an operational or strategic scope.[26]

The UNC's position at Panmunjom sapped all the vigor from Eighth Army. Van Fleet was extremely disappointed, and he showed it in his instructions to the Eighth Army's corps commanders, which read, "Eighth Army should clearly demonstrate a willingness to reach an agreement while preparing for offensive action if negotiations are unduly prolonged to this end . . . reducing operations to the minimum essential to maintain present positions regardless of the agreed-upon military demarcation line. Counterattacks to regain key terrain lost to enemy assaults will be the only offensive action taken unless otherwise directed by this headquarters."[27]

To ensure that any withdrawal of forces did not incidentally compromise the MLR and its OPLR, Eighth Army was ordered to "make frequent and sufficient contacts to maintain a firm, unquestionable line of contact at least two kilometers forward of the outpost line," and it was to accomplish this "by vigorous patrolling, raids, and reconnaissance in force." However, any offensive action designed to restore a "marginal position" was limited to a battalion size, unless directed. Finally, and most disconcerting for all, was the injunction, "Constant effort will be exerted toward insuring [sic] against unnecessary casualties."[28] In other words, keep fighting the war and kill communists, but don't get any GIs killed.[29]

Although Active Defense made sense to Ridgway, who was taking his strategy cues from Washington, Van Fleet and his subordinate commanders now faced a very different prospect to achieve Truman's political and strategic objectives. It is war's nature for battle to be the defining characteristic to resolve the conflict between political wills, and it is the essence of generalship to determine where, when, and how best to fight and defeat an enemy in battle. If World War II had taught nothing else, it illustrated vividly that the destruction of the enemy's armed forces was the only sure path to the strategic goal. The past few months of Van Fleet's fighting experience only solidified the theory: to bring the Communists to terms required the destruction of his armies and the taking of his ground—military objectives that could only be achieved through offensive battle. Battle for the sake of any reason other than those stated was sure to be both unprofitable and a cut at Eighth Army's morale and fighting spirit. Ridgway's directive effectively removed the UNC's most useful tool from use and set the stage for the long and bitter stalemate to follow.[30]

Naturally, when war correspondents caught word of Van Fleet's directive, which was in no means contrary to Ridgway's intent, it caused a public furor, embarrassing both the president and Ridgway and causing the latter to chastise Van Fleet: "I do wish to point out that . . . your letter of instructions . . . to your Corps Commanders assumes a function entirely outside of the field of responsibility of Eighth Army."[31] Van Fleet was to continue to follow Ridgway's Active Defense directive, but the truth was finally out of the bag. When it came to military options to pressure the Communists, ground attack was off the table, and the disappointing endurance of the November 27, 1951, de facto cease-fire embarrassed the UNC. The Communists had scored the more significant triumph. Whatever the UNC's future plans, Mao's generals were now certain that both the threat of a second march to the Yalu or their own military defeat in the field had been dispatched.[32]

Meanwhile, American commanders felt the effects of Eighth Army's "peace at hand" tactical posture. Hill 281 and Hill 395, west of Chorwon, and the future scene of intense and bloody fighting in the fall of 1952, became flashpoints for the I Corps commander, General O'Daniel. The idea of withdrawing two kilometers and giving up such precious ground in the process was dismaying, especially as he read the Chinese tactics, called "touch-base" raids, focused on "driving us off ground that we should retain." Prohibited from expanding UNC controlled ground through offensive action, the Americans were forced into a game of challenge and response. The Communists would pick the place to fight over, and the Eighth Army would respond by retaking lost ground but would refrain from expanding the battle zone to threaten the Communists with territorial loss elsewhere. In the short run, this strategy appeared to promise a reduction in casualties, but it in fact simply ceded military initiative to the Communists, precisely when Eighth Army's military pressure was producing results in the negotiations.[33]

To Ridgway, Van Fleet, Weyland, and Joy, these tactical conditions were more than marginally influential. The enemy remained strong, resistant to military pressure and logic, and was obviously digging in for a long duration. The flexibility of American policy may have suited Washington's purposes domestically and internationally, but it placed Truman's military commanders in a poor position. Admiral Joy and his delegation, even Ridgway for that matter, stood on shaky ground, and they knew it. Joy captured the dilemma of the military men dispatched to fine tune the outcomes of this inchoate policy. He said, "[We] never knew when a new directive would emanate from Washington to alter our basic objective of obtaining an honorable and stable armistice agreement . . . it seemed to us that the United States Government did not know exactly what its political objectives in Korea were or should be. As a result, the United Nations Command delegation was constantly looking over its shoulder, fearing a new directive from afar which would require action inconsistent with that currently being taken." It was a bitter critique of how America pursued this limited war in Asia. Joy was soon to be even more disconcerted by "new directives" originating from Washington in the coming months.[34]

Winter War

With the demarcation line established, a lull settled over the peninsula, despite Ridgway's insistence that Active Defense meant continued fighting. Van Fleet worried that the Chinese might try to nibble away at his OPLR, constantly edging the line of contact south so as to force the UNC to give up strategic points when the two sides withdrew to form a demilitarized zone. He already recognized the shift in Chinese tactics, noting the absence of "sea of men" assaults. Instead, CPVF attacks were more controlled and carefully planned, with adequate artillery and usually three-to-one superiority at the point of assault. The road and rail centers at Kumhwa and Chorwon (at the base of the Iron Triangle) were particularly vulnerable to this type of pressure, but Ridgway continued to deny Van Fleet authority to conduct major attacks as winter began to set in fully by December, which encouraged a slowdown to combat activity.[35]

American soldiers did not understand the politics behind the UNC's strategy and the tactical stalemate that appeared to grant the communist armies the chance to recover and rebuild, and they questioned the purpose of continuing the war. Col. Lloyd R. Moses reported to the X Corps headquarters as the G-3 (Operations) officer in the dead of this stalemated winter. His sense of the American soldiers' martial attitudes worried him: "They referred to their bunkers as high-rise, low cost, speculation housing. . . . One sign advertised a job opening, another one claimed overtime. . . . The winter cold had imprisoned them in their bunkers. It was as unglamorous as murder in a back alley." Eighth Army morale was sinking, and Moses was certain that "Big Jim" Van Fleet knew it. Active defense had produced a stalemate akin to "having our 'full house bluffed by a pair of deuces.'"[36]

With offensive activity limited to patrols, the Americans characteristically assumed that more was better. And in another characteristic move, underemployed corps and army headquarters staff began to track individual patrols—their planning, conduct, and debriefs—with the level of detail previously reserved for larger actions at battalion or regimental level. This bureaucratic emphasis gained significant life after December, when Eighth Army captured only 247 prisoners, a quarter of the previous month's total. In the I Corps sector, subordinate divisions received orders that every patrol must make an enemy contact. The American and Korean divisions took the directive in stride. The British and Canadian Brigades thought the edict silly and easily manipulated. The edict also demanded unnecessary risk, as the Chinese now showed little inclination for aggressive action, meaning that any patrol determined "to make contact" would have to wander dangerously close to the enemy's main defensive areas.[37]

If patrols could not satisfy corps commanders, the prodigious expenditure of artillery would try "to keep the heathen Chinese off balance by hitting him every time he stuck his head up, even if we saw only one enemy soldier at a time." One American officer, writing after the war a scathing critique of the army's command culture suggested that the informal competition between commanders to rack up the highest number of enemy "killed" resulted in unnecessary waste of munitions and unnecessary risk to FOs and patrols tasked to determine the battle damage from an artillery strike.[38]

It was precisely this fake war situation that promoted schemes such as Operation Clam Up (known as Snare in the Commonwealth Division). Clam Up was designed to reverse the situation and entice the Communists to assume greater liability by becoming more exposed tactically. "Deceit keynoted the plan" and required efforts to convince the enemy that UNC troops had withdrawn from the MLR. All patrolling would cease, all artillery fires were canceled, no close air support strikes would occur, daylight vehicular traffic was eliminated and night traffic held to a minimum, and soldiers would not shoot unless expressly ordered by a senior commander. It was hoped the Communists would then send patrols toward the MLR and subject them to "ambushes and [artillery] fire concentration" to destroy and capture them.[39] The short time between Eighth Army's letter of instruction (February 4) and execution (February 10) gave division, regimental, and battalion commanders less than one week to prepare the show and make it convincing. Fundamentally, the deception hinged on the assumption that the Communists were willing to assume an offensive posture *operationally*; that is, they would be willing to vacate their own carefully prepared positions and move south to occupy UNC positions on ground they had already ceded at Panmunjom in late November. The Communists were content. It was to their advantage to remain defensive so long as the Eighth Army did likewise.[40]

When Operation Clam Up terminated on February 16, Eighth Army had to face the fact that the results did not live up to the aim—not even close. The Communists across the front did end up emerging from their lines "to investigate," but they rarely loitered, frequently breaking contact immediately on confirming the presence of UNC troops. Across all three corps, sixteen POWs were taken. It was nearly impossible to take prisoners in these conditions as nearly all challenges to surrender were met by a barrage of small arms fire and a shower of hand grenades. The operation was a flop and most viewed the weeklong combat hiatus as yet another unearned respite for the communist soldiers to improve their defenses unmolested. The outcome of this "idea cooked up by some wild-eyed dreamer at Eighth Army HQ" put the Chinese in a stronger position tactically.[41] They "profitably used the period of comparative safety to improve existing fortifications and [begin] the construction of new ones," thereby nullifying many of Eighth Army's previous efforts to push the Communists' outpost line back.[42] Colonel Moses afterward grudgingly allowed, "The enemy has been very military . . . [and] mature . . . in his reaction. . . . They reacted about as we would have [done]."[43]

An exception to the rule of limited military activity in the winter of 1951/52 was a ROK army offensive behind the lines to clear out guerrilla forces in southwestern Korea. The successful prosecution of this counterguerrilla campaign in the Chiri-san mountain region east of Kwangju showed the ROK army in a much more positive light and indicated a way forward for the Americans to retain the initiative in a war that Washington was losing interest in, at least in terms of fighting on to a military solution. At the conclusion of the Chiri-san campaign, Van Fleet set into motion steps to reorganize the ROK army that would improve its fighting capabilities and increase its burden in the battle just as the two sides were reaching their climax of impatience at Panmunjom.

On November 14, 1951, Maj. Gen. Paik Sun-yup reported to Eighth Army headquarters to receive instructions on his next assignment. Remnants of the KPA defeated along the Naktong River in the late summer of 1950 had joined indigenous southern socialist partisans and former South Korean troops who had defected to the communist cause. Together they represented a hard core of trouble threatening Eighth Army's rear area and the Rhee government's legitimacy. Van Fleet was aware of Paik's experience in counterguerrilla operations, both as a commander in the ROK army and as an officer in the Japanese-sponsored Manchurian army that fought Korean partisans during World War II. He told Paik, "You've got to take charge of this thing. We can temporarily pull two divisions out of the line for this mission, and I'll leave it up to you which ones we use."[44] Paik planned to eradicate the guerrilla strongholds in the Chiri-san area with Eighth Army support: photo and signal intelligence, transportation and logistics as needed, and two frontline ROK divisions. Sixty American advisors (part of the Korean Military Advisory Group or KMAG), led by Lt. Col. William A. Dodds, who served with Van Fleet in Greece and was handpicked by the Eighth Army commander, were detailed to support what was in effect a Korean corps-level headquarters. Paik recalled the invaluable assistance KMAG provided in operations, liaison with Eighth Army, communications, and psychological warfare. Van Fleet ordered the operation, known as Ratkiller, to begin by December 1.[45]

Task Force Paik became operational on November 25, 1951. The Korean divisions (the Capital and Eighth Divisions plus one security force police division) began combat operations a week later. Van Fleet was true to his promise, organizing logistics, air support, auxiliary forces, and intelligence information. The overwhelming force of three divisions piled on the guerrilla strongholds and compressed the estimated eight thousand partisans into an ever-shrinking sanctuary. Paik's constant presence in an L-19 liaison aircraft gave him the chance to direct operations and assess results in a manner unheard of before in the ROK army. Climatic conditions (no foliage and a light dusting of snow) exposed enemy movement and eased the Paik's intelligence-gathering operations. Paik's forces also coordinated numerous air strikes flown by South Korean pilots. Paik, like his soldiers, appreciated the bravery and competence of South Korean airmen bombing and strafing the surprised and exposed guerrillas in daily missions. Fifth Air Force also participated, assigning a Tactical Air Control Party (TACP) of one officer and two enlisted men to support the two ROK army divisions. Paik's headquarters also had an American air force liaison officer assigned to assist planning and coordinating US air support.[46]

A KMAG report described Paik's tactical plan as "the contraction of three concentric rings about a common point." The inner ring, making the initial contact with guerrillas, was made up of the regular army regiments of the Capital and Eighth Divisions. Youth militias and police regiments composed the middle ring to block the escape of guerrillas scattered by the strike forces, while national police held the outer ring to follow up and occupy cleared-out areas and prevent a resurgence or reappearance of antigovernment forces. ROK forces appeared to achieve total surprise, with the army troops converging on Chiri-san after only five days of active operations. Cornered, hundreds of guerrillas attempted to go to ground, but the ROK troops continued to press forward. ROK and Fifth Air Force planes killed hundreds, who were caught in the open with nowhere to run. Phase I was declared complete on December 14, with 2,706 partisans counted killed or captured.[47]

After the successful convergence of the ROK divisions' strike forces, Task Force Paik began Phase II on December 19 with each division tasked with searching out and destroying guerrilla remnants in an expanded zone of operations north and west of Chiri-san. The regiments and battalions in these operations performed very well and employed sophisticated blocking and encirclement tactics to trap and kill or capture the rebels. Phase III lasted from January 6 to February 1, 1952, bringing Paik's divisions back to the Chiri-san region for a "thorough and complete mopping-up in the areas of Phase I and II operations." Phase III also had the distinction of producing the largest aggregate enemy losses of Ratkiller.[48] Overall, ROK forces claimed 10,103 guerrillas killed and 9,676 captured along with 3,132 individual and crew-served weapons. At a cost of 352 killed and 39 missing, Task Force Paik broke the back of military resistance in the Chiri-san region and established a template that the ROK army would follow in successive counterguerrilla operations.[49]

The success of Ratkiller highlighted an additional aspect of the war. Negotiations and the declaration of active defense had reduced the tempo of fighting sufficiently that Van Fleet could pull two entire divisions away from the battle line, transport thousands of troops by rail and sea, and throw them into a major campaign lasting two months confident that the tactical situation would remain stable.[50] More importantly, Paik and his staff demonstrated their ability to command and control a complex and fluid operation involving three divisions with engineers, air support, logistics, intelligence, and civil-military units. In Van Fleet's mind, the gamble had paid off and Paik Sun-yup proved he—and the ROK army—was ready for the next step in the evolution of American strategy.

For their part, the CPVF took full advantage of Eighth Army's active defense posture and the thirty-day truce. They improved their fortifications and began work on extensive tunnels and underground shelters to stockpile supplies and ammunition, and to provide concealment and cover from air attack. The rotation of fresh troops to their own MLR increased capabilities even if the number of troops on the front line actually decreased. Chinese gunnery was noticeably improved with an increase in artillery tubes and greater proficiency at defensive fire support. The Eighth Army G-2 at the end of the year ruefully noted that Chinese combat effectiveness "is now as high as it has ever been."[51]

The Chinese volunteers had learned some hard lessons in the first eight months of negotiations. Fundamental to the CPVF's tactical renaissance was the successful transition from mobile to positional fighting. Marshal Yang captured the essence of positional warfare best. In his communications with the Sixty-Third Army during the late summer fighting, Yang observed, "Units should be permitted to have gains and losses. Having lost, they would win again, and having gained, they would lose again. . . . The soldiers ought to be cherished; the soldiers ought to be loved. As much as possible [we should] preserve their combat ability."[52] The CPVF's flexible approach to the forthcoming battles would give it tactical resilience in the face of American firepower superiority and allow China's meager military resources to have an outsized strategic impact in Korea.

7

TRUMAN DECIDES ON THE POWS

The exchange of prisoners of war, agenda Item Four, was not expected to become the major issue of the armistice negotiations. But the nature of the conflict had transformed following the expiration of the de facto truce agreed to on November 27. Propaganda maneuvers, both in and outside of Korea, now occupied the central battleground. It was a paradigm shift American military leaders were slow to grasp, and when they did, they found it difficult to communicate meaningfully with Washington the new rules by which yards were gained in the battle for men's minds. As the military stalemate solidified in the winter months of 1952, the propaganda contest assumed even greater importance until the linkage between propaganda and fighting was clearly established.[1] How this conflict unfolded nearly derailed the UNC's strategic and policy objectives, and it provoked the most bitter round of fighting since the previous fall.

Up to this point, the UNC delegates avoided delving into political concerns, preferring to defer these to a postconflict conference. Compared to the six months of wrangling to get agreement on the demarcation line and the implementation of the armistice agenda, Item Five, the political conference to settle "Korean issues," proceeded at a lightning pace. Both sides were content with the vague language and low expectations of Nam Il's proposal, slightly modified by the UNC, for a conference to convene ninety days after a cease-fire to settle the Korean question.[2] Admiral Joy expressed amusement after the war on how Nam Il nearly choked on his own proposal when the UNC delegates quickly accepted it, as it only bound the respective governments to discussion and recommendations. It seemed harmless, but the Communists were immediately suspicious that they might have trapped themselves. After a two-day recess, Nam Il delivered "a long statement full of escape clauses affecting his own proposal." Staff officers were directed to discuss the matter further, but nothing changed, and the delegates appeared to move one step closer to a settlement.[3]

As the issues were being narrowed, the Chinese were busy digging, receiving reinforcements and equipment (artillery in particular), and increasing the costs on American airmen attempting to freeze the military situation through aerial interdiction. For UNC ground commanders, there was no perceived advantage to expose their forces in large-scale military operations, suffering casualties to seize terrain that had no permanent value. From now on, the fighting on the ground would take on a different character, for different purposes, attempting to apply pressure without paying too high a price.[4]

Narrowing the Issues

As 1952 approached, only three substantive issues remained to be settled: the composition of a Neutral Nations Supervisory Commission (NNSC), the question of communist airfield construction and rehabilitation following an armistice agreement, and the exchange of prisoners of war.[5] The first task following the fixing of the thirty-day demarcation line was to tackle the rules and procedures to ensure a complete and enduring cessation of hostilities. Now serious work began to frame the mechanisms necessary to establish and enforce an armistice, agenda Item Three, "the crux of the armistice" as defined by the Americans.[6] Unfortunately, "the negotiations began poles apart" as each side had completely different viewpoints on what constituted fair machinery to implement an armistice. The UNC proposed a series of intrusive but reliable protocols and restrictions on troop increases, introduction of military equipment into Korea, and airfield construction and rehabilitation. Additionally, Joy wanted unrestricted joint inspections and aerial surveillance rights over the peninsula. Nam Il countered that the withdrawal of all foreign troops was sufficient guarantee. This response was no more acceptable in December than it had been the previous July. And it was a depressing reminder that so much bloodshed had not yet sufficiently greased the skids to a settlement.[7]

The initial JCS directive to Ridgway emphasized the need for unlimited inspections throughout the Korean peninsula to ensure compliance with armistice terms and the freezing of the military equilibrium. Washington clearly anticipated that the armistice would be the precursor to a peace deal, and neither side should be able to act in bad faith, using the cessation of hostilities as a cover to increase their military power. This included the construction of modern airfields in North Korea, something that greatly concerned Ridgway and Weyland. Ridgway even proposed breaking off negotiations if airfield reconstruction were not prohibited.[8]

This was a reasonable stand to take, as Ridgway, Weyland, and Joy recognized that a great portion of the UNC's strength lay in its mastery of the skies over the battlefield.[9] Keeping high-performance Communist aircraft confined to MiG Alley provided Van Fleet's army with significant advantages. Although the JCS sympathized with Ridgway's view, they recognized the improbability of enforcing a ban on airfield construction over the long term, especially after Ridgway expressed doubts that the Communists would accept anything more intrusive than limited inspections at designated ports of entry. In fact, the Communists insisted that activities of any supervisory bodies be contingent on unanimous agreement of its members composed of representatives from neutral nations, which from the communist perspective included socialist states such as Poland, Czechoslovakia, and the Soviet Union—a proposal that was utterly unacceptable to the Americans.[10] Further, the Communists vehemently rejected the UNC's proposal to allow aerial reconnaissance through North Korean air space. The situation left Ridgway in a quandary, as the Communists appeared to agree to certain structures of an armistice but refused to give those structures the authority or the assurance against a resumption of hostilities. Nam Il cheerfully pointed out that any foreign supervision of military activity in North Korea would "obviously involve political questions" and that such supervision would "constitute a direct interference in the internal affairs . . . and are absolutely not to be tolerated."[11] The two sides worked through agreements on most of the issues regarding troop rotations, withdrawal of paramilitary forces, disengagement of conventional forces, and limits of aerial surveillance. By March 15, it appeared that barring airfield construction and Soviet participation in the NNSC, agenda Item Three was solved.[12]

Seeing how laborious and acrimonious debate on agenda Item Three was, Joy attempted to gain time by proposing subdelegate talks for POW exchange simultaneously with the remaining items. The Communists were reluctant, but in the end realized stalling the opening of additional talks was not going to make good press. In any event, the Communists were sure that the final terms of any exchange would be "all for all," and Li Kenong believed "to reach agreement on this issue should not be too difficult." The first subcommittee meeting on POWs occurred on December 11.[13] General Lee Sang-cho and Colonel Chai Chengwen represented the KPA and CPVF while Rear Admiral Ruthven E. Libby and army Colonel George W. Hickman Jr. spoke for the UNC. The Communists proposed "that both sides release all POWs held by them after signing of arm[istice]." The UNC countered with two general principles that the early exchange of prisoners be effected on "a fair and equitable basis" and that both sides would ensure "humanitarian treatment, safety, and comfort of prisoners" during the exchange. The UNC then requested the immediate exchange of POW data (previously requested on November 27) and the admission of Red Cross representatives to all POW camps.[14] The Communists were puzzled as the exchange of POW lists appeared to be a technicality as opposed to an agreement. Whatever had passed for difficult up to this point was nothing; here the real trouble began.[15]

The UNC's response requires explanation. The Communists believed (and continue to do so) that the Americans were interested only in using POWs as a smoke screen to draw out the negotiations. However, the evolution of the UNC's POW policy was long and not firmly established by the time the subject arose at Panmunjom, and this was the foundation for the difficulty the negotiators found themselves in as the subject moved to center stage. This evolution began early in the war as more nations joined the UNC coalition, when it was determined that US forces would assume responsibility for all aspects of POW operations. There was special concern that ROK units might mistreat or kill POWs at the slightest provocation. However, ROK troops would be used to the maximum possible extent, "under close supervision by US Army personnel" to reduce the number of American forces required for that mission.[16]

The UNC had captured tens of thousands of Korean (both Communist and non-Communist) and Chinese soldiers. Truman and others felt the repatriation of these prisoners, as required by international agreement, would have a significant impact on how the Korean War was viewed in terms of its ideological consequences. Aggression had to come with a price tag, "not only repulsed but punished in the present," as William Stueck observed.[17] The UNC failure to achieve a decisive military victory on the peninsula only magnified the imperative. The probable cease-fire line gave the Republic of Korea a marginal net gain in territory, the key word being "marginal." The uncomfortable reality for the UNC's political success in Korea, which Truman saw as the means by which to seize victory in a conflict limited for realistic reasons, was the political exploitation of the many anti-communist POWs in the UNC's control. Truman was also keenly aware of the humanitarian dimension of the POW issue, and this personal conviction likely was far more decisive than any other in the deliberation. The president expressed doubts about the wisdom of forcing repatriation on perhaps thousands of human beings likely to be "immediately done away with" by the Communists.[18] The resolution of this political dilemma was to have significant military consequences.

Prisoner of war operations are always sensitive and carry great risks. From the beginning of the war the UNC's POW system suffered from disorganization and low priority. Even though the value of immediate interrogation and exploitation of prisoner information and knowledge was recognized, by October 1950, when the tempo of UNC offensive operations accelerated, the number of POWs held by the UNC multiplied by thousands, and the entire system for handling POWs, such as it was, completely collapsed. The confusion regarding Eighth Army's capability to stay on the peninsula following Chinese intervention exacerbated the already difficult challenges POW administrators faced. Further, the docility of these early captives soon collided with the attention deficit Eighth Army gave to POW operations. The entry of Chinese troops into Korea, and the large numbers captured during the failed Fifth Campaign, changed the calculus surrounding the POW issue. Van Fleet scrambled to establish command responsibility while retraining new ROK troops as security forces, increasing housing construction, and improving sanitation.[19] By the summer of 1951 it was clear that full repatriation was going to be problematic, as General Collins recalled, for prisoner disturbances were already becoming commonplace.[20]

The presence of large numbers of hostile personnel in Eighth Army's rear area posed a condition and strategic dilemma of staggering proportions, which the Americans were unprepared to solve. Prior to the Inchon operation, the Pusan Logistical Command operated one POW enclosure holding fewer than two thousand KPA prisoners with a staff of five officers and twenty-seven soldiers. On September 19, 1950, just days after the Inchon landing, the Pusan Logistical Command was deactivated and replaced by the Second Logistical Command. This organization continued to be responsible for POW collection and holding, but by the end of September, the Second Logistical Command's prisoner population had swollen to 10,829. KPA prisoners were being brought in at such a rapid rate that some 10 percent of POWs were housed in wire-fence compounds without any type of shelter. Worse was to come. Just a month later, the Americans held 116,822 POWs. ROK forces held thousands more captive.[21]

To alleviate overcrowding and potential sabotage of the port facilities at Pusan—already a congested cesspool teeming with homeless, destitute, and desperate civilians—internment camps and supporting facilities were hastily built on Koje-do, a mountainous island 240 square kilometers in size located southwest of Pusan. There was little open space to support extensive construction, and the island already was home to more than 200,000 residents and refugees. Compounds intended to hold a thousand prisoners soon were bulging with many times that number. Because Koje-do was an island, Eighth Army presumed its POWs did not "present an immediate threat to UNC/ROK operations."[22] Van Fleet devoted few Eighth Army resources to Koje-do, entrusting its management to the Second Logistics Command under Brig. Gen. Paul F. Yount. Yount's responsibilities focused on the major port and rail operations in Pusan. He had little interest in managing prisoners, but he did keep Van Fleet informed about the inadequacy of the guard force, which failed to suppress clashes that resulted in several deaths even before the major riots in May 1952.[23] The Americans simply had no experience with warfare "behind the lines." The Second Logistical Command slowly recognized its problematic position, and it lobbied for additional resources and personnel, but these were not forthcoming. Eighth Army was focused on the front and did not realize, until it was too late, that the front was about to invert itself.[24]

At the time that negotiations began on agenda Item Four, the POW rolls had expanded to include more than 169,000 Koreans and Chinese. Among the thousands of KPA prisoners were an unknown number of South Korean soldiers impressed into the KPA and ROK civilians (labeled "Civilian Internees"—CI) policed up during the pursuit phase of the war who were initially held as potential guerrillas. Although they were not strictly POWs, the UNC continued to classify and hold them as such until both sides focused on accounting for their POW lists. It was a sloppy mistake to make, but understandable at the time when no one knew for sure what course the war was going to finally take. Additionally, many of the captured Chinese soldiers were veterans of Chiang Kai-shek's defeated Nationalist army, who wanted to repatriate to Taiwan. What should come of these prisoners?[25]

Militarily speaking for the Americans, the forcible return of these men to the Communist side was objectionable not only on humanitarian grounds. The Americans had no desire, through an "all-for-all" exchange, to reconstitute the KPA to a level greater than its prewar strength, especially without clear mechanisms to guarantee a durable armistice. At the same time, they did not necessarily want repatriation to be the road block to an armistice. JCS instructions to Ridgway on December 19 offered little clarification other than to insist that "any position requiring forced return of personnel must have prior approval by Washington."[26]

The problem was that Washington's own mind was divided. Secretary Acheson, with an eye toward securing the unencumbered release of all allied POWs held by the Chinese and North Koreans, initially opposed any policy or scheme that might delay their return. Defense Secretary Robert A. Lovett believed "all for all" was the right policy, especially if the Communists refused to negotiate on any other basis. The JCS, after a brief flirtation with the idea of exploiting POWs for psychological warfare purposes, eventually agreed with Acheson. Other functionaries pointed out the likelihood of retaliation against UNC prisoners and the effect any delay to repatriate might have on the European allies' will to continue fighting in Korea. John D. Hickerson, the assistant secretary of state for United Nations Affairs, urged caution. He wrote to deputy undersecretary of state H. Freeman Matthews, "I further recognize that the stand one takes on this must necessarily be a matter of individual judgment since there are about as many arguments on one side as on the other."[27] Crucially, the president was unconvinced, believing that an all-for-all exchange ought to be part of a larger settlement that included substantial concessions from the other side; however, no further guidance was sent to Panmunjom, leaving Joy's team to muddle through with some inde-fensible proposals.[28]

The exchange of lists, accomplished December 18, immediately blew an al-ready tense situation apart. North Korean propaganda had loudly trumpeted the figure of 65,000 captured UNC and ROK soldiers, but when it came time to name names, they presented a list of only 11,559 allied prisoners: 7,142 ROK, 3,198 American, and 1,219 other nationalities. These numbers con-trasted sharply with the UNC's list of 132,747 communist prisoners.[29] If both sides' figures were accurate, then more than 80 percent of allied and South Korean prisoners had either died or simply disappeared, while the Chinese were disappointed to see that of their 25,600 reported missing soldiers, only 21,700 were included on the UNC's roster; four thousand had "disappeared forever."[30]

Meanwhile, Lt. Col. James M. Hanley, a judge advocate officer and combat veteran (he had commanded in the 442nd Regimental Combat Team, a Japa-nese American volunteer outfit renowned for its fighting spirit and motto, "Go for broke") was charged with organizing the UNC's War Crimes Divi-sion and with gathering evidence of North Korean and Communist Chinese atrocities.[31] Hanley's team did its work well, perhaps too well. UNC intelli-gence agents and informants operating among North Korean and Chinese POWs gathered stories and testimony of brutality and murder. In an effort to counteract Chinese propaganda of "humane treatment of prisoners," Han-ley drafted a statement regarding the unpredictable fate of US and ROK sol-diers who fell into communist hands. It is unclear now who approved the release of the material that later would become known as "the Hanley re-port," but it turned into a public-relations bombshell just as the issue of pris-oner accountability was being addressed in Washington and at Panmunjom. Ridgway denied any direct knowledge of Hanley's work even as Collins sug-gested a "disclaimer of any connection with armistice negotiations would be most helpful."[32] Hanley's "evidence" accused the Chinese of killing 2,513 US and some 250 other UNC prisoners since November 1950. The North Kore-ans had a significantly lighter burden, responsible for 147 UNC POW deaths in the same time frame. But Hanley went on to accuse the KPA of being the real mass murderers of the conflict, responsible for the deaths of over 25,000 South Korean captives. Eventually, additional testimony surfaced that the KPA may have killed or allowed to die through neglect up to 6,000 more Ameri-cans.[33] The feeling of mistrust and deep suspicion Hanley's report engendered was going to affect how the UNC negotiators approached the POW question at Panmunjom.

Despite the utter imbalance between the two sets of numbers, Admiral Joy remained convinced that an all-for-all exchange was the right way to go.

"Non-forcible repatriation" or "voluntary repatriation" posed several serious risks for the UNC. Based on the numbers involved, the UNC negotiators feared that voluntary repatriation would jeopardize the return of all UNC and ROK prisoners. Knowing that the Communists were unlikely to agree to voluntary repatriation, negotiations were likely to be protracted unnecessarily, extending both the captivity of prisoners and the number of casualties as the war continued. Additionally, the principle was arbitrary, lacking support from precedent and international agreements; any precedent that would be set in Korea might rebound to the West's disadvantage in another conflict where the ratios of captured personnel were reversed. Finally, voluntary repatriation was clearly a political issue with implications well beyond the Korean battlefield that had no place in a military armistice agreement. In Admiral Joy's view, a political question by definition was likely to affect any military settlement in a negative way.[34]

When the two sides exchanged their lists, Hanley's report—which had sparked a significant outcry in the United States demanding a strict accounting of POWs and American soldiers declared missing in action—suddenly assumed strategic importance. Unsurprisingly, Joy and his delegates applied pressure on the Communists to produce, or at least shift responsibility for, that accounting. With a straight face, Lee Sang-cho patiently explained that it was the policy of the KPA to release South Korean troops at the front as a form of voluntary repatriation. Clearly, his argument ran, these soldiers decided to change sides, deserted to their own homes, or were lost in the press of refugees and perhaps ended up in UNC prisoner cages. Lee concluded, "Those many persons who are released and who have gone back home . . . will certainly know that we are really serving the people . . . you shouldn't ask us about persons which we do not detain in our prisoner of war camps."[35] The UNC saw through the verbal gymnastics and recognized that many South Koreans were likely never to be seen or heard from again. At the same time, Joy insisted that CI would no longer be classified as prisoners and would not be repatriated. The UNC hoped the Communists would concede to this scheme, which they did, but the resultant poisonous atmosphere set the stage for the tough deliberations ahead with respect to the repatriation of the remaining 132,000 Chinese and North Korean POWs.[36]

The stubborn fact animating the Americans' dilemma regarding Item Four was the Geneva Convention protocol of 1949, which stipulated quick and compulsory repatriation of all prisoners of war. Ironically, the compulsory aspect was aimed at the capturing power, in this case the Soviet Union, which had forcibly retained thousands of German and Japanese prisoners after the end of World War II. There was no exception to cover prisoners who resisted repatriation, as many Soviets captured by the Germans did and who were subsequently forced back into the Soviet embrace by the western Allied powers. Furthermore, the United States, along with North and South Korea, had pledged to abide by the Geneva Convention. The Americans' ambiguous stance put Dean Acheson, who was the president's closest advisor, in a precarious position. He had approved of repatriation of Soviet prisoners who collaborated with or served in German army units, but he had felt misgivings about returning eastern European civilians to Soviet control. Nevertheless, in Korea he was an early opponent of voluntary repatriation, pointing out its legal inconsistencies and pitfalls, along with the likelihood that such a policy would "jeopardize the prompt return of all United Nations and Republic of Korea prisoners of war."[37]

Against this background of accountability, the memory of Soviet non-repatriation following World War II, the desire to recover UNC prisoners, and the Communists' vociferous demands to return every soldier in UNC custody, Rear Admiral Ruthven E. Libby, heading the subdelegation negotiating the POW issue, reluctantly proposed on January 2, 1952, a complicated formula for voluntary repatriation, which attempted to reconcile Communist and UNC definitions of "prisoner," "repatriation," and "civilian internee." Joy urged the Communists to accept "the release of all persons who are or should be classified as POW, and the repat[riation] of those who desire to be repatriated" as a fair and equitable pathway to an armistice agreement.[38] Despite Joy's various arguments and perspectives to make voluntary repatriation tolerable to the Communists, Lee Sang-cho responded with charges that the UNC proposal was "a barbarous formula and a shameful design." A day later, Communist delegates insisted on adherence to the Geneva Convention Article 118 and called the UNC proposal "absurd, unreasonable, and useless." The Chinese showed particular sensitivity to the idea of individual choice, declaring, "The Chinese people's movement of safeguarding their homes, defending their fatherland, fighting against the American partisans is supported by all the people of the People's Republic of China. If anyone dares to hand over any of the personnel of the CPVF captured by the other side to the deadly enemy of the Chinese People [Chiang's Republic of China on Taiwan], the Chinese people will never tolerate it and will fight to the end."[39]

Delighted to find themselves on the side of international law, the Communists insisted the language in Convention Article 7 and Article 118 could have no other possible meaning than the compulsory return of all prisoners, regardless of any personal desires.[40] Insistence on any plan that was not a complete exchange of prisoners was "placing an insurmountable stumbling block" to an armistice.[41] For the Americans, this stance was the worst possible outcome. Joy now found himself wedded to voluntary repatriation, if for no other reason than to avoid appearing to concede a major issue at the time when the Communists were being so inflexible on the mechanisms to implement the armistice. Inconclusive back and forth produced a deadlock as the UNC delegates never knew for sure that Washington would not change its position, especially when other significant issues affecting the armistice remained to be worked out. If Joy and his colleagues felt Washington was wishy-washy on some of these positions, they were about to receive very straight-forward and difficult instructions to implement.

President Truman felt strongly the United States had a moral obligation not to return POWs who faced an uncertain future in the home territories. This was particularly true of those POWs who were in fact Koreans from the ROK, who had been swept into the KPA in the summer of 1950. As a subsidiary argument, a stand on this moral principle could also have significant propaganda and psychological effects to discourage communism generally and to perhaps also dissuade further acts of subversion or outright conflict in Asia. On February 8, Acheson—whose own views were now shifting—provided Truman the fundamental choice regarding the disposition of POWs. The president's thinking was focused and personal: "We will not buy an armistice by turning over human beings for slaughter or slavery," he later wrote.[42] His decision to remain firm that no prisoner would be forced to return to a communist state was the crucial American policy directive of the negotiations period of the war.[43]

Recognizing that this position was a bitter pill, Truman authorized the JCS to direct Ridgway to concede airfield rehabilitation. If the Chinese and North Korean delegates refused this quid pro quo, then Ridgway was to screen prisoners to determine those who would violently resist repatriation and strike their names from the overall POW list. The new accounting would then be presented as the basis for an all-for-all exchange. According to Ridgway, this package offer "should be our final position."[44]

However, from a military standpoint, Ridgway did not agree with his commander in chief. Not only did a policy of voluntary repatriation violate the Geneva Convention, it was also certain to prolong the war at a cost of an unknown additional number of casualties. There was also the fate and welfare of UNC, Korean, and American prisoners to consider. He was also aware of the problematic conditions of UNC facilities and control exercised in the POW camps. Prisoners ran individual compounds, terrorizing ideological enemies and intimidating potential dissenters, making any truly accurate and willful declaration of repatriation unlikely. A meaningful prisoner screening would have to be overt, that is, done during the daylight hours of a single day. Ridgway also informed Washington that the Chinese were unlikely to be easily moved, especially since their military position was currently stronger than at the beginning of the armistice negotiations. Chinese airpower was potentially menacing, while the extent of communist fortifications "would require an additional corps of three divisions and greatly increased casualties" to force the issue through military means.[45] But Truman was in no mood to concede any further time or advantage to the Communists. He was at a moral crossroads. There would be no "victory" in Korea, but somehow the Communists needed to pay a military and political penalty. His private diary reveals the supreme leader of the free world engaging in a militaristic diatribe that would have made nearly all but Gen. Curtis LeMay balk at the possible cataclysm. The depth of his frustration at being unable to bring Korea to a satisfactory close probably influenced strongly his stance on POWs and set the conditions for both the political and military impasse that followed.[46]

Admiral Joy did not buy into these political arguments, but he reluctantly carried out his tentative instructions to pursue voluntary repatriation along with the packaged offer.[47] Shocked by the American proposal, the Chinese immediately objected to any repatriation plan that fell short of "all for all."[48] Mao himself had dictated precise terms that emphasized the Communists' position, but he did allow for each side to "allow and assist" so-called civilian detainees to repatriate to their chosen side of the demarcation line. The Communists presented this significant concession (though it was disguised in a tirade alleging POW abuse at the Koje-do prisoner camp) that accounted for nearly 40,000 POWs on March 5.[49] Three weeks later, on March 27, the Communists again made allowance for guerrillas, impressed civilians, and other soldiers "caught" on the wrong side to choose to repatriate to their home location rather than the army from which they were captured. Admiral Joy recorded in his journal, "Commies [sic] ended session by saying they agreed 'to apply the prin[ciple] of vol[untary] repat[riation] to the group of about 40,000 captured personnel of our side.' [They] only did so to settle questions [and] differences between both sides."[50] The bargaining was intense, both sides accusing the other of failing to offer any meaningful concessions while asserting concessions came only from their own side.

This was at least some kind of progress, but Joy and his team had the hard task of convincing the Communists with their words that "our side [the UNC] cannot participate in forced repatriation of those POWs of your side who would violently oppose such repatriation. The sooner your side realizes that this is a minimum position of our side, the sooner we can reach an agreement to this Agenda item."[51] Informed speculation figured that the Communists would likely accept some figure of repatriates around 100,000 as acceptable. Ridgway's staff estimated that "approximately 5,000 North Korean POWs and 11,500 CCF [Communist Chinese Force] POWs could be expected violently to resist repatriation to the Communists." Ridgway also recognized that it was not just numbers, but the nationality of the POW that mattered. In his view, the large percentage of Chinese resisting repatriation (more than half of the total captured) would likely generate a reaction "much more difficult than that of Korean POWs."[52]

Without meaningful military pressure, the Communists had no incentive to go along, and they had plenty of semantic tools to deny the legitimacy of voluntary repatriation. After weeks of further wrangling, the Communists at last agreed in principle to a screening process, even going so far as to provide a letter assuring all repatriating prisoners they would rejoin their families and live a peaceful life. The UNC had now reached a point of no return. Having agreed to carry out a screening process, the course of American policy—and to a great extent the contour of its military strategy to implement that policy—was in the hands of an unknown number of non-repatriate Korean and Chinese soldiers. Sheila M. Jager assesses the UNC's position well: "By agreeing to carry out the screening process, the UNC was now fully committed to the principle of voluntary repatriation and would henceforth be honor-bound not to return those who had identified themselves as anticommunists."[53] And here is where the Americans, who depended on the moral force of voluntary repatriation, found themselves entangled in their own strategic trap. The neglect the UNC showed toward prisoner operations would come back to frustrate Truman's policy and prolong the conflict far beyond what Ridgway or his subordinates imagined.

While the delegates sparred at Panmunjom, the UNC moved forward to determine exactly what number of forcible repatriates they could expect. A tentative initial screening begun in February 1952 pointed to the real dangers embedded in Truman's policy. American units had failed in the most basic tenets of handling prisoners, which stipulated that capturing units would secure, segregate, and speed to the rear captured enemy personnel. This process had practical benefits: no infantry battalion wanted to be encumbered with prisoners, and the potential to question and gain intelligence information could only be realized at division and corps levels. However, it was expected that a minimum level of processing would occur at the battalion level, namely, to identify officers from enlisted men, tag and attach captured documents and other equipment, and provide a brief narrative of the circumstances of capture. Experienced intelligence personnel would use this baseline information to determine whom, and how best, to exploit in follow-on interrogation. Unfortunately, through inexperience, confusion in the fluid operations characterizing the first twelve months of the war, and professional neglect, capturing units rarely did even this level of basic intelligence work to identify and then segregate officers from enlisted men.[54]

The confusion was so bad that by early 1951, fewer than 2 percent of all arriving POWs at Pusan were properly screened, identified, segregated, tagged, and their intelligence value assessed. Many POWs never halted at forward prisoner enclosures at division or corps level but were shipped directly to Pusan. From there, POWs were transshipped to Koje-do, where they were held in overcrowded compounds guarded by a small number of American and ROK soldiers.[55] Authorities later discovered many high-ranking and important officers managed while in transit to lose or exchange identity cards with ordinary soldiers, thereby assuming the name and POW number of an enlisted man and escaping attention and avoiding interrogation.[56] Neglect encouraged further disorder. Some POW compounds were completely controlled by die-hard Communists who refused to submit to screening, even resorting to violent resistance, which was clumsily put down with force. Other compounds, conversely, were equally anti-Communist, and UNC guards and camp administrators failed to interdict the infiltrating stream of South Korean and Nationalist Chinese agents who easily established non-communist enclaves that used violence and other means of coercion to undermine the credibility of the UNC's screening efforts. The very process of screening aggravated the already tense situations in the camps, where both sides were waging war against the other sides' POWs under their influence. The Americans, in honest reflection, understood they could not be certain that weaker-willed POWs had not been intimidated into silent acquiescence.[57]

Even as voluntary repatriation became the strategic touchstone of American policy in Korea, reality—or as Acheson later admitted, "Circumstances unforeseen and embarrassing"—intruded. No one knew just how many Communist prisoners would in fact resist repatriation. Privately, UNC leaders hoped the number would be small enough to be inconsequential compared to the benefits of an armistice agreement.[58] But no one really knew just how the Chinese (Kim Il-sung was ambivalent about POWs and more focused on ending American bombardment of what was left of North Korean cities) would react when the true figures became public. The key appeared to be the size of the final repatriation list, and the number of Chinese on it.[59] In fact, the Chinese appeared resigned to accept that a modest number (approximately 10 percent) of Communist prisoners would somehow avoid repatriation, a sort of rational admission that POW "wastage" was a legitimate form of attrition in the "other front" fought in the UNC's rear area.

Finally, the UNC was ready to present an estimated figure, 70,000, of those accepting repatriation: 5,100 Chinese, 53,900 North Koreans, and 11,000 South Koreans.[60] When these initial figures were presented on April 25 at Panmunjom, the Communists were shocked speechless. For their part, they were prepared to repatriate 12,000 prisoners: 7,700 ROK troops and 4,400 UNC and Americans.[61] The loss of 62,000 of 132,000 POWs held by the UNC was a serious propaganda blow, a great loss of face they could not accept. The fact that nearly three out of four Chinese volunteers indicated they would violently resist repatriation was a significant stab at the legitimacy of Mao's China.[62] Col. Chai Chengwen loudly accused the UNC of using voluntary repatriation as a ploy to retain prisoners and lengthen the war. Nam Il went further, accusing Joy and his delegates of overthrowing "the basis for further negotiations."[63] Even when the UNC dropped airfields and proposed a NNSC of two truly neutral states (Sweden and Switzerland) and two communist bloc countries (Poland and Czechoslovakia), Nam Il declared the talks "inconsequential" and moved for an indefinite recess. Ridgway saw that the UNC had hit a nerve and boxed itself into a strategic corner. He was well aware that the military balance in Korea did not support such an aggressive negotiation demand. In a war over men's hearts, the repudiation of one way of life over another would go a long way to expose winners and losers in a war that officially had neither. There was no way to compel the Communists to agree to a ceasefire that included the right of prisoners to determine their own fate. And for his part, he was ready to accept an "all-for-all" exchange that would guarantee the speedy return of allied prisoners *and* end the war on terms acceptable to the United Nations. It was for him a simple and obvious settlement.[64]

UNC negotiators attempted various stratagems to bundle the POW problem with airfield construction and Soviet participation in the NNSC. Ridgway, ever sensitive to the grand strategic ramifications of appearing to concede too much to the Communists, cautioned the JCS that under the current conditions only by sacrificing essential principles would the UNC be certain to get its armistice agreement. Furthermore, he was confident that Eighth Army could hold if the talks broke down.[65] Finally, Ridgway was directed to present a "package proposal" that conceded airfield construction, excluded the Soviet Union from the NNSC, and exchanged POWs on the principle of voluntary repatriation. Joy's team made the UNC's final proposal three days later, on April 28, in a charged atmosphere. The Communists recessed the talks and then returned an hour later to read a prepared statement: "Having studied the total . . . of captured personnel . . . this figure by no means can be a basis for further discussion." Then, to underscore the seriousness of the UNC's position, the Communist spokesman, Col. Chai Chengwen reiterated, "If your side is willing to negotiate for a solution of the POW matter on a fair and reasonable basis, we request your side to reconsider fundamentally this estimated figure. *I repeat, this figure absolutely by no means can be a basis for further discussion* [original emphasis]."[66]

On May 2 the Communists agreed to drop the Soviets from the NNSC; airfield reconstruction was ignored—there was nothing for the UNC to do about enforcing a ban anyway. But the Communists insisted on the all-for-all formula of repatriation. There would be no compromise.[67] By May 7, it was clear the war of words at Panmunjom was at an impasse. Admiral Joy, in response to further Communist denunciations and propaganda, could only reply, "I have no statement to make. Our position should be very clear to you by this time. If you have nothing constructive to offer, I suggest we recess until such time as you may desire." General Ridgway, ever a loyal soldier, underscored the finality of the UNC's offer: "Our position is one from which we cannot and shall not retreat."[68] Joy summed up the unhappy situation when on May 22 he delivered his final statement as chief of the UNC's armistice commission: "After ten months and twelve days I feel that there is nothing more for me to do. There is nothing left to negotiate."[69]

This was the situation Gen. Mark W. Clark inherited when he replaced Ridgway as the FEC and UNC commander in May 1952. The communist forces were well-entrenched, battle experienced, and prepared to react violently to any local UNC efforts to push the line of contact farther north. Ridgway and Clark saw the tactical situation in similar terms: "there always was the lure of the next highest hill just ahead of you. The enemy had it . . . you wanted it . . . [to] look down his throat. But you never really did, for always there was just one more hill, a little higher, up ahead of you. Each hill soaked up doughboys, cost lives."[70] Clark would continue to restrict Van Fleet's tactical reach, requiring (and usually denying) permission to make any attack involving more than one battalion. The war of words would go on, and Clark would have to find a way to end it, without sacrificing the one strategic goal that could possibly justify the continued bloodletting at the front or in the UNC's rear.

8

A STRATEGY OF PERSISTENCE

The CPVF's Adaptation to Modern War

THE WAR HAD reached a genuine stalemate. Both sides now began to grapple seriously with the problem of protracted war. The Americans resorted to their strong suit of technology and applied firepower, which influenced both tactical and strategic actions designed for the same purpose: coerce the Communists to accept voluntary repatriation. Mao, on the other hand, had received political advice from Stalin to take a hard line and not be hurried into concluding an armistice. Stalin pledged substantial military aid as well: arms, ammunition, and equipment along with twelve air divisions including 72,000 pilots, technicians, ground service personnel, and air defense troops.[1] Fresh Chinese troops arrived in Korea to ensure stability along the line of contact and give CPVF commanders flexibility and opportunity to turn the military situation to their favor. By November 1951, the number of Chinese troops in Korea had reached its high point since intervention a year earlier. Combat forces totaled 880,000 men organized into four army groups, including seventeen armies (organizationally equivalent to a US corps) with fifty-two infantry divisions, eight artillery divisions, four antiaircraft divisions, and four tank regiments. Rear area troops added 220,000 men organized into four railroad engineering divisions, one rear-security division, and fourteen engineering regiments. Combined with the airfield construction corps, the total number of Chinese forces in Korea reached 1,150,000.[2]

With this level of Chinese commitment, the Sino-Korean armies were not in danger of suffering a strategic military reverse. Despite the territorial losses from the Eighth Army's fall offensive, both Mao and Stalin were content with the political deadlock. In mid-November 1951, as the de facto truce agreement on the demarcation line was about to emerge, Stalin wired Mao, "We consider your position on the definition of the line of demarcation . . . to be correct." Stalin believed the Americans were the ones needing an armistice; therefore, the Chinese should not feel pressured into a premature agreement.[3]

The Communists' power to resist UNC military pressure derived mainly from the influx of Soviet materiel and logistical sustainment of the CPVF in Korea. The modernization of Chinese forces complemented their ideological commitment to defend the PRC by fighting in Korea. Soldiers and units endured substantial punishment, yet their morale and will to fight never faltered. Continuous political education and friendly propaganda ensured that the Chinese soldier understood why he was fighting and what was at stake, and the CPVF devoted substantial resources and leadership to this aspect of resistance.[4]

When Chinese forces entered Korea they had the unenviable distinction of possessing arms and equipment from practically every major war material producing country. It was not unusual for Chinese units to enter battle armed with weaponry of American, Japanese, Russian, German, Belgian, Polish, Czech, and Swiss manufacture.[5] Such an eclectic array negatively affected combat performance and complicated an already tenuous supply system. Mao's agents worked hard through 1951 to get the CPVF more modern and standardized equipment. In May, the Chinese dispatched a delegation to Moscow with PLA representatives for the air force, industry, science and technology, artillery, and operations. Gen. Xu Xiangqian negotiated for the purchase of weapons and equipment to outfit sixty divisions along with technical and material assistance to build indigenous ordnance factories capable of producing 152 mm artillery and ammunition. After four months of hard bargaining, and at a time when the Chinese and Korean forces were being pummeled by UNC ground and air forces, Stalin finally agreed to fulfill his commitment to help rearm the Chinese army. But, excepting aircraft, he stopped short of providing the modern equipment such as tanks and artillery the Chinese desired. Although devoted to maintaining his proxy Asian forces in battle against the UNC, there were limits to his support.[6]

As negotiations began in July 1951, the Communists recognized that their political demands to restore the 38th parallel lacked any military basis. The farther Eighth Army forces ground forward, the worse it looked. Having fought the Americans and their UN and South Korean allies to a standstill, Mao could not then risk loss of face and prestige by slowly retreating even farther from the 38th parallel. Mao's strategic vision was clear: "Expecting that the negotiations will be drawn out for another half year or year, we have moved toward economizing on our human and material forces in the Korean theater of military operations and we are pursuing the tactics of a long, active defense, with the goal of holding the position we presently occupy and inflicting great manpower losses on the enemy, in order to gain victory in the war."[7]

Marshal Peng's devotion to Mao's intent and principles gradually earned him a better relationship with the chairman and allowed him to lead the renaissance in Chinese strategy and tactics specifically designed to keep their forces adequately supplied; reasonably protected from UNC bombardment, artillery firepower, and ground assault; and capable of limited offensive action to support their political demands at Panmunjom. The Sino-Korean armies had to find a way to diminish the impact of UNC air and artillery on their massed troops. Therefore, both political and military considerations compelled the Chinese to adopt a form of fighting that was on its surface anathema to the PLA's tradition of mobile guerrilla warfare employed successfully against the Japanese in World War II and the Nationalist armies in the Chinese Civil War. To ensure that the CPVF could survive until Soviet aid made itself felt, Peng settled on a dualistic approach emphasizing strong positional defenses supported by artillery to blunt any UNC offensives, increased air presence by Soviet and Chinese air forces, and increased logistical capacity while exploiting propaganda and subversion by opening a front in the United Nations rear, their prisoner of war camps. In this way, Peng hoped to make the *niupitang* adage "the longer we fight, the stronger we will be" operative while on the defensive and maintaining the communist armies' relevance at the strategic level of the war.[8]

UN soldiers who participated in Operation Commando noted the early evolution of this philosophy. The Chinese fortifications were based on the concept of a ridge-line defense with certain knobs and fingers as strong points to cover the likely routes of approach. A long communication trench dug in on the reverse slope (the opposite side of the hill hidden from the attackers' visibility) of the ridge extended to other hilltops. From this main trench, smaller trenches led to rifle, automatic weapons, and mortar positions located on the forward slope just below the military crest. Most of these early firing positions lacked overhead cover. However, bunkers had been constructed at certain points that had exceptionally good fields of fire. Individual artillery pieces were dug in on forward slopes, mounted on carts, wheeled out to shoot and wheeled back under cover to reload, giving these guns increased accuracy and survivability. On the reverse slope were numerous personnel shelters large enough to accommodate four to eight men. These structures were generally bombproof and used as living quarters as well as protection from artillery, mortar, and aerial bombardment (figure 8.1).[9]

Despite assumptions about "Chinese ways of war" or Mao's obsession with "guerilla war," many parallels exist between the American Eighth Army and the CPVF counterparts. Both sides stressed the importance of firepower, fortifications, and patrolling. In establishing their MLR defense, the Chinese followed practices similar to the Eighth Army, while still maintaining the integrity of their own military tradition and culture.[10] To avoid further territorial losses after their unsuccessful defense against Van Fleet's fall campaign of limited objective attacks, and about the time negotiators reconvened

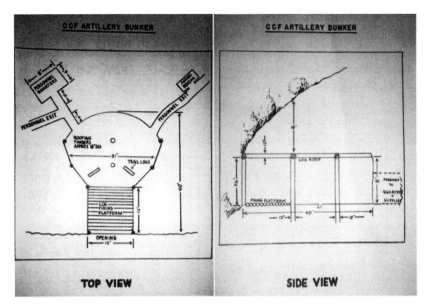

Figure 8.1 Chinese field defenses during Operation Commando. Source: Head-quarters, I Corps, Operation Commando, Annex B, 1–2, USAHEC.

at Panmunjom in October 1951, CPVF commanders instructed all first-line forces to construct tunnel-based fortifications with overhead protection at least five meters thick. Called the "Pivotal Defense System Centered Around Tunnels," key terrain defensive positions—geographic features that provided dominating observation and fields of fire—were organized for all-around defense, often including connecting tunnels to permit lateral movement and safe summoning of additional reinforcements from the rear area. Extended outposts were placed to the front and on the flanks, with small groups of soldiers armed with grenades and automatic weapons such as burp guns and light machine guns with the mission of delaying UNC probing attacks and countering patrols. Further, all tunnel works were expected to withstand 155 mm bombardment, have multiple branch tunnels for ventilation, and have protection from flame and gas attacks.[11] A Commonwealth engineer described these improved Chinese defenses west of Chorwon: "Most of [their] digging consisted of tunneling into the reverse slope of the hill, leading to dank and dark chambers where three or four men apparently dwelt. Apart from a few spare bits of clothing, there was neither bedding nor furnishing of any kind, not even boxes—just a part bag of rice to each hole, and quantities of small arms ammunition and grenades."[12] Backing up the positional defense were the reserve and counterassault forces. Reserves were carefully controlled to feed fresh troops into the battle, while the counterassault force was equipped and trained to launch hasty attacks to recover lost ground.[13] Yang Dezhi called these positional defenses "underground great walls," and he noted with satisfaction that the Chinese and North Korean troops' living and fighting conditions had markedly improved from the war's first year "hand-to-mouth" experience.[14]

The result was a modern military miracle. From these defenses, carved out of the living rock, the Chinese soldier was enabled to live, fight, counterattack, assault enemy hills, and if necessary die to defend every foot of hard-won Korean ground. By June 1952, CPVF forces had constructed 7,789 tunnels totaling nearly 200 kilometers in length. The KPA added another 90 kilometers of 1,730 tunnels. Across the breadth of the peninsula, the two Communist armies built 784,000 defensive works consisting of bunkers, tunnel entrances, and protected firing caves supported by 100,000 fortified command posts, observation posts, infantry fighting positions, and other strongholds. All of these were connected by 3,600 kilometers of open or covered trench lines. In the summer of 1952, any UNC effort to coerce a concession on POW repatriation would have to tangle with a defensive complex 233 kilometers long and 15–20 kilometers deep, extending from the mouth of the Imjin River in the west to the east coast.[15] The CPVF gained sufficient experience and confidence in their large-scale defensive battles that eventually led to the adoption of general field guidelines to pursue "protracted war and active defense" for the remainder of the conflict.[16]

The CPVF's defensive resilience was impressive, but in a significant tactical innovation, they also learned to use tunnels offensively, to bring large numbers of troops close to an objective unobserved and shielded from air attack. The concentrated assault stood a good chance of overwhelming the defenders with firepower and mass. Peng attempted to launch four to five of these kinds of limited attacks a month. When the UNC fought offensively themselves, such as during the attack on Old Baldy (see chapter 10), or at Triangle Hill and Sniper Ridge, the tunnel defensive system demonstrated its utility to keep large Chinese formations in contact with the American and ROK troops for extended periods of time with most of the defending troops remaining safely protected underground. On order, or by a prearranged signal, these troops "come running up from their deep shelters in time to meet the advancing enemy infantry" or to stage a powerful counterattack.[17] The system worked and it saved the CPVF from slow destruction. Peng assessed that the victory at "Sangkumryung Ridge" (Triangle Hill) was due fundamentally to the CPVF's defensive works and tunnels.[18]

The Chinese capability to build and rebuild fortifications was daunting for the GIs who observed it firsthand. One marine artillery observer remembered how friendly air and artillery would demolish enemy positions by day and then the infantry soldiers would watch or hear those same positions being reconstructed by night. The cycle was then repeated. He summed it up: "They build at night, and we blow it up in the daytime and nobody ever really accomplishes anything." It was prima facie evidence of the absurdity of "active defense," and it jaundiced American fighting men in particular to the point where they did not care whether the war ended or not, only that they would live long enough to redeploy home.[19]

For the American soldier or marine accumulating his four points a month on the front line, it was an uncomfortable fact that as the Americans increased the volume of their artillery support the Communists were doing the same. The Chinese proved adept at the technical adaptation necessary to integrate artillery fire with infantry maneuver and assault. "They make exuberant artillerymen," and their progressive improvement was critical in giving their infantry equal ground on which to fight.[20] By the fall of 1951, when the Communists possessed an estimated 530 artillery tubes, noticeable improvement in both timing and accuracy were observed, especially the increased coordination between Chinese infantry and their artillery support. For those who felt the CPVF was "an army of simple foot soldiers who, if they achieved anything, did so by sheer weight of numbers," increasing artillery was an unpleasant surprise, "an entirely new discovery" in some cases. Some marveled at how the Chinese in Korea had suddenly emerged as "better artillery men than the Germans."[21] One reluctant infantryman testified, "the shelling would last no longer than ten minutes, but time stood still . . . hoping not to take a direct hit. The noise was awesome, and there was nothing we could do but wait it out. There was no way to get used to the shelling. This was a constant part of our existence, and I always got the feeling that death was right around the corner and the next shell had my name written on it."[22] The Chinese were learning Soviet doctrine and organization in addition to receiving Soviet artillery. In practice, this meant the CPVF began to rely more on firepower to accomplish tactical tasks to capture and even hold ground that previously would have consumed men. "In Korea our troops have encountered enemy artillery fires of an intensity few veterans of World War II ever experienced," recalled Maj. Mark M. Boatner III, an experienced infantryman and veteran of both conflicts. He continued, "American troops [were] driven out of defensive positions by *fire power alone*. American troops . . . had counterattacks stopped short of their objectives . . . by *fire power alone* [original emphasis]."[23]

Chinese attacks based on "fire power alone" intensified in the summer of 1952. In the I Corps sector, Canadian Lt. Col. E. A. C. Amy believed the Chinese were "a much more dangerous foe" now that they possessed enough artillery to "concentrate one hundred guns to blanket a single company po-

sition."[24] Between April and July 1952, the Chinese deployed their largest increase in artillery, adding thirty battalions to their front-line strength, bringing their tube count to 1,246, a 33 percent increase. Further, the Chinese
order of battle now included five artillery divisions and four independent artillery regiments equipped with Soviet 122 mm howitzers to augment the infantry divisions' 76 mm guns. The 122 mm howitzer gave the Chinese greater
range, flexibility, and capability to conduct counterbattery fire against Eighth
Army artillery, an unwelcome development for American gunners grown accustomed to uninhibited firing. They also began to master Soviet methods of
shooting deliberate preparatory bombardments, sometimes independent of
and sometimes in support of, but always timed and coordinated with an infantry assault.[25] The result was a strong artillery arm "capable of delivering effective, concentrated fire in support of his defensive positions and of limited
objective attacks" and "accurate, effective counter-battery fire" (table 8.1).[26]

The doctrinal (and historical) response to such concentrated bombardment was to extend the depth of the defensive belt, defending forward positions lightly, if at all, and husbanding counterattack forces to give elasticity
to the overall defense. This technique, however, required a mindset that accepted the loss of ground, even if only temporarily. Eighth Army, however,
adopted the opposite course of action, attempting to gain depth by pushing
the outpost line farther north toward the Communist MLR. Further, it was
deemed that these outposts had to be defended at all costs. It was a rare battle
that was fought on the MLR: Old Baldy, Porkchop Hill, and Outpost Kelly
were all forward of the MLR. Fortunately for Eighth Army, communist artillery tactics remained conservative. Guns were emplaced farther to the rear
than was the American practice, and the dispersal of artillery pieces, combined with logistical constraints, reduced their ability to mass and shift fire
from multiple locations without extensive coordination. Consequently, most
artillery fire remained concentrated "in intense bombardments of very small
areas in support of local actions." Small comfort indeed for the UNC soldier
occupying that "very small area."[27]

The air war in many respects was a mirror image of the ground war. Despite Stalin's promises for military support, Mao remained dissatisfied with
Soviet assistance, whether on the ground or (especially) in the air. The consequences of the Fifth Campaign highlighted the difficulties of surviving and
fighting under the Americans' superior airpower. The CPVF leadership had
to find alternate methods to remain relevant. Here again Chinese strategy
followed two tracks: (1) reducing the Americans' ability to attack their logistical communications while (2) making those lines of communication more defensible and resilient. The first involved the skillful employment of the People's
Liberation Army Air Force (PLAAF) and increased deployment of antiaircraft

TABLE 8.1. MONTHLY ARTILLERY EXPENDITURES
(DECEMBER 1951–DECEMBER 1952)

Month	UNC/ROK	Communist (estimated)
December 1951	611,700	19,700
January 1952	928,200	17,500
February	625,400	11,900
March	661,800	18,500
April	684,000	29,200
May	701,600	43,500
June	909,900	77,300
July	791,200	57,000
August	759,200	70,400
September	932,600	104,700
October	1,740,900	220,600
November	866,900	106,700
December	859,600	51,000

Source: Eighth Army, "The Employment and Effectiveness of the Artillery," 43, USAHEC.

artillery while the second focused on the repair, building, concealment, and redundancy of rail and road transportation.[28]

Chinese airpower in Korea had modest beginnings. In July 1950 Stalin agreed to provide MiG fighter-interceptors to the PLAAF along with training to prepare Chinese pilots to fly in Korea. Mao worried that an adequate number of pilots would not be combat ready before the spring of 1951, long after he intended to intervene in Korea. The arrival of the Soviet 151st Guards Interceptor/Fighter Aviation Division in Shenyang, Anshan, and Liaoyang confused the issue, as the Russian commander was torn between air defense missions of China proper, providing defensive air cover for Chinese ground forces preparing to cross the Yalu River, and training Chinese pilots.[29]

Chinese troops therefore crossed the Yalu River in late October 1950 and fought their first engagements with ROK and American divisions without the benefit of air cover. Soviet MiG-15s only flew their first combat missions over the Yalu on November 1, surprising American fighter-bombers who had grown accustomed to "milk runs" along the North Korean–Manchurian border. The appearance of swept-wing jet fighters promised to change the calculus American airmen had wagered to maintain and exploit air supremacy to blunt the threat of Chinese intervention. Later that month, additional Soviet MiGs deployed to Manchuria, specifically tasked to defend the Yalu bridges at Andong, prevent UNC planes from attacking hydroelectric facilities, and provide general air cover for the Andong-Sinuiju complex, which was the crucial bottleneck and vulnerability for CPVF supplies and reinforcements.[30]

Although this level of protection did enable the Chinese volunteer to enter the conflict and carry the battle as far as the 38th parallel by New Year's Day, 1951, CPVF supply lines extended well beyond the protective umbrella that Soviet MiGs could provide. FEAF interdiction attacks between Pyongyang and Seoul inflicted serious losses and did much to sap the Chinese of their offensive momentum; Ridgway's revitalized Eighth Army did the rest.[31]

In private talks with Mao on February 21, 1951, Peng complained that mounting casualties and inadequate supplies made further offensive planning futile. He estimated that UNC airpower was interdicting up to 40 percent of the CPVF's logistics and reinforcements. Mao was moderately impressed by Peng's plea and allowed for an extended pause before resuming the strategic offensive, but he could do little to satisfy his marshal's lust to see Chinese airmen sacrificing themselves in a manner commensurate with his infantrymen. Peng allegedly confronted the PLAAF's chief, Liu Yalou, and barked, "This is a problem and that is a problem. You need to go to the front to see what the soldiers are eating and wearing. There are so many casualties. . . . At present we have no planes, very few [antiaircraft] guns, and the transportation at the rear has no protection [from air attack]."[32]

Liu's pilots were in the battle, but their inexperience was glaringly obvious. Although outnumbered, American F-86 Sabrejets—hastily deployed in December 1950—still ruled the sky, keeping the PLAAF MiGs at bay as other UNC aircraft continued their deadly work of interdiction and strategic bombing. Any attempt to project Chinese airpower south of the Chongchon River, let alone to support Peng's offensive in April–May, would have produced few positive results. The fact is that Mao rushed to fight a modern war before he had developed a modern military. Duped by Stalin's rubber checks that promised specific air support in exchange for Chinese infantry to fight the Americans, Mao's strategic genius was left exposed for what it was—antiquated and romantic. Peng was a bit more clear-sighted, and he refused to press forward with a sixth campaign in the late summer after negotiations at Kaesong began to bog down on the initial agenda item of setting the demarcation line, and then again as the Eighth Army was grinding up North Korean troops in the Punchbowl. Instead, he resolved to solve his logistics and force protection problems without the PLAAF.[33]

Stalin may have disappointed Mao by reneging on the implied offensive air support, but Soviet contributions to the air war should not be minimized. Within tight constraints, Soviet pilots, technicians, and air defense gunners played a crucial role defending air space over the Yalu River, keeping open the routes over which CPVF troops and Soviet trucks, supplies, munitions, and weapons flowed. Without this level of support and the Soviet air shield Stalin did provide, it is unlikely Peng could have maintained his forces in strength as far south as he did. Additionally, the Soviet effort to train and equip Chinese air divisions eventually gave Mao more flexibility to prosecute both the air and ground war.[34]

A key component of PLAAF's Korean strategy was to construct jet-capable airfields south of the Yalu River. Early plans anticipated the deployment of twelve air regiments (about 350 planes) to North Korea by April 1951. The UNC recognized the game-changing threat PLAAF airfields established south of Yalu represented, and FEAF spared no effort to ensure that MiGs or ground attack planes never took off from Korean soil. Air reconnaissance maintained continuous surveillance to track construction progress, and when it appeared that an airfield approached operational capability, the Americans struck, pounding runways, revetments, taxiways, and service roads to pitted rubble. As fast as construction crews could repair damage, the bombers returned, seventy-two times during the months of April and May 1951 alone. Despite significant increase in antiaircraft weapons defending these targets, during these two months, over 6,800 bombs hit runways and other critical facilities, rendering the construction effort moot.[35]

The Chinese never gave up on their airfield basing plan, but it soon became overshadowed by the urgent need to get the PLAAF into the war. On September 12, 1951, the PLAAF's Fourth Aviation Division, fifty-five MiG-15s, moved to Langtou airfield near Andong and flew its first combat operation two weeks later, tangling with twenty F-86s flying cover for thirteen F-80s attacking a bridge over the Chongchon River. The fighter-bombers were distracted, but the engagement was inconclusive, with the Chinese losing one MiG destroyed (along with its pilot killed) and one damaged in exchange for damaging one F-86 Sabrejet. Still, a week later Mao cited the Fourth Division pilots, lauding their "courage and spirit" in the confrontation with the more experienced Americans. Such plaudits fitted well with Mao's style and ethos, the spirit of the man was always considered more important than the weapon, and there is evidence that his young aviators responded to his compliments. On October 5, the Fourth Division was back over the Chongchon, flying cover for CPVF troops crossing the river. A group of F-80s had just completed a bombing run when the Chinese MiGs pounced in a disciplined attack. The PLAAF claimed three Shooting Stars destroyed and two damaged. Two weeks later, October 19, the Fourth Division withdrew to Shenyang, having claimed twenty American jets shot down (US records admit to zero losses) for four-teen MiGs lost. The next division to deploy to Korea was the Third Aviation Division, and it showed that it absorbed many lessons to improve their surviv-ability while inflicting losses on UNC aircraft. The Third Division performed well against F-80 and F-84 jets flying unescorted missions along the rim of MiG Alley. By December it became clear that the Communists could field enough MiGs that unescorted fighter-bombers were at serious risk in prose-cuting Strangle targets between the Yalu and Chongchon Rivers.[36]

The Third Division's success prompted a more aggressive air strategy. It was also important that Peng Dehuai had once again interjected his influence, rhe-torically suggesting, "If the air force with such wonderful aircraft could con-trol the enemy activities like the ground forces, [we] could defeat the enemy much sooner."[37] Peng's gently sarcastic push was politically motivated. In No-vember both sides agreed to a thirty-day tactical freeze to allow negotiators the opportunity to finalize a settlement. Much as Peng's American counter-parts looked to their air arm to maintain military pressure without violat-ing this agreement, the CPVF commander looked to his comrades above the ground to do the same.

PLAAF leadership agreed to fulfill a new role, independent of the Sovi-ets. The Third Division was encouraged to seek out large-scale battles with its Sabre enemies to gain control over the skies of North Korea. While it is un-clear exactly how PLAAF or the CMC expected air superiority to materialize, or what they would do to exploit this condition, Chinese pilots paid a high price for the switch in strategy. By January 15, 1952, when the Third Divi-sion withdrew from its combat tour, it had lost sixteen MiGs along with sev-eral pilots, but it claimed to have fought twenty-three air battles and downed fifty-five UNC aircraft.[38]

The Chinese always fought the war with one eye over their shoulder. Mao's ability not only to fight the Americans and aid North Korea but also to build his own modern military force depended entirely on Russian largesse. If the war in Korea ended too soon, the Soviet's interest in Chinese military growth could diminish when placed against competing priorities. The prospect of a truce in November 1951 increased Mao's desire to get as many Chinese pi-lots as possible not only trained and sitting in a jet fighter but also to have combat experience. Eventually the Chinese built a force of ten fighter divi-sions and two bomber divisions, with nearly one thousand pilots and sixty thousand support personnel based in Manchuria. Even though many pilots were not considered fully qualified for combat operations, PLAAF leadership decided to increase the flow of aviation units to Andong and let them engage in five to seven large air battles.[39]

Xiaoming Zhang documents how these formations, which did not have the benefit of Soviet tutelage, gradually immersed themselves into the air war. Based on the experience of the Third and Fourth Divisions, new pilots started off slowly, flying into areas without enemy opposition then gradually moving into more complex and dangerous engagements with fighter-bombers and small groups of Sabers. In February 1952, however, Mao urged more opportunities for real combat experience, and more of these inexperienced divisions found themselves thrown into the maelstrom over the Yalu River. For the rest of the war, the PLAAF contribution to Peng's CPVF remained at three to four air divisions, totaling between 150 and 200 MiG-15s.[40]

The PLAAF's efforts never lived up to Peng's expectations. He was therefore forced to rely more on ground-based air defenses. Compared with what American airmen faced in Europe during World War II, communist ground-based air defenses were too weak in numbers and types of weaponry to be decisive, but they still took a heavy toll on UNC aircraft prosecuting interdiction strategies in 1951 and 1952. Both the KPA and CPVF used Soviet-made heavy and light guns. Intelligence estimates at the beginning of the war assessed that the KPA possessed thirty-six heavy anti-aircraft guns and fewer than one hundred automatic weapons dedicated to air defense. A large number of infantry weapons were subsequently adapted to anti-aircraft roles, such as the 7.62 mm Maxim machine gun, either on a dual-purpose mount or an anti-aircraft (AA) tripod.[41] By May 1951 the inventory had grown to 278 heavy guns and 800 automatic weapons, and by the end of the war heavy guns increased by a factor of three (720) while lighter guns enjoyed a more modest 50 percent increase to 1,300. Many of these lighter AA weapons were deployed along the line of contact and were used aggressively to defend the MLR and its supporting assets: artillery, supply points, and command centers.[42]

The principal heavy anti-aircraft gun was the Soviet-manufactured 85 mm Model 1939. These guns, capable of firing fifteen to twenty rounds a minute, defended Yalu bridges, rail marshalling yards, and the North Korean capital Pyongyang. They were most effective against level-flying bombers flying at medium and high altitudes, like the B-29. At lower levels, and more lethal against smaller aircraft, were the 37 mm automatic gun and the 12.7 mm machine gun. These mobile weapons defended railroads, supply dumps, artillery parks, and command posts. They were the guns interdiction and close air support pilots were most likely to tangle with, and they proved to be the deadliest. From January 1 to April 30, 1952, Fifth Air Force lost 828 fighter-bombers destroyed or significantly damaged—21.6 planes out of action per 1,000 sorties. Fifty percent of hits were inflicted below 2,500 feet, within easy reach of 37 mm guns.[43] Despite these losses, the AA problem was far from insurmountable, but it involved tactical compromises. The true effectiveness of these guns was to drive bombing altitudes higher, resulting in greater aircraft survivability but reduced accuracy and additional sorties required to destroy or neutralize a target. As a measure of how AA guns affected FEAF's interdiction campaigns and effectiveness, analysts determined that dive bombing accuracy declined from a Circular Error Probable (CEP) of 75 feet in 1951 to a CEP of 219 feet by the end of 1952. The increased CEP, a radial measurement where 50 percent of dropped bombs could be expected to land, indicated that per sortie, air attack was one-third as effective by 1953 as it was two years previously.[44]

As effective as air defense weaponry was at frustrating FEAF's interdiction effort, the biggest factor that limited the impact of aerial interdiction operations was the skilled and unskilled manpower the Communists mobilized with astonishing speed and proficiency. China mobilized a total of 600,000 civilians to serve in rear supply and supporting service units during the war. At the height of Operation Strangle, 200,000 Chinese civilians fought the rear-area war side by side with their North Korean partners.[45] The North Korean Railroad Bureau controlled three brigades of engineering troops and could call on the free labor of South Korean prisoners of war along with thousands more North Korean civilians—men, women, old, and young, who were all conscripted to fight against the technological might of the United States.

Over time, repair crews learned to anticipate where repair supplies and materials needed to be stockpiled. Relying on local materials and muscle power, these crews filled pitted roads, shored up frames of damaged bridges, and straightened out bomb-bent rail irons. FEAF intelligence estimated that hasty repairs such as these could be accomplished in as little as two to six hours. More solid repairs would be accomplished later; in the meantime, light vehicular and rail traffic would continue on, gingerly, southward to feed the front-line troops with only a modest delay.[46]

When it came to bridges, communist engineers pulled out all the stops: constructing multiple bypasses and underwater bridges, cannibalizing heavily damaged bridge planking to shore up those less damaged, extending fill material from the riverbanks as far out as possible and then bridging the much narrower gap, and emplacing wood and sandbag piers to reinforce and provide redundancy to the concrete ones. Other work involved replacing dropped bridge spans with interlocking timbers cribbed up to support the track on a bed of wood. This work could be done quickly and provided a stable enough platform to support immediate rail traffic (figure 8.2).[47]

However crude the Communist system of road and repair was, it did the job and proved the adage that quantity has a quality of its own. In this case, numbers did matter in a contest of man versus machine. After the war Van Fleet paid the appropriate eulogy to these brave and skilled railroad troops: "Without modern equipment, but with seemingly unlimited labor, they were

Figure 8.2 Communist repair of interdiction damage. Korean laborers constructed bypasses to keep track in operation. The upper bypass has been put out of action. A passenger train, caught on the lower bypass and destroyed by air attack, has been pushed off the embankment. Repairs to restore the line to the operation have already begun. Source: US navy photo.

able to replace or by-pass track just about as fast as we could knock it out, and in the end their restorative capacity defeated our destructive capacity."[48] The air force also had its say. Brig. Gen. Darr H. Alkire, FEAF's deputy commander for material, marveled, "It has frequently been stated by commanders in Korea that the one man they would all like to meet when the war is over is the G-4 [logistics officer] of the Communist forces. How he has kept supplies moving in the face of all the obstacles is a real mystery."[49]

The Logistics Miracle

After the war, Van Fleet marveled at the "amazing logistical performance of the enemy," who "displayed astounding ingenuity in finding methods to circumvent our efforts" to strangle the tendrils that made up the CPVF's lifeline in Korea.[50] The man responsible for this "amazing logistical performance," and the one man every Chinese commander in Korea wanted to meet, was Hong Xuezhi.

Logistics difficulties had long affected modern Chinese operations.[51] Mao's volunteers had a long tradition of equipping themselves at the enemy's expense. Mao boasted, "We have claim on the output of the arsenals of London as well as Hanyang and, what is more, that output will be delivered to us by the enemy's own transport corps."[52] This logistical philosophy may have been adequate during the Sino-Japanese war or the Chinese civil war, but against the Americans Peng needed someone to fight the battle in his rear area to ensure a continuous flow of the material of war. Hong—reluctantly—accepted the assignment as deputy commander for logistics.[53]

The spectacular success of Peng's Second Campaign, resulting in a nearly thirty-day pursuit of Eighth Army, masked the fact that Peng really could only sustain about ten to fourteen days of serious combat and maneuver. During the American counterattack (January 25–February 16, 1951) following the Third Campaign, Peng's forces adopted a mobile defense to compensate for his lack of supplies and munitions. Trading space for time and avoiding a set-piece battle allowed Peng to restrain Eighth Army's advance until his major formations reformed, received reinforcements, and recuperated in time to launch the largest communist offensive of the war. The results of the Fifth Campaign, though, called into question the military efficacy of Mao's shoestring strategy, and Peng understood that his forces could not compete in the positional warfare that emerged after July 1951 with a mobile defense posture.[54]

As the Chinese acknowledged, Van Fleet's limited objective attacks in the summer of 1951 threatened their field forces with annihilation or starvation. UNC air interdiction was most effective when combined with ground pressure that forced the Chinese to take more risks transporting ammunition and other supplies to the front. In late April Hong had returned to Beijing and implored Zhou Enlai for greater support. He detailed the severe losses UNC airpower inflicted on the volunteers, particularly effective were the "black widows" (night-flying B-26s) that "dropped bombs everywhere" there was a lucrative target. For Chinese soldiers, the rear area was just as dangerous as the front lines. Chinese lines of communication were very long and lacked adequate air defenses, although Fifth Air Force losses suggested the gradual proliferation of anti-aircraft artillery along main road routes *was* taking a toll. CPVF logistics units were also primitive and lacked the mobility necessary to keep up with combat troops. In the long term, as both sides grappled with stationary warfare and political battle at Kaesong and Panmunjom, it would be "transportation, rear supply, and logistics service" that would determine both the tactical resilience and the strategic relevance of communist armies for the remainder of the war.[55]

Zhou convinced Mao and the CMC to reinforce Peng with fresh combat formations and a greater logistics effort. The Eleventh and Sixteenth Armies were called forward to give Peng a strategic reserve and to help even the odds tactically, giving the Communist negotiators something with which to resist UNC demands at Kaesong.[56] At the same time, the CPVF Logistics Department was established June 1 with Hong directed to fight "the Korean War in our rear." Hong need not have worried as the CMC was determined to "win the war in the rear while supplying the front." Consequently, Hong was invested with wide-ranging authorities and power to take charge of all logistics forces, including supporting troops (meaning air defense), road and rail repair personnel, and rear supply units. American intelligence reports already suggested that as many as 23,000 North Koreans were organized into specialized rail-repair units and stationed at all major stations and marshalling yards, ready to move out immediately to begin repairs inflicted by enemy aircraft. To this number would be added thousands more Chinese soldiers and civilian volunteers, many of whom would dig purposeful revetments, shelters, and trenches to hide trucks and locomotives during the day.[57]

The reform and rationalization of the rear area battle, combined with the addition of two fresh armies, came just in time for the emergence of positional warfare that characterized the front following the start of truce talks. Peng's force now consisted of seventeen infantry armies, six artillery divisions, four anti-aircraft divisions, one tank division, and 60,000 draft animals. The relaxation of military pressure allowed Hong to organize specified "locational supply" units responsible for supporting any and all front-line forces located in their respective sectors. Importantly, as opposed to the early CPVF campaigns, no offensive battle ever was called off and no defensive position was abandoned for want of logistical support. Whereas the conclusion of the Fifth Campaign exposed the CPVF's strategic long-term vulnerability in Korea, by the fall of 1951 Mao and his generals believed that the worst was past, and that if the Chinese could not win the quick, lightning victory, they could— through other means—attempt to win a slower one that exhausted the UNC.[58]

The best tactics cannot have any enduring meaning without adequate resources. In other words, unless Peng could put his logistics house in order, *niupitang* operations would have nothing to offer strategically. For the first time in the PLA's history, the logisticians became vital components in supporting the Communists' political objectives. By "making adequate preparations for protracted war and striving for ending the war through peaceful negotiations" Mao's generals prepared to confront the UNC and the American political leadership with a strategic conundrum that defied clarity and tested the patience and resolve of the UNC coalition. Thereafter, Chinese military strategy evolved from an attempt to annihilate large American and Korean formations to a more deliberate and scaled combination of defensive and offensive actions designed to seize key terrain and hold the UNC in the close embrace of attrition. Holding the current battle line, sustaining capable forces, and reducing unnecessary casualties became not only military goals but also political necessities.[59]

By 1952, Mao was in a much stronger position to resist UNC pressure, both on the ground and in the air, than ever before. CPVF soldiers were more numerous, experienced, and better equipped with modern Soviet guns, small arms, trucks, and ammunition. The CPVF's elaborate system of trenches, tunnels, and protected positions reduced vulnerability from the air and provided a bulwark to resist a ground assault. The Chinese flexibility in their various operational approaches to counter American firepower and maneuver formed the basis for prolonged and successful negotiations that would justify the PRC's expense in manpower and treasure to confront American influence in northeast Asia. The pivotal "Defense System Centered Around Tunnels" reduced communist casualties to a more sustainable level. CPVF sources claim that in the summer of 1951, forty UNC artillery rounds produced one Chinese casualty. By January 1952, the ratio had climbed to 264 shells per casualty, and by April 1952, the UNC could only inflict one casualty by firing nearly 650 shells. The PLA's Military History Research Department concluded, "the apparent increasing success by CPVF and NKPA forces against UN forces had demonstrated the effectiveness of the tunnel centered defense works built . . . in the winter of 1951 and spring of 1952." The same assessment also credited the tunnel-centered system for tactical success in both defense and attack operations. Mao's legions had found a way to exist on a battlefield dominated by American air and artillery firepower.[60]

One American officer, a veteran of Peng's slow and deliberate war of posts, later reflected, "We call the enemy mostly Joe (for Stalin) or Joe Chink, and I have developed a deep respect for his abilities as a fighting man."[61] Whatever Mao's desires for an armistice, he was hardly desperate. It was surely one of the most disappointing discoveries for the Americans to make in the summer of 1952.[62]

9

"A SITUATION BEYOND REPAIR," MAY–AUGUST 1952

BRIG. GEN. S. L. A. Marshall (frequently known as "SLAM") was a regular guest lecturer at the Command and General Staff College located at Fort Leavenworth, Kansas. The General Staff College was a highlight for any army officer's career. Here he learned the fundamentals of corps and division combined arms operations, rubbed shoulders with experienced staff and faculty, networked with his peers, and took the measure of his professional competition. The curriculum focused on tactics and operations from the perspective of commanders and staffs. SLAM was present at Fort Leavenworth in January 1952 to help the class of army majors "understand the other end of the problem." In other words, SLAM was going to give a tutorial on the individual soldier's experience, facing the enemy, living in the elements, and wondering when someone was going "to resolve the situation which by its nature may be beyond repair except as a possible solution may come in time out of a greater world convulsion."[1]

"The greater world convulsion," was, of course, an allusion to the outbreak of a third world war. This was an event the Truman administration was working hard to prevent, but the American political-strategic apparatus found itself tied in knots. The day after the UNC delegation dropped its package proposal at Panmunjom (Tokyo time), President Truman announced a command change in the Far East. Ridgway was appointed to replace Gen. Dwight D. Eisenhower as the Supreme Allied Commander in Europe, while Gen. Mark W. Clark, former commander of the American Fifth Army and the Fifteenth Army Group in Italy during World War II and current chief of Army Field Forces in the continental United States, would take over as the commander in chief, Far East Command and United Nations Command. In making the appointment, Truman emphasized that "General Clark will continue the policies which have been so ably carried out by General Ridgway with regard to the United Nations actions in Korea, including, if possible, the achievement of an honorable armistice." Truman's statement was one of confidence and warning:

a change in command did not indicate a change in policy. Clark would have his military options just as circumscribed as Ridgway, and the war would remain limited and confined to the Korean peninsula. On May 12, 1952, General Ridgway said farewell to the Far East as Clark assumed command of the defense of Japan and its surrounding waters as well as of the war in Korea.[2]

Clark arrived in Japan on May 7, the same day that the deadlock at Panmunjom was publicly announced. His combat command experience did not necessarily make him a standout selection to be Ridgway's replacement. The Italian campaign he directed from September 1943 until May 1945 was more famous as a slow, casualty intensive slugfest under very difficult political conditions. He also endured a reputation as a mediocre commander, "and at times insufferable as a person," according to Rick Atkinson's history of that campaign.[3] The bloody and futile assault crossing over the Rapido River in January 1944 continued to haunt Clark long after the war, with members of the Texas National Guard going so far as to demand congressional hearings into Clark's "inefficiency, inexperience, and useless sacrifice of American youth" during the battle. The brutal mountain fighting also left a deep impression on Clark, who was criticized even by his friends. "There is always another mountain mass beyond with the Germans dug in on it," one of his division commanders and former mentors lamented.[4] The sad military truth was that Italy had been a side show, and Clark earned little glory and much resentment for his "calculated risk" mentality. Korea, with each passing day of deadlock and stalemate, was beginning to assume an uncanny resemblance to that unfortunate campaign, and Clark would go to great lengths to avoid provoking comparisons. The military problem he was handed, a situation that appeared politically unwinnable and strategically untenable in the long term, would tax his abilities to the utmost. Perhaps Italy had been the perfect proving ground after all for the new UNC commander.[5]

Despite Clark's negatives, he was disciplined, personally fearless, and capable of thinking broadly—joint service cooperation and coalition politics seemed to come naturally to him. He also was not burdened as Ridgway had been by inheriting the FEC mantle following MacArthur's relief. Therefore, he was not beholden to Ridgway's narrow thoughts on attrition and strategic options. Clark recognized the war could only be won through a prolonged process of wearing down the enemy physically, psychologically, and politically, and he was for the moment willing to reverse Ridgway's defensively attrition-oriented approach to one that was more muscular. His was still an attrition strategy, but he was willing to countenance actions that provoked a communist response, thereby bringing his forces out to be killed or his propaganda positions and arguments to be confronted. He was also willing to take the gloves off when it came to airpower, and he successfully lobbied Washington to approve a substantial increase in ROK ground forces and capabilities. Clark hoped these two military measures would increase the price tag for intransigence while maintaining limited liability both strategically and tactically. At issue would be the definition of winning and whether Clark's strategic approach was an acceptable bridge linking American policy to the military outcome in Korea. In this regard, his only misstep was his engagement with president-elect Dwight D. Eisenhower when Eisenhower went to Korea following the US presidential election in November 1952. Both Clark and Van Fleet misconstrued Eisenhower's purpose, and their argument to expand the war received a cold reception.

But that was still several months in the future, and in the immediate days following his assumption of command, Clark's political sense and military equilibrium were immediately tested. Several crises erupted at once: the POW riots on Koje-do and the associated fallout at Panmunjom, the ROK constitutional crisis, and the inauguration of an air pressure strategy (APS) that unleashed American airpower against hitherto restricted civilian targets in North Korea.

Prisoners of War and the Chinese Propaganda Offensive at Panmunjom

In Korea the UNC faced a new type of prisoner, one who did not surrender his intent to resist while in captivity.[6] Ridgway confessed, "But I did not know then, nor do I know now, how far the communist command might have gone in its readiness to sacrifice the lives of its own people in order to achieve a propaganda victory."[7] Nor did the Americans anticipate the violent antipathy between anti-communist and pro-communist prisoners, and the toxic reactions that were bound to occur in compounds where partisans from both sides were housed. Many of the Chinese prisoners captured in May were in fact ex-Nationalist soldiers, who quickly surrendered when faced with starvation, exposure, and superior firepower. Operation Scatter, the attempt to screen POWs in February 1952, aggravated and exposed the tensions between the two sides. Koreans and Chinese rejecting repatriation attempted to control or persuade their uncommitted brethren through psychological coercion, intimidation, and at times outright violence. For their part, North Korean and Communist Chinese prisoners returned reports to Panmunjom through intermediaries regarding collaborators, conditions in the camp, and propaganda opportunities to exploit. They too were not above using coercive tactics to advance their cause. In some exceptional cases, the communist high command deliberately allowed senior officials to be captured or pretend to defect. Instead, these agents brought orders to provoke the UNC into actions that would cause the UNC to lose the moral high ground in the ideological contest surrounding voluntary repatriation. Much as the UNC put high stock in air attack to pressure the Communists, the Communists returned the favor in the arena where they held all the cards and had the will to play them.[8]

Communist prisoners on Koje-do had been secretly organizing over several months. The initial impulse was self-preservation. Camp guards never ventured into the compounds at night, which is when the most severe intramural clashes occurred, and anti-communist POWs, both Korean and Chinese, capitalized on the surety of their position, especially when the policy of voluntary repatriation was announced. Senior KPA and CPVF leaders responded with organizational efforts of their own. CPVF political commissar Col. Zhao Zuorui was captured in the spring of 1951 during operations along the Soyang River following the collapse of Peng's Fifth Campaign. Concealing his identity and rank, Zhao was shipped off with a thousand other POWs to Koje-do, Compound 72. Immediately he asserted his position to organize his fellow officer POWs to "continue to fight the Korean War on Koje Island. It was the second front of the Korean War."[9]

Zhao's task was simplified by the island command's negligence. Little was done to segregate prisoners from the island's indigenous and refugee population or to supervise them adequately. POWs had been issued picks and shovels for road work on the island, but camp authorities neglected to take the tools back when work was done. Enterprising prisoners dug tunnels connecting compounds to each other, which allowed free passage for leaders and sometimes for entire compounds to switch places. They had even dug tunnels leading outside of the camp, which enabled North Korean agents to cultivate sympathetic islanders to pass and receive information.[10]

American and ROK guards declined to interfere in the "running" of individual camps ruled by anti-communist prisoners (the UNC called them "Trustees"). Trustees compelled fence-sitters, or—if they felt secure—even pro-repatriates, to be tattooed with anti-communist slogans and to participate in mass rallies and demonstrations in favor of prisoner screenings. They also used psychological tactics, telling prisoners that screening was merely a ruse to identify communists for later punishment or even execution. When the trustees went too far and resisters were beaten or killed, Communist leaders like Zhao began to mobilize and inspire their fellow soldiers to resist both inside and outside the wire pressures. They sang KPA songs, created homemade banners in praise of the North Korean forces and Kim Il-sung, and openly displayed their contempt for American and ROK soldiers.[11] Each compound soon created secret cells led by reliable party-member cadres and disciplined through a strong hierarchical structure that culminated in April 1952 with the establishment of the Communist United Front. Colonel Zhao was its first secretary general.[12]

The first serious outbreak of prisoner violence against POW screening was on February 18, 1952. A team of ROK soldiers backed by a US infantry battalion entered Compound 62, which was under communist control, to screen 5,000 CI. The predawn entry of the security force appeared to have successfully intimidated the prisoners when a few minutes later, more than a thousand CI attempted to force their way out of their barracks, armed with steel pickets, spiked wooden clubs, barbed wire flails, metal tent poles turned into spears, and iron pipes. Rocks and knives rounded out the improvised armory. US troops forced the CI back with fixed bayonets and concussion grenades. When this proved insufficient, the Americans opened fire, killing 77 and injuring 139. One American soldier died and 23 were injured in the clash.[13]

The Communist ringleaders clearly had forewarning about the operation and were well prepared to orchestrate a propaganda headache for the UNC. They remained in control of Compound 62, and when further attempts at screening met similar resistance, the resultant violence fed further propaganda assaults at Panmunjom, the communist delegates charging the UNC with negligence resulting in "a bloody incident in which many of our prisoners were brutally killed." General Clark later recalled that the camp commander (identified by Boatner only as "Colonel Fitzgerald") did not even know how many prisoners were in custody, as it had been several months since any attempt was made to enter and control the compounds.[14]

Two days after the riots in February 1952, Van Fleet dispatched from his own staff Brig. Gen. Francis T. Dodd. Dodd's mission was simply to restore order and prevent a repetition of violent responses to further screening.[15] As General Collins later reflected, he "proved to be an unfortunate choice." Perhaps, but without experienced American units and relying on a poorly manned and trained ROK guard force, Dodd had little to work with except to trust in the POWs' good behavior. On the one hand, it was later suspected that some of the South Korean guards were passing messages and intelligence from the camps to communist agents on the mainland.[16] On the other, the camp leadership appointed former Nationalist POWs as "trustees" to control the camps. Phil Manhard, a US embassy official, personally observed conditions on Koje-do and how the Chinese trustees discharged their duties: "These trustees exercise discriminatory control over food, clothing, fuel and access to medical treatment" and their fellow Nationalists "maintain control over the Chinese compounds by means of force and coercion . . . to intimidate the majority of Chinese POWs."[17] This was bad enough, but Dodd quickly lost control as the screening process to support the segregation of communist and non-communist POWs became imminent. Operation Scatter finally went into effect on Koje-do on April 8. It proceeded smoothly until an attempt was made to enter and poll the communist-controlled compounds. Communist leaders refused entry, and based on the February 18 incident, it was decided to forego screening and extrapolate figures to present at Panmunjom. This concession to avoid violence merely postponed the final reckoning, as UN officials visiting Koje-do at the end of March witnessed horrendous conditions for both the guards and the prisoners: "He [Dodd] is living on the edge of a volcano and on any day there might be fresh outbreaks of violence and more deaths."[18] A late April inspection by the army's provost marshal general produced similar observations. He informed Ridgway that a "dangerous lack of control" existed in the Communist-dominated compounds.[19] These warnings unfortunately went unheeded and additional security was not provided as the FEC implemented its next attempt to separate the various POW factions.

Operation Spreadout commenced on April 19 to remove some 82,000 non-repatriate POWs (including 14,200 Chinese) and CI from Koje-do to new camps on Cheju-do island or on the Korean mainland. This action was precisely what the Communists strove to prevent as it would break the influence of competing ideologies and reduce the threat of POW violence, thus removing an essential propaganda tool from the Panmunjom arena. As General Clark prepared to take over the Far East Command, Ridgway relayed to Clark that prisoner aggressiveness increased in direct proportion to the sensitive progress of prisoner exchange talks. On April 29, Ridgway informed the JCS, "It now appears clearly evident that in those compounds at Koje-do yet to be screened, any screening and segregation program will meet with violent resistance." Ridgway explained the intensive organization the Communist POWs had achieved and his view that "the risk of violence and bloodshed" would not warrant further screening. In his opinion, it was best simply to list all POWs in the unscreened compounds as repatriates. Any last minute changes could be dealt with at the time of the armistice and final exchange.[20]

What the two generals did not know was the extent of the Communists' organization and detailed planning. A mid-April announcement indicating that the prisoner population on Koje-do was to be reduced through Operation Spreadout likely accelerated Zhao's plans.[21] Using the camp's infirmaries as message drop points, Zhao coordinated with his North Korean counterparts an elaborate ruse to lure Dodd into the compound areas. On May 2, the Communist POW leadership presented a letter of grievances to Dodd. Protests and a general hunger strike followed the next day. Zhao informed Dodd that only his personal attention to the prisoners' concerns would end the strike. On May 6, Dodd agreed to meet to hear their complaints, and the prisoners agreed to end their hunger strike.

The POWs executed their plan on May 7, when General Dodd again agreed to discuss camp conditions and the progress of additional screening with a group of North Korean prisoners at Compound 76. Inexplicably, Dodd relaxed his guard (an armed security platoon was present but positioned about ten yards away) and allowed the prisoners to gather around him and his military police battalion commander, Lt. Col. Wilbur R. Raven. Without warning, the prisoners closed ranks and whisked the unfortunate Dodd into the compound.[22] Van Fleet sent Brig. Gen. Charles F. Colson, who was then the I Corps chief of staff, to take over at Koje-do on May 8, but he reserved the use of force to effect Dodd's release. Unfortunately, though Ridgway urged him to restore order, Van Fleet delayed as he awaited the arrival of an infantry battalion and a company of tanks. Colson demonstrated force by surrounding the camp with armored vehicles and soldiers, but the impasse continued. The prisoners' initial demands were bold: authority to form a prisoner association with by-laws, as well as the administrative apparatus to run such an association: "an intercompound telephone . . . additional tents, desks, chairs, reams and reams of paper, ink, fountain pens, mimeograph machines and even two three-quarter ton trucks."[23]

For three days Dodd stood trial in a "people's court," but what the Communists really wanted was a confession to discredit the process of prisoner screening and the American policy of voluntary repatriation. The Communists presented Dodd four demands: (1) stop the abuse and murder of prisoners; (2) stop the repatriation screenings; (3) agree to the organization of a "Chinese-North Korean Prisoner Delegation to coordinate camp activities"; and (4) terminate all voluntary repatriation efforts, termed "unlawful screening." He initially refused, but after hours of interrogation and psychological pressure, he finally gave in. On May 10, Dodd stood up after another round of prisoners' testimony of abuse and neglect and said, "I am responsible for what happened here. And I am guilty." Dodd then signed the prisoners' petition.[24]

Meanwhile, the pressure was on General Colson. Prisoners clearly ruled the island. Van Fleet continued to withhold use of force, which limited the harried commander's immediate options. Exuberant prisoners defiantly displayed homemade communist flags and propaganda banners decrying the injustice of prisoner screenings. Verbal insults and passive disobedience cowed the guard force, which further encouraged the demonstration leaders. Dodd had frequent conversations with Colson, where he pleaded the prisoners' case and passed their suggestions to Colson for his responses to their demands. All of this added to the psychological pressure Colson felt, but he was being played. Reluctant to act and unfamiliar with the POW situation on the island, Colson accepted the prisoners' demands and publicly acknowledged UNC mistakes in the camps. He further promised, "in the future POWs can expect humane treatment," that there would be "no more forcible rescreening," and that prisoners would be entitled to appoint representatives to negotiate with the American command.[25]

Although Dodd was immediately released unharmed and further prisoner violence was prevented, Colson had acted far outside his authority, particularly with respect to suspending repatriation screening. What is more, his actions and statements generated significant strategic and political effects that threw both the UNC and Washington on defense.[26] Clark immediately issued a press release denouncing Colson's ransom statement as having "no validity whatsoever" and pointing out the unlawful behavior of the prisoners who even in captivity struggled to achieve strategic aims, by "carefully prepar[ing] to manufacture propaganda for the purpose of beclouding the whole prisoner-of-war issue at [the] Panmunjom negotiations."[27] Clark's analysis was certainly correct that the prisoners were "acting under instructions from outside agents" and that Van Fleet was incapable of handling this crisis while also commanding Eighth Army's operations.[28] To ensure complete control over the island, Clark dispatched the 187th Airborne Regimental Combat Team from the theater reserve. He then summoned Brig. Gen. Haydon L. Boatner, in Japan at the time, to FEC headquarters and directed him to "reestablish and maintain control of the POWs." At this time no instructions were given regarding the segregation and movement of the POWs.[29]

On Koje-do the Communists found a way to continue the war by means other than uniformed armies arrayed in battle and subjected to attack. At Panmunjom, the Communist negotiators at last had an angle with which to attack voluntary repatriation. Nam Il crowed, "The unshakable fact is that public confessions by the commandant of your prisoner-of-war camp indicate that you have engaged in an endless series of blood-shedding incidents which you justified by your so-called screening to detain the prisoners forcibly."[30]

Admiral Joy worried how the Communist delegates actively exploited the POW situation to provoke the UNC either to compromise or to terminate conference talks. On Clark's first day of command, Joy urged that "the issue must now be squarely faced." That is, either the UNC would make its position plain and risk terminating the negotiations as a statement of resolve, or the Communists would be allowed to use Panmunjom as a forum of propaganda without any penalty for delaying a final settlement. It would then be up to the UNC to make concessions to break the logjam.[31]

As the JCS took up Clark's endorsement of Joy's proposal to announce a unilateral suspension of the conference, Van Fleet at last moved to reestablish control over Koje-do. On May 14, he issued his own instructions to Boatner, emphasizing the need to regain discipline and control over Koje-do. Van Fleet also dispatched two Commonwealth (one British and one Canadian) infantry companies, one Greek infantry company, the 430th Engineer Construction Battalion, three American tank companies, and the Third Battalion, Ninth Infantry. Three days later, Clark's 187th Airborne Regimental Combat Team arrived to give Boatner overwhelming fighting power: 14,000 troops and four dozen tanks.[32]

Boatner had unusual experience for an American general in Korea. He had served two years as a junior officer in the Fifteenth Infantry Regiment stationed in Tianjin (Tientsin), China, and four years as a Chinese language student between the wars. During World War II, he was Lt. Gen. Joseph "Vinegar Joe" Stilwell's chief of staff, spending forty-four months as a senior leader in the Chinese army. Fluent in Chinese, he understood the unique military mentality of the Chinese soldier. He employed both his experience and talents to formulate a deliberate military plan to solve the Koje-do crisis.[33]

Initially, Boatner did nothing regarding the POWs, but he expressed his displeasure "with just about everything he saw—from the array of uniforms, lax discipline, and general sloppiness." One directive he did issue immediately was to lift the ban on guards carrying loaded weapons.[34] Meanwhile, he reorganized his own forces to ensure no missteps when it came time to move aggressively. Gradually, the American troops (reinforced with Dutch, Australian, British, and ROK forces) restored their presence among the compounds and set to repairing wire fences, relocating guard towers outside of the POW compounds, and, on the arrival of building materials, began construction of five-hundred-man compounds within new and properly secured enclosures. The construction effort was considered the most decisive, and so Boatner refrained from making any provocative moves until the new compounds were ready to be occupied. Work on the new enclosures proceeded rapidly with workers on a two, twelve-hour shift day, seven days a week.[35]

Simultaneous with construction, Boatner began giving precisely calibrated orders to the POWs, using direct language and expecting to be obeyed. He felt it was important that prisoners received time limits for compliance, and that adequate force was on hand and visible should compliance not be forthcoming. Other measures Boatner took included the removal of unreliable ROK guards, the relocation of the island's civilian population, and the assignment of a FEC military lawyer as an inspector general "to insure that my orders and conduct were in accordance with the Geneva Conventions." He never negotiated with the POWs or acknowledged "their association." These small-scale engagements had the desired effect: POWs got used to being controlled and the American guard force gained confidence in using a combination of restraint and coercion.[36]

Boatner tolerated no ambiguity about who was in charge on Koje-do. He later wrote, "I was effective in these incidents because I was polite and dignified and I assumed I would be obeyed and did not act apologetically. I made very certain that I was understood and then when necessary I acted firmly and decisively."[37] Boatner's troops moved deliberately to implement Operation Breakup. New enclosures constructed on Koje-do's south side and two islands off Koje's southern coast, Yoncho-do and Pongam-do, all fell under the command of POW Camp 1 and consisted of four to eight compounds, each with accommodations for five hundred POWs.[38] Clark called it an operation planned "as carefully as for any orthodox military campaign. . . . We knew the Communist POWs were active combatants and had to be dealt with as soldiers, not prisoners in the traditional sense."[39] Troops first used tanks and bayonets to move into some of the compounds to remove communist signs and banners. Three days later American infantry backed by tanks moved into Compound 607 and split the compound into two sectors, divided by a barbed wire fence. No resistance was encountered, but the Communists knew the final blow was imminent.[40]

That blow fell on June 10, a month after Dodd's release. Paratroopers with leveled bayonets used tear gas and concussion grenades to break into Compound 76 and overcome prisoner phalanxes armed with improvised spears, swords, knives, gasoline bombs, and rocks. The melee lasted three hours before the prisoners realized they faced overwhelming force, and the crisis quickly petered out as the ringleaders were identified and captured. One US soldier was killed and fourteen injured; thirty-one POWs died and another 131 suffered injuries, mostly from the concussion grenades. POWs in Compounds 78 and 77 submitted without resistance or incident (fifteen POWs, presumably anti-communist, were found dead shortly after Compound 77 was vacated).[41] No other incidents occurred over the next ten days as pro-communist prisoners were forcibly relocated to smaller more secure compounds where they could be controlled.

Although those accepting voluntary repatriation relocated to secure camps on the mainland or Cheju-do island, and casualties were low relative to the number of hostile POWs extracted and moved to other more secure enclosures and camps, the Communists at Panmunjom milked the Koje-do incident for all it was worth, extolling their martyrs and heaping abuse on Maj. Gen. William K. Harrison, who had replaced Admiral Joy on May 22 as the lead UNC delegate.[42] The Dodd incident had inflicted significant short-term damage to the UNC's moral position as it gave those who wanted to believe in the UNC's brutality the opportunity to do so. It also called into question the competence of the UNC's POW screening program and therefore threatened to undermine Truman's voluntary repatriation objective. Furthermore, the disturbances underscored a reality that dawned slowly on the Americans. This was no mere "incident." It was a full-fledged communist offen-

Figure 9.1 Communist soldiers arriving at their new POW compound, June 1952.
Source: Norman Isler.

sive, "another battle" in which the POWs "obviously considered themselves
still combatants . . . ready to attack and attempt to overwhelm our troops."[43]
It was war by other means.

Fortunately for the UNC, the effort to segregate and limit the size of the
new prisoner compounds (in some cases compound populations declined
from five to seven thousand down to five hundred or fewer) made future
prisoner-led disturbances very difficult if not impossible to execute. Organized prisoner resistance to voluntary repatriation was never again as effective as it was in May. Therefore, the long-term consequence of the "second
front" campaign evolved as a moral and strategic advantage for the UNC.
The Americans moved to implement the rescreening process that proved unencumbered by further prisoner disturbances or communist objections. Recalcitrant prisoners were effectively isolated and unable to further influence
the UNC's position on voluntary repatriation. POWs were informed specifically of their rights and limitations as prisoners and the actual mechanics of
repatriation options. Eventually it was determined that 83,000 POWs would
not resist repatriation and would return to Communist control—an increase
of 13,000 from the original screening estimate.[44] More than 14,200 Chinese
POWs would exercise their option to repatriate to Taiwan instead of returning

to Communist China. This was a stinging blow to Mao, one that could only be assuaged through significant battlefield action in the summer of 1953.[45]

The ROK Constitutional Crisis

South Korea was a nation still prostrate after forty years of Japanese exploitation. The five years between liberation and the outbreak of the war were substantially lost in the multiple crises of food shortages, disease, and sociopolitical turmoil that finally erupted into civil violence. Two years after the North Korean invasion, some estimates claimed that from a prewar population of thirty million, one of every nine South Korean men, women, and children had been killed as a result of the war. An additional ten million were wounded, sick, displaced, or homeless in a country whose infrastructure was thoroughly wrecked. Inflation was out of control and agriculture production had fallen by a third. The military had first claim on the nation's resources, wealth, and human potential.[46]

By the time the tactical stalemate had produced the strategic frustration of the summer of 1952, Syngman Rhee had been struggling for over half a century to liberate and unify Korea. It had been an all-consuming task, relentlessly pursued. Rhee had rarely seen eye to eye with American policy toward Korea, especially that which appeared to leave Korea to its own fate prior to 1950. Consequently, Clark recognized "that [Rhee] had come to identify himself as the living embodiment of Korean patriotism, the sole prophet who could show the way to unity and freedom for Koreans. Opposition to Rhee's ideas seemed to him to be anti-Korean, not anti-Rhee." He was, continued Clark, a man to be respected because of his determination and single-minded patriotism, but also one who was "as exasperating an ally as anyone could have."[47]

Rhee's confidence in himself was borne out time and again in his dealings with his reluctant patrons. The American prewar occupation commander, Lt. Gen. John R. Hodge, did not care for the manipulative ways, blustering rhetoric, sycophantic street thugs, and high appeals to democratic principles on display whenever Rhee disagreed with occupation policy. When confronted with the consequences of failing to work within American policy, as happened on numerous occasions during the war, Rhee broke out in self-serving rants, accusing the Americans of being faithless, dupes, or immoral appeasers. During the summer of 1952, Rhee told the American ambassador, John Muccio, that not only was President Truman "ill-informed" about Korean government, but that the president, his administration, and the ambassador all should "have more confidence in [Rhee] and in his reputation as [an] upholder, not destroyer, of democracy." Anyone who disagreed with Rhee or his methods not only was guilty of being "taken in by bad elements in Korea" but also ran the risk of "destroy[ing] affection Korean people" held for Americans.[48]

Rhee tirelessly advocated the expansion of the ROK army at American expense, along with a limitless flow of arms, equipment, and resources to put the youth of Korea into uniform. With the experience of the Chinese Fifth Campaign still recent memory, Van Fleet, Ridgway, and Clark held their peace and worked behind the scenes to make the ROK army better before making it bigger. That patient approach did not sit well with Rhee. He never understood the reluctance to confront and destroy the communist enemy in Korea, and he was unafraid to be vocal about it. Paik Sun-yup remembered Rhee's rhetoric at the inauguration of the ROK II Corps in April 1952. "Our army now has the personnel and the material resources to fight. We must punch through the barbarians and advance north, unifying the entire country," Rhee intoned.[49] He was not kidding, and although many American officers privately agreed with the Korean patriot, *puk chin* ("go north") was an empty slogan that promised little more than higher casualties and greater strain on an already strained UNC coalition.

During the months of military crisis and fluidity along the front lines, it was easy to look past these political differences. But in the summer of 1952, Rhee was increasingly fearful that the Americans' insistence to come to terms with the Communists would leave Korea divided. Compounding his fears was the state of South Korean politics, which were not favorable to Rhee personally. Over the previous six years Rhee had neutralized many capable Korean political leaders because of their personal opposition to him. Whatever could be said about the ROK president, he was an autocrat, a man used to getting his way. As in the United States, 1952 was an election year. The ROK constitution provided for indirect election, through the National Assembly, for the office of president. The Korean National Party, the largest of Rhee's political support groups, suffered heavily just one month before the North Korean invasion, winning only twenty-four seats for its 154 candidates in the May 1950 elections. Independents emerged as the most powerful legislative force, with 126 members. As the war continued, Rhee's support appeared to be dwindling even further, aggravated by spiraling inflation, resentment, and factionalism among Rhee's own cabinet on domestic issues. In January 1952, the National Assembly decisively rejected Rhee's proposed constitutional amendment to place the election in front of the people at large. In a society where "face" is everything, and for a man as personally driven as Rhee was to be Korea's savior, he could not countenance anything but an affirmative vote. His political gravitas stalemated as effectively as the armistice talks at Panmunjom. The Americans feared he would use the crisis and an extralegal solution "to establish a personal machine which henceforth will stifle all opposition."[50]

Rhee's solution was simple. On May 24 he declared martial law for the regions around Pusan (the wartime seat of government) and then had his most strident political enemies arrested when the National Assembly balked at reconsidering a change to the constitution. Rhee ignored a National Assembly vote to terminate martial law, and by the next day Rhee's police arrested the most "unreliable" assemblymen and intimidated enough of the rest to prevent further quorums from an embarrassing vote to end martial law.[51] Rhee's street machine broke up any demonstrations with brutal efficiency. The political theater then turned serious as Rhee's henchmen, led by the new Home Minister Yi Pom-suk, threatened to recall ROK divisions from the front. When Rhee talked about dissolving the National Assembly and reseating one that would return the required constitutional vote, the Americans prepared to hit the panic button.[52]

Rhee miscalculated. Washington immediately communicated its displeasure that martial law had the potential to exacerbate the already fragile state of South Korean politics. Even more pressing from the JCS perspective was the possibility of the UNC's member nations withdrawing their active support for Rhee's regime and the American effort to save it. Rhee's actions were so extreme, the Americans feared a pro-communist revolt in the Eighth Army's rear area. Clark advised the JCS that should Rhee move forward with his threats to dissolve the National Assembly or otherwise manipulate the constitutional process to assure himself another presidential term, the consequences "might endanger the supply lines of the 8th Army and the mil[itary] situation in general. In the event that such disturbances seriously interfere with mil[itary] operations, it will be necessary for me to assume control."[53]

Tough talk from General Clark who only days before assumed command in the Far East, and whose political experience was limited to two years of military governance in postwar Austria.[54] Despite Clark's assurance, the fact was that the Americans were not in a strong position to be decisive. Despite a stern warning from President Truman on June 2 that "it would be a tragic mockery of the great sacrifices in blood and treasure which the people of many free nations and of Korea have made in the past two years if any changes considered necessary in the political structure of the ROK cannot be carried out in accordance with due process of law," Rhee informed his cabinet of his intent to present the National Assembly with an ultimatum.[55] They would have twenty-four hours to pass his constitutional amendment or he would dissolve the assembly. Ambassador Muccio reported to Washington rumors that thousands of Rhee supporters were projected to descend on Pusan. On Rhee's orders, ROK security forces were not to impede the mobs; indeed, Muccio suspected that Rhee's martial law commander, General Won Yong-duk, along with home minister Yi, had generated the hysteria surrounding the political crisis. General Won liberally used his authority to detain recalcitrant assemblymen and generally to put South Kyongsang province under lockdown.[56] Clark also saw the "popular protests" in Rhee's favor as staged for American and international consumption. These were crude and simpleton-like methods aimed at coercing the UNC to turn away from the ROK's internal turmoil.[57]

Of additional concern to the UNC and the US State Department was the growing evidence of antiforeignism, which Muccio ascribed to Rhee's exhaustion and his inability to control or influence his more xenophobic supporters. After a personal engagement with the president, Muccio reported, "I have just spent the most futile hour with Pres[ident] Rhee I have ever spent with him. . . . I mentioned my concern over the posters throughout the city damning foreigners for interfering with Korean affairs." Rhee immediately turned to his "chief of the palace guard, Capt[ain] Kim" and berated him loudly in Korean. Rhee then tried to turn the tables, decrying Truman's ignorance in attempting to influence what was a Korean problem and using the machinery of the United Nations and threats to withhold much-needed economic assistance. Muccio concluded, "I have been forced to the conclusion that we cannot expect effective leadership from Pres[ident] Rhee."[58]

The pressure was on Clark to generate a credible military option to rein in President Rhee. E. Allan Lightner, the chargé in Pusan, worried openly that Clark and Van Fleet failed to communicate the seriousness of the American position to Rhee, which simply emboldened him to wait out the opposition. The idea to use force to overthrow Syngman Rhee and replace him with some other candidate was distasteful, as Clark recognized that the Eighth Army had neither the troops nor the desire to fight against the ROK government and its paramilitary—or worst case, army—forces. Clark warned his diplomat counterparts that unless the overall military situation were drastically threatened, any plan to use force against Rhee would be a bluff, as the UNC could not spare troops from the front, Koje-do, or Japan to hold Pusan as well. Furthermore, there was no figure in the ROK who possessed Rhee's stature or ability to maintain political conditions favorable to the UNC's ground forces. Clark believed the United States "might well have to swallow pride . . . and go on working with Rhee even after watching him overthrow democracy."[59]

Lightner disdained Clark's and Van Fleet's reluctance to confront Rhee, and after the war he claimed that ROK chief of staff Lee Chong-chan stopped by Lightner's quarters one evening and offered to place Rhee, Yi, and Won under house arrest, without any American action or bloodshed. Lee (according to Lightner) then promised that once a new government was formed, the army would back out of the political scene. The potential solution was clean, if a suitable candidate could be found, and Lightner was confident one could.

Clark, on the other hand, bungled his chance early to influence Rhee by stating the UNC did not care about Korean politics so long as the lines of communication and logistics remained and that the front-line forces could fight. "Well," said Lightner, "that's all Rhee needed [to hear]."[60]

Lightner's story is incredible as the ROK army remained studiously aloof from the political chaos in Pusan. With the exception of the martial law commander, nearly all ROK senior officers appeared supportive of the constitutional process. A State Department summary of options and consequences of American intervention cited Eighth Army intelligence conclusions indicating "the leaders of the ROK armed forces appear to be solidly against Rhee's tactics. This is the most important asset we have in this crisis . . . we should take care not to stimulate involvement of the ROK armed force in politics, after General Van Fleet and KMAG have put so much successful effort into taking them out of politics." Further encouragement was the probability that even if Rhee rescinded his delegation of control over ROK forces to the UNC, "Korean military leaders would ignore such an act and remain loyal to the UNC."[61]

As the crisis deepened, the JCS instructed Clark to come up with a plan that could be executed with little to no warning. In early July, Clark finally informed the JCS that he was prepared "to take action in case widespread disorders affecting my mission suddenly break out," but he preferred that any action taken would be informed by a political decision from the countries involved in the UNC. Clark's plan, Operation Everready, was simple, but it failed to account for Rhee's suspicious nature and his unquenchable desire to lead a unified Korea under his terms. The president would be "invited to visit Seoul or elsewhere" on some pretext to get him out of Pusan. Then, a designated UNC commander—presumably an American with American troops— would move in and arrest key Rhee supporters, establish security of all UNC installations, and exercise martial law control through the ROK chief of staff Lee Chong-chan. Rhee would then be informed of the fait accompli and "urged to sign a proclamation lifting martial law" while permitting freedom of action to the National Assembly and liberties of press and radio without interference by Rhee supporters that Muccio called "goon squads." If Rhee refused to cooperate, then Clark would work through the ROK prime minister to gain the same result. If that option likewise failed, for any reason, the UNC would then "take further steps [for] a UNC interim gov[ernment]."[62]

Clark never had to execute the coup. After five weeks of martial law and staged demonstrations and protests, the opposition had had enough. By July 3, Rhee's strong-arm tactics had worked. After an eight-hour meeting with Van Fleet, Rhee finally allowed ten anti-Rhee assemblymen to be freed, but the National Assembly still amended the constitution, allowing Rhee to stand in a popular contest. Martial law was lifted on July 28, but the issue was never in doubt, with Rhee winning a second term by an overwhelming margin (5.2 million out of 7 million total votes cast). Two weeks later General Clark sent a begrudgingly congratulatory message to Rhee. The Americans recognized the fact that Rhee's ability to manipulate Korea's internal conditions bore significantly on the UNC's overall mission to terminate the war while maintaining the security and interests of the United States in east Asia. Although never implemented, Operation Everready remained on the shelf to the very end of the conflict.[63]

The Propaganda Campaign Intensifies

The debacle at Koje-do had put the Americans on strategic defense, and it sapped the UNC's April 28 package offer of its diplomatic strength at a time when the political content of the talks had assumed significant proportions. In a flawless *jujitsu* move, the Communist delegates at Panmunjom had parried American military strength into a moral liability. But POW disturbances were not the only uncomfortable surprise. The Chinese in particular found their own propaganda theme, and the timing coincidence between the UNC repatriation proposals and increasingly aggressive germ warfare accusations suggest a deliberate linkage. The North Korean government claimed as early as May 1951 that American planes had sprayed smallpox virus on their territory, but no one took that allegation seriously. However, a full-scale blitz occurred beginning February 2, 1952, in the UN General Assembly. Soviet ambassador Yakov Malik announced that the UNC had employed toxic gases and biological agents in North Korea, sparking outbreaks of smallpox and typhoid. By the end of the month, both Pyongyang and Beijing radio picked up the charge and ran it farther down the field. In addition to dropping "germ bombs," American airmen were guilty of releasing infected flies, snails, and rodents. Communist newspapers throughout the world picked up these "stories," and a worried UNC held a special press conference on March 6 to deny the allegations.[64]

Although logically false—flies, snails, and rodents could not be expected to survive a fall from high altitude in the dead of a Manchurian winter—the allegations of germ warfare constituted a significant challenge to the credibility of the UNC and its legitimacy in intervening in Korea. Importantly, the Communists acted as if the allegations were true, going so far as to initiate public health and propaganda campaigns aimed at their own soldiers as well as world public opinion.[65] Just a few weeks into the new year, the Chinese released the first two of thirty-eight "confessions" from American pilots, admitting to participating in an illegal campaign to spread disease among innocent civilians. The effect was to put the UNC on trial for war crimes. In the public's perception it was even more damaging than the prisoner riots, since there was no way the United States could prove its innocence while prosecuting an aerial bombardment campaign specifically designed to destroy North Korea's infrastructure and undermine its will to resist. As a barometer of the damage that germ warfare allegations inflicted on the UNC, General Clark's memoirs devoted substantial space to refuting the idea that American or allied air forces dispersed bacteriological agents from the air.[66]

The Chinese were sophisticated advocates of the germ war idea. Their claims of UNC planes flying over Manchuria to drop "black flies," "a kind of flea," and another insect similar "to both ticks and small spiders" were specific enough to be credible but also completely unverifiable.[67] As Clark noted, such claims accomplished several objectives, few of which had to do with a good faith effort to end the war in Korea. Should the charges stick at all and play a role in limiting offensive air activity in Korea, that would be welcome relief, but it was clear that the real target was domestic and international political opinion. As explanations for poor harvests, unchecked rampage of smallpox and other lethal communicable disease, and failing progress of public medical care, the grainy images of Chinese peasants picking up black specks in the snow, over captions reading, "germ-laden flies" dropped from American planes, carried a lot of weight. At the same time, the Communists produced written "peace appeals" from captured American personnel, urging the UNC to soften their stance on repatriation.[68] As a foil to the Americans' broadly trumpeted refrain of opportunity and freedom, the twin pillars holding up (at least publicly) the voluntary repatriation policy, biological warfare allegations were peerless.[69]

Maj. Gen. William K. Harrison, who had joined the UNC delegation on January 23, 1952, assumed the unpleasant duty of confronting the Communist propaganda offensive. A scion of American nobility, a devout Christian, inquisitive scholar, and experienced soldier, Harrison demonstrated his suitability to replace Joy, but he was asked to accomplish much without a lot of political or military support.[70] His reliance on the Bible and the Lord, who "put those words in my mouth," may have discomfited some, but he impressed his own delegation with his calm and cheerful demeanor—no mean feat given the circumstances—and his utter contempt for the Communists, "whom he considered as common criminals."[71]

His seemingly bizarre and nonchalant behavior made a strong impression on the Chinese and Korean negotiators. Colonel Chai called him "uneducated and uncivilized"; Harrison would have considered that a compliment.[72] A 1917 West Point graduate (Ridgway, Collins, and Clark were his classmates), Harrison had no illusions about his position: "The only good way to have an armistice is to initiate discussions when the enemy is really defeated."[73] Otherwise, the Communists had little incentive to negotiate but plenty of opportunity to talk. "They would meet there with us and they would say what they wanted to say which would be for propaganda and had nothing to do with getting an armistice." Harrison admired their skillful exploitation of media and the staged news conference. "They use words in the same—for same purpose that they use bullets. . . . Same thing exactly." A frustrated Harrison later reflected, "We were just playing their game for them—that was all we were doing."[74]

Harrison was no fool. He knew that he had a part to play in the war, and he was intent to make every day count and do his best to convince the Communists the UNC had presented its final proposal. He gave his team firm instructions to break off plenary sessions and subdelegate meetings when the Communists became outrageous or abusive. The Communists knew him as the delegate who would walk in and then walk out, often after less than five minutes in the tent. Harrison himself set the record by walking out of a subcommittee meeting after only fifteen seconds. When he did not feel like getting up, he would sit disrespectfully, pretending to be bored as he listened to one diatribe after another. His biggest complaint was that "their propaganda does not even have literary value."[75]

Militarily, Clark was willing to increase pressure from the air, but that was about all. There would be no major UNC offensive as in the previous fall to give the Communists something to worry about. Washington determined almost immediately that there would be no breakdown in the talks, at least not that would be construed as the UNC's responsibility. Although the JCS wanted Joy (and subsequently Harrison) to "take greater advantage . . . to engage in a propaganda and psychological offensive against the Communists," Harrison saw he had little to work with. A week after the Koje-do riots, Bradley recognized the delegates were "in worse shape . . . now than [they] were a few days ago."[76] The Communists had the initiative, and there was no way for Harrison to talk tough or to take the offensive in the war of words. He had to sit and listen to hours of invective that Nam Il and his colleagues could dish out with gusto. In short, he was captain of a team playing defense.

Prior to his retirement, Joy outlined for Clark the UNC's fundamental negotiating situation and the disadvantages the current policy of continued meetings with communist delegates caused. By appearing uncommitted to the April 28 proposal, the UNC delegates had convinced the Communists that they were not serious about the finality of their stand and that further concessions were likely, even expected, through the constant repetition of "vituperation and abuse which, although unfounded, leaves the [UNC] delegation with the only alternative of becoming mired in a propaganda morass." The

Americans had to figure out their own strategic approach to exploit the aftermath of Koje-do while attempting to regain the initiative on prisoner screening and convincing the Communists to agree to voluntary repatriation.[77]

Clark soon realized that the status quo was an unacceptable means by which to win the armistice terms that Truman had laid out for Ridgway the previous July. The talks were supposed to be limited to military factors only, which by mid-1952 had declined to minor importance. In trying to negotiate his own side's policy constraints, Clark began by recommending to the JCS that the delegates be authorized to present to the Communists the final tally of POWs to be repatriated, and then to be prepared, pending Communist rejection, to recess unilaterally the talks "until such time as the Communists accept our offer or break [off the] negotiations." Clark intended to exercise this course of action once the situation on Koje-do was satisfactorily resolved.[78]

Clark's play was a bold one, which would have shaken the Communists' position by denying them a forum to prosecute the war of words with immunity. It probably would have provoked a Chinese military reaction earlier in the year, but it is doubtful that the Communists would have been sufficiently impressed to give in on POW repatriation. The military situation was not as bad as it had been eight months previously when they had conceded the actual line of contact as the final military demarcation line. Air interdiction had not starved the Communist armies, and the lack of UNC ground pressure did not jeopardize their field forces in any meaningful way.

Political logic overrode Clark's strategic objections. On June 5, the JCS informed Clark that the delegates would have to continue meeting at Panmunjom, as the UN allies would not support a unilateral suspension of talks, and the administration worried that a suspension would give the Soviets an opening in the United Nations Security Council, which they chaired in the month of June, to link other questions with a Korean settlement. Even after the Communists subjected the UNC delegates "to a particularly vicious and emotional type of propaganda," continuing to charge "slaughter" of Chinese and North Korean prisoners, they insisted on meeting in plenary session each day, and Harrison had to sit and endure a constant stream of berating and insulting language.[79] The only relief the JCS was prepared to offer Clark was permission to "indicate without explanation [the delegation's] inability to meet for 2 or 3 days so that UNC Del[egation] is not placed in pos[ition] of being continuously responsive to Communist urging for m[eetings]."[80] Clark's argument that communist "statements" at Panmunjom amounted to nothing more than propaganda with "no bearing on the problem at hand [of achieving an armistice]" failed to move the Joint Chiefs. International considerations were paramount.[81]

With Clark's backing, Harrison declared a unilateral recess on June 7. The

Communists objected strenuously, recognizing that without a forum at Panmunjom, their diplomatic offensive would be effectively blunted. Nam Il insisted on meeting the next day, but Harrison replied, "Your side can surely come to the meeting tomorrow, but our side won't attend." He then stood up and left, saying only that he would return on June 11.[82] The Communists were beside themselves. On June 9, they informed General Clark of the deplorable UNC stance on voluntary repatriation, the only "problem preventing an armistice." They further accused Harrison of refusing to negotiate, refusing to explain UNC statements, and "even refusing to come to the [delegate] meetings."[83] Clark remained unmoved and supported Harrison's walk-out tactics. The shift in tenor at Panmunjom was matched by increased aggressiveness in central Korea as the two sides clashed over a small outpost known as Old Baldy.

In late June the UNC had completed rescreening its POWs in a carefully controlled process observed by the International Red Cross and members of the press. Clark was now confident in his numbers and reported to the JCS the final accounting: 62,169 North Koreans, 6,388 Chinese, 4,560 South Koreans, and 9,954 civilian internees for a total of 83,071 out of 169,938 prisoners desired repatriation. Rather than causing relief that the 70,000 number was revised upward, the JCS and other Department of State experts worried that releasing the new figure would actually complicate the UNC's position, implying that the more the Communists stalled at Panmunjom, the higher the number of repatriates would grow. On the same day (July 3) that Clark informed the JCS of his readiness to make the numbers public, Harrison reported that the Communist delegation appeared to make a significant concession to the UNC's position and desired to enter in executive sessions. But five days later no progress had been made, as the Communists continued to insist on 20,000 Chinese repatriates and a "realistic" number of Koreans. American diplomats feared the Communists had misunderstood previous statements and assumed the UNC was preparing its *own* concessions.[84]

On July 13, General Harrison presented the UNC's final tally of repatriate POWs that included 6,400 Chinese. The reaction was not a happy one as the Chinese delegates again demanded the return of all 20,000 of their countrymen. The talks recessed for six days, but when the two sides came back together, the Communists had hardened their position further. They now required the return of 116,000 POWs. Harrison was exasperated. Clark fumed and suspected that something was up. Chinese forces were then in the middle of a large-scale engagement over Old Baldy, which the Americans seized in early June. It appeared the Communists were now resorting to military pressure to support their propaganda offensive and position at Panmunjom.[85]

In response, on July 26, Harrison informed the Communist delegates that because recent talks "had been futile" the UNC was observing a seven-day recess. After a plenary session that lasted only thirty-two minutes, with no prospect for progress, Harrison requested another seven-day recess, which the Communists granted. In August, the UNC upped the pressure by unilaterally recessing for seven days at a time, which the Chinese dubbed "the first escalation of the 'escaping the meeting' tactic."[86] Plenary sessions would convene only six more times in the next two months, many of these meetings lasting only half an hour. With no constructive proposals coming from the communist side, and Van Fleet's own pessimism deepening, it appeared that the deadlock was complete. On July 31 Van Fleet informed reporters, "Present trends show less chance for an armistice than ever before," while the US Defense Department tabulated American war dead in Korea at 19,979 with another 93,709 wounded and missing.[87]

The Air Pressure Campaign

Following the presentation of Admiral Joy's "package proposal" to the Communist negotiators on April 28, the UNC's worst fears materialized. There was neither momentum at Panmunjom nor adequate military options at acceptable cost available to Ridgway. The war was stalemated both politically and militarily. It would be Clark's decision how to attempt to break the impasse. He saw the outcomes of American policy in the Far East in stark terms. The UNC had to win the war, get an armistice, or get out of Korea—while still defending Japan. Ground forces alone were unlikely to accomplish either of the two positive objectives at an acceptable cost, and the UNC's air superiority appeared to be scoring only modest gains at best. However, immunity from enemy air attack *did* provide Van Fleet with a significant military advantage off-setting the Communists' preponderance in manpower and their strong defensive positions. Once again airpower appeared to offer a way to maintain military pressure against the Communists and hold their forces in place while inflicting damage at relatively low cost. Although Communist forces continued to gain strength in resources and manpower in the summer of 1952, prolonged air attack had made an effective general Chinese offensive highly unlikely, but the Americans admitted "that the Communists were not being subjected to intolerable pressure by the rail [interdiction] attacks [as] indicated by their . . . obstructionist maneuvers at the armistice negotiations."[88] Behind their lines, nothing moved by day; by dawn trains and trucks were camouflaged or tucked into tunnels and caves. They remained immobile until dusk, when the Communists' logistics tail began to snake forward again, but now the network was so dispersed as to offer few lucrative targets to the inefficient nighttime B-26 attacks.[89] Although not on a scale of the Fifth Campaign, in the autumn of 1952 the Chinese would demonstrate tactical and operational offensive capabilities, showing that despite tremendous UNC efforts the CPVF still packed a significant fighting punch. Clark recognized that the key strategic question was how to make the Communists see the war the same way Washington did.[90]

The next evolution of air targeting, which developed substantially against civilian infrastructure targets, was in fact a deliberate effort to push the Communists to accept the UNC's position at Panmunjom, as opposed to destroying their ground forces. In March 1952, FEAF planners presented Ridgway options to attack North Korea's hydroelectric dams. Ridgway refused over political concerns that the dams' primary use was for civilian power, but the desire to do something was overpowering. A FEAF staff study in April pointed out that rail interdiction was indecisive and wasteful of airpower's strategic potential. The Americans were exchanging half-million-dollar aircraft and trained pilots for the occasional truck, train locomotive, small supply dump, or a few enemy troops. According to its authors, the best way FEAF could contribute to a useful and early settlement of the war was "by inflicting maximum pressure on the enemy by causing him permanent loss." Trucks, train tracks, and locomotives were easily replaced, but air pressure directed at "supplies, equipment, facilities, and personnel as would represent a permanent loss and accumulative drain to the enemy's strength" was something else entirely.[91]

The air pressure strategy (APS) developed that spring was specifically conceived to address the doctrinal and technical weaknesses that had undermined Strangle and Saturate. Interdiction struck directly at the enemy's capability to continue fighting and only indirectly at his will. The intransigence of communist negotiators at the height of the interdiction campaign appeared to support this interpretation. The APS, however, intended to attack both capability and will directly and simultaneously by inflicting maximum punishment on military related facilities and infrastructure that were also essential for civilian livelihood and well-being. Clark was about to cross a line that Ridgway dared not approach.[92]

Under the APS plan, interdiction attacks declined significantly from May to July, such that army units reported an increase in communist activity, effective artillery fire, and UNC casualties.[93] Even FEAF's intelligence chief, Brig. Gen. Charles Y. Banfill, warned "although rail interdiction may not prove decisive, statistical evidence indicates that immediate resumption of the rail interdiction program is warranted." The FEAF targeting committee generally "agreed that a limited amount of air effort would have to be employed" to keep North Korean railways at suboptimal efficiency, but interdiction would not be permitted to interfere with "the primary purpose of our program," meaning the strategic air pressure campaign.[94]

The fact was that the air force had tired of the unprofitable interdiction effort that appeared to do little but risk valuable aircraft and trained pilots for ephemeral damage to the Communists. The APS was therefore billed as a shift in emphasis to attack better targets rather than a new interdiction campaign so as not to arouse army suspicions regarding the availability of additional close air support sorties (although Fifth Air Force did agree in July to increase its close support in response to Van Fleet's request).[95] Rail bridges and marshalling yards remained scheduled as secondary targets to be bombed only if pilots were unable to strike their primary targets. Sorties dedicated to interdiction tended to focus on roads and truck traffic, but no serious effort was made to challenge communist lines of communication beyond infrequent attacks focused in time and limited in scope.[96]

In June, FEAF commander General Weyland presented Clark a broadened campaign to attack the Japanese-constructed hydroelectric power plants along the Yalu River, arguing intelligence assessments judged that North Korea had reconstituted many war industries in dispersed and underground locations that operated with electricity from these facilities. Clark approved the addition of these power-generating facilities to the target list, the most important of which was the Suiho (Supung) plant, a well-designed and modern installation responsible for supplying 10 percent of electric power to Manchuria. It was the largest generating plant in the East, and the fourth largest in the world. As a target, Suiho presented unique technical challenges. The dam, a massive concrete structure 349 feet high and 2,950 feet long, was a problematic target, but FEAF targeteers assessed that the destruction of nearby transformers and powerhouse buildings might make it unnecessary to strike the dam itself. Other power generators at Fusen (Pujon), Choshin (Changjin), and Kyosen (Pungsan) rounded out the target system, and their destruction was expected to disrupt North Korean and Chinese industrial production. In Washington, Hoyt Vandenberg convinced the JCS to remove targeting restrictions on the Yalu power plants, and Clark, sensing this may be his strongest ace to use to get a settlement, agreed to set June 23 or 24 as the start of the new air offensive.[97]

At 1601 hours (local time), June 23, 1952, more than five hundred air force, navy, and marine corps aircraft descended on all four power plants. The most spectacular part of the air assault was the attack on the Suiho plant, involving 108 F-86s, 79 F-84s, 45 F-80s, 35 AD-4 Skyraiders, and 35 F-9F Panthers. The navy F-9Fs, flying from carriers based in the East Sea, swooped in first to suppress air defenses; three dozen Skyraiders with 5,000-pound loads followed. Ten minutes later, the air force F-84s and F-80s arrived to continue the pummeling, while the F-86 Sabres provided air cover, which proved to be unnecessary. A total of two hundred tons of bombs demolished the target area. Photo reconnaissance showed the plant to be completely out of commission.[98] Some two hundred MiG-15s remained idle at Antung. No Chinese MiGs rose to contest the blitz, and the cost was only two American aircraft lost. It was a magnificent display of airpower, "brilliant and effective," and called by one historian "the outstanding strategic air strike of the war."[99]

By 1800 hours that day electric power production in North Korea abruptly halted. Additional attacks succeeded at demolishing nearly 90 percent of the Yalu's electric power, plunging much of North Korea and neighboring regions reaching as far as central Manchuria and northern China in darkness and severely curtailing Chinese industrial production. Fifth Air Force fighter-bombers returned to Fusen and Choshin plants, and navy bombers struck Kyosen. All plants showed continuing fires and smoke, indicative of the severe damage and the surprise obtained that the Communists were unprepared to respond to such devastating attacks. Two more days of "mopping-up operations" provided the denouement, ripping up transmission lines and destroying transformers, substations, generator houses, and penstocks. By June 26, "all lights went out in North Korea."[100]

The anemic response to FEAF's devastating assault on these targets begs examination. Official communist sources claim inclement weather grounded their planes. The Soviet commander of the Sixty-Fourth Fighter Air Corps cited a powerful storm front with low clouds and heavy rains that completely blanketed the MiG bases around Antung. There would have been no chance for MiG pilots to land safely even if they succeeded in taking off and engaging the Americans. Given the level of damage FEAF did inflict on these critical targets, and the possibility of a massive strategic and propaganda victory if Communist airpower had successfully intervened, falling back on "weather" as an excuse seems inexcusable. However, as American sources suggest that MiGs in general that month were "conspicuous by their absence," it is likely that a rotation of inexperienced Chinese pilots was responsible.[101] Whatever the reason, the Communists had to face an uncomfortable truth that the Americans did possess a potent weapon if they chose to employ it. The successful attack put the Sino-Korean allies in a political dilemma. Who knew how far the Americans now might be willing to go, and with demonstrably inadequate air defenses effective resistance was unlikely. In other words, FEAF's air pressure operations had suddenly exposed a vulnerability in the Chinese's persistence strategy.[102]

July was even worse for the North Koreans. Nearly all of Kim Il-sung's industrial manufacturing was already destroyed, not to mention 600,000 houses, 5,000 schools, and 1,000 hospitals reduced to rubble. Industrial production was already 40 percent of its 1949 level.[103] Pyongyang had not been hit in nearly a year. Now it topped the list of military-industry-supply complexes slated for destruction. On July 11, 1952, every available fighter-interceptor, fighter-bomber, and attack plane, to include sixty-five B-29s, flew in Operation Pressure Pump—an eleven-hour assault—to blitz simultaneous targets in Pyongyang, Sariwon, and Hwangju. Attacking in three waves, the American and allied pilots bombed, strafed, and napalmed suspected factories, ammunition dumps, vehicle parks, repair shops, storage buildings, and military headquarters. The damage reported was "extensive" (Radio Pyongyang admitted 1,500 buildings destroyed), and air opposition was again negligible due to an effective F-86 screen that kept responding MiGs far from the battle.[104] Pyongyang was hit again at night by fifty-four Superforts, the largest nighttime strike of the war up to that point. The strike destroyed another six hundred buildings in and around the capital city, leaving "hardly a house standing on the surface." At the end of the month sixty-three B-29s demolished the Oriental Light Metals Company at Yangsi, a strategic asset located only five miles from the Yalu River that now made the target list. Once again, there was no effective opposition.[105]

Soldiers on the MLR were privately pleased at FEAF's new aggressiveness. Many felt the Chinese especially benefited from an unearned truce to regain their balance after the fall and early winter battles at the end of 1951.[106] The political consequences, however, were neither predicted nor positive. Many interpreted the UNC's aggressive posture as a provocative and counterproductive escalation. Allies, politicians, newspapermen, even other Air Force leaders questioned the utility of the hydroelectric attacks.[107] The British reaction was especially disturbing as it opened up a substantial misunderstanding regarding coercive tactics employed from the air and the degree of consultation with allies that Clark would undertake before making major military moves with political significance. The subsequent massive air raids against Pyongyang and other North Korean cities in July 1952 simply amplified the criticism.[108]

Despite the political fallout, no one told Clark to stop. In August the FEAF ratcheted up the pressure, swarming 1,104 air force and navy fighter-bomber sorties that month against Pyongyang alone.[109] In addition to fighter-bombers pummeling Pyongyang, B-29s hit a series of manufacturing targets on August 5 (Hoechang ore processing plant), August 11 (Hokusen steel mill), and August 13 (Anak supply center). In all cases, the bombers left a swath of destruction, leveling up to 90 percent of buildings and storage areas. The B-29s returned to Pyongyang and its surrounding areas on August 20, 23, 26, and 30 to blast other military facilities identified through photo reconnaissance and other intelligence sources.[110]

Unsurprisingly, Kim Il-sung loudly cried out for more material assistance and greater Chinese efforts to respond with something more than passive defense. The Soviets did agree to dispatch additional antiaircraft units, and both Chinese and Soviet air force commanders met with their North Korean counterparts at Antung to assess the measures that needed to be taken to strengthen air defense operations and protect key targets. But Mao declined to prosecute a large-scale offensive as a retaliation for FEAF's air attacks, and he rejected as unwise later North Korean demands for the PLAAF to bomb Seoul.[111]

An Asian delegate at the United Nations pointed out the precarious position in which the UNC had placed the world body, in whose name it was destroying North Korea to restore peace to the peninsula: "It seems to me to be a dangerous business, this policy of mass air attacks while the truce talks are going on. Knowing the Chinese, I think it likely that they would regard the signing of an armistice under such military pressure as a loss of face."[112] And this was precisely the dilemma Clark faced. The JCS recognized the paradox of explicitly using airpower to coerce an agreement was likely to "seriously engage" Communist prestige, and thereby reduce the chances for a settlement. For his part, Clark had to continue to treat the air pressure campaign as just another military option, something to do that did not carry heavy political expectations.[113]

This policy, of course, was a ridiculous proposition, and it demonstrated how deeply the Americans were enmeshed in the policy consequences of fighting a limited war they did not want to fight. The application of pure force whether in the form of aerial assault or turning loose the Eighth Army risked undermining the UNC military strategy's moral influence over the North Koreans and Chinese. From voluntary prisoner repatriation to strategic air attack to increased pressure on the ground, the Chinese in particular were unlikely to yield and willingly agree to a cease-fire that looked like defeat. Some other political or moral path to victory would have to be found.

10

THE SUMMER CAMPAIGN

AMERICAN STRATEGY FOR Korea was never as well defined as it had been from 1942 to 1945. Although the Truman administration had outlined early in the war strategic goals for the UNC to achieve, there had been no sophisticated articulation of the military means to accomplish even those minimal political objectives in Asia. The elegant simplicity of "Germany first," or the operationally prescriptive cross-channel attack or Combined Bomber Offensive directives of World War II were not part of the Americans' strategic debate for Korea. (Although from a global perspective, the United States adopted a "Europe first" vision that drove MacArthur to distraction; after all, he argued, the Communists were actually fighting in Asia, not in Germany.)

It was not until June 1951 that Ridgway had policy guidance specific enough to formulate a militarily coherent strategic approach to Korea. This guidance remained relatively unchanged over the next twelve months, and it was successful at getting the Communists to come to the truce talks. When these initial talks did not bear fruit, limited offensive action combined with the interdiction air assault was enough to get an agreement on a demarcation line that reflected military reality and to bring a settlement within apparent reach. However, when Truman decided on voluntary repatriation of POWs as a strategic objective, he "moved the goal posts" on Ridgway. Truman's demand expanded the moral costs of an armistice for the Chinese, and it created a situation American military leaders did not fully comprehend. Ridgway did not receive any additional military resources to prosecute what amounted to a new war against the Chinese, and following the phony thirty-day truce at the end of 1951, the UNC commander was in a tough spot. There was little military leverage he could employ against the Communists. His support for Van Fleet's reform of the ROK army, however, sowed the fields that Clark would reap as expanding Korean forces provided new means to bring pressure against the Communists without increasing American liability or requiring increased commitment from the UNC nations contributing troops to Korea. It was an accidental windfall that Clark was smart enough to rec-ognize and convert into a viable strategic path to gain an armistice. Unfor-tunately, its effectiveness would not begin to assert itself until January 1953.[1]

Meanwhile, Mark Clark did not like sitting on defense at Panmunjom or on the battlefield. Shortly after taking over as UNC commander in chief, Clark expressed his dismay to General Collins in Washington. The lack of military pressure, particularly against the Chinese, was counterproductive, al-lowing the Communists to dictate the flow of events and the tempo of battle on the ground. Clark realized that the forces available to him were too weak to try a major offensive, so he settled for the Air Pressure Strategy. Clark hoped for chances to inflict enough damage on the enemy's will to fight while de-priving him of key terrain features that could provide a useful jump-off point for a more aggressive posture later. Ultimately, Clark would face disappoint-ment that summer in the search for a new military strategy, but the fighting in the air and on the ground during the summer and fall of 1952 would in fact solidify the military equilibrium and set the conditions that would influence the final negotiations in the late winter and early spring of 1953.

The Korean Army

A key question about Clark's strategic approach was the assessment of Com-munist military capabilities and intentions. In response to a United Press cor-respondent's question, "In what respect have the two opposing forces used the past ten and one-half months to strengthen their positions and capabilities," Clark addressed ground and air force strengths, logistics, and defensive po-sitions. He noted that since July 1951, the tactical situation had reduced the tempo of battle sufficiently that the fighting strength of Communist ground forces rose from roughly 500,000 men to nearly 1,000,000, with many CPVF "divisions hav[ing] been brought to full effective combat strength." During the same time period, Communist air activity had increased equally dramati-cally, with the number of aircraft doubling to 1,000 jet fighters.

Apart from numbers, Clark also pointed out the increased capacity for modern warfare the CPVF units demonstrated. Chinese operations enjoyed not only increased numbers of men but also more effective support from artil-lery, mortars, tanks used as artillery, and antiaircraft artillery. The antiaircraft artillery were especially worrisome as Communist AA artillery was at "a point where it is a serious threat to our air operations over North Korea." Conse-quently, the Communists had "vastly improved his logistics picture" and was capable of "mount[ing] a powerful offensive." Furthermore, improved logis-tics and increased manpower had enabled the construction of elaborate for-tifications, extending up to twenty miles to the rear.[2]

On the UNC side of the ledger, Clark highlighted successful counterguerrilla operations in the winter of 1951/52, the most celebrated of which was Operation Ratkiller, led by Paik Sun-yup. The South Korean troops performed ably, and their leadership showed significant improvement in their ability to plan and conduct joint operations with air and paramilitary assets. Junior leaders demonstrated skill with small unit techniques, employing blocking and envelopment tactics to identify, track, trap, and capture or kill the guerrillas. Of more lasting importance for Clark, and for the progress of armistice negotiations, was the overall improvement, reorganization, and retraining of ROK army divisions. Begun in the late fall of 1951, General Van Fleet determined to fix his "Korean problem" by creating an army more reflective of the American army. This meant increased firepower, mobility, and logistics. It also meant better leadership, individual soldier training, and unit reorganization and rehabilitation. Finally, and most importantly, it meant expansion. Both Van Fleet and Clark knew that under the circumstances no additional American forces would be forthcoming. However, by using South Korea's untapped manpower, properly equipped, trained, and led, the Americans could indeed find off-book ways to increase military pressure on the Chinese and North Koreans without incurring additional political liabilities or limitations. Given the ROK army's record, it was a bold gamble. Van Fleet was willing to roll the dice.[3]

Van Fleet's first step was to approve a plan to add artillery battalions to ROK divisions. The standard Korean infantry division had only one light battalion of 105 mm howitzers. American divisions had three such battalions and one medium battalion of longer-range 155 mm howitzers. Ridgway agreed that the lack of equipment and training in fire support procedures put Korean divisions at a disadvantage, particularly under the new conditions of fortified positional warfare. He also acknowledged that additional battalions of Korean light and medium artillery would permit greater mutual support between all divisions and help make up in firepower what Eighth Army lacked in manpower.[4] In September 1951, Ridgway approved Van Fleet's authorization for KMAG to raise, equip, and train four 155 mm howitzer battalions, a significant increase in range and capability over the airborne pack 105 mm howitzer then in the ROK inventory. Van Fleet also initiated a plan to activate additional 105 mm battalions along with their corresponding headquarters batteries, giving each ROK division an artillery group of four battalions, significantly improving its fighting power, at least in terms of organic fire support.[5]

From September 1951 through December 1952, the ROK army activated and qualified for combat twenty-four 105 mm battalions and six 155 mm battalions. KMAG officers supervised the activation of these units by using cadres from existing battalions, training them for three months at the Artillery School at Kwangju, and equipping them in Seoul. Many Korean officers also received training at the US army's artillery school at Fort Sill, Oklahoma. KMAG provided the equipment, ammunition, fuel, radios, other necessary supplies, and advice for each battalion of six hundred soldiers, eighteen howitzers, and seventy vehicles.[6] The newly equipped battalions then deployed to a US corps sector to complete their organization and training under the tutelage of an American artillery unit, while participating in combat fire missions. These additional battalions made an immediate impact on the battlefield by multiplying the number of artillery tubes available to the Eighth Army's corps and division commanders. Appropriately equipped and organized, these battalions promoted confidence and self-sufficiency among the Korean divisions, making their soldiers less reliant on American artillery or close air support.[7]

On-the-job training taught the Korean gunners tactical techniques such as illumination missions and the devastating TOT. The effect of these techniques impressed the Koreans, and by the end of 1952 they boasted a total of forty artillery battalions. Activation of additional howitzer battalions continued every month thereafter. This fivefold increase in Korean artillery firepower argued persuasively that this was no longer the ROKA of 1950–51, and in a large measure it inspired the Korean soldier to stand his ground. It certainly impressed Van Fleet and Clark, who intended to rely more on the South Koreans to carry weight during the climactic battles in the fall of 1952.[8]

Creating a more muscular South Korean army was one thing. True combat effectiveness hinged on the officers, soldiers, and units themselves to use their equipment, tactics, and command procedures to fight modern war and to adapt to the Chinese innovations in both attack and defense. It was in training this reborn army that Van Fleet's faith in KMAG paid the greatest dividends and laid the foundation for increased American reliance on the ROK army.

New officer training was the most immediate need for the ROK army, both for providing proficient leadership at lower levels and for setting the foundation for all other officer training programs. The demand for junior officers remained high throughout the war, but the need was especially acute during the negotiations period. Patrolling, ambushes, and small unit actions placed a premium on skills such as initiative, combat instinct, fire planning and control, and communications. As a result, junior officer training had to be both extensive and specifically tailored to conditions at the front.[9]

The next pillar in KMAG's reformation of the South Korean army was individual soldier training.[10] ROK army replacement training centers had been producing soldiers in quantity, but their utility on the battlefield remained problematic. Van Fleet promoted three initiatives: a separate command to supervise individual replacement training, the creation of a centralized combined arms Korean army training installation, and the establishment of a Field Training Command to supervise an eight-week retraining program for all ROK infantry divisions. Its mandate was to build on soldier skills and teach fighting tactics at platoon, company, and battalion levels. The visible slowdown in tactical operations following the initiation of truce talks gave Van Fleet time and space to pull Korean divisions off the line and reestablish them as training organizations. Progressive training with rearmed and re-equipped units culminated during the final training week with a battalion-level field problem in conjunction with a command post exercise for the division and regimental staffs.[11] The result was a new Korean army that was vastly improved, more resilient in battle, and capable of dishing out severe punishment both in attack and defense. According to Paik Sun-yup, a division and corps commander during this period, KMAG's retraining program likely did more to save the Korean army than anything else done by the Americans. The Korean divisions that completed this training tended to reduce casualty and equipment losses by 50 percent over their less-trained counterparts. These same units also "revealed an élan and confidence quite superior to what they had shown before going through the training."[12] It was precisely this tactical confidence that would be tested during the CPVF's autumn counteroffensive campaign.

Clark did not get to see substantial ROK army expansion prior to 1953, but he certainly realized the potential that a larger Korean army could help realize on the battlefield and at Panmunjom.[13] Providing for a larger Korean army was the only way he could increase ground pressure against the Communists without increasing American casualties or inducing a political commitment to expand the war. A corollary advantage was that ROK army expansion inevitably threatened to destabilize the military equilibrium that the Communists exploited in their negotiation tactics. The Chinese began to feel the pressure on the ground, in the form of Eighth Army's limited thrusts west of Chorwon, while the North Koreans endured increasingly effective and devastating bombardment from the air. In July 1952, Mao informed Stalin, "We must continue operations so as to find in the course of the war . . . a means for changing the present situation."[14] The CPVF planned to raise the stakes through sustained offensive action in the summer and fall of 1952. It is plausible the Chinese recognized the political and military dangers of unchecked ROKA expansion and were forced into conducting military action early to seize the initiative and intimidate Korean forces before the UNC gained irreversible momentum in capabilities, confidence, and capacity to wage war indefinitely using Korean manpower.

Operations Counter, Creeper, and Buckshot 16

Eighth Army activity along the front had remained subdued through the winter and spring of 1952. Due to the expectation of armistice talks producing a settlement, Ridgway tightly controlled Van Fleet's activity, circumscribing plans that promised American casualties to capture indefensible terrain or to inflict only temporary damage through large-scale raids. One particularly promising operation, called Chopstick 16, a two-division thrust in eastern Korea to clear North Korean forces south of the Nam River, was approved in April. However, the presentation of the UNC's package proposal on April 28 caused Van Fleet to call off the attack the following day. Although fighting occurred frequently as patrols clashed between the respective MLRs and artillery duels continued unaffected by negotiations, the UNC held itself in check, content to defend against local attacks that at times were described as "heavy" in official reporting. Most of the ground fighting was characteristic of that reported in May, when the largest enemy action comprised two single company-size attacks against outposts and numerous platoon and squad-size probes across the peninsula. An operational lull settled over the battle lines. All that was about to change in the early summer.[15]

The Forty-Fifth Infantry Division's arrival in Korea in December 1951 to replace the First Cavalry Division heralded a new American chapter for the Korean conflict. Shortly after the American intervention in July 1950, the JCS recommended the call-up of four National Guard divisions. Two of these, the Fortieth and the Forty-Fifth Infantry Divisions, activated for two years of federal service deployed to the Far East. The Forty-Fifth Infantry Division ("Thunderbirds") was a Guard division from Oklahoma with a storied past in World War II. The division was no stranger to winter and mountain warfare, having been part of Mark Clark's Fifth Army in Italy, 1943–44. It was also well acquainted with hardship, having been battered by the Germans at Salerno and Anzio. Korea, however, would be a new test for these citizen-soldiers called to active federal service in a limited war.[16]

Ridgway was not enthusiastic about taking the National Guard divisions to war. Because they had had a year of training, he preferred to draw on them for replacement soldiers for those troops rotating out of Korea. Collins disagreed and for reasons political and institutional, he got his way. The Thunderbirds went to Korea where they occupied the eastern portion of the I Corps's sector along Line Jamestown, not far from Chorwon and the western apex of the Iron Triangle.[17] Its MLR ran along the ridgeline of Hills 477 and 487, the "Bloody Angle" seized by the Third Infantry Division during Operation Commando. This position was the western rampart for IX Corps's hold on Chorwon. Its loss would undo the gains from Commando and jeopardize Eighth Army's position facing the Iron Triangle.[18] The division had arrived in Korea in substantially better shape than its regular army counterparts twelve to fifteen months earlier, but it entered a war that was not what many of the divisions' experienced officers and noncoms expected. Instead of pitched battles, maneuver, and serious fighting, the Guardsmen experienced the dreary pattern of patrols, raids, and exchanges of mortar and artillery fire. Many of the specialty units—anti-aircraft, tank, and reconnaissance—found themselves unemployed, or employed in nontraditional ways. Artillerymen were initially frustrated at the lack of observable targets and their inability to strike at Chinese guns that could shoot and then hide without a trace.[19]

In January 1952, the division mounted its first significant raids; unfortunately, these moves provoked a strong reaction from the Chinese. American inexperience and Chinese skill at camouflage and fire discipline typically combined to cede the initiative to the Chinese on most occasions that the division's patrols encountered the enemy. On January 24, a reinforced rifle company from the 279th Infantry Regiment attempted a raid against Hill 266, known as Old Baldy, southwest of a large T-shaped hill known simply as "T-Bone," standing between the two MLRs. Intense fire and stiff resistance turned the Americans away with four dead, twenty-three wounded, and three missing; a similar attack mounted by the 180th Infantry Regiment fared just as poorly.[20]

The division commander, Maj. Gen. James C. Styron, recognized the symptoms for his regiments' lackluster inauguration in battle: poor small-unit leadership, lack of proficiency in basic infantry skills, and inexperience under fire. The 279th Infantry Regiment's commander thought his troops were "too dependent" on artillery and that "more forceful leadership" was required from his platoon and company leaders. A veteran artilleryman himself who fought in Sicily and Italy, Styron had incoming officers taken to a stationary dug-in tank overlooking no man's land to fire the main gun. Although Lt. Francis G. Boehm could see nothing of the phantom Chinese, after several officers performed the task, "the air was filled with incoming artillery rounds from our invisible enemy . . . and exploded in the valley behind us. We knew now that we were at war."[21] More productively, additional specialized training was given to all incoming soldiers beginning in March 1952 (by July the entire division would have changed over from National Guard to mobilized reservist, regular, and draftee officers and men). Styron stressed the virtues of patrolling, declaring, "This patrolling is the finest training I have seen. We would not know where the enemy is without [it]. It can be compared to life insurance: some day [sic] it is going to pay off. I want the men to know that we are doing it for their protection."[22]

Like other divisions facing a new style of warfare, the Thunderbirds improvised with innovative approaches to American doctrine, such as the creation of special, all-volunteer "Raider" groups. Raider patrols tended to end with contact more frequently, resulting in more Thunderbird casualties, but also inflicting more damage against the enemy. The Chinese began to respond in kind, increasing artillery and infantry attacks against the division's MLR. The

CPVF's 349th Regiment of the 117th Division, Thirty-Ninth Army, focused on what appeared to be the division's Achilles' heel, a small knob located on the southwest end of the line, known on military maps as Hill 200. Defended by a reinforced platoon of fifty-five soldiers, Hill 200 guarded the opening to a stream valley that snaked behind the division's MLR based on Hill 477. It also neutralized Hill 255 ("Porkchop Hill") from being a Chinese outpost and provided observation and direct fire into the flat paddy lands to the division's front. Chinese occupation of this hilltop position would immediately put the division into a close fight to preserve its own left flank.[23]

Since May 20, enemy patrols had probed the hill but without much vigor. The Americans of Third Platoon, F Company, 179th Infantry, reinforced by an additional rifle squad and two heavy machine guns, sensed something was coming, but they did not expect to get hit by an entire battalion just before midnight, May 25. Prisoner interrogations after the fight revealed that the Seventh Company, Third Battalion, had been reprimanded by its political officer for "the poor showing of its patrols." As punishment, the entire company was ordered to seize Hill 200 and bring back prisoners. Eighth Army apparently was not the only headquarters distressed about patrols and prisoners. The other two companies in the Chinese battalion received similar missions.[24]

It was a particularly severe infantry assault, supported with 2,245 artillery and mortar shells falling in just thirty-five minutes. Under almost no natural illumination, the Americans called for all the artillery and machine gun fire support available. Fortuitously for them, the Chinese chose to make their main push on the northeast face, which was gently sloped, but also exposed to the punishing fire of eight machine guns positioned on the Americans' MLR. A further six guns swept the southern and southwestern slopes of Hill 200. Two lieutenants, Perry E. Gragg and William J. Moroney, and one experienced noncommissioned officer, Msgt. Cecil Tackett, led the defense, calling artillery, shoring up the line of riflemen, distributing ammunition and grenades, and caring for the wounded. After several hours of close fighting, the Americans were barely holding their position, then an air force flare ship arrived overhead to illuminate the field and expose the Chinese to accurate artillery fire, which finally broke their stranglehold on the hill. Once the quick reaction platoon from the MLR began pushing against the Chinese rear, the attackers' momentum "was materially diminished," and the Chinese broke contact.[25] Reinforcements sweeping the valley floor just before dawn recovered three wounded prisoners and found thirty-two Chinese dead along with evidence to report an estimated additional 130 killed and wounded. Seven Guardsmen died in the battle and fifty-four were wounded.[26]

Although a successful defense, the battle illustrated several tactical problems for the division commander, Maj. Gen. David L. Ruffner (who had just replaced Styron four days earlier) to consider. A regular army officer, Ruffner (older brother of Maj. Gen. Clark Ruffner, former commander of the Second Infantry Division) was a 1917 graduate of the Virginia Military Institute and a field artillery officer. He served in Italy as the Tenth Mountain Division's artillery commander from January 1945 until the war's end.[27] Compared to Styron, he was far more abrupt with subordinates and tended to be oblivious to the reactions his presence on the MLR provoked from the Chinese. His judgment was also quick and harsh: his troops needed more skill, confidence, and aggressive leaders. At Hill 200 the counterattacking platoon was slow getting into position, the division's artillery played little role in stopping the assault, and the outpost's own machine guns were late opening fire, allowing the hill's perimeter to be easily breached.[28] How a battalion-size attack could mass itself against one platoon was also a mystery. Two days after the battle, the division's reconnaissance determined the Chinese were advancing their own outpost line, occupying Pokkae ridge as well as digging entrenchments on Hills 191, 150, and 266 (Old Baldy). At nighttime, his infantry was occupying Hills 180, 190, 255, and 266.[29]

A quick study of the map, a survey of the ground in front of the division, and the intuitive sense derived from his own mountain warfare experience dismayed the Thunderbird's new commander. The Chinese held the high ground near the small villages of Mabang-ni, Agok, and Hasakkol, plus the northern face of the T-Bone (Hill 290), and they were too close, in too great strength, for comfort. The terrain generally sloped upward, south to north, such that the Chinese almost always had a height advantage and corresponding benefits in observation and artillery concealment from UNC counterbattery fire. Hill 200 could not be a secure outpost if Porkchop Hill remained in no man's land, or worse, if permanently occupied by the enemy. Ruffner wanted some breathing room on Line Jamestown to reduce the division's vulnerability and the ease with which the Chinese could, at their whim, bring significant forces against the outpost line. He continued Styron's training programs and tactical schools for junior officers, but he wanted to gain an additional margin of security before the Chinese could test the division again. He planned to seize in a *coup-de-main* twelve terrain features that would be incorporated into a new outpost line abutting the Yokkok River and giving the American troops better warning and more opportunities to kill Chinese with close air support and artillery rather than rifle bullets and bayonets (figure 10.1).[30]

On June 1, the 180th and 279th commanders received orders to formulate attack plans for Operation Counter. Ruffner intended to pick a fight, and he directed, "Once taken, [troops on] combat outposts will be withdrawn only under extreme enemy pressure and by order of the regimental commander concerned. Sharpen your bayonets! Be alert!"[31] He further ordered Counter's

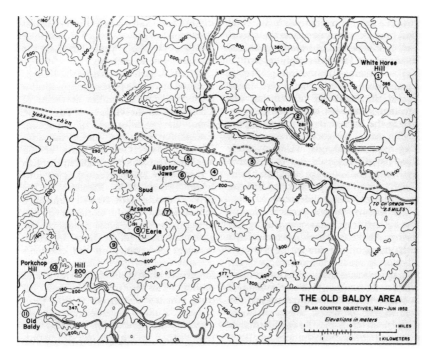

Figure 10.1 Operation Counter, June 1952. Source: Hermes, *Truce Tent and Fighting Front*, 286.

objectives seized at night and construction supplies, defensive equipment, and additional ammunition to be supplied before daybreak so the troops could dig in and prepare for the expected counterattacks that night.

Operation Counter may not have been the "brilliant tactical maneuver" lauded in the division's history, but the nighttime rush against several objectives at once did take the Chinese by surprise. On the night of June 6, the two regiments began their movement forward and quickly seized their objectives. Only at Hill 255 (Porkchop) and Hill 266 (Old Baldy) did the division run into any significant opposition. Hill 255 was secured after nearly an hour by two platoons. The wrestling match for Hill 266, though, was more prolonged, with Company A, 180th Infantry, employing artillery and flanking moves to finally drive the Chinese defenders back. Almost immediately the Americans were beating off probing attacks. The troops dug in even as Chinese artillery crashed around them.[32]

Once the outposts were seized, the key task of organizing them for the defense got under way. This quick exploitation of terrain won was the deciding factor in allowing the Americans to hold against furious counterattacks that occurred in June and July. The ubiquitous Korean Service Corps personnel brought in on their backs construction and fortification materials and worked through the night to build bunkers with overhead protection (proof against VT proximity shells),[33] ring the outposts with barbed wire, and emplace mines along the avenues of approach. Whenever possible, the troops sited their machine guns and recoilless rifles in positions to support adjacent outposts and cover their obstacles and avenues of approach. Signal personnel set up communications to the rear and laterally to other outposts by radio and wire. Incoming Chinese artillery lent urgency to the situation and provided the incentive to dig. By morning the new outposts were manned and ready to withstand counterattacks and keep the Chinese away from the MLR.[34]

Almost immediately the Chinese launched several company-size attacks. The artillery FO supporting Company A, 180th Infantry Regiment, 1st Lt. Francis Boehm, was responsible for calling artillery in support of nightly patrols that often made contact with the Chinese attempting to infiltrate behind the American defenses. "Several nights a week," he later remembered, "the Chinese troops with whom we were in contact would mount an attack, complete with bugles blaring and rockets being exploded for effect, but we pummeled them with artillery concentrations that had been registered during the day to assure accuracy [at night]."[35] When three rifle companies from the 180th Regiment seized a position known as Outpost Eerie, the Chinese responded fiercely, having seen and recognized the division's intent to elbow them out of the Yokkok River valley. For two days the Chinese fought back, throwing a battalion of infantry and five thousand artillery and mortar shells at the Americans, who struggled to hang on to their sliver of newly won ground. Eventually the Americans' firepower prevailed. Fifty-eight close air support sorties and 44,000 shells fired by the corps artillery blunted the Chinese's ability to maintain their offensive pressure.[36] The division's 145th Anti-Aircraft Artillery Battalion fired more than a million bullets from its half-tracked M-16 quad .50 cal. machine guns. Intercepted Chinese communications revealed the devastation these weapons caused. During the battle for Outpost Eerie, the local Chinese commander was ordered, "Turn off the running water!" as heavy machine gun bullets scythed down Chinese soldiers by the score.[37]

By June 14, Ruffner achieved his local objective to extend his defensive zone and to place down a marker along the Yokkok River. Expecting further counterattacks, Ruffner maintained an entire infantry battalion, fully motorized, on one-hour alert. He also posted several tanks from the 245th Tank Battalion on Outpost Eerie to steel the confidence of the beleaguered infantry.[38] These measures were prudent, as strong attacks up to regimental strength and "supported by artillery fires of unprecedented volume" in late June and early July were beaten back with heavy losses inflicted on the Chinese. From

Tokyo, Clark reported to the JCS that the Forty-Fifth Infantry Division was responsible for inflicting 3,500 casualties since June 6. It was an impressive undertaking to turn these outposts into a serious fortified line that would endure nearly until the end of the war.[39]

The success of Counter inspired Maj. Gen. Lyman L. Lemnitzer, commander of the adjacent Seventh Division, part of the IX Corps, to approve Operation Creeper with a similar objective to increase the depth of his defensive line and give the Chinese a nudge from their positions overlooking Kumhwa on the east side of the Iron Triangle. Lemnitzer deferred the tactical planning to Col. Lloyd R. Moses, now commanding the Thirty-First Infantry Regiment. Moses was also about to get his baptism as a combat commander in Creeper. Having just served a few months as the X Corps G3 (Operations) officer, Moses was eager—"itchy for a unit of my own"—to engage in an aggressive operation. The corps commander, Maj. Gen. Willard Wyman, also hoped that Creeper might provide some intelligence and extra insurance should the Chinese be planning to launch a major offensive from the Iron Triangle.[40]

Lemnitzer approved Creeper on June 16, and Moses lost no time ordering his Second Battalion to move one company forward to occupy a new outpost line and its support platoon to commence work on what would become the new MLR. New defensive works went up quickly and without much interference, so Moses decided two days later to move the Third Battalion forward. However, the enemy's reaction was unanticipated. Heavy mortar and artillery shelling disrupted the building work and convinced Moses to send all three of his battalions to establish the new outposts, reasoning that giving the enemy six target areas to focus on as opposed to two would lessen the intensity of fire on any one outpost. The new outposts were on ground that the enemy himself often used for the same purpose, and the Chinese were not about to watch with equanimity the sudden move forward against the southern face of the Iron Triangle, but they were not prepared to meet the American's effective infantry-armor-artillery combination that finally drove them away from the contested outposts. Creeper did succeed in advancing the division's lines forward, but it also provoked a series of sharp clashes throughout the summer. It also would have another, more ironic, effect. The new outpost line was like a stick in the eye of the Chinese, bringing the Americans too close for comfort to their own outpost line based on Triangle Hill and extending east to Sniper Ridge. Both positions were critical to safeguard Hill 1062, Osong-san, the CPVF's citadel of the region. Creeper was therefore simply a prelude to the showdown that was to come in mid-October.[41]

In late June, after Counter, the Forty-Fifth Infantry Division tried to capture prisoners employing a reinforced infantry battalion. The results were disappointing: three Chinese soldiers pulled off the objective all died before they could be brought safely to the MLR. Two weeks later, Clark approved another battalion-size effort, named Buckshot 16, this time executed by the ROK Eleventh Division to capture a North Korean prisoner. One ROK battalion crossed the Nam River in the ROK I Corps sector and ran into a considerable defensive position. When the battalion withdrew, it had suffered thirty-three soldiers killed, 157 wounded, and thirty-six missing, inflicting estimated losses on the enemy of ninety killed and eighty-two wounded. Not a prisoner was taken.[42]

The results of these abortive raids and the difficulties encountered in trying to straighten out a line here, or erase a bulge there, convinced Clark that the UNC losses in efforts to militarily pressure the Communists were not worthwhile. Van Fleet may have hoped that the change in commanders from Ridgway to Clark might result in less restriction on his activity along the front, in particular, his desire to strike at the Iron Triangle and eliminate the font of Chinese fighting power in central Korea. Clark quickly disabused him of that illusion. After the war he called it "the lure of the next highest hill ahead of you." There would always be another hill or one more bulge to take out, and it seemed that the Chinese were nearly always willing to lose men just to give the UNC "a local black eye."[43] The situation reflected Clark's ambiguous strategic posture. The opportunity to gain intelligence of enemy positions, give the UNC troops experience, destroy enemy stockpiles, and use US firepower and ROK manpower made no impression on Clark, who still worried in the short term about the possibility of adverse effects on negotiations, the numbers of friendly casualties involved, the lack of UNC reserves if a heavy enemy counterattack followed, and the unprofitable nature of an advance beyond Pyonggang (the northern apex of the Iron Triangle) without further exploitation. Perhaps even more important, though unsaid, would have been more bad press in an already discouraging summer.[44] A Canadian reporter admitted that "it can truly be stated that this is a twilight war. But somehow one feels as though we are sitting on a powder keg."[45] Unless the Eighth Army commander felt an attack was imminent, Clark did not think the potentially high casualty rate incurred in offensive raids and limited attacks was justified. He preferred to let the Chinese do the attacking, and hopefully most of the dying, too.[46]

The CPVF's Counterpressure

The CPVF's relative inactivity across the front came to an end in June. Chinese infantry, increasingly in conjunction with accurate and sustained artillery and mortar support, resumed aggressive patrolling and conducting sizable raids on Eighth Army positions that increased in intensity throughout July across the front, but particularly focused on those locations Korean or

American troops recently occupied. One division commander ruefully reflected that as summer progressed, Eighth Army appeared to have lost the initiative: "It cannot be said any longer that we dominate no man's land—it has become a battleground for patrols with the enemy holding at least one good card in the form of expendable manpower."[47]

The continuing deadlock at Panmunjom encouraged the Chinese to play their "one good card." The focus for the Chinese's attention initially fixed on Hill 351, defended by the ROK Thirty-Fifth Regiment, Fifth Division, and Hill 266, Old Baldy. Although the struggle for Old Baldy dominated the Americans' attention, ROK troops from the Fifth Division fought their own seesaw battle for Hill 351. This hill, much like Old Baldy, was a sore spot for the Communists, who endured accurate naval gunfire and air attack directed by observers on Hill 351 against their own MLR along the Nam River. From July 10 to July 14, the Koreans defended their outpost against daily attacks. Close air support played a strong role in the defense, with napalm used repeatedly to blast Communist troops when they reached the crest and just before the ROK soldiers mounted their own counterattacks. This excellent coordination between air, artillery, and infantry forces proved very costly to the Communists, who lost 372 dead (counted), 265 wounded (estimated), and four prisoners. The Korean defenders suffered much more modest losses: sixteen killed, 308 wounded, and thirty-eight missing—and they retained Hill 351.[48]

By contrast, the fight over Old Baldy was a costly engagement for both sides. Two attacks, the first involving a reinforced battalion and the second elements of a regiment, unsuccessfully attempted to storm Old Baldy on 27 and 29 June. Thousands of Chinese shells had blasted the top of Hill 266 over the last two weeks of June, giving the hill its distinctive bald look compared to the surrounding hills. On the night of July 3–4, the Chinese launched three separate attacks against Old Baldy. The last was battalion-size with "the bitterest hand-to-hand fighting" yet seen on the bare crest, but it was no more successful at wresting control over the key hill than previous efforts.[49] The Americans' defenses were for the moment too strong and the firepower brought to bear on the attacks too effective to permit the Chinese from massing their infantry to overwhelm the defenders.

The Second Infantry Division, commanded by Maj. Gen. James C. Fry, relieved the Forty-Fifth Infantry Division shortly after this final set of attacks. General Fry was a 1922 West Point graduate who served in a variety of infantry and tank assignments until the outbreak of World War II. His experience as a regimental commander in Italy impressed him with the tactical problem he faced to fight the Chinese over this mountainous terrain. His division's relief of the Thunderbirds began on July 16 and lasted two days. The new soldiers took stock of their surroundings and gained an appreciation for Clark's reluctance to wrestle over hilltop positions in no-man's land.[50] From the division's MLR the Chinese controlled the high ground to the east and west, and they held a hill mass jutting from the north end of Hill 266, known as Chink Baldy. Pvt. Rudolph Stephens and his fellow soldiers got their first glimpse of Old Baldy at night, "The moon was shining bright as day . . . cast[ing] an eerie glow on the rear slopes, and we could see many shell holes from the top to the bottom." The effects of the battle had rattled and exhausted the defenders, who greeted their relief with hardly a glance or greeting as they "left their position and ran down the hill. This was unnerving to us," Stephens remembered. Quietly and quickly the Second Infantry Division troops occupied the trenches and tried to establish their defenses along the crest, facing Chink Baldy. They would not wait long.[51]

The Chinese had taken nearly a two-week pause in the Mabang-ni area to prepare to renew the fighting for Old Baldy and Porkchop Hill. The CPVF leadership took the loss of these hilltop positions as serious indicators of Eighth Army's aggressive posture to bring pressure on their negotiators.[52] A week-long seesaw battle began the night of July 17–18, just as the two American divisions were exchanging positions, when Chinese infantry managed to claw their way back onto Old Baldy. Elements of two companies from the Twenty-Third Infantry Regiment defended the hill from dilapidated bunkers and partially collapsed trench lines and fighting holes. After an initial burst of shelling, Chinese bugles, not more than fifty meters off, sounded their eerie calls to assault. Flares illuminated the mass of Chinese infantry who pressed forward despite the losses caused by the Second Infantry Division's guns.[53]

Eventually, intensive artillery and mortar fire suppressed the defenders long enough to allow Chinese reinforcements to surge over the hill and into the northern salient of the outpost. From there, they fanned out east and west into the trenches to clear the defenders. The fighting was close and brutal. Hand grenades and bayonets were preferred over rifle and carbine. Still, the Chinese continued to press forward on either side of Old Baldy, and eventually they overwhelmed the center of the hill. The survivors withdrew under artillery cover to the Twenty-Third Regiment's MLR positions. There they learned the ugly truth of this kind of war. No ground, to include a flimsy outpost, could be lost without significant political costs. The Twenty-Third Infantry was going back to Old Baldy. "We would bleed and die for an old ugly hill that to the men in the trenches wasn't worth throwing lives away for, just so we could see Chinese movement to the north . . . we just did what we were told and didn't question the motives."[54] The question now, and which would continue to be asked through the fall campaign, was whether the Chinese felt the same way.

The Chinese attack stunned the regimental commander, Col. George Mergens, and his staff. Mergens had assumed command of the regiment in January and spent most of the following six months away from the MLR. This was his first experience with battle (he had served successive assignments as an inspector general, the most recent at FEC headquarters in Japan), and his staff was equally flummoxed by the requirements of coordinating a relief while fighting a major engagement. Command and control both fell apart quickly and were not regained until the division commander made significant personnel changes in the regiment's leadership structure.

As an example of the regiment's dysfunction, Mergens directed his executive officer (and second in command), Lt. Col. Ralph D. Burns, to form an ad hoc battalion after the Third Battalion commander was wounded on Old Baldy and evacuated. Burns organized two companies from First Battalion (A and B) and two companies from the Third Battalion (I and L) with one additional heavy weapons company and one platoon of tanks in support. The two surviving battalion commanders were assigned to Burns's ad hoc command as were the regimental S2 and S3 officers. He was permitted a five-minute personal reconnaissance and ordered to begin the attack to seize both Old Baldy and Chink Baldy by 1600 hours.[55]

Burns planned a double envelopment, but the disorganized nature of his four attacking companies frustrated the potential of this tactical maneuver. Company B stepped off first at 1625 hours and immediately ran into a wall of Chinese artillery and mortar fire. Burns reported that it took these men over an hour to clear themselves of the impact area; the unit was scattered and shocked. It made no progress up the old ugly hill. Then men from Company I, seeing what Company B endured, stopped to set up "a blocking position" instead of advancing against the right (north) side of Old Baldy. Only Company L made any attempt to climb the hill, and they went to ground only two-thirds the way up the slope. A heavy rain then made any forward movement impossible.[56]

By now Burns had lost communications with the attacking companies and had no idea where his soldiers were. An exhausted runner claimed Company L was in position at the top of the hill, but the volume of small arms fire coming down the hill belied the positive report. Curiously, the executive officer from the Ninth Infantry Regiment, Lt. Col. Robert W. Garrett, appeared out of nowhere, causing Burns to question what was going on. He reported to Mergens and complained that the staff was not providing adequate assistance to control the attacking units or coordinate logistics and fire support. Mergens meekly acknowledged and said that he had little control over the situation as "the generals [were] running the show."[57]

In fact, Fry had determined to replace Mergens and Burns almost as soon as the battle kicked off. Just a few hours after Burns's attack went forward, the division commander called Mergens at his command post and gave him a tongue-lashing for being too far in the rear. "You're not doing any good up there. Put the heat on," Fry urged. Mergen's responses were sufficiently timid that Fry exploded, "I expect you to get on top of that [hill]." At 2200 hours Fry contacted Garrett, a Ranger battalion veteran of World War II, at the Ninth Infantry Regiment's command post and directed him to "move in and put that staff to work and straighten it out." Mergens "needs rest," he continued, and had allowed the regiment to become disorganized with "a little of it spread out everywhere."[58]

What Fry did not reveal to Garrett was the intense pressure he was under from I Corps and Eighth Army to recapture Old Baldy. Just minutes after Fry spoke to Mergens, Lt. Gen. Paul W. Kendall, who had only just assumed command himself of I Corps, called to tell Fry to kick the Chinese off the hill. That night, when it became clear that Burns's group had failed, Fry reported to Kendall that a deliberate attack was required. Kendall, an experienced and distinguished combat veteran of the Italian campaign (1944–45), where he had been Fry's superior officer, agreed and told Fry to take his time. "Work it over" with artillery for a day or so, he counseled. Then the regiment could "be set on it to do a better job with less casualties."[59] The rebuke was clear, and it validated Fry's instinct to remove Mergens from command.

Burns prepared again to commit elements of two battalions to retake Old Baldy just before nightfall on July 19. Some of the men selected for the assault were survivors who had only escaped with their lives barely twenty-four hours earlier. It was a half-hearted attempt as the division's artillery was not yet prepared to provide the necessary fire support. Burns discovered that the Americans had unwittingly kicked over a hornet's nest. The Chinese were not going to accept idly aggressive moves on the battlefield at the same time they were stymied at Panmunjom over voluntary repatriation, an issue of immense strategic and political importance. Before daybreak on July 20 the Chinese were already coming back, emerging from their fortified tunnels on Chink Baldy and pressing hard against the remnants of Company L defending the center of the American-occupied trench line.[60] The exhausted American infantrymen had to endure a tremendous artillery pounding as their reward for braving enemy machine gun fire and mortars. With no means to shelter themselves from the Chinese artillery, it was unsurprising that the hill remained in Chinese hands. Fry was mollified somewhat when Garrett called that night to render his assessment. Garrett, though he was junior to Burns, was a confident leader, and his report portrayed both judgment and resolve. Something needed to be done about the Chinese artillery before the regiment could be expected to seize and hold Old Baldy. He said, "I am just not sure that we aren't playing into the Chink's hands. There is nothing up there anymore; that's the worst piece of artillery pounding I have seen anything take." Fry asked if the hill as an outpost was worth having. Garrett responded, "I don't see a damn bit of use in that terrain anymore."[61]

Garrett's analysis was surely right, but that did not matter. The Chinese, now defending their outpost again, were fighting a smart attrition battle. With about two platoons backed by a single battalion feeding fresh troops to hold their defenses, mortar, artillery, and small arms took a heavy toll on the Americans. Despite repeated attacks and their own powerful air and artillery bombardments, "it appeared as if this condition might continue indefinitely."[62]

Kendall called on Fry in the morning to ask what the situation was. Fry paraphrased his conversation with Garrett the night before, emphasizing that "two good officers" said they "never went through such artillery" before. Kendall was unmoved and impatiently insisted Fry prepare a full effort for that night, applying pressure all across the front. "You got my message?" he demanded. "I want that hill. That is the one task that lies before the Second Division." Perhaps to soften the blow, Kendall confided, "There are big things at stake, and the pressure is [coming] all the way down."[63]

Garrett, now the regiment's acting commander, followed Fry's instructions and prepared Company K to assault that night, but this time with greater artillery preparatory support. The division's artillery commander ordered his guns to fire 1,000 rounds per hour leading up to the attack.[64] The soft muddy ground on Old Baldy absorbed much of the explosive power of the bombardment, however, and heavy Chinese mortar fire was enough to decimate Company K before it reached the top with only twenty-four effective men. But the important news was that they were holding. Garrett ordered Burns to get Company G to send a platoon to reinforce Company K. Early in the morning on July 21 the Americans were making slow but steady progress across the top of Old Baldy. Fifth Air Force contributed fifty-two close air support sorties during the day to keep the Chinese at bay.[65] The news was sufficiently good that Fry optimistically reported to Kendall that "most of a company [was] up on Old Baldy." Ominously, he added, "We seem to have bad luck with company commanders being hit." There were too few officers, and when one became a casualty, the impetus of the attack, or the will to defend, inevitably faltered.[66]

At 2100 hours, July 21, the rest of Company G moved up to the crest of Old Baldy and joined the remnants of Companies K and L. The surprising absence of a Chinese counterattack induced a sense of security for Fry, and he instructed Garrett to pull back the two shattered companies. He also urged Garrett to get the regimental staff more involved in controlling the battle. Fry ordered his assistant division commander, Brig. Gen. Lionel McGarr, to keep Mergens out of the way. McGarr concurred, acknowledging the regiment was still in a mess organizationally. Unfortunately, in the early morning hours, the Chinese launched such a powerful attack (unusually in daylight) that Company G was easily pushed off the hill, which precipitated the final crisis for the regiment. The regiment had already reported forty-two killed,

403 wounded, and ten missing—and now the seemingly easy loss of the hill when it looked as if Company G was set indicated that the Chinese were nowhere near to conceding. In frustration, Fry called Mergens, who was out of the battle though still nominally in command of the regiment. "When you get squared away, get your staff squared away," Fry spit out. He continued to elaborate on the regimental commander's failing: weak command and control that resulted in individual companies fighting piecemeal battles, which produced high casualties with no positive result.[67]

Meanwhile, Burns was trying to organize a coherent defense on Old Baldy. He recognized that the infantrymen needed ammunition, timber, and above all, water. KSC porters refused to carry the supplies up the hill (one of the rare occasions when the KSC failed at the critical moment). Burns, who had no communications to the rear, came off the hill to find the regimental S-4 (Supply) officer. What he found instead stunned him: seventy men from Company G and fifteen more from various other companies at the forward supply point sitting on the side of the road. Seeing the potential to resupply the hill with men and materials, Burns ordered the men to "fall in," that is, to form up in ranks. The men refused to move.

Burns had by this point been awake and under fire for nearly four continuous days. It is amazing that he still attempted to continue his mission to get reinforcements to Old Baldy. After a few moments of cajoling, he contacted the regimental command post. Mergens responded, and after hearing Burns's explanation, ordered him to shoot a few of the men. Burns tried again to convince the men to move. Other leaders split the men into small groups and pleaded with them to go up the hill one more time. Mergens repeated his order, and when Burns made it clear he would not follow it, Mergens relented and agreed to have the men placed under arrest and driven to the rear.[68]

At noon on July 22, the Chinese remained in control of Old Baldy. Kendall was not happy, and he reiterated his order that the Americans hold the hill. "They are not both going to stay up there," he told Fry. "It is either going to be one or the other, and I want our boys to stay up there!"[69] General McGarr, who had spent every day at the Twenty-Third Infantry Regiment's forward command post, understood it was not going to be so easy. Two junior officers he interviewed stated, "Getting up is not the job, but staying up [there] is." McGarr told Fry that the materials to construct defensible and survivable positions did not exist. The men were lying in the open trying to make their bodies sink as low as they could in the rain-drenched and shell-obliterated slit trenches that crisscrossed the bald hilltop. They needed tanks, McGarr added, and for them to get to the hill they needed a major engineering effort to shore up the collapsing trails.[70] Before Fry could act on McGarr's suggestions, the summer monsoon deluge brought an end to the battle as the rains and mud made the movement of men and supplies nearly impossible; the fighting could not be maintained.[71]

In Tokyo, Clark blanched at the July casualty figures for the Twenty-Third Infantry's effort to defend the Forty-Fifth Infantry Division's modest gains: three officers and fifty-three enlisted men killed, nine officers and 310 enlisted men wounded, and a further eighty-four missing. On the other side, the Chinese were willing to pay an estimated 1,093 killed and wounded.[72] Nevertheless, the logic of using tactical gains to leverage strategic pressure dictated a return to Old Baldy. The division and regimental staff used the weeklong pause to prepare the deliberate attack Fry had advocated on July 18. Two companies from a single battalion would make the assault with heavy artillery and air support to suppress Chinese mortars and disrupt any counterattack.

By late evening of July 31, the rains had finally stopped and American artillery was already smashing the Chinese defenders as the Americans supported by six tanks moved toward the base of Old Baldy. No one fired until the crest was reached, and then the troops opened up as groups "leap-frogged," alternating fire and movement, over the top of the hill. The American tactics paid off, despite the incessant mortars that inflicted the majority of casualties and continued to harass the American survivors through the night.[73] The two-company assault succeeded with light casualties in driving off the defending Chinese by 0900 hours August 1. Additional reinforcements, along with significant engineering efforts to construct bunkers, lay mines and barbed wire, and other obstacles, foiled further Chinese counterattacks so that by August 4, the Americans were holding, and would hold, Old Baldy for the rest of the year. It became a valuable patrol base, and the Chinese never lost interest in its neutralization and eventual recapture.[74]

Other Eighth Army units executed a number of raids in July 1952 to destroy defensive positions, kill soldiers, and capture prisoners. In all these attacks, Eighth Army units performed well, using armor, artillery, and close air support to minimize their own casualties while inflicting serious damage on local targets.[75] Although individually these actions were of little overall significance, taken together along with FEAF's muscular air pressure campaign, they probably confirmed for the Communists that Clark was preparing for a more belligerent approach. Anticipating that "the enemy is likely to make a new move" elsewhere along the front line, the Chinese decided to preempt the UNC's challenge and began to return the favor, picking over the Eighth Army's outpost line for favorable terrain to target with their own artillery and infantry assault.[76] Overlooking the UNC's road to Panmunjom, the US marine outposts known as Bunker Hill and Siberia were tempting targets for the Chinese to aim at to counterpunch the UNC's recent aggression. Beginning during the night of August 11–12, the marines fought a four-day battle over these two outposts. Marine gunners with the Third Battalion, Eleventh Artillery Regiment, poured water through their gun tubes all night long as they fired more shells at Siberia and Bunker Hill in a one-day period than at any other point in the war up to that time. The Chinese replied with their own effective fire support, slinging 6,000 shells at the marines on August 12 alone. When it was over, the marines retained their hilltop outposts, but the CPVF had demonstrated tenacity and closer coordination between assaulting infantry and their supporting artillery fire.[77]

The Chinese expanded their probing attacks in early September with "unusually intensive efforts" beginning September 6–7. Chinese infantry returned to Bunker Hill, trading control of the hill multiple times in a ten-day seesaw battle. Other Chinese probes and attacks erupted in early September. UNC troops attempting to conduct patrols often found themselves immediately engaged after leaving the security of their own entrenchments. The Chinese made nightly reconnaissance around Hill 355, known as Little Gibraltar, identifying the defending Canadians' standing patrols (what the Americans called outposts), cutting and removing wire obstacles, and scouting and clearing avenues of approach to the MLR. On September 8, a standing patrol reported "the enemy were throwing stones into the wire," presumably to entice the patrol to open fire and expose its location.[78]

Eighth Army counted 43,531 indirect fire shells impacting along their outposts and MLR positions in September—a record high. For the month the daily average of indirect fire rose to more than 1,200 artillery and mortar shells hitting the Eighth Army's lines.[79] CPVF tactics had evolved to something the Americans now recognized as effective attrition. American intelligence assessments captured the dilemma produced by stalemate at Panmunjom and the tactical equilibrium obtained at the front. It appeared that neither side was prepared to risk a significant military move to break the impasse. The Chinese in particular appeared content to wait out the UNC by defending its positions. They exercised the tactical initiative only when it suited them, which was usually in response to Eighth Army aggressive moves. It was equally clear that without a significant increase in ground troop strength and approval to expand the theater of operations, the UNC probably could not apply sufficient military pressure to compel a settlement or induce a withdrawal of the Communists' forces. The fights for Old Baldy and Bunker Hill were typical of the savage and localized battles that substituted for the military strategy more familiar to Van Fleet or Clark. The war appeared to have become an endless twilight struggle for control of prosaically named hilltops, one after the other.[80]

11

WHITE HORSE MOUNTAIN, SEPTEMBER–OCTOBER 1952

THE AIM OF military intelligence is to interpret an adversary's actions and determine, as closely as war's inherent ambiguity will allow, his capabilities and intentions. Too often, a misreading of clues will lull decision makers to disregard intentions, despite the evidence of capabilities. Throughout the summer, the Chinese demonstrated their increasing capabilities, particularly their willingness to return to local attacks with better artillery support and reduced casualties. The interrogation of captured communist soldiers, typically a reliable gauge of future intent, failed to reveal any definitive offensive plans. But the increase in pressure in early September did catch the attention of Eighth Army analysts and commanders. They sensed a major offensive was coming, only its timing and scope remained unknown.[1]

Tactical Counteroffensives

Chinese commanders worried that the status quo developed under General Ridgway was jeopardized by Clark's willingness to extend American military power in the air and on the ground. Operations Counter and Creeper had moved Eighth Army's MLR much closer to the Iron Triangle. The Chinese perceived other indicators that suggested an increased threat of an amphibious attack or some other offensive move. The additional air and naval forces making their presence felt along the coasts and in the interior of North Korea only added to their suspicions.

MacArthur's decisive Inchon attack had made such a deep impression on the Chinese that they continuously feared an amphibious "end-run" against their flanks. Deng Hua, acting CPVF commander (Peng was convalescing in Beijing), assessed that the political deadlock combined with the tactical capabilities at the UNC's disposal made the area around the Iron Triangle, particularly the region of Pyonggang, of vital importance. The loss or neutralization of this town would severely compromise the Communists' ability to supply and move their troops from west to east, or vice versa. Pyonggang would be the key pivot to defend against an amphibious attack against either coast. After significant planning, Deng announced to his subordinate commands, "We are proposing tactical, continuous offensive campaigns in order to retain the initiative, smash the enemy's plans, and let newly arrived troops have more combat experience." Deng ordered this campaign of autumn "Tactical Counterattacks" to buy some breathing room around the Iron Triangle and inflict casualties on ROK and American units. He directed the campaign to begin by September 20 and finish thirty days later.[2]

Deng issued on September 12 the tactical counterattack order explaining the strategic situation facing the Chinese and North Korean armies and his intent to seize the initiative. It was the first detailed guidance for an offensive campaign since May 1951. The CPVF Thirty-Ninth, Twelfth, and Sixty-Eighth Armies were to "conduct continuous tactical counterattacks on three to five selected targets to wipe out enemy troops and inflict substantial enemy casualties." Deng further instructed commanders to conduct thorough reconnaissance on their objectives and insert "elite groups" to the rear and flanks of the targeted positions. It was critical that the attacking troops could identify all defensive positions, artillery emplacements, reserves, and obstacles. Artillery and infantry operations needed to be strictly coordinated to exploit the construction of caves and tunnels leading to the attack assembly areas. This technique would enhance surprise and reduce casualties from UNC air attacks and artillery fire. In line with *niupitang* tactics, if first- and second-echelon forces suffered inordinate casualties, then the action should be suspended, but, if the combination of constant infantry pressure and artillery fire could lure defenders "out of their defense works . . . it would be well worth it . . . [to] encourage annihilation battles at the front."[3]

The first phase of tactical counterattacks lasted eighteen days, and the Chinese gained several advantageous positions. Entire divisions massed against individual objectives, but the Chinese did not rely on human waves to swarm the defenders. Companies and battalions launched deliberate attacks to expose the defenders to effective artillery fire. Only once a position was sufficiently weakened did the infantry charge forward to overrun the defenses. Chinese gunners even engaged in limited counterbattery fire against American artillery battalions supporting the Koreans. The Chinese were getting more proficient and more prolific with their fire support, and engagements at Outpost Kelly and Capitol Hill inflicted hundreds of casualties against US and ROK units.[4]

But from a strategic viewpoint, the results were disappointing. Although Clark convened an emergency meeting with his Eighth Army commanders, there was no major shuffling of units, and, most importantly, no new situation at Panmunjom. The UNC continued to insist on voluntary repatriation. Therefore, Deng and his commanders decided to launch a second, even more ambitious, set of counterattacks. Deng signaled his army group commanders "to further disperse enemy forces and firepower and to deliver harder blows [against the] enemy." This second stage of tactical counterattacks would differ from the previous by timing and intensity. Whereas the earlier attacks involved elements of three armies and were conducted sequentially as units felt prepared, the CPVF commanders now decided to launch simultaneous attacks employing elements of seven armies supported by 760 artillery guns.[5]

During this second stage of tactical counterattacks (beginning October 6), Chinese troops claimed to have stormed twenty-one of twenty-three targeted UNC positions. However, the main effort in the CPVF's Thirty-Eighth Army's sector failed to capture Hill 395 after an epic ten-day battle, which cast a pall over the Communists' effort to force political concessions through military action. It also directly encouraged the UNC to launch its own counter-counter-attack campaign in an attempt to wrest the initiative from the Communists.[6]

White Horse Mountain

Hill 395 was the dominant terrain feature overlooking the Korean town of Chorwon, located at the southwestern apex of the Iron Triangle in the Yokkok River valley. It was virtually surrounded by the Yokkok River, which meandered around the hill's eastern, southern, and western slopes. Hill 395 and its neighbor to the west, Hill 281 ("Arrowhead Hill"), were the only two UNC positions on the north side of the river, the loss of which would compel the IX Corps to withdraw substantially south of the river, uncovering the flank of the I Corps and undoing the gains of Operation Commando. Further, loss of the valley's head opened a potential avenue to threaten Seoul. The corps would have also lost its lock on the southwestern apex of the Iron Triangle, which would have imperiled its ability to supply and support UNC forces farther east. It was therefore a vital UNC position, and its importance, both tactically and strategically, was such that the IX Corps commander, Maj. Gen. Reuben Jenkins, was not going to treat Hill 395 as just another outpost.[7]

The battle for Hill 395 (subsequently known as White Horse Mountain for its shape on the map resembling a horse lying on its side) lasted ten days and developed in four distinct periods, one of preparation and three of close fighting. Each of the fighting periods was punctuated by a major Chinese effort to dominate the hill and beat back any Korean counterattacks. However, backed by overwhelming artillery and air support, the Koreans inevitably returned and flung the Chinese off the hill. The battle ended with the utter exhaustion

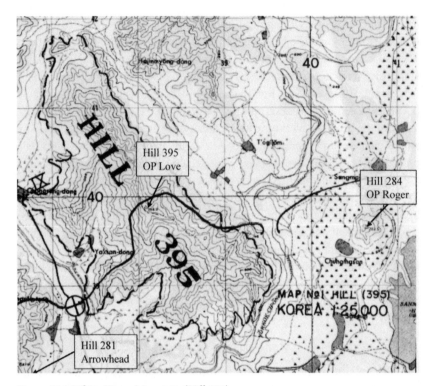

Figure 11.1 White Horse Mountain (Hill 395).

of the CPVF Thirty-Eighth Army and the triumph of the ROK Ninth Division, which became known as the White Horse Division.[8]

The ordeal at White Horse Mountain began with an intercepted Chinese communications message that prompted the Americans to establish a field site in the IX Corps sector to exploit tactical messages more quickly. This technique, called Low Level Intercept (LLI), was a Korean War innovation to put collection equipment and trained personnel close to the front lines and in direct contact with staff intelligence officers advising unit commanders. Analysis of LLI identified the Chinese units assembled and then forecasted the date and time of the first attack wave. These LLI reports continued to keep US and ROK forces informed of the location of Chinese units during the battle. Occasionally, analysis of Chinese signals identified potential targets for American artillery.[9]

Further intelligence information corroborated the LLI reporting. On October 1, ROK patrols discovered propaganda leaflets and a series of red, white, blue, and yellow colored flags emplaced near the Korean lines. These markers were likely guide points for unit assembly areas and attack corridors. American artillery observers and aircraft also noted increased enemy movement and activity, "the highest number of vehicle sightings ever recorded in this portion of the IX Corps sector."[10] But the great intelligence prize came two days later, when a CPVF officer deserted his unit and was captured by ROK soldiers on nearby Hill 284, just to the east of Hill 395. Thanks to an American artillery officer's intervention, the anonymous prisoner was sent to the rear where he revealed the intention of the CPVF 114th Division to assault Hill 395 and Hill 281 between October 4 and 5. He indicated the size of the units involved (six companies from one regiment) and the *niupitang* techniques of the assaulting elements to seize the crest and then briefly withdraw to allow artillery to inflict maximum losses against the expected Korean counterattack.[11]

Although not totally convinced by the prisoner's story, Jenkins ordered the repositioning of corps artillery, armor, anti-aircraft, and engineer units to support the ROK Ninth Division. The Korean troops defending Hill 395 also took additional measures. In addition to the whole of the Thirtieth Regiment already on the OPLR, the division commander, Maj. Gen. Kim Jong-oh, redeployed the third battalion of the Twenty-Eighth Regiment into a support position close to the hill. The rest of the regiment was designated to act as a reserve counterattacking force. In division reserve, Kim held the ROK Fifty-First Regiment, a newly formed and as yet untested unit. American artillery fired missions to interdict and disrupt Chinese activity and to suppress their artillery, which became more active on October 4. When the expected attack failed to materialize that night, Kim ordered all troops to hold their current positions for at least another three days.[12]

American forward observers (FO) had two observation posts (OP) supporting the ROK Ninth Division, one on White Horse itself and one on Hill 284, about 1,500 meters to the east. These observation positions, nicknamed OP Love (Hill 395) and OP Roger (Hill 284), played a key role to defend White Horse. From these two locations, the Americans observed the valley between the Chinese-held Hill 396 and the Korean lines on White Horse. Hill 284 also had good observation northward covering part of the back side of Hill 396. The FO at OP Roger, one of the few Americans on the ground throughout the battle, had clear orders to shoot all observed targets, "no matter how insignificant they seemed."[13] Throughout the first week of October the FOs identified likely Chinese artillery and mortar positions, infantry bunkers, assembly areas, and final attack positions where troops concentrated prior to launching an assault. Having identified these potential targets, the FOs recorded the map coordinates and target descriptions as target reference points (TRP). A TRP enabled an FO to request support using an abbreviated procedure that resulted in a faster response from the firing batteries.[14]

The corps commander's crucial decision was to reorganize artillery command and supporting relationships. The ROK First Field Artillery Group (FAG) was directed to support the ROK Ninth Division with its three Korean 105 mm battalions. Two US medium (155 mm howitzer) battalions, the 213th Field Artillery Battalion and the 955th Field Artillery Battalion, were ordered to provide "general support, reinforcing fires" to the First FAG. This meant that the American artillery would fire in response to the First FAG's requests to engage targets either out of range of the smaller Korean howitzers or when the heavier firepower of the American battalions was required. The 937th Field Artillery Battalion (155 mm gun), with range to shoot well beyond the limits of visual observation, provided counterbattery punch. Finally, to ensure artillery dominance Jenkins had his artillery command assign a "reinforcing" role to Battery B, Seventeenth Field Artillery, and Battery A, 424th Field Artillery. Both batteries employed massive 8-inch howitzers, giving the Americans destructive bunker-busting and antipersonnel capabilities. Additionally, because its FOs were calling for and adjusting fire, the 213th's fire direction center was designated as the artillery command and control headquarters for the entire corps artillery capable of firing in support of the ROK Ninth Division. This arrangement allowed the Korean commander, through the American FOs, to call on an unprecedented weight of explosives and metal in support of a Korean unit, and it was the singular factor influencing the battle's outcome. The 213th also assigned artillerymen as liaison officers to the Korean artillery battalions to coordinate targets and avoid fratricide. Because of this careful alignment of firepower, along with the prepositioning of tanks and other supporting troops, William Russell, a combat correspondent for Eighth Army, recalled that nowhere "was an army more prepared for an attack" than was the IX Corps.[15]

The importance of the IX Corps artillery was demonstrated even before the battle began. During the night of October 5–6, Chinese mortars had begun their bombardment, and soon heavier Chinese pieces added to the volume of shells falling on Hill 284 and White Horse. Lt. Jack Callaway and his team on Hill 284 were the first to observe and report on the Chinese preattack preparations. Callaway observed mortar teams on the southern slope of Hill 396, which was the Thirty-Eighth Army's main support position. Calling first for illumination rounds, he then called for and adjusted two to six rounds of 155 mm shells to scatter or kill each team he observed. This was done under strenuous conditions as Chinese artillery fell around and on top of OP Roger. After nearly twenty-four hours of this heavyweight game of hide and seek, Callaway spotted the first Chinese infantry formations and called for a TOT with VT fuses. The results were devastating and severely disrupted the Chinese assembly prior to the attack.[16]

Meanwhile, General Kim ensured that no Chinese infiltrators could outflank the division by positioning tanks, searchlight batteries, and anti-aircraft weapons along the flank approaches. The anti-aircraft weapons, with their high rate of fire, proved especially effective against massed infantry.[17] On the hill itself, the troops worked hard to improve their positions, stringing 725 rolls of concertina wire and 2,000 rolls of barbed wire, and emplacing 2,000 mines and 500 trip flares. Engineers constructed additional fortifications and bunkers using 450,000 sandbags and 6,400 board feet of heavy timber.[18]

On the morning of October 6, the Chinese destroyed the dam levee of the Pongnae-ho reservoir, which flooded the Yokkok River valley. Fortunately for the Koreans, the water level rose less than one meter and served only to alert the defenders.[19] As the sun set that evening, elements of two battalions from the CPVF 340th Regiment moved forward against the northern slope of Hill 395. Simultaneously, one battalion from the CPVF 113th Division began a supporting attack against nearby Hill 281. Additional artillery fire was directed against the Seventh Infantry Division on the Koreans' east flank.[20]

The Chinese attack was well planned. Nearly 2,500 shells of all calibers hit the defending Koreans during the first six hours of the battle (1900–0100 hours), when the Chinese first occupied the crest of the hill. Despite the tremendous American and ROK artillery fire, they still managed to overrun the ROK outposts on the northeastern tip of the hill and then seize the crest by midnight. One American eyewitness to the assault said, "It looked as if each little group had its own specific objective on the hill. Each group headed doggedly for this spot and seemed indifferent to the fate of adjoining Chinese formations."[21] These were assault troops, well drilled, rehearsed, and determined to reach their assigned objectives.

Three American artillerymen, Lt. Joseph Adams, Sgt. Roland Oxendale, and Cpl. Joseph Augustyn, occupied OP Love just below the crest on White Horse's northern slope. By 0200 hours on October 7, the Chinese had forced the First and Second Battalions of the Thirtieth Regiment back and had advanced to the southern slope of the hill, but the Americans remained firmly ensconced in their well-built bunker, although a direct hit did crumple the northwest side and knock down a piece of timber that hit Corporal Augustyn, who escaped with minor cuts, bruises, and a punctured eardrum. But the radio was damaged, and the shelling had cut wire communication lines to the rear, severing their lifeline to the artillery fire direction center. A sudden silence then left them in an ambiguous isolation. Unknown to Adams, the Koreans were reorganizing, and the Chinese had passed them by, taking the sounds of the battle to the other side of the hill.[22]

Adams decided to go out and look for himself. Exiting the outer bunker entrance into the trench line, Adams's senses struggled to appreciate the devastation. A nearby explosion caused him to duck just as a rifle shot rang out.

A moment later Adams was flung to the ground. A Chinese bullet had hit the top of his helmet, creased his scalp, and exited through the helmet's front. Stunned briefly, he gained awareness as he heard the distinctive eruption of a Chinese burp gun. Adams dashed back to his bunker and bowled over Sergeant Oxendale as he dove through the narrow entrance. Shouting that the Chinese were right behind him, Adams rushed to the radio and yelled into the handset, "THE CHINESE ARE ALL OVER THE . . . PLACE START SHOOTING AT MY BUNKER."[23]

Miraculously for the Americans, at the fire direction center of the 213th Field Artillery Battalion, Adams's last transmission broke through the static. Lt. Col. Leon Humphrey, the battalion commander, ordered a corps TOT including the ROK 105 mm battalions and the US 8-inch howitzers. The call was risky as an accidental impact, especially by one of the heavy 8-inch shells, could easily destroy the OP and kill its occupants. But the FO's call left no doubt as to the tactical necessity. Callaway heard the battalion's fire commands and immediately began to call adjustments. As each volley of shells exploded over OP Love, Callaway requested to shift the next concentration by forty meters. Three adjustments after the initial volley completed a full box around the target area. Inside the bunker, the Americans curled up under cover while the Chinese outside were cut down. The dozens of air bursting shells ensured nothing above ground level could survive. Some shells failed to detonate or were mistakenly fused at impact. Each time one of these hit the ground, the bunker shuddered, but held. The shelling was so severe that when Callaway ordered, "Cease-fire," he could not tell if the bunker had survived. For several days he was sure that his friend Adams and his team had perished.[24]

The bombardment of OP Love shattered the Chinese attack. The ROK infantry managed to disengage, reorganize, rearm, and bring up the reserve troops from the Twenty-Eighth Regiment to counterattack. By sunrise on October 7, the Koreans had recovered their original positions at a cost of fewer than 300 total casualties and were digging in, anticipating the next Chinese move.[25]

During the first twelve hours of the battle the CPVF's losses had been severe. The Koreans counted 587 dead left on the hill and estimated an additional 143 enemy killed. They also recovered four recoilless rifles, ten light machine guns, thirty-eight automatic rifles, and three mortars, indicating that two, possibly three, battalions had been roughly handled.[26] In response, the Thirty-Eighth Army immediately committed four more battalions from the CPVF 114th Division. Once again, overcome by the size of the Chinese force, the Koreans had to abandon their main positions. Just after midnight October 7–8, the Chinese again controlled the heights. General Kim responded by recalling the ROK Thirtieth Regiment and ordering the ROK Twenty-Eighth Regiment to assume responsibility for the battle. He also redeployed the ROK Fifty-First Regiment to cover the eastern portion of the division's line (including Hill 284), and repositioned the ROK Twenty-Ninth Regiment to support the attempt to recapture the hill in the early hours of October 8.[27] Radio intercepts revealed the strain of the battle on the CPVF: "Situation is bad. Need reinforcements; cannot hold out much longer; 7th and 8th companies very short of men. Need more artillery."[28]

By midnight on October 8–9 neither side owned the crest. The Chinese attempted one final surge with three fresh battalions advancing in successive echelons and supported by heavy concentrations of artillery. Within two hours they had complete control over the hill's peak, crest, and the ridge running from the crest to the northwest. Kim and his staff prepared a deliberate attack, with American artillery and tactical aircraft to support the First and Second Battalions of the ROK Twenty-Ninth Regiment. A nighttime counterattack supported with over 17,000 shells, bombs, napalm canisters, and tank rounds brought the Koreans to the hill's crest for the sixth time since the battle began four days earlier.[29] On the following night, October 10, a Chinese company attempted to cross the Yokkok River between Hill 395 and Arrowhead Hill. Thanks to coordinated illumination support, Company C, Seventy-Third Tank Battalion, turned back this effort with severe casualties for the Chinese. Indeed, throughout the day, tank support had been critical for the Koreans' endurance. Korean and American tank crews fired 585 rounds of 90 mm tank gun shells, 62,975 .50-caliber machine gun rounds, and 56,250 .30-caliber rounds.[30]

At 2200 hours, though, the Koreans were moving forward again, which signaled another transition in the battle as the IX Corps began now to take more aggressive actions against the battered Thirty-Eighth Army. Jenkins saw an opportunity to exploit the Americans' mobility and get more firepower into the battle. He ordered the 140th Tank Battalion to prepare one company to team up with a Korean infantry company and conduct a raid about half a kilometer north of the MLR.[31] At 0400 hours on October 11, Company B accompanied by a company from the ROK Fifty-First Regiment moved forward to a position due east of Hill 396. Unopposed, the tankers fired round after round at Chinese infantry, artillery, and logistics units on Hill 396 and the north slope of Hill 395. Later the same day, a similar task force composed of Company B, Seventy-Third Tank Battalion, and the Second Battalion of the ROK Thirtieth Regiment attacked up the western draw separating Hill 395 from Arrowhead Hill. After two hours of heavy fighting, the Chinese recognized the danger of this position on the flank and they spared no effort to wipe it out. Although the Koreans held the crest, by nightfall the western flank position had to be abandoned.[32]

On October 12, General Kim sensed that the intensity of the Chinese attack had diminished, and he ordered his units to begin a "leapfrog" advance to keep the pressure on the Chinese and inflict maximum casualties while maintaining fresh troops in reserve to guard against a Chinese counterthrust. The staff planning and artillery preparation that accompanied this plan demonstrated how far Korean leadership had progressed over the past year, as such an attack was clearly an advanced and difficult maneuver. However, the Korean troops and officers were up to the task. Elements of the Third Battalion, ROK Thirtieth Regiment, were eager to get at the enemy and strike a severe blow. As they passed through the ROK Twenty-Ninth Regiment, they were met by a strong Chinese thrust. Having reached a point one hundred meters north of the crest of the hill, the Koreans dug in and remained to defend throughout the night. Chinese efforts to force them back came to naught. An intercepted Chinese headquarters message reported, "We have stopped our artillery. You start attacking position number five." The troops on Hill 395 radioed back, "We have no strength [to attack]."[33]

At 0300 hours on October 13, Kim ordered the ROK Twenty-Eighth Regiment to move forward and continue the attack. One battalion went straight over the top of the hill while a second moved around the west side to flank the Chinese still struggling to hold on to their part of the northern slope of Hill 395. The two battalions closed the pincers and cleared their respective objectives. Early in the morning the following day, the ROK Twenty-Ninth Regiment moved forward after a sharp and brief preparatory bombardment. Chinese resistance was ineffective as Korean companies overwhelmed Chinese platoons. By the end of the day the fighting lines were substantially farther north than they had been the previous days. Between midnight and 0200 hours on October 15 the firing died off as White Horse Mountain was cleared of all Chinese troops. In a final action, the ROK Twenty-Ninth Regiment passed through the Thirtieth Regiment's forward line and cleared the last Chinese outposts remaining on the ridge extending to the northwest from Hill 395. Having full control over White Horse Mountain, and as attention in the IX Corps sector had already transitioned to the east, General Kim ordered his troops to dig in. The battle, and the Koreans' crucible of combat, had ended.[34]

The Will to Win

As American and Korean officers assessed the results of the battle, the statistics were impressive. The Chinese had never suffered so many casualties and loss of equipment in fighting a single ROK division. The Koreans claimed

TABLE 11.1. CHINESE WEAPONS AND EQUIPMENT
CAPTURED ON HILL 395, OCTOBER 5–15, 1952

Heavy machine guns	8
Machine guns	40
Mortar, 60 mm	22
Mortar, 82 mm	3
Automatic rifles	27
3.5" Rocket launchers	22
Radios	4
Light machine guns	57
Recoilless rifles, 57 mm	11
Submachine guns	312
Rifles	530
Anti-aircraft machine guns	2

Source: KMAG Command Report, October 1952, Annex F-50,
ROK Ninth Division, 59, RG 407, NARA II.

3,244 enemy killed (counted), an additional 1,966 estimated killed, 4,021 estimated wounded, and 54 prisoners. Even allowing for exaggerated reporting, the CPVF Thirty-Eighth Army had suffered a significant defeat, using up by October 15 two divisions against White Horse Mountain and a third assaulting neighboring Hill 281 (table 11.1).[35] According to prisoner reports, company strengths in the assaulting regiments were down to an average of only fifteen to twenty men. They also revealed that because of effective air and artillery interdiction of the CPVF's supply line, coupled with a lack of evacuation facilities, Chinese dead far exceeded their number of wounded.[36]

The Chinese attributed their failure to capture the two heights to three reasons: "the corps [Thirty-Eighth Army] had made too hasty plans on the operation, selected inappropriate targets, and had the plan leaked by a defector."[37] These points certainly played a role in the battle's outcome, but the Chinese failed to give due credit to their enemies. They assumed that the ROK Ninth Division, whose fighting record up to this point was mediocre, would be easily pushed off the hill. They also underestimated the Americans' willingness to defend their positions north of the Yokkok River. These two assumptions led the Chinese to attempt too much by assaulting both Arrowhead Hill and White Horse Mountain with the same army formation. These two positions were geographically linked, and the failure to seize Arrowhead complicated an already difficult tactical problem.[38] They also committed too few troops to the initial assault and were unprepared for the amount of attrition they would suffer under UNC artillery bombardment, which made the ROK counterattacks more challenging to resist.[39]

Korean gunners, freshly graduated from intensive on-the-job training with the ROK First Field Artillery Group, also contributed to their countrymen's support, firing thousands of shells and enabling them to survive repeated Chinese assaults and the more than 43,000 shells fired at them by Chinese artillery and mortars (table 11.2).[40] KMAG officers testified to the effectiveness of artillery, reporting "TOT's involving several battalions time and time again hit the enemy at critical periods in the battle and played a major part in his inability to hold ground gained. Likewise, [CPVF] reinforcements were dispersed . . . when their commitment to the battle could have been influential." The net result was a decrease in Chinese artillery effectiveness, isolation of the battlefield that prevented Chinese infantry from bringing to bear their numerical advantages, and a large casualty list presented to the CPVF Thirty-Eighth Army.[41]

American and Korean armor crews also turned in an impressive performance over ground that was not "tank country." Jenkins's employment of armored forces showed once again the value of imaginative combined arms fighting. Tank-mobile firepower interdicted all routes of approach against the flanks of Hill 395, forcing the Chinese into a series of frontal attacks on ground already saturated by air strikes and artillery fire. At the same time, Korean troops could maneuver along these same flank approaches when required, as they did in the battle's last period. Korean tank units also received their baptism by fire at White Horse Mountain. Twenty-two M36 tank destroyers from the ROK Fifty-Third Tank Company covered the eastern flank of Hill 395 and played a key role observing and interdicting the movement of Chinese reinforcements.[42]

As important as these technical factors were, the Korean victory was also a vindication of Van Fleet's soldier and officer training initiatives. The ROK Ninth Division completed its Field Training Command rotation in October 1951 and continued its own unit training program to keep their skills sharp and provide officers with additional experience planning and executing unit operations tasks. General Kim and his staff performed magnificently to command and control the tempo of the battle. Both during offensive and defensive actions, Kim enforced a periodic rotation of units to keep troops fresh and prevent battle losses from undermining unit cohesion and effectiveness. Friendly casualties, which were substantial for a ten-day period of "stalemate" fighting, included 505 killed, 2,415 wounded, and 391 missing (prisoners or

TABLE 11.2. ARTILLERY FIRED IN SUPPORT OF ROK NINTH DIVISION

Unit	Rounds fired (October 061500–151100)
51st Field Artillery Battalion (Korean) 105 mm	21,689
52nd Field Artillery Battalion (Korean) 105 mm	56,056
50th Field Artillery Battalion (Korean) 105 mm	17,343
30th Field Artillery Battalion (Korean) 105 mm	48,661
955th Field Artillery Battalion (US) 155 mm	22,011
213th Field Artillery Battalion (US) 155 mm	36,326
937th Field Artillery Battalion (US) 155 mm	9,378
A/2nd Heavy Mortar Company (US) 4.2-inch	15,868
B/17th and A/424th FA Battalions (US) 8-inch	10,080
2nd Rocket Battery (US) 4.5-inch	6,678
Total	246,090

Source: KMAG Command Report, October 1952, Annex F-50, ROK Ninth Division, 106, RG 407, NARA II; Headquarters, IX Corps, Special After Action Report, Enclosure B.

presumed killed), yet the visible presence of Korean officers played a prominent role to ensure the Korean soldier focused on the enemy in front of him rather than the potential escape to his rear. Keeping the Korean soldier in the trenches, or conversely, bringing him up the slopes repeatedly to face automatic weapons fire and hundreds of grenades, was an incredible feat of leadership, perseverance, and patriotic motivation.[43] Van Fleet's investment in Korean troops was paying dividends and potentially pointing a way forward to apply additional military pressure against the Chinese.

The Chinese Assessment of the Autumn Counterattack Operations

Despite the disappointing results at Hill 395, Deng Hua on October 21 signaled his commanders that the counterattack operations had been a stunning success. "Our forces have gained tremendous experience," he wrote, "and have inflicted heavy casualties [against] U.S. and its [ROK] forces." With another intense battle (Operation Showdown) already in progress, Deng prudently alerted his commanders that retaliation attacks should be expected. "All [armies] must now go back to regular active defense operations starting on October 22." But the pressure of the American-Korean offensive at Kumhwa, at the opposite side of the Iron Triangle, caused Deng almost imme-

diately to countermand his order. He and his senior commanders decided to
extend the counterattack campaign at least until the end of the month. During the last week of October, CPVF units across the front launched attacks
against twenty-one additional objectives.[44]

The Autumn Counterattack Campaign was the first major offensive operation the Chinese and North Korean forces initiated since UNC forces had assumed their own active defense in the late fall of 1951. Even if the UNC did
not react to the campaign as the Chinese hoped, the operations had been tactically beneficial. The Chinese believed these attacks had taken the UNC by
surprise, inflicted numerous casualties (27,000 claimed by the Chinese), and
seized valuable terrain, thereby disrupting Clark's (supposed) plan for a major
offensive. The units involved learned to make elaborate and deliberate preparations for each attack, to include rehearsals and extensive political indoctri-
nation to explain the purpose of the attack to the troops. The most successful
attacks typically involved a small-scale "annihilation operation" based on the
Communists' fortified defensive tunnel and cave positions. They also tended
to use fewer troops and more artillery than in previous offensives. The campaign showed the Chinese capable of a limited general offensive across the
front.[45] Even if White Horse Mountain was a failure, the battle could still be
carried on elsewhere. Mao boasted to Stalin that the CPVF had learned great
lessons and inflicted serious damage against the UNC during this campaign.
He further explained that "the reason we have achieved such an enormous
victory . . . is—in addition to [the] bravery of [the] troops and commanders,
solid works, appropriate command and adequate supplies—the ferocity and
accuracy of the artillery fire, which *turned out to be the decisive factor* [em-
phasis added]."[46]

The Chinese proficiency with artillery was plainly manifest and docu-
mented by the Americans, illustrating how sophisticated the Chinese had
become using artillery in support of the infantry battle. In the ten days prior
to the Battle of White Horse Mountain, the Thirty-Eighth Army had visibly
increased its artillery positions, engaged in more counterbattery fire than before, and integrated additional reinforcing artillery. Few registration rounds
were required for these new units, indicating Chinese gunners had a thorough
understanding of enemy positions and the capabilities of their own guns. As
a result of these enhancements, artillery fire during the attack was "timely,
accurate, and usually effective."[47] The supply of communist artillery was also
assessed as adequate as the number of rounds fired into the IX Corps sector
reveals (table 11.3).

The counterattack campaign produced two additional influences that conditioned the military and political interactions between the CPVF and the
UNC. The first is that from the Chinese perspective, their tactical military ef-

TABLE 11.3. ARTILLERY FIRED AGAINST IX CORPS,
OCTOBER 5–15, 1952

Time period (1800–1800 hours)	Number of rounds (excluding mortar shells)
October 5 to 6	1,468
October 6 to 7	10,980
October 7 to 8	2,226
October 8 to 9	12,024
October 9 to 10	4,474
October 10 to 11	4,840
October 11 to 12	3,430
October 12 to 13	5,467
October 13 to 14	5,768
October 14 to 15	4,631

Source: IX Corps Special AAR, 30–31.

forts, excepting the rebuff at Hill 395, were an unqualified success. The Sino-Korean armies could look back on the two-months' fighting with satisfaction that they had made the UNC pay for its unreasonable intransigence at Panmunjom, and they had seized the initiative for the first time since May 1951. A Canadian officer serving in the Commonwealth Division ruefully noted, "It was obvious then [fall 1952] that the Chinaman could smash our existing defences almost any time he chose."[48] Furthermore, the Chinese in particular learned crucial lessons fighting modern war that translated into further strategic confidence. The transition from mobile to protracted war was working. Mao could, with equanimity, let the strategic impasse continue without fearing a major military reverse or penalty for *his* intransigence.[49]

Second, the campaign appeared to show that the Communists had battlefield momentum that threatened the military equilibrium, and they were using it to score cheap tactical victories without paying any political penalties on the world stage or at Panmunjom. Clark reported to Washington his assessments of the CPVF's moves, characterizing them as "limited objective attacks" displaying strength and firepower to dissuade a UNC offensive or to spoil such a move by forcing the UNC to divert resources and effort to counter the Communists' moves. A secondary objective was considered to be the seizure of valuable terrain to use as bargaining chips.[50] In either case, the Chinese's initiative on the battlefield was upping the ante and making it harder to bargain for an end game that accomplished the UNC's military goals and the Truman administration's policy objectives in Korea. The UNC would have to respond with its own political and military initiatives.

The US army's official historian, Walter Hermes, correctly noted that the new UNC commander had been as reluctant as Ridgway to step up military pressure on the ground just to gain real estate. This sound reasoning was forgotten that fall as Clark became more alarmed by Communist intransigence at Panmunjom combined with their recent offensive in central Korea. Van Fleet was ready to go: "The situation is about the same, but more and more I am of the opinion that we should do something to end it—and first with a military victory," he told Collins in late September.[51] A few days later, on September 29, in response to a JCS inquiry, Clark replied that the reason an armistice had not been obtained in Korea was not "the apparent impossibility of agreement on repatriation of POWs." Rather, it was the failure of the UNC to exert "suf[ficient] mil[itary] pressure to impose the [requirement] for an armistice on the enemy."[52]

After the war Clark clearly spelled out his viewpoint: "To my mind an armistice was an objective that had to be won by military means."[53] Negotiation was a supporting effort only. Clark was convinced, as were his principal subordinates—to include Lt. Gen. William Harrison (promoted on September 6)—that the Communists would only respond to loss on the battlefield. Therefore, Clark considered it a great strategic move forward when President Truman agreed in mid-September to give Harrison the authority at the height of the CPVF's tactical counteroffensive to suspend further meetings at Panmunjom until the Communists agreed to bargain on the basis of voluntary repatriation of prisoners.

On September 26 the JCS directed Clark to present three packaged alternatives to use to resolve the POW deadlock. All three involved bringing prisoners to the DMZ and then essentially releasing them to choose whether to travel north or south. Two days later, Harrison delivered the final menu of options that would satisfy the UNC's objective and permit the Communists to assuage their stated fears of forcible retention. He then proposed a ten-day recess to give the Chinese and North Korean delegates the opportunity to study the proposals. The delegates reconvened on October 8, when Nam Il broke out into a rehash of old accusations. He agreed to an exchange point at the DMZ supervised by a Neutral Nations Supervisory Commission, the return of Korean prisoners to the home, north or south, but Chinese prisoners would all be returned to Communist control.[54] Nam did not recognize that Harrison had presented a "take it or leave it" deal. Between July 8, 1951, and October 7, 1952, the two sides had met in 121 plenary sessions,

179 subdelegation meetings, and 138 staff officer sessions. The UNC had had enough. After observing that Nam's reply was unsatisfactory in resolving the impasse, Harrison asked one last time if the Communists rejected the UNC's latest proposal. After confirming that the Communists would not accept any proposal or offer one of their own, Harrison made a final statement that the UNC was not terminating the talks but would be available should the Communists accept one of the UNC proposals on POWs or submit in writing their own constructive offer. He then declared the talks indefinitely recessed and walked out of the conference tent. He did not return until April 26, 1953.[55]

At nearly the same time, Secretary Acheson affirmed the UNC's stance during a press conference in Washington. The Truman administration at last appeared to be siding with its negotiators, noting that the talks at Panmunjom had degenerated into a forum for "Communist abuse and propaganda harangues." The secretary reiterated that the three proposals put forward would meet the administration's intent to follow voluntary repatriation while safeguarding the Communists' right to interview each prisoner and ascertain in the presence of a neutral party that prisoner's repatriation desire. Significant to Acheson's argument was the need to "preserve the humanitarian principles" of repatriation and not "compromise on the principle that a prisoner should not be forced to return against his will. For us to weaken in our resolve would constitute an abandonment of the principles fundamental to this country and the United Nations. We shall not trade the lives of men."[56] It was a passionate defense of Truman's policy, perhaps the most passionate to date. It also tied the prestige of the United States and its armed intervention in the Korean War to the September 28 proposals tabled by Harrison. There could be no going back.[57]

As military men, both Clark and Van Fleet understood the calculus. Not airpower, psychological pressure, or logic could break the deadlock. The Chinese advances over the previous two months would have to be met by an equally forceful offensive, if nothing else to demonstrate that the failure to agree to an armistice carried a price tag. To reverse the perception of Communist momentum in the fall of 1952, Clark on October 8—the same day that General Harrison broke off talks at Panmunjom and as the Chinese assault on Hill 395 was reaching its climax—gave approval for the limited attack that came to be known as Operation Showdown.[58]

12

OPERATION SHOWDOWN, OCTOBER–NOVEMBER 1952

OPERATION SHOWDOWN WAS originally conceived as a regiment level attack to counterbalance the Chinese thrust at White Horse Mountain and to demonstrate UNC resolve to fight for the hills.[1] If successful, the Americans assumed severe losses inflicted on the enemy would keep the Communists off balance, forcing them to commit their reserve forces and lessening the pressure against other critical areas (the ROK sectors in particular). Its architect dreamed the operation might even "persuade the Communists to begin bargaining in good faith at Panmunjom."[2]

But Operation Showdown was a risky enterprise. Van Fleet's idea to seize the tactical initiative with an attack against the southeast apex of the Iron Triangle promised to upend the delicate operational balance, and therefore should have called into question Showdown's basic premise, that a limited attack against a strongly defended and important terrain feature would not provoke a significant enemy response leading to a costly battle of attrition—a battle the UNC might not be able to afford to win. Ridgway had employed attrition tactics very well, inflicting large losses while preserving the UNC's ground combat strength. The objectives of Showdown, two terrain features known as Triangle Hill (Hill 598) and Sniper Ridge, did not promise by themselves tangible operational gains, even if successfully captured.[3] Showdown was also an isolated attack that failed to engage the Communists' reserves or support other offensive efforts. There was no synergy at the army level, where such an operationally significant effort would pay the greatest dividends. Therefore, Showdown was at variance with the Americans' operational approach, and it should have provoked a more deliberate and thoughtful plan on the part of the Seventh Infantry Division, the IX Corps, and Eighth Army.[4]

However, the Chinese offensives in September and then the fight for White Horse Mountain demanded a response. With negotiations suspended since October 8, Clark recognized that the arena for strategic positioning had shifted back to the battlefield, and he may have been comfortable with the opportu-

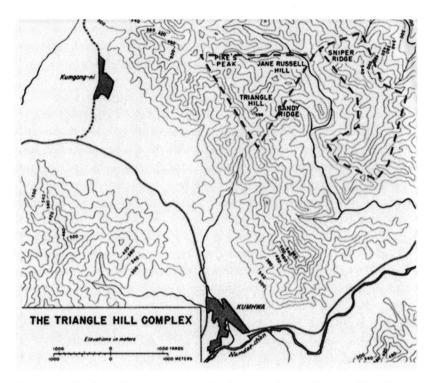

Figure 12.1 Kumhwa–Osong-san region, October 1952. Source: Hermes, *Truce Tent and Fighting Front*, 312.

nity to unleash American firepower and duplicate the ROK's success at White Horse Mountain in an offensive context. If Clark thought he could influence the Communists with tactical pressure, he, along with every American and Korean soldier involved with Showdown, would come to understand that Triangle Hill and Sniper Ridge were not ordinary hilltops, but critical Chinese outposts with strategic and potentially political consequences.[5]

After a year of positional combat, American commanders were familiar with Chinese *niupitang* tactics and why they were effective: artillery and manpower. In September 1952, the Chinese for the first time in the war tied focused preparatory bombardments with a significantly higher volume of shelling.[6] The Chinese had learned to economize, and though they were ready to throw men into any cauldron if the payoff were attractive, it was always for a purpose. Clark observed, "The enemy was able at any time to mass enough men to dent our line [and] if the Communists had taken terrain features important to our defense line we had to counterattack to recapture them. That is where we suffered our heaviest casualties."[7] Through the summer and fall campaigns, UNC troops had to contend with the enemy's new proficiency at combined arms fighting, which promised to make any attack against prepared positions costly. No matter how well planned and executed, Showdown was going to be expensive for its limited gains, which was problematic for a war that was supposed to be limited.

The Americans would get the fight they sought. However, for such a valuable tactical objective, the UNC's initial plan did not accord enough respect to the Chinese. As the plan developed, the Americans assumed the attrition contest for White Horse Mountain had worn down the resistance of nearby CPVF units. The employment of sixteen artillery battalions—nearly three hundred guns ranging from 105 mm to 8-inch howitzers—teamed up with hundreds of preplanned fighter-bomber sorties to pulverize dug-in enemy forces would make the infantry task to advance two hundred to five hundred meters to occupy their objectives and hold against Chinese counterattacks relatively easy. Based on the sanguine estimates from the army down to the regiment conducting the attack, Clark approved the operation, expected to cost two hundred casualties.[8] Frustrated by the extended military and political confrontations, Clark was willing to try a trial of strength on the battlefield to influence the suspended clash of wills at Panmunjom.

Deng Hua had anticipated that the Chinese tactical counterattacks might provoke a "regional attack as retaliation."[9] To the east of the Kumhwa valley was the Kumsong salient, protruding north and menacing the east side of the Iron Triangle. The Chinese had expected Clark to launch a major offensive, and the Kumsong area was a likely jump-off point. Able to read a map as well as the Americans, the Chinese recognized their vulnerability. Osong-san would have to be heavily defended. Even as Deng directed that tactical counterattack operations would continue through the rest of the month, he instructed the Third Army Group command and staff to look after the Kumhwa defenses. The CPVF's Fifteenth Army commander, Qin Jiwei, was directed to "work out every detail but also to get ready to pay a high price" to keep the UNC forces away from Osong-san, "the key point in the middle of our entire cross-peninsula defensive line." Yang Dezhi, commander for CPVF operations, remembered, "We had to win this battle."[10]

Osong-san (Hill 1062, dubbed "Father Mountain" by American soldiers), was the linchpin to the Chinese defenses guarding the Iron Triangle in the vicinity of Kumhwa. From this vantage point, the Chinese had complete observation of the Kumhwa valley. Just as importantly, from Hill 1062, which bristled with guns and hidden artillery emplacements and tunnels, the Chinese could mass troops and artillery out of sight and beyond striking range of all but the heaviest caliber artillery. Efforts to seize additional outposts or to drive the Chinese back onto their own MLR were frustrated by Osong-san's indomitable presence.[11] Lt. Richard Ecker, upon getting his first view of the Chinese-held mountains north of Kumhwa, remarked, "The hills closing around us were steep and tall, rising a thousand feet or more above the valley floor. But they were all dwarfed by the mountain that appeared directly in front of us, perhaps five or six miles to the north . . . that's 'Papa-san,' Hill 1062."[12] Another American soldier, a combat correspondent, was equally impressed by Papa-san. "You could drive for miles to the rear and look back and see 'Papa-san' staring down at you. It was kind of spooky to know that the Chinese were watching you for miles."[13]

Defending Osong-san was the CPVF Forty-Fifth Division, part of the Qin's Fifteenth Army. Elements of its 135th Regiment and 133rd Regiment held two outpost positions on Hill 598 and a protruding ridgeline to the east known as Sniper Ridge.[14] The troops defending these positions had cut forty-eight tunnels (each at least ten meters in length), dug multiple trenches, emplaced obstacles, and sowed hundreds of land mines. Other logistics preparations included the allocation of 8,000 hand grenades to each infantry company along with food, water, and other necessary supplies to sustain three months of combat. Qin reorganized his army's artillery and ordered to the Osong-san region the Twentieth Howitzer Regiment, one battalion of the Eleventh Howitzer Regiment, the Sixtieth Army Artillery Battalion, and the 209th Rocket Artillery Regiment—a total of 185 howitzers and rocket launchers. Tang Wancheng, the CPVF Forty-Fifth Division's vice commander, assumed command and control of all artillery to ensure "full support to infantry in operations."[15]

The CPVF Third Army Group shared Deng's and Yang's complete confidence in Qin's preparation, commitment, and leadership. Operationally, the Chinese looked on this battle as an extension of their Autumn Tactical Counterattacks Campaign. Therefore, successful resistance was necessary not only to pressure the UNC to return to Panmunjom, but also to maintain the strategic initiative, strike a heavy military blow against the UNC, and vindicate Chinese methods for defensive warfare, which attempted to neutralize American firepower and technology. Qin's cool handling of the battle demonstrated the degree to which Chinese tactical commanders had matured in the conduct of modern combined arms fighting.[16]

Significant for Qin's conduct of the battle, the regions around the Iron Triangle had profoundly transformed since the end of Operation Piledriver in June 1951, giving the Chinese three crucial advantages. Fortified positions and tunnels in depth factored prominently in the Chinese ability to carry on fighting. As long as CPVF troops could retreat into tunnels and caves, UNC forces could never really control the surface above. Counterattacks facilitated by tunnel forces could quickly reclaim lost ground and drive enemy troops off with significant casualties. A second advantage was that tunnels neutralized air interdiction, close air support, and artillery effects on the battlefield. They protected the movement and storage of necessary supplies (food and ammunition being most critical) for a protracted battle and gave the Chinese more staying power. Finally, defending troops no longer needed to mass in open areas subject to air and artillery bombardment, which shortened the distance and time required to stage counterattacks and increased surprise on the objective.[17] All of these factors strongly influence the course of the battle during Showdown.

Van Fleet's Vision

Unusual for this period, the genesis for Showdown came from the bottom up. Immediately after Operation Creeper, Col. Lloyd R. Moses, commander of the Thirty-First Infantry Regiment, recognized the terrain advantages the Chinese had by holding Triangle Hill. On July 23 he directed his staff to begin planning to neutralize or seize Hill 598 outright. Moses was eager to prove himself as a combat leader and enthusiastic about his offensive ideas. He reflected in his daily journal, "I believe every commander (that includes me) has to come under fire and get the feel of a perfect fighting animal, untiring, cold, cunning, ruthless, quick of decision, incredibly brave (bold), and [able to] see thru the 'fog.'"[18] True to his own ideal, Moses made several personal visits to Hill 598, either overhead in a light aircraft or on the ground as a patrol member with the regiment's Intelligence and Reconnaissance platoon. These scouting trips gave Moses a good appreciation for the difficulties involved: a maze of zigzag trench works studded with bunkers, excellent observation toward the south, no covered or concealed avenues of approach or ways to outflank the enemy, and multiple strong points defended with machine guns. It was a good position, and a successful attack would require a tremendous amount of firepower and support.[19]

By October (and before the battle for White Horse Mountain had begun), the IX Corps commander, Maj. Gen. Reuben Jenkins, understood the military dilemma along with the importance of his corps's position astride the Chorwon-Kumhwa valleys. The Chinese grip on Hill 1062 posed a strategic threat to his corps and the Eighth Army as a whole should the Communists return to a general offensive. A spoiling attack aimed at Osong-san could disrupt the Chinese plans and help Van Fleet seize the initiative tactically. Jenkins and his staff accepted the Seventh Infantry Division's plan to use Moses's Thirty-First Infantry to seize Triangle Hill. The modest casualty estimate should have caused greater reflection, but to increase the chance for success against Hill 598 Jenkins agreed to add the ROK Second Division to the attack and give it a similar mission to seize Sniper Ridge and tie the Chinese down defending two positions instead of allowing them to focus on just one.

Van Fleet, ever looking for a way to push the Chinese back, immediately concurred with the plan and on October 5 wrote to Clark expressing support and requesting approval. Van Fleet was concerned the Chinese tactical counterattacks threatened the precarious military balance and had swung the initiative to the Communists. He argued, "Our present course of defensive action in the face of the enemy initiative is resulting in the highest casualties since the heavy fighting of October and November 1951." It was time to give the Communists something they had to defend.

Van Fleet's second argument was tactical. He claimed that the two sides' OPLRs were, in some cases, only about 200 meters apart. A successful thrust to capture Triangle Hill and Sniper Ridge would force the Chinese back more than 1,200 meters to the next significant terrain feature, Osong-san, which would then bring the Chinese citadel to the forefront of the battle, compromising its value as an observation point, artillery position, and supporting area for the Fifteenth Army's MLR. Van Fleet felt "the resulting wider no-man's land is very desirable tactically." He declined to go further, as he could have, to suggest that a successful offensive could have potential to generate momentum for more gains in the Iron Triangle at the Communists' expense.

Finally, Van Fleet was concerned that Eighth Army was losing its combat edge. Nearly a year since Ridgway directed Eighth Army to assume active defense, the Communists still resisted a final settlement, while the highly tuned and aggressive Eighth Army had slowly become a weakened force through troop rotation and inactivity. Van Fleet believed an offensive effort would be "good for training and morale" and that US public opinion "will support [us] doing something aggressive, even though on a small scale." He understood that the UNC could not accept increasing casualties without any apparent progress either at Panmunjom or at the front lines.[20]

While Van Fleet lobbied Clark, Jenkins continued to flesh out the Showdown concept. He did not intend to make any significant changes to his corps's disposition with three divisions forward: from west to east the ROK Ninth, Seventh Infantry, and the ROK Second. The Fortieth Infantry Division's three infantry regiments remained in reserve, but its artillery, tanks, and engineer troops were available to support the attack. On October 9, IX Corps issued Operation Plan (OPLAN) 32 to the ROK Second and Seventh Infantry divisions and the corps artillery. The plan, only five pages long, ordered: "IX Corps attacks D day to seize and hold Hill 598 and Sniper Ridge, adjusts MLR accordingly, and inflicts maximum casualties on the enemy." It was seemingly a straightforward, infantry-oriented offensive mission: take ground and kill the enemy.[21]

Both divisions received nearly identical tasks. One infantry battalion was to attack and seize its respective objective, consolidate, and establish a new defensive line north of the MLR. Air and artillery fire were to provide the killing power for the infantry to exploit in a fast-moving thrust that would hopefully catch the Chinese by surprise, divert attention from White Horse Mountain, and compel a hasty and costly counterattack. Each division was also ordered to maintain a reinforced battalion prepared to assist in the consolidation phase, a prudent directive that anticipated a Chinese reaction. The corps expected the attacking battalions to establish their new defenses by the end of the first day and the divisions to have detailed plans for defensive artillery fire and air support to pummel any Chinese counterattacks. For unknown reasons Van Fleet and Jenkins assumed the entire battle would last only five days.[22]

To reduce the risk to his attacking infantry, Van Fleet promised "to use fire power to the maximum extent . . . in addition to my own [artillery] fire power, we will have adequate air support, about 86 sorties daily."[23] Both divisions had their direct support artillery (the Fortieth Infantry Division's artillery was attached to the ROK Second Division), consisting of three 105 mm howitzer battalions and one 155 mm howitzer battalion. To reinforce these battalions, the corps attached two Korean battalions to each division, giving each division commander a total of four 105 mm and two 155 mm howitzer battalions in a direct support role. In general support to each division's artillery were an additional 155 mm howitzer battalion from the corps artillery and heavy mortars (4.2-inch). One 155 mm and one 8-inch howitzer battalion remained under corps control to fire in support of the entire corps front. Preattack bombardment was to commence five days prior to D-day, with the full weight of the corps's massed guns to begin just twenty minutes prior to the infantry assault—280 guns and howitzers from sixteen battalions. On the day of the attack, 24,750 rounds were planned to hit Chinese lines.[24]

Van Fleet expected the Fifth Air Force to "soften up" defenses on the objectives and isolate the Chinese by interdicting their ability to resupply and reinforce their positions. American pilots were wary about attacking communist positions that were protected by effective small arms, automatic weapons, and anti-aircraft guns, so IX Corps staff officers developed a new tactic to coordinate better air-to-ground actions and suppress enemy air defenses. When air force liaison officers at the corps headquarters cued their army counterparts, corps and division artillery would fire on known and suspected air defense positions just prior to friendly aircraft making a bombing run. This collaboration was extremely effective: during the month of October only one plane was lost out of 1,816 close air support sorties supporting the IX Corps, despite a tripling of Chinese flak guns in the Triangle Hill and Sniper Ridge area of operations.[25]

The planning for air and artillery support was vital to minimize UNC casualties and justify the relatively small troop commitment, but air sorties allocated for D-day minus five (October 9) through D-day minus three (October 11) were diverted to other areas in the corps sector, primarily Hill 395. Neither Van Fleet nor Jenkins envisioned the scale of the battle for White Horse Mountain, which pulled a lot of artillery and air support away from Showdown's preparatory phase. Nevertheless, they agreed to proceed with the attack as scheduled.[26] From D-day minus two through D-day plus one (October 12–15) 245 fighter-bombers, nearly half of all aircraft devoted to close air support, pummeled the Showdown sector.[27] Ninety-eight sorties struck Chinese reserve positions and supply depots behind Triangle Hill and Sniper Ridge on October 12 and 13. B-29 medium bombers flew five consecutive nights prior to D-day, relying on radar guidance to drop nearly a thousand tons of high-explosive and fragmentation bombs, but their effects were insufficient to isolate the battle zone. Once the battle began, close air support to the attacking infantry did enable the Americans to seize the eastern side of Triangle Hill on October 15. Over the next ten days, air attack sorties dropped off dramatically, with an average of only eighteen aircraft supporting both divisions daily.[28] The artillery bombardment that was to start on October 8 was also delayed, until October 12. Two artillery battalions ordered to reinforce the Seventh Infantry Division did not move into position until the night of October 12–13, which complicated the efforts to register the guns, coordinate with the infantry units, and determine the details for offensive and defensive supporting fire. Effective counterbattery fire, which was another key component to the plan, was subsequently and considerably reduced, leaving most of the Chinese artillery undisturbed by the time the infantry soldiers were ready to step off their start lines.

The Divisions' Preparation for Showdown

The Seventh Infantry Division was a longtime veteran of Korea, having landed at Inchon as part of the X Corps in September 1950. After a second amphibious landing at Iwon, about 107 miles northeast of Wonsan, it then participated in MacArthur's march north. Elements of its Seventeenth Infantry Regiment reached the Yalu River in northeastern Korea in November 1950. The CPVF's Second Campaign cut short the division's occupation of North Korea, and following its withdrawal and reconstitution, the Seventh Infantry Division fought in the hills of central Korea. By the fall of 1952 the division was defending along Line Missouri, which had been established following Operation Creeper, and it would be responsible for conducting the first American offensive since Van Fleet's limited objective attacks in September–October 1951.[29]

Combat losses and the irregular flow of replacements created personnel problems in the division, especially among its junior leaders such as company commanders, platoon sergeants, and squad leaders. The theater rotation plan for front-line soldiers ensured that experience was always in short supply. By 1952, the most experienced veterans were dead, wounded, or had already served their turn in the Far East. The majority of troops by this point in the war were new draftees. Enlisted noncommissioned officers, even if longer-term soldiers, lacked experience in troop leading under combat conditions. The veteran noncommissioned officers—"the very type of men" required to lead a complex attack—were the ones most rare in the squads and platoons charging up Triangle Hill.[30] But the policy, deemed fair to those expected to carry the burden of fighting, had foreseeable consequences: "We no sooner got a team working effectively than key men were through with their part of the war and were sent home, to be replaced by recruits . . . or at times, by Koreans [KATUSAs]."[31] Officers fared no better. For the Seventh Infantry Division, rotation meant that none of its company or battalion commanders had ever attacked a fortified Chinese defensive position. Although personally brave and aggressive, the division's officers lacked experience planning and controlling company- and battalion-size attacks. Half of the company commanders in the Thirty-First Infantry were lieutenants (captains normally command companies), and three of the four battalion commanders assigned to Moses's command were majors instead of lieutenant colonels.[32] War is a team exercise and offensive tactics are inherently complex, relying on interplay between units and fighting arms: artillery, engineers, tanks, and infantrymen. It normally takes months of practice and gradually accumulated experience to forge a team that can react instinctively and move aggressively to close with and destroy the enemy. Showdown was a poor choice of action in which these platoon, company, and battalion teams would receive their baptism by fire.[33]

To compensate for their inexperience, the troops were expected to spend two weeks training specifically as squads and platoons, practicing on ground that resembled their objectives on Triangle Hill. Unfortunately, these measures fell short of their potential as demands elsewhere in the IX Corps sector took priority. In addition to the delayed deployment of artillery battalions and air sorties expected to provide preattack bombardment, the Thirty-First Infantry was ordered to move out of its training area to occupy a blocking position southwest of Chorwon to prepare a counterattack to reoccupy Hill 395.[34] The crisis on White Horse Mountain did not pass until after October 10, which gave the Third Battalion, Thirty-First Infantry, only two days to rehearse its deliberate attack. Then, the battalion's dress rehearsal scheduled for D-day minus one was canceled due to the absence of the regiment's commander and key staff officers. But one thing did become clear during the planning process: the terrain, enemy situation, and the necessity for speed to take the two assigned objectives, Sandy Hill and Jane Russell Hill, dictated a coordinated two-pronged attack. The division commander, Maj. Gen. Wayne C. Smith, approved Moses's plan to employ immediately a second battalion, First Battalion, Thirty-First Infantry. Moses's headquarters would direct both units as it would have been impossible for a single battalion commander to control the divergent efforts. It was understood though, that the total number of companies committed would not exceed in aggregate one battalion. Having two battalion commanders was a good decision, for the reasons already identified and to place a regimental headquarters with its larger staff and resources to coordinate air and artillery support in overall command. Smith also attached the Second Battalion, Thirty-Second Infantry, to Moses as a reserve. But these decisions were made late, and the two assaulting battalions were never able to rehearse together under the Thirty-First Infantry's command. Giving Moses control over four infantry battalions also set the IX Corps on the path that would see Showdown morph into a much larger fight, with much higher stakes, than Van Fleet or Clark had anticipated.[35]

To the east of the Seventh Infantry Division, the ROK Second Division was going through a similar, though simpler, planning process. Van Fleet, as he had the previous year at Bloody Ridge, approved Jenkins's decision to employ the Koreans in the attack. The Korean army was still young, and its commanders, who maintained an inferiority complex when it came to facing the Chinese, were inexperienced in leading large combined-arms formations. Not only did Van Fleet want to showcase the Koreans' improved combat capabilities, he also saw Showdown "as a means of putting the finishing touches on the training of General Chung Il-kwon prior to moving him to be Deputy Corps Commander, IX Corps."[36] Chung had been doing well in the defensive combat his division had seen since he took over in the late summer, and Van Fleet wanted to see him in offensive action. However, the ROK Second Division did not enjoy the same level of planning and training that the Seventh Infantry Division did.

Unlike in the American sector, the Koreans had all three of their regiments on the MLR, with each regiment holding one battalion in reserve. This arrangement did not give the Korean troops the same opportunity to train, as the demands of maintaining the MLR kept Korean units constantly in rotation forward to the front line. Although the Sniper Ridge objectives were assigned to the ROK Thirty-Second Regiment, Chung attached the Second Battalion, ROK Seventeenth Regiment, to the Thirty-Second as its second assault battalion. Bringing in an outside unit on short notice to an unfamiliar sector, and then assigning it a mission to attack over unfamiliar ground, is a recipe for failure. Despite the fact that General Jenkins urged the Koreans to make full training and logistical preparations for Showdown, Chung remained confident that American artillery and airpower would overcome the Chinese defenses. KMAG's official report for October notes that Korean patrols from D-day minus five to D-day minus one averaged fewer than forty a day, with only one of nearly two hundred making "minor contact."[37] Since no prisoners were taken, little accurate intelligence was available to Chung's staff or the attacking battalions. Although the first objective was only two hundred meters from the MLR, the Koreans remained blind to the enemy's disposition, strength, or supporting elements.

Unfortunately for the infantry soldiers ordered to assault Qin's strong positions, this limited attack contained the seeds for extensive risk and danger. The IX Corps and the respective division plans were structurally flawed in this respect. There were no options (called "branches" in military planning language) to account for unforeseen obstacles or opportunities. Just because an attack is limited in objective does not mean that the planning can be half-hearted. The seizure of valuable terrain objectives required risk to the corps MLR, risk that Jenkins and his subordinate commanders shied away from. Operation Showdown would begin with an entire division, the Fortieth Infantry, parked in reserve, and the ROK Ninth Division still recovering from the ordeal at White Horse Mountain. Neither division's infantry units participated in the battle. Jenkins's two assault divisions would comfortably hold their positions on the MLR as two companies from each of the four attacking battalions ventured into the early-morning darkness to confront in close combat veteran Chinese infantry that was dug-in, prepared, supplied, and well supported by artillery and mortars. Risking battalions to kill Chinese was a poor tactical trade-off, but that is precisely what happened.

The Battle Begins

The Seventh Infantry Division began its attack on October 14 with three diversionary raids to destroy defensive positions opposite the MLR and gather intelligence. One reinforced platoon from First Battalion, Thirty-Second Infantry, attacked and cleared several bunkers while a combat patrol from the same regiment's Third Battalion engaged a Chinese platoon and destroyed three bunkers on its objective. These were minor, routine actions, and both raiding parties returned to their original positions on the MLR by 0700 hours.

A more significant engagement erupted when elements of Company C, First Battalion, Thirty-Second Infantry, attempted to seize and hold a Chinese outpost less than two thousand meters west of Hill 598. Even though the attackers moved out of their MLR positions in the predawn morning, they were soon spotted and received accurate and sustained artillery and mortar fire before reaching their attack position. The patrol leader reported that fifty to seventy Chinese defended the outpost. By 0520 hours, the Chinese were reinforcing their defenders and their artillery continued nonstop. A second platoon from Company C arrived to reinforce the assault team. The Americans were able to fight their way to the objective, but intense small arms and automatic weapons fire had taken a toll. At 0625, both platoons withdrew and the Chinese remained king of their hill.[38]

This action for an objective known only as Hill 472 was a foretaste of what was to come. Despite intense preattack bombardment, the Chinese were prepared to hold their ground, relying on their own weapons to pin down advancing forces. Accurate and heavy shelling made the final assault expensive in killed and wounded. The American soldiers testified that they "never could see [the enemy]," but they moved under fire from Chinese cannon almost continuously. Chinese gunners were protected from observation and indirect fire, and they did not fear to fire their 76 mm guns in "direct lay" from positions on Triangle Hill.[39] Finally, the movement of reserves allowed the Chinese to maintain their level of fire or to counterattack any American penetrations of their position. The CPVF's effective coordination between infantry, artillery and mortar fire, and timely reserves was to be a salient feature of the main battle to come.[40]

While the Thirty-Second Infantry was reinforcing its attack on Hill 472, the division's main attack began after a two-hour artillery bombardment. Two companies from the Thirty-First Infantry's Third Battalion advanced toward Hill 598, the southern apex of Triangle Hill, and one company from the First Battalion launched its attack to seize Sandy Ridge and Jane Russell Hill. A few hours earlier the Thirty-First Infantry's antitank and mine platoon cleared a path between the MLR and the slope of the objective. Two squads employed forty Bangalore torpedoes, thin metal tubes filled with explosives, to clear lanes through suspected minefields along the regiment's planned approach march to Triangle Hill. The noise alerted the Chinese who responded with mortar and artillery fire.[41]

Although the element of surprise was lost, the de-mining work enabled the assault troops from the Third Battalion's Company K (commanded by Lt. Bernard Brooks Jr.) and Company L (commanded by Lt. Charles Martin) to move out at 0524 and reach their final assault positions only thirty-five meters from Hill 598 by 0630 without any casualties.[42] Lieutenant Brooks looked at his objective, only five hundred meters distant horizontally from the MLR, but at an average slope of 30 degrees and the final angle closer to 70 degrees. The sandy shale slope was so steep the men had to climb hand over hand, with rifle, pack, and ammunition slung across their backs. There was little vegetation for concealment and no cover from the incoming mortar and artillery fire. A half hour later, Brooks's soldiers had reached the crest of the hill only to be thrown back by a sudden deluge of small arms fire and hand grenades. The defenders were well hidden from view behind the military crest, impossible to engage with direct-fire weapons or artillery. Those exhausted soldiers lucky enough not to have been hit crawled into any crevice or depression they could to find protection from the bullets and shell fragments raining down on them.[43]

Seeing all the company's officers, Brooks and his three platoon leaders, killed or wounded in the initial rush over the crest, Lt. Col. William H. Isbell, the assistant Division Artillery commander, took charge. Isbell's presence as a senior division officer on Triangle Hill was unusual, as each infantry company had several FOs capable of calling for and adjusting artillery fire. A 1931 West Point graduate, Isbell served in World War II as an artillery staff officer but did not see action with a combat unit. Showdown was probably the only opportunity he would have had to serve in a forward position.[44] A captain expressed his disbelief: "The Colonel didn't have any damn business up there." But there he was, and seeing the attack stalled just short of the crest, he dashed forward armed only with a hand grenade and his .45-caliber pistol. After clearing a bunker with his paltry weaponry at close range, Isbell sprinted back to bring the line of infantry forward. A sergeant remembered the colonel's act as "the most remarkable example of courage I've ever seen." Moments later a mortar shell mortally wounded the "Old Colonel."[45] Lieutenant Martin immediately brought up his company, while calling in tank fire to suppress or scatter the Chinese. His attempt to rally survivors was also short-lived, as the attack on Hill 598 stalled in a pure infantry slugfest at close range.[46]

For the next six hours the Americans tried to seize the crest from two companies of the 135th Regiment supported by fifteen mountain guns and twelve mortars. By 1300 hours most of the field works were destroyed by the artillery bombardment or captured by the Americans. The defenders stubbornly held their ground, relying on hand grenades and preplanned mortar fire. Each American assault over the crest of Hill 598 was met by an increasing volume of fire as the Chinese brought forward fresh troops.[47] The battalion commander, Maj. Robert Newberry, now made a fateful decision. He ordered his reserve, Company I (commanded by Capt. Max Stover), to climb Sandy Ridge and take Hill 598 from the east.[48] Showdown was only six hours old and the carefully calibrated commitment of troops, meant to limit tactical liability and casualties, was already being discarded by the commanders on the ground. Company I did secure a firm defensive position around which Companies K and L could rally, but the Chinese were too strong. All three companies hunkered down, exchanging fire with enemy infantry who held the high ground and had plenty of mortars in support.[49]

On the east side of Triangle Hill, Lt. Col. Myron McClure committed Company A (commanded by Lt. Edward R. Schowalter Jr.), to seize both Sandy Ridge and Jane Russell Hill. Company B (commanded by Capt. William Young) followed to reinforce Schowalter's assault or secure the ground taken. By 0650 hours, Schowalter's company made contact with the Chinese on Sandy Ridge. Within minutes the company lost twenty-five men, and by 0800 hours, McClure recognized Schowalter had little chance to advance farther. He then ordered Young to seize Jane Russell Hill. The pattern established by the Third Battalion on Hill 598 now repeated itself. The Americans advanced to a position just below the crest of each objective. Chinese mortar fire and showers of hand grenades prevented the attacking infantry from gaining the high ground. To break the impasse, McClure then committed Company C (commanded by Capt. Roy Preston) at 1030 to consolidate the hold on Jane Russell Hill. As in the Third Battalion's zone, the fighting was tough, but Schowalter rallied his surviving soldiers. He personally led one platoon attack after another through a hail of grenades and small-arms fire. Severely wounded twice, he was later found stacked among dead Chinese. At last the American attacks drove the Chinese off Jane Russell Hill. They now controlled both terrain features on the east side of Triangle Hill.[50]

But the Chinese did not go far. By late afternoon Moses received several intelligence reports that reinforcements were already en route from Hill 1062 to the north. The Americans tried to dig in and prepare for the counterattacks they knew were coming. Moses estimated at least a full battalion was thrown at Jane Russell, with heavy artillery and possibly a second battalion in support. Already outnumbered, running low on ammunition, and facing increasingly powerful attacks against Hill 598 as well as Jane Russell, Moses ordered both battalions to withdraw. By 2045 hours the Americans were streaming off of Triangle Hill. Two hours later, the remnants of the Thirty-First Infantry's attack were safely tucked into the Thirty-Second Infantry's front-line position. The attack to seize and occupy Triangle Hill had failed.[51]

Simultaneous with the American attack 1,500 meters to the west, the ROK Second Division launched two companies, with a third in support, from Third Battalion, ROK Thirty-Second Regiment, against Sniper Ridge. The Korean troops advanced rapidly along the axis of the ridge and seized their initial goal, known as Objective A, at 0600 hours, where they then met stiff resistance and artillery fire. They pushed on, aided by the gentle topography, which did not give the Chinese the same tactical advantages they enjoyed on Triangle Hill. By 1530 hours, the main objective, Y, was also overrun and an hour later declared secure.[52]

The Korean troops had suffered heavy casualties, many due to their own artillery, which typically fired much closer to advancing troops than American doctrine prescribed. The Korean technique was more effective in suppressing the enemy longer, but its disadvantages became more clearly revealed as the same topographic situation that had facilitated their successful advance during the day now turned against them once night fell.[53] At 1900 hours, a strong Chinese force, using their underground tunnels, massed against Objective Y and struck the weary Koreans. Supported by heavy artillery and mortar fire, the Chinese closed for hand-to-hand combat, nullifying the effect of the Koreans' artillery support. The Koreans struggled to hold their ground with grenades, bayonets, rifle butts, and fists. Although the Chinese also suffered terrible losses they forced the Koreans off of Sniper Ridge before midnight. A furious Chung Il-kwon ordered the Second Battalion, ROK Seventeenth Regiment, to recapture Sniper Ridge.[54]

The IX Corps's complete failure provoked a swift reaction. Shortly after midnight on October 15, General Clark demanded to know why two battalions were committed against Hill 598 when the plan had called for only one; why friendly casualties were much higher after one day than Van Fleet's five-day estimate; and, what did Van Fleet intend to do next? For some reason, Clark did not express a corresponding concern about ROK casualties or General Chung's handling of the battle on Sniper Ridge. Clark intimated that Van Fleet's plan was ill-advised and underresourced. It was a disingenuous accusation, as Clark—like Ridgway before him—was certain to disapprove any limited attack that did not look limited.[55]

That night the Seventh Infantry Division and Thirty-First Infantry staffs worked furiously to salvage what they could of Showdown. The First and Third Battalions of the Thirty-First Infantry had been badly mauled, suffering thirteen killed, fifty-eight missing, and 331 wounded. Van Fleet was also disappointed. He reported to Clark, "The position [on Triangle Hill] was lost during the night . . . due solely to leadership within the Infantry units. . . . It was not good Infantry action."[56] The division's command report for October noted that Chinese troops did not hesitate to attack through their own artillery, and they enjoyed accurate fire from (supposedly) captured recoilless rifles—powerful, portable, and accurate supporting weapons. The G-2 (Intelligence) section had previously identified the Eighth Company, 135th Regiment, defending Triangle Hill, but by the early morning hours of October 15, it assessed the Chinese to now be in battalion strength, with regimental support to reinforce and provide additional firepower.

General Smith fretted that the insufficient preattack bombardment allowed the Chinese "artillery and troop movements [to be] much more active than had been anticipated and contributed to the early commitment of substantial reinforcing elements."[57] Seeing that a significant number of American casualties were due to Chinese artillery and mortar fire, Smith's contention probably has merit. However, the fact remains that the infantry units involved were unprepared for the rigors of a deliberate attack against an entrenched enemy. The failure to conduct a full-dress rehearsal with key battalion and regimental leaders was the most egregious oversight, particularly considering the inexperience of the assaulting battalions. The restricted terrain also prevented more imaginative tactics, causing the Americans to funnel themselves into the obvious kill zones at the hill's summit. But once committed to the action, Smith rationalized that only the addition of fresh troops could compensate for the greater enemy resistance. Moses convinced Smith to release one battalion from the Thirty-Second Infantry along with Moses's own uncommitted Second Battalion to attack in the morning of October 15. The division's portion of Showdown was now becoming a limited offensive that would soon consume two entire regiments, the majority of the Hourglass Division's combat capability. Contrary to Clark's intent, the Americans were now engaged in an attritional struggle.[58]

At the same time, Qin Jiwei was reinforcing and resupplying his victorious troops. The lessons from White Horse Mountain told him that he was in the stronger position, defending against unsupported frontal attacks. His flanks were secure, and support from his rear area was unimpeded. Sensing he had the battle that the Chinese had been looking for to inflict substantial casualties and a serious defeat on the UNC, he directed his regimental commanders to "concentrate all your strength . . . organize continuous small counterattacks for killing and wounding large numbers of enemy soldiers."[59] Qin also directed the consolidation of regimental and division command posts to increase the capability of the Chinese command and staff to control and support their companies in the battle. Simultaneously, the army commander initiated key preparations for a massive counterthrust, which included calling forward four companies from his reserve 134th Regiment. The tunnel system from Hill 1062 allowed these troops to move unmolested and position themselves unobserved on the north side of Hill 598.[60]

Around 0200 hours, October 15, Colonel Moses gave orders to the two commanders who would lead the morning's attack. He stressed "boldness in leaders, speed in seizing the objective and preparing . . . to meet enemy counterattacks, and the movement of ammunition forward . . . to companies and their men after reaching their objective." Bold leadership and effective logistic support were the two obvious lessons from the day before. Moses also instructed his supply officer to mobilize every M39 armored carrier to haul ammunition up the hill and bring casualties back down. At the same time General Smith negotiated with IX Corps to return to division control the First Battalion, Thirty-Second Infantry. This change was accomplished by 0300 hours, and the troops moved to a new assembly area and were prepared to attack in conjunction with Moses's Second Battalion by 0930. First Battalion, Thirty-Second Regiment, drew the assignment to take Jane Russell while the Second Battalion would storm Hill 598.[61]

A two-battalion attack was required, but the hasty deployment of these battalions, combined with the unfamiliar command and control Moses and his staff had to exercise over another regiment's battalions, meant the attack would have to take place in daylight. H-hour was set for 1000. Artillery fire and air attacks pounded Triangle Hill, and the attacking Americans, benefiting from a drizzling rain, fog, and morning mist, managed to scramble up the eastern slope of Hill 598 and Sandy Ridge before encountering serious resistance.[62]

After a brief but bitter hand-to-hand struggle, the Americans occupied their objectives and began to dig in. However, as Chinese troops overlooking the Americans from the west (a hill known as Pike's Peak) began lobbing grenades and mortar rounds throughout the day and into the night, it became clear that Hill 598 could not be secure unless the Americans also controlled the western apex. Company E (commanded by Lt. William Knapp) set out to the northwest and ran into stiff defenses and mortar fire. The Chinese mounted several immediate small counterattacks to push the Americans back, using bugle calls to muster and control troops before and after each attack.[63] Maj. Warren Phillips, the battalion commander, sent in his two other companies to secure Hill 598 and extend the attack against Sandy Ridge and Pike's Peak. Company F (commanded by Capt. Joseph Giesemann) drew the assignment to take Sandy Ridge, which he did, while Company G occupied Hill 598 allowing Company E to press on toward Pike's Peak on the western apex of Triangle Hill.[64]

Pike's Peak was never a planned objective, but it became clear to General Smith that Hill 598 could not be held unless he expanded the zone of attack to include Pike's Peak and Jane Russell Hill. It was equally clear that the Chinese were not going to give way easily. By 1600 hours, Moses moved his tiny command post to Hill 598, signifying a tenuous hold on the hill. Of the defenders' tenacity, he recalled, "I never saw a more fanatical foe. They endured our [artillery] fires, stayed above ground and even made a strong counterattack against our troops, indifferent as to [their own] casualties."[65] Moses estimated that each of his battalions faced a Chinese regiment, and only numerous TOT fires managed to stop the onrushing Chinese and give the Americans a foothold for the night.[66] With two battalions holding on tight to Triangle Hill, the division commander transferred control of the battle to Col. Joseph R. Russ, commanding the Thirty-Second Infantry. He also alerted one battalion from the Seventeenth Infantry to be prepared to reinforce the new defensive positions.[67]

In truth, the Chinese defenders mustered elements of two battalions, about one thousand men. They proved stubborn and well prepared, even with the vast destruction they endured during the all-night artillery bombardment. Company commander Zheng Yanman remembered that the first two days of shelling and heavy fighting had nearly obliterated any recognizable terrain feature on the hill.[68] Close air support missions attempted to suppress and destroy reserve positions north of Triangle Hill and to interdict the flow of troops and supplies, but the elaborate trench lines and fortifications degraded the threat of air attack. Artillery fire too was of limited effectiveness. Mortars with their higher trajectory arcs were more effective at reaching the reverse slope, but they lacked the range and the punch needed to demolish fortified positions. Direct fire from tanks positioned far back along the MLR helped to alleviate some of these problems. From the MLR artillery forward observers, using 50-power telescopes, radios, and landline telephones, communicated with regimental and battalion commanders to pass information about enemy movements and ensure that friendly troops would not be in the line of fire.

On the second day of the battle, Lt. Belisario Flores, attached to the Colombian Battalion as a bilingual liaison officer, clearly observed from his outpost on the MLR the northern slope connecting Jane Russell Hill and Sandy Ridge. He was stunned by the number of Chinese infantry moving forward literally under the noses of the American troops on the other side of the crest. A nearby M4 Sherman tank saw the same situation and asked Flores to spot rounds. After a complex exchange of telephone calls to one headquarters and then another, Flores soon found himself talking to the regimental commander. Moses brusquely asked if Flores could see both enemy and friendly troops. When Flores replied he could, Moses directed him to shoot. Flores scampered back and forth from the tank's turret to his telescope to ensure the gunner was aligned on the target, which was only thirty meters away from the friendly infantry. After several trips back and forth Flores was satisfied. He told the tank to fire. The first round fell short by only ten meters. A small adjustment preceded the second shot, which struck true, causing the Chinese to scatter.

Although they could slow down the supply line, the tank's 76 mm cannon had no effect on bunkers. Moses also observed the "peashooter" effect of the fire, and he directed a platoon of M47 tanks, with 90 mm guns, to report to Flores's positions. Only one tank at a time could fit into the firing position, so Flores kept up a stream of shells until the barrel got too hot to fire; another tank waiting its turn then moved forward and the process began again. The margin of error was very small throughout the battle, and Flores sweated heavily the initial shot of each tank, lest he accidently send a projectile into the American lines. Flores and his tanks kept up a steady stream of fire until darkness fell. The fire support effectively sealed off the east side of the battlefield from reinforcement and allowed the Americans to dig themselves in on the eastern slopes of Triangle Hill.[69]

The transfer of command from Moses's Thirty-First Infantry to Colonel Russ and the Thirty-Second Infantry signaled a phase change in the American plan. Moses's task had been to capture the hill and kill Chinese counterattackers. He assumed, and every general officer in his chain of command agreed, the attack would terminate after five days, meaning that the Chinese would accept not only defeat but also the loss of tactically valuable terrain at a time when every hilltop battle started to assume profound strategic importance. It was an irresponsible assumption, giving little credit to the Chinese and vibrantly illustrating another core problem with the Americans' plan. Reliable intelligence was almost nonexistent. The division knew what units confronted them, but they did not know Qin's depth of reserves, artillery support, or will to engage in a prolonged battle. Triangle Hill and Sniper Ridge were altogether different from White Horse Mountain, where the Chinese were in control of the battle and could call off the attack when the pain became too severe, having lost nothing but men. To lose the hill complex that guarded Hill 1062 and the Iron Triangle would cause the Chinese to lose face as well as a strong tactical position with strategic importance. Qin would not let that happen.[70]

Correspondingly, Moses's regiment had paid a high price to secure Triangle Hill, having worn itself out fully three days before the fight was supposed to end. Smith now realized he had provoked a serious battle requiring division command and control, which prompted him to bring in the Thirty-Second and alert the Seventeenth Infantry to be prepared to join the fight. Meanwhile, the Americans on Sandy Ridge and Jane Russell both beat off platoon-size attacks early on October 16. With clearer skies air force fighter-bombers provided excellent close support and were a key factor in helping the infantry hold their ground.[71] Col. Joseph Russ then ordered both battalions to continue their advance to secure all of Triangle Hill. Pike's Peak became the focus of a pincer movement from the southeast and the east by the remaining Thirty-First Infantry troops, which failed to secure the high ground but did kill a lot of Chinese caught in a TOT. That afternoon, the Second Battalion, Seventeenth Infantry, came under Russ's control, and two of its companies set out from the MLR to occupy Jane Russell Hill, but Pike's Peak held out for another two days, when it was attacked successively by three different companies from the Second and Third Battalions, Thirty-Second Infantry. Finally, as night fell on October 18, a platoon from Company I advanced beyond the crest of Pike's Peak and engaged the enemy in close fighting under an intense Chinese mortar and artillery barrage. Having suffered severe casualties, Russ ordered the company to withdraw to the southern side of Pike's Peak and prepare its defense.[72]

The first three days of battle had been a brutal meat grinder for the Chinese. The Forty-Fifth Division commander was shocked by the loss of fourteen out of sixteen positions between Jane Russell Hill and Pike's Peak. Casualties in the 135th Regiment ran as high as 550 killed and wounded in only one day of defense. Despite the bloodletting, Qin knew that his defensive concept was sound: "sacrifice a finger to save an arm."[73] As long as the battle remained localized, the Chinese could control the losses to front-line units by exploiting their tunnel network. Fighting from caves, trenches, and deep tunnels, the Forty-Fifth Division kept up seemingly endless waves of counterattacks that gave the Americans no respite, especially at night.[74]

Smith continued to reorganize his uncommitted battalions to support those hanging on at Triangle Hill. He also made the extraordinary decision to form a "Divisional Provisional Battalion" from headquarters and service personnel from across the division. Smith planned for this unit to free up other infantry or to provide depth to the division's defensive line, depending on the circumstances. The Seventeenth Infantry received orders on October 16 to be prepared to relieve the remaining Thirty-First Infantry troops. The next day the Third Battalion, Seventeenth Infantry, came under Russ's control and relieved the Second Battalion, Thirty-First Infantry, which had occupied Hill 598 for two days without reinforcement or resupply and had suffered nearly 100 percent of its officers killed or wounded. The Thirty-Second Infantry now had four battalions working for it to control Triangle Hill. Sporadic fighting continued through the night until Pike's Peak was finally seized on the eighteenth. Showdown was now five days old.[75]

On the night of October 19–20, three companies of Chinese infantry initiated a long and bitter struggle centered on Pike's Peak. Supported by the CPVF 209th Rocket Artillery Regiment, the Chinese surged forward, repeatedly advancing against American rifle, machine gun, and artillery fire.[76] By morning, the Third Battalion, Seventeenth Infantry, was nearly wiped out, its three companies hanging on to their shredded bunkers and trenches by their fingernails. In two days the battalion suffered fifteen dead, 112 wounded, and sixty-three missing. The figure of the missing, sixty-three, was an eerie portent for a unit defending such a compact area where tens of thousands of shells had detonated, churning and rechurning the earth, mixing the gray soil with the bodies of the dead and dying.[77] Chinese prisoners taken during the melee revealed they had been ordered to fight on to the death; no retreat was permissible. By 0600 hours on October 20, the Chinese once again owned Pike's Peak, taking up their positions in the many caves and tunnels the Americans had paid so dearly to clear out just two days prior.[78]

For the next week, although US troops assaulted the heights daily with strong artillery and air support, they could not consolidate their possession long enough to hold it from the strong counterattacks that followed, usually at dusk and continuing into the night. The division's intelligence officer had identified elements of all three regiments from the CPVF Forty-Fifth Division present on Triangle Hill. One Chinese commander recalled, "In one of our front tunnels . . . twenty-four soldiers who continued to the fighting [sic] were from thirteen different companies."[79] By October 20, Smith estimated that the Thirty-Second Infantry faced seven Chinese battalions, who gave no indication of being willing to give any respite to the Americans on Pike's Peak.[80]

An apocryphal story told by Yang Dezhi suggests the depth of the struggle. According to his retelling, the Sixth Company had only sixteen men still standing when a battalion signalman, twenty-two-year-old Huang Jiguang, volunteered to lead two other soldiers against a machine gun position. "I go," he exclaimed as the three companions rushed forward and hurled grenades in a vain effort to silence the gun. His comrades pinned down, Huang finally leaped forward and threw himself across the blazing muzzle, his body absorbing the burst of bullets, which allowed the remaining men to bypass the position and attack it from the rear. Yang memorialized Huang as "a kind of symbol . . . a kind of power . . . always a model who urges us forward."[81]

The Korean Battle on Sniper Ridge

Just across a steep ravine from Hill 598, and along the length of Sniper Ridge, Chung Il-kwon faced a similar dilemma as Smith did to achieve Showdown's objectives. The first day's attack produced nothing but casualties and disappointing results. As added pressure, Van Fleet paid a visit to the ROK Second Division to encourage Chung and see for himself how his new Korean army was faring in its first significant offensive battle. Chung responded much like Smith did: he ordered fresh troops into the fight and he made plans for further units to be prepared to reinforce those already committed.[82]

After an intense artillery barrage, Korean troops from the Second Battalion, ROK Seventeenth Regiment, attacked Objective A at 0900 hours, October 15, and secured it five hours later. The Chinese launched immediate counterattacks, one of which managed to penetrate the Korean positions with a company-size element that managed to hold the crest of the ridge despite numerous Korean probes and artillery strikes. Just after midnight, Chung's troops, reinforced by the Second Battalion, ROK Thirty-Second Regiment, attacked again and held on to Objective A despite numerous Chinese efforts to reclaim the ridge. KMAG officers observed additional Chinese troops occupying positions on Objective Y while the volume of artillery fire, 4,541 rounds of all types, continued to increase.[83]

The following day, Chung reorganized the division's line by extending the eastern boundary of the ROK Thirty-Seventh Regiment to free up the ROK Seventeenth Regiment and make it available to control the battle on Sniper Ridge. As on Triangle Hill the Chinese showed no inclination to quit the struggle, and the ROK Seventeenth Regiment had to fight off several counterattacks during the day, one of which lasted nearly six hours. For the next two days both sides poured in fresh troops and the artillery duel continued, the Chinese firing an astonishing 16,833 rounds at the Koreans.[84]

Generals Van Fleet and Jenkins both visited Chung on the eighteenth and conferred with the KMAG advisors. The fighting was tough, but the division was holding its own due to effective artillery and air support and a continuous stream of replacements, though Korean casualties exceeded the flow of new soldiers. Chung's attacking battalions had lost 155 killed and 673 wounded, but just 436 new soldiers had joined the division. As worrisome for Lt. Col. Sidney Carpenter, the division's senior advisor, was the shortfall in logistics, particularly transportation for ammunition. The division received one transportation company, but its ten trucks were overburdened supplying the division's artillery and the front-line troops. Van Fleet was not about to let the Koreans fail for lack of support, and he directed IX Corps and KMAG to expedite supplies and replacements.[85]

Even though elements of two CPVF regiments were defending the ridge, Chung, perhaps stung by the corps and army commanders' visit, decided to lunge forward and seize Objective Y on the nineteenth. Already exhausted after five days of intense fighting, the Korean troops made little headway against stiff resistance. Fighting from caves and tunnels, which protected them from their own artillery, the Chinese pinned down the exposed Koreans until a final counterattack drove them back. By the end of the battle's sixth day, further attacks had pushed the Koreans entirely off of Objective A.[86]

Qin's Counterattack

The Chinese on Triangle Hill and Sniper Ridge were still full of fight even though Qin's Forty-Fifth Division was now a battered shell of its old self. Attacking out of their tunnels by night and scurrying underground during the day, attrition had depleted their ranks and exhausted the survivors. But they

had denied Van Fleet the quick victory he hoped to have and made the UNC
pay a stiff price for the small parcels of ground they tenuously held. Deng
Hua proudly informed his soldiers, "Although all hills and positions have
been turned into torched soil, our troops are still holding their tunnels. Our
forces staying inside tunnels have not only made facilitation to our counterattack operations but also have made independent assaults on the enemy."[87]
The CPVF's tenacity impressed the Americans. The inability to interdict the
flow of infantry soldiers through the tunnels or to disrupt the increasingly effective Communist artillery spelled disaster for the UNC and put Showdown
on the books as a decisive defeat for Eighth Army. Wave after wave of advancing Chinese were seemingly consumed in the maelstrom of artillery fire,
yet they continued to press forward "in local attacks aimed at overwhelming UNC forward positions," and despite being "repulsed with heavy losses"
time and again, they would not abandon their ground.[88]

As the fighting died down on October 20, the attacking troops had the
illusion of respite as Qin ordered his troops to go underground and leave
the surface to the Americans and Koreans during the day. Company commanders directed nighttime sorties to prevent the attackers from locating
and sealing up the tunnel entrances. This technique kept Chinese casualties
at a sustainable level and allowed the Chinese to maintain some of the tactical initiative.[89] Qin also ordered additional troops from the CPVF Twenty-
Ninth Division forward to be responsible "for making counterattacks until
all lost positions were recovered." The CPVF Twelfth Army also deployed
supporting troops forward to Osong-san, giving greater depth to Qin's defensive scheme. Deng Hua recognized the political opportunities hinging on
the outcome of the battle, and he shifted two divisions, the CPVF Thirty-First
and the Thirty-Fourth, with additional artillery batteries to support the Fifteenth Army's counterattack battle.[90] Deng also encouraged his Twelfth and
Fifteenth Army commanders, reminding them "the enemy is making a serious mistake by storming our fortified positions . . . it presents us a good opportunity of decimating the enemy troops in a large number." The "opportunity," though, was expensive for the troops of the Forty-Fifth Division who
had to keep on fighting while the Twenty-Ninth Division made its way forward to Triangle Hill.[91]

The Chinese came out in force on October 23, launching no fewer than
four company and battalion attacks against the Second Battalion, Thirty-
Second Infantry's, positions south of Pike's Peak and against Third Battalion,
Thirty-Second Infantry, defending Hill 598. Lt. William J. White was a platoon leader with Company F, Thirty-Second Infantry. As the tempo of Chinese shelling increased dramatically, he witnessed the Chinese "charging out
of an old mine shaft [to which] our automatic weapons had a clear field of

fire . . . their firing was taking an unimaginable toll, but the Reds kept right on coming right over their dead and dying, as if they had an endless supply of men, and we, a short supply of bullets."[92]

The final American attack on Pike's Peak began in the afternoon of October 24, when a reinforced platoon from Second Battalion, Thirty-Second Infantry, immediately ran into a dense minefield laid out the night before. Artillery helped clear a path and allow the infantry to maneuver up the slope to their objective. They arrived to within thirty yards of the crest before a curtain of Chinese artillery stopped them cold and forced their withdrawal at 1900 hours. A second reinforced platoon also nearly reached the crest at 0400 hours, October 25, when it too was subjected to twenty minutes of heavy shelling and small arms fire. The platoon withdrew and the Americans prepared to be relieved by Chung's Korean troops.[93]

Clark was not happy. After twelve days neither division controlled its objective nor could the limited gains be economically defended. The Chinese had been sucked into a contest of flesh against steel, but the attrition tactic was cutting both ways. US and ROK casualties had been much higher than expected, and the ground gained was ultimately insignificant in Clark's view. He was not keen to continue a face-saving slugfest, upping the ante to match Chinese manpower, not to mention their surprisingly heavy and accurate artillery fire. It was time to bring Showdown to a close.[94]

The problem was that Van Fleet did not want his Korean troops to feel that they had been beaten. Since Showdown began Chung's division lost 324 killed and over 1,000 wounded or missing. It was important for the ROKs to believe that White Horse Mountain and Sniper Ridge had been Korean victories against a powerful enemy. Jenkins was willing to continue the battle with Korean troops, and Chung agreed to bring up his reserve regiment, the ROK Thirty-Seventh Light Infantry, to man the MLR while the ROK Thirty-First Regiment moved west to relieve the US Thirty-Second Infantry on Triangle Hill. The ROK Second Division continued to press the fight on Sniper Ridge, reoccupying Objective A and committing yet another battalion from the ROK Seventeenth Regiment to assault Objective Y without success on October 22. By October 25, the ROKs were barely holding on to Objective A against strong Chinese probes and attacks.[95]

On this same day, Qin and his staff began assembling additional troops and planning a counterattack to recover Triangle Hill and Sniper Ridge. The CPVF Twenty-Ninth Division received the mission to devote five companies to each objective. Another division, the CPVF Thirty-First, detailed one regiment as a reserve force, and three more of its battalions were devoted to waging the battle of supply immediately behind the front lines. Earlier in the war such a concentration of enemy troops would have been most welcome to Eighth Army and Fifth Air Force targeteers. However, now the proliferation of tunnels and underground shelters allowed the buildup to take place unhindered and generally unobserved by UNC intelligence.[96]

With Chung's division now bearing the entire brunt of the Chinese effort to reclaim Triangle Hill and Sniper Ridge, the Koreans found their command and control stretched beyond their capabilities. Qin was ready to strike as the Chinese fed a continuous stream of companies and platoons, supported by thousands of shells, to throw the Koreans back to their starting positions. As darkness approached on October 28, a furious Chinese assault on Sniper Ridge pushed the ROK Thirty-Second Regiment off of Objective A until the following morning when the Koreans returned. On Triangle Hill, the back and forth fighting continued until the end of the month, when on October 30, a two-battalion assault, composed of troops from both the Twenty-Ninth and Forty-Fifth Divisions, advanced through their own artillery bombardment to overwhelm and wipe out the better part of a ROK battalion and thrash another as it attempted to counterattack. After five hours of intense fighting, the ROK Thirty-First Regiment was barely hanging on to a mere outpost line on Hill 598. Even American 8-inch howitzers could not stem the tide.[97] The Koreans suffered the heaviest loss of terrain since they took over the fight. A newspaper report quoted an Eighth Army staff assessment that "the combined Red and Allied barrages probably were the greatest of the war." The same report called that day the "worst setback since the battle of the central front heights broke out 18 days ago."[98] On Sniper Ridge the situation was a little better, as Chung figured out the secret to the fight being to cycle in fresh troops daily. Elements of the ROK Seventeenth Regiment reentered the battle on October 30 to counterattack advancing Chinese, which culminated in a fierce fight that left the Koreans in possession of Objective A, but Objective Y remained far out of reach.[99]

Every ROK thrust at Objective Y had failed to hold as the Chinese counterattacks invariably drove them back to Objective A, but Jenkins noted that Objective A was always stubbornly defended. The situation on Triangle Hill was more complicated. The ROK soldiers were unfamiliar with the ground, received less effective fire support compared to the Seventh Division troops, and contended with an enemy who could exploit the elaborate tunneling system on the hill complex to mount attacks from nearly all directions.[100] The Chinese showed skill in massing their troops to coincide with intense mortar and artillery fire and utter disregard for the hazards of close combat. There was no effort to interdict the flow of fresh troops from Hill 1062 to the north. Poor weather also limited American close air support, denying the Koreans an important capability to even out the numerical odds.[101] In an attempt to even those odds, Jenkins ordered Chung to hold the ROK Thirty-First Regiment in place while the ROK Thirtieth Regiment was ordered forward from

Field Training Command #5, where it was in the process of refitting and re-training after its ordeal on White Horse Mountain. On October 31 the ROK Thirtieth Regiment came under the division's control and prepared to attack Triangle Hill.[102]

Despite October being "the year's most costly month to the Communists," Qin showed no sign of quitting the fight.[103] On November 1, he commit-ted the CPVF Thirty-First Division to the battle, flinging its Ninety-First Regiment, which had been in reserve since October 25, directly against the ROK outpost line. These troops were backed by a fresh artillery regiment.[104] The ROK troops were now consolidated on a position near the line from which Moses's Thirty-First Infantry had begun two weeks earlier. Between November 1 and November 3, the ROK Thirtieth Regiment along with other elements of the ROK Second Division and the Ethiopian Battalion unsuc-cessfully attacked both Jane Russell Hill and Hill 598. Chinese mortar fire continued to drive the attackers to the ground just a few yards from the crest where they were easily swept back by sharp infantry counterattacks. The Ko-reans managed to defend their line on Sniper Ridge against a single battalion that had made a small penetration on Objective A.[105] But as evidence even the Eighth Army was losing interest, Chung Il-kwon gave up command of the di-vision to Maj. Gen. Kang Mun-bong on November 3 and moved up to be the IX Corps deputy commander. With the Koreans fully in charge of the fight-ing in the IX Corps sector, it was still important to showcase the Korean con-tribution. Moving Chung up to the corps level accomplished this, and it al-lowed Van Fleet to give Chung experience in managing a corps-level battle.[106]

The change in command did not alter the course of the battle at Triangle Hill. The uninterrupted influx of fresh Chinese regiments was decisive. The CPVF Thirty-First Division was now responsible for Triangle Hill and had deployed its three regiments to consolidate its defense and reconstitute re-serve counterattack forces to keep the Koreans back. The CPVF Thirty-Fourth Division, with two additional regiments, was in Qin's operational reserve.[107] A final Korean assault on Hill 598 took place on November 5, which was defended by two Chinese companies. The attackers advanced to within ten meters of the crest, where they stalled amid a barrage of hand grenades and mortar shells. After enduring hours of the close fighting, the Koreans with-drew off the hill entirely and retired to the MLR. Jenkins judged the casual-ties too high and the probability for success too low to justify continued ef-forts against Triangle Hill. Reluctantly he suspended further attacks in this zone and focused all the corps' efforts to retain the ground gained on Sniper Ridge.[108]

Just as Jenkins suspended further ROK attacks on Triangle Hill, Van Fleet wrote to Clark to summarize the progress of Showdown and to attempt some damage control with the Far East commander in chief. Van Fleet focused most of his analysis on the artillery arm of both sides. It was in his view "the deciding factor." Infantry occupying open hill positions were destined to be blasted off by opposing cannon and mortars—nothing could survive above ground when the bombardments began in earnest. To help the ROK Second Division's infantry, now mired in a grim battle of attrition that one observer reported "had turned the Korean fighting into a minor simulacrum of World War I, with its trench lines, its heavy artillery barrages and its struggles for gains measured in yards," he ordered an artillery destruction mission as an "experiment" to be applied in other "limited objective attacks."[109] Additional heavy artillery temporarily joined the IX Corps guns: three battalions each of 8-inch howitzers and 155 mm guns. They were supported by airborne photographic intelligence and tactical reporting from the First Field Artillery Observation Battalion's sound/flash and radar detection platoons. Van Fleet hoped the concentration of heavier caliber guns would throw enough weight of explosive steel to batter down the tunnels and fortified positions the Chinese artillery used to protect themselves during Showdown. Then the Korean troops might gain time and space to organize their defenses better to resist the Chinese counterattacks.[110]

Col. David W. Gray, Van Fleet's liaison with the corps artillery command, later reported the results of the artillery battle. After four days and more than 14,000 shells, IX Corps claimed thirty-nine artillery pieces, fourteen antiaircraft guns, and eighty-five "positions" destroyed and a further seventy-nine emplacements "damaged." Fifth Air Force sorties accounted for an additional nine guns and six positions "destroyed" and twenty-four positions "damaged." However, the 155 mm guns gave disappointing results. Due to the degree of terrain masking and strength of fortifications—typically twenty-foot-thick overhead rock or concrete cover—only the 8-inch howitzer had the trajectory angle and weight of shell to make an impact. Gray assessed that one enemy artillery piece "kill" required more than fifty shells to be fired; a near miss was almost always useless. In his opinion, Eighth Army could not justify the expenditure of ammunition required for future destruction missions except in emergency situations.[111]

As the American artillery opened fire on the Chinese north of Sniper Ridge, Operation Showdown went through another metamorphosis as the ROK Second Division now concentrated solely on maintaining its MLR in the vicinity of Triangle Hill and defeating any Chinese attacks against Objective A on Sniper Ridge. For nearly a week the battle seemed suspended as both sides settled in to patrol and launch occasional probing attacks, never committing more than a platoon-size element. By this time the Chinese had also made significant changes, replacing the Fifteenth Army with the Twelfth Army. The Thirty-First Division assumed responsibility for defending both Triangle

Hill and Sniper Ridge. Then on November 11 the Chinese, supported by seventy artillery pieces, twenty mortars, and twenty-four rocket launchers, swarmed down from Objective Y and overran the ROK Thirty-Second Regiment, which had just relieved the ROK Seventeenth Regiment. These fresh troops were from the Thirty-First Division's Ninety-Second Regiment, which combined with elements of the Twenty-Ninth Division still determined to retake Sniper Ridge. The Koreans launched several counterattacks during the next two days, and both sides remained locked in close combat, each bringing in fresh battalions in an effort to overwhelm the other.[112]

In an attempt to gain a positional advantage, the Koreans extended their attacking frontage to the east and seized Rocky Ridge, a finger extending northeast from Sniper Ridge. By the end of November 17, every battalion of the ROK Seventeenth Regiment was committed to Objective A and Rocky Ridge. The final battle for Rocky Ridge was especially intense, as Korean troops skillfully withdrew a short distance to allow the ROK First Field Artillery Group to blast the exposed Chinese off the crest. The ROK Seventeenth Regiment's Second Battalion attacked through the Third Battalion and in a two-hour hand-to-hand struggle firmly planted itself on Rocky Ridge and began digging in. The Koreans were learning hard tactical lessons, and the final assault on Rocky Ridge showed how far they had come. Previous attacks often took place with indiscriminate shelling falling among the attacking troops, causing as many casualties among the Koreans as among the Chinese. The Second Battalion, however, coordinated its advance and fire support so precisely that the Korean gunners were able to shoot over the heads of the infantry in the minutes just prior to the assault, ensuring that the Korean soldiers would arrive on the objective to overwhelm the stunned defenders.[113]

Showdown entered its last phase on November 18 and ended seven days later. The Korean army defended its forward positions on Sniper Ridge tenaciously against repetitive probes and assaults, but the intensity of the Chinese offensive pressure was visibly slackening. Chinese artillery did most of the killing in this phase as Qin limited his exposure to nighttime platoon attacks that generated little more than sporadic firefights from one ridge to another.[114] American artillery and fighter-bombers continued to hammer the Chinese, but there was little fight left in the Koreans for them to capitalize on American firepower. Fifth Air Force continued to devote half of its aerial sorties to close air support missions on Triangle Hill and Sniper Ridge.[115] American pilots proved their expertise to support the ground troops; bombs were needed, and the fighter-bombers showed up. Many an American and South Korean soldier owed their survival to the UNC's mastery of the air.[116]

Then, seemingly as if by mutual agreement, the fighting died out in the early morning on November 24. The next day the ROK Ninth Division relieved the ROK Second Division and assumed the defense of Sniper Ridge and the MLR extending into the Triangle Hill sector. The Seventh Infantry Division had earlier been replaced by the Twenty-Fifth Infantry Division. The Chinese also rotated out the shattered remnants of the Forty-Fifth and Thirty-First Divisions to the rear of Osong-san for reorganization and reconstitution. On December 1 the Twenty-Ninth Division handed over its sector to the Thirty-Fourth Division. After December 3, the Thirty-Fourth Division was content to engage in squad-size harassment "sorties" that made no impression. With all the major fighting units pulled back to their rear areas, the front settled back into its old routine of patrol and posts. The battle for Osong-san was over.[117]

The Worth of a Hill

After the war, General Clark reflected, "We suffered more than eight thousand casualties, mostly ROKs, a loss out of proportion to our gains. The enemy lost at least half again as many men, but I considered the operation unsuccessful."[118] One American participant in the battle was far less generous. In his view, there was "no compelling tactical reason for these proposed assaults [against Triangle Hill and Sniper Ridge]. At the time the Korean conflict was essentially on hold, with each side . . . waiting for the negotiations . . . to work out a peace settlement." Even worse, "this operation was nothing but a show for the big brass."[119] Assuming that Clark's intent for Showdown was to produce a strategic benefit, to show the Communists that obstruction of an armistice would cost them, it should be asked, "What went wrong?"

The battles for Triangle Hill and Sniper Ridge were the biggest and bloodiest contests of 1952. Operation Showdown lasted forty-two days and cost the UNC more than 8,000 casualties.[120] It was a bloodletting that the Americans were unaccustomed to during this period of active defense. Casualties were especially severe among junior leaders. Of the fifty-two noncoms and six officers present for duty at the beginning of October in Company E, Seventeenth Infantry Regiment, only twenty-four noncoms and one officer remained by the end of the month—nearly 50 percent losses among enlisted leaders and 83 percent among the officers.[121] Lt. Peter R. Johnston, a smoke platoon leader, remembered the toll the battle took on the division: "On a few occasions I dined with the staff of a regimental service company. The warrant officer in charge of recovering the dead never smiled."[122] The Chinese acknowledged losing 15,792 soldiers killed, wounded, and missing. The CPVF's Forty-Fifth Division, which started the campaign with more than ten thousand soldiers, had been utterly crippled: 3,076 killed and 5,676 wounded. Losses among junior leaders were most severe. The 134th Regiment lost 65 percent of its company commanders, 89 percent of its platoon commanders, and 100 percent of its section (squad-level) commanders.[123] Nevertheless, after nearly a month and half and with forty times as many casualties as originally forecast, the UNC controlled only the southern half of Sniper Ridge. Triangle Hill was completely ceded to the Chinese. The Koreans were willing to declare victory, which was not entirely inaccurate, given the intensity of fighting and the ability of the ROK Second Division to remain committed to the grueling battle without collapsing. The ROK army certainly displayed an improved fighting ability and spirit, but there were several factors that tempered the Americans' enthusiasm for what the ROKs had achieved.[124]

American intervention was critical to keep the Korean regiments filled with replacements and supplied with ammunition. For much of the battle, Chung's division was fighting at 80 percent of its authorized strength, and as the KMAG advisor pointed out, the losses were more telling among noncommissioned officers and the company-grade lieutenants and captains—key leaders who were not being replaced, and the effect of their absence was felt on Sniper Ridge throughout the battle. KMAG personnel advisors helped coordinate replacements and their integration with the fighting battalions. IX Corps personnel and logistics officers were also temporarily detailed to assist the KMAG detachment. One tangible result was "a marked improvement in the clothing, equipment and physical condition of replacement [soldiers]."[125] Another contribution was the dedication of corps transportation assets to move replacements and supplies from rear support areas to the MLR. They also assisted KMAG to evacuate and salvage damaged or destroyed equipment and weapons. All of these measures contributed to the resilience of the ROK Second Division and allowed the division staff to focus its energy on the battle as opposed to the requirements to support the battle. However, these efforts simply papered over the real deficiencies that the Korean divisions had when it came to sustained combat operations. It was clear to the KMAG advisors and to the American commanders involved that the ROK army was still too reliant on the Americans.[126]

The Americans and Koreans had learned a bloody lesson in attrition tactics and had paid for underestimating the will and the skill of the Chinese infantrymen opposing them. Although elements of two battalions were committed at the outset of the battle by both divisions, the total strength of each division's attack initially amounted to only one battalion. Frequent heavy enemy counterattacks and intense enemy artillery, mortar, automatic weapons and small arms fire immediately forced the employment of additional units of these battalions as well as other elements of the divisions to save the lives of the men in the initial attacking units and to attempt to carry the operation to any kind of successful conclusion.[127] For their part, the Chinese demonstrated a willingness to risk casualties to keep a continuous cycle of fresh troops surging into the battle zones, emerging from their own mortar and artillery bombardments to overrun and engage US and ROK troops in close combat. The Americans marveled at the proficiency of Chinese gunners and how they were "utilized at every opportunity in support of his major attacks with an approximate daily average of over 18,000 rounds of artillery and mortar fire."[128]

At Osong-san the CPVF celebrated a significant victory of manpower and technique over technological firepower. Commander Deng and his subordinates handled the battle masterfully, ultimately committing four infantry divisions (Forty-Fifth and Twenty-Ninth from the Fifteenth Army and Thirty-First and Thirty-Fourth from the Twelfth Army) along with two artillery divisions (Second and Seventh), one additional artillery regiment from the Sixtieth Army, and one rocket regiment (209th). These formations represented the fighting power of 40,000 men, 114 artillery pieces, 24 rocket launchers, and 47 anti-aircraft guns that "repulse[d] 25 enemy attacks of battalion size and beat back 650 enemy attacks of smaller scale."[129] The most important method of Chinese fighting, given the UNC's absolute superiority in firepower, was the intricate and extensive tunnel system. The Chinese credited their tunnels with "preserving the defense forces, harassing UN forces when they occupied the surface positions, and facilitating the main counterattack forces in wiping out UN troops on top of the tunnels." Strengthened artillery support also played a critical role, but it was the tunnel defense that greatly boosted the CPVF's confidence and determination to maintain their positions along the line of contact.[130] Mao was greatly encouraged. On November 8, 1952, he commended the lessons of the "seesaw" battle to his field commanders and implied that a militarily successful conclusion was still in his scope of strategic outcomes: "If we continue to employ such methods of fighting, we will surely bring our enemies to their knees and force them to come to terms so as to end the war in Korea."[131]

Unfortunately for the American policy of limiting the conflict in Korea while relying on military pressure to gain strategic objectives, Eighth Army was not prepared to fight this kind of battle at this time, and the lack of preparedness contributed in large measure to Showdown's failure. American tactics (and Korean to a lesser extent) by this point had evolved to an unsophisticated reliance on heavy artillery fire using impact fuses to secure approaches to the objective and give the infantry a chance to drive off the Chinese. When the enemy returned, as they nearly always did, the Americans called final protective fires employing variable time fuses and hunkered down. The buzz saw of screaming shrapnel shards cut down anyone standing. But, as a matter of statistics a large enough force would eventually prevail against the Americans' limited commitment of troops. Eventually, there were too few remaining, and the Americans were compelled to fall back to restart the cycle.[132]

Operation Showdown required nearly the entire Seventh Infantry Division to fight for twelve days to occupy ground that could not be defended and that did not serve its purpose to punish the Chinese for failing to meet the UNC's political demands at the conference table. The ROK Second Division likewise had to commit elements of all its regiments just to hold on to a sliver of Sniper Ridge. Although the Koreans did not break, their fighting did not much impress the Chinese, who still regarded them contemptuously and continued to undervalue their capabilities. Contrary to the Korean army's official history, Showdown did not secure advantageous outposts on the line, demoralize the enemy, or allow the UNC to seize "the initiative along the whole front line . . . contribut[ing] a great deal to establishing a favorable political position in the truce talks." The results were just the opposite: a lot of casualties for blasted earth that would either be abandoned or remain in enemy hands at the end of the conflict. Worse, Showdown was a severe blow to the morale and prestige of the UNC, and to the Americans' belief in military operations to solve their policy problem in Korea.[133]

Colonel Moses, whose regiment led the initial assault on Hill 598, captured Showdown's tactical lesson with a warning: "War in any place is a nightmare, but the battle for outpost positions in Korea was savage."[134] William Russell, an American combat correspondent in Korea, was more direct. He recalled that "the price of real estate in Korea was exorbitantly high."[135]

13

SETTLING FOR A SETTLEMENT, NOVEMBER–DECEMBER 1952

GENERAL CLARK NOW grasped the reality of the UNC's strategic dilemma. After the war, he wrote, "Since it was not our government's policy to seek a military decision, the next best thing was to make the stalemate more expensive for the Communists than for us, to hit them where it hurt, to worry them, to convince them by force that the price tag on an armistice was going up, not down."[1] Unfortunately for the Americans, the disparity between Showdown's promise and its actual achievements turned their tactical thinking upside down with respect to using military action to push negotiations in a favorable direction. Militarily, the lessons the Seventh Infantry Division identified offered instructive perspectives to the American commanders and politicians directing the war. The division staff compiled ten pages of "after action" reporting that addressed everything from squad leadership, the need for training and rehearsals, fire support planning, and best use of close air support. For veteran soldiers, these were lessons in basic military practices, combined arms tactics, and leadership. The fact that these issues were addressed in this manner indicates the degree to which the Eighth Army as a whole had atrophied in the eleven months of "active defense," making problematic any future effort to rely on offensive battle to force concessions at Panmunjom.

The army's greater manpower crisis exacerbated Van Fleet's deficit of combat leadership as experienced commanders eventually rotated out of Korea and were replaced, in many cases, by junior officers and noncoms who were more likely to avoid risk in a situation of strategic stalemate. A prime indicator was the mismatch of rank to position of command. The US army authorized a captain to command a company, a lieutenant colonel to command a battalion, and a colonel to command a regiment. Each officer was expected to have maturity, judgment, and experience commensurate with the responsibility to lead his respective echelon in combat, employ its various weapons and systems effectively, and to provide for the care and well-being of the men. By the fall of 1952, in the Seventh Infantry Division it was typical for a lieutenant to lead a company, a major to command a battalion, and—on occasion—a lieutenant colonel to head a regiment. These younger officers were understandably keen to avoid mistakes. Doing too much fighting, incurring too many casualties, firing too many shells—these were the kinds of things to avoid. The consequence was timidity, misjudgment, lost opportunities to gain tactical advantage, and occasionally outright incompetence when the Chinese did come calling.[2]

The American soldier had lost some of his hard-won knowledge fighting the Chinese, a deficit in fighting proficiency that would ensure that the gap between tactical capabilities and strategic imperative to force a settlement would remain unbridged. The tactical premise of Showdown was that artillery and airpower would inflict intolerable casualties on Chinese troops attempting to retake ground lost to the Americans. The Seventh Infantry Division soldiers, however, were not prepared to move aggressively under fire, and when they did occupy an objective, they did not automatically organize an effective defense with communications wire, reserves close to the expected battle area, and other basic security measures to prepare for a counterattack. As a result, the Americans were often surprised by the timing, location, and strength of enemy attacks, and they were unprepared for the casualties such back-and-forth fighting demanded.[3]

Even more damning for the future of Eighth Army's offensive potential and spirit was the loss of confidence among the men being asked to charge up another hill bristling with machine guns and pounded by mortars and artillery. Although serving in a different division, Pvt. Rudolph Stephens was familiar with Hill 1062 and the futility of attempting limited attacks under its shadow. "We wondered sometimes how the big brass who planned these missions had sense enough to even get out of bed in the morning without breaking a leg."[4] Some of the most respected officers were those, typically of junior rank, who ran no unnecessary risks with their men's lives, but they did so by deliberately avoiding contact with likely enemy positions.[5]

Van Fleet acknowledged the decline in his army's offensive potential in the twelve months since the Punchbowl battles. In September, just as the CPVF's Autumn Counterattack was gaining momentum, he lamented "it is a damn hard job to keep an army ever fit, ready, and eager to fight—especially when they go home faster than we can train them."[6] Reflecting back on the failure of Showdown, Van Fleet admitted, "We simply don't have the leaders and the skills in the lower grades, or *sufficient hard combat* to produce an outfit fully combat effective [emphasis added]."[7] Active defense and the war of patrols had not kept Eighth Army sharp, calling into question the feasibility of

Van Fleet's, Clark's, or anyone else's plan to expand military operations beyond the MLR.

By the end of November 1952, American forces were suffering 1,000 casualties a week, a significant spike and the heaviest casualty rate for the year. Since the truce talks began the previous summer, the Pentagon reported that 44,700 Americans had been killed and wounded, and that the tonnage of bombs dropped, and the number of shells and mortars fired, had reached World War II proportions. Yet, the Communists appeared to be getting stronger, not weaker, and as Showdown demonstrated, their defenses were tough. Any breakthrough battle premised on a limited attack promised only more casualties for small returns.[8]

Under these military conditions, the American political scene appeared to offer the generals a lifeline. Even as Showdown was winding down to its bitter conclusion, Mark Clark received a boost in confidence as his friend and former boss in the World War II European theater, General Dwight D. Eisenhower, had just been elected to succeed Harry Truman as president of the United States. Eisenhower's victory rested to a great degree on the assumption that as a military man he possessed some secret insight to solve the Korea knot. Eisenhower did not discourage such speculation, famously declaring at a campaign stop in Detroit on October 24 that if elected, he would go to Korea. It was an ambiguous commitment that was politically brilliant. He did not promise he would actually end the war in either victory or with an armistice, but the American electorate interpreted that, somehow, he would change its sad course.[9]

Anticipating the president-elect's visit to Korea, Clark seized the opportunity to present an ambitious strategy articulated in a document known as OPLAN 8-52. This plan called for an escalation to bring the Communists to terms with a military victory in Korea—a significant departure from previous plans that sought merely to increase military pressure to leverage bargaining concessions.[10] Clark had previously sent three staff officers to Washington to convince General Collins and the JCS to support the plan's force requirements: three US or UN divisions (one each infantry, airborne, marine), two ROK divisions (the Twelfth and Fifteenth Divisions were already formed and undergoing unit training), two Chinese Nationalist divisions, twelve field artillery battalions, and the support and supply organizations necessary to support two additional corps.[11]

It was an ambitious shopping list, but the key element of the proposed strategy was what the military calls the "scheme of maneuver," how these forces were to be used. Over a three-week period, UNC forces would conduct a three-phase operation to seize a line stretching roughly from Pyongyang to

Wonsan—back to the so-called narrow waist of northern Korea. A massive frontal assault to break the enemy's lines in the west, followed by a grand encirclement and battle of annihilation, would collapse the Communists' defenses and leave Pyongyang exposed to capture. If the capture of Pyongyang did not do the trick, then an advance to the Yalu was contemplated. Major amphibious and airborne attacks would envelop Communist forces on either coast and in their operational depth; expanded sea and air operations (requiring one additional battleship, six cruisers, two carriers with full air complements, forty-one destroyers, one hundred B-29 and B-26 bombers, and more than one hundred F-86 and F-84 fighter and fighter-bomber aircraft) would target China's industrial and military capacity in Manchuria and north China.[12] Atomic weapons were not required, but "serious consideration" would be given to their employment—the plan allowed for up to 600 such weapons to be used against Manchurian and North Korean targets. Nothing was said about the Soviets—a critical omission given that Clark knew that the font of China's strength was located in Soviet Russia (tables 13.1, 13.2, and 13.3).[13]

OPLAN 8-52 was deeply flawed because it was worse than a MacArthur do-over. It lacked strategic imagination by being entirely reliant on military pressure to produce a political settlement that was unacceptable to the Communists. Clark informed the JCS, "I have had this subject under active study to determine the extent of aggressive action in Korea nec[essary] to establish conditions whereby the enemy will be compelled to seek or accept an armistice on our terms."[14] It also contained several unverifiable assumptions about Soviet and mainland China military reactions, such as Mao's massive reserves of manpower, which if fully mobilized in Korea could easily spell disaster for the exposed UNC ground forces operating far north of the 38th parallel. Clark's own intelligence apparatus believed that up to twenty-seven PLA divisions could be available from China within ninety days to reinforce the twenty-seven divisions already in Korea as a reserve to the sixty-eight CPVF and KPA divisions committed to holding the front line. It is hard to see how the modest UNC augmentation called for would not only compensate for, but actually overmatch, the additional Communist forces that could be thrown into the battle. Furthermore, the plan explicitly discarded three of Washington's four strategic proscriptions: violating the Manchurian border, employment of Nationalist Chinese forces, and the imposition of a general blockade of the PRC's southern and eastern coasts. The fourth prohibition, the employment of atomic weapons, was observed only by omission, but certainly not ruled out. Eisenhower and his entourage could hardly have believed that the UNC ground forces would be able to blast their way through prepared

TABLE 13.1. GROUND FORCE AUGMENTATION TO UNC OPLAN 8-52, 1952

Type	Augmentation required	Total available to OPLAN 8-52
UN Division	3 (Marine, Infantry, Airborne)	11
ROK Division	2	12
Nationalist Division	2	2
105 mm How Bn	1	4
155 mm How Bn	7	16
8-inch How Bn	4	8
AAA AW Bn	12	16
AAA Gun Bn	8	12

TABLE 13.2. NAVAL FORCE AUGMENTATION TO UNC OPLAN 8-52, 1952

Type	Augmentation required	Total available to OPLAN 8-52
Battleship	1	2
Cruisers	6	10
Carriers w/aircraft	2	6
Destroyers	41	91
Minecraft	16	48

defenses—like those encountered in Operation Showdown—using conventional firepower alone. Atomic bombs would be required to destroy enough enemy forces to give the UNC the room to maneuver that the plan required.[15]

OPLAN 8-52 contained, moreover, several fatal operational flaws that should never have gotten past experienced soldiers such as Van Fleet and Clark. Although the air and ground augmentation surely would increase the UNC's fighting power, it was equally clear, especially by the fall of 1952, that such augmentation would not give the UNC a sufficient relative superiority in the theater to force a breakthrough and put the Communists on the run. The plan already envisioned a *division* of force with an amphibious landing, not a militarily significant concentration along the MLR. Furthermore, an experienced general understands that any offensive inevitably loses momentum

TABLE 13.3. AIR FORCE AUGMENTATION TO UNC OPLAN 8-52, 1952

Type	Augmentation required (squadrons)	Total available to OPLAN 8-52
Fighter-bomber F-80, F-84	3	18
Fighter-interceptor F-86	9	16
Fighter-interceptor (all weather) F-91	4	3 (one squadron retained in Japan)
Light bomber B-26	3	9
Medium bomber B-29	6	15
TACP (close air support)	3	8

over time. A blow that did not produce substantial destruction of communist armies would only ensure a stalemate a little farther north of the current line of contact. Operation Showdown convincingly showed that a major breakthrough just was not in the cards, and one to two additional infantry divisions would not supply the weight of men and firepower needed to maintain enough momentum to achieve a useful military result.[16]

Could Clark really have believed that a massive offensive as described would have permitted Nam Il and Deng Hua to remain equipoised at Panmunjom, nodding in anxious agreement at whatever terms for an armistice the UNC offered? His intelligence analysis suggested that is precisely what would happen: "The Communists will intensify their efforts to obtain an immediate armistice once any chance for any significant UNC success is evident." This assessment completely contradicted the evidence of how the Communists actually behaved both at Panmunjom and in the field when UNC forces attempted to increase military coercion. FEC intelligence did meekly suggest that Mao might substantially reinforce Korea "to take advantage of a weakness in the UNC position," meaning that if the ground attack failed, or significant UNC forces were destroyed in the effort, Clark's position in Korea might actually become materially worse. It was a substantial risk that Clark seemed to accept without much worry.[17]

Clark was suggesting a completely new war for the new president to wage, and he was advocating a return to the operational methods that had produced the Americans' strategic conundrum in the first place. A strategy aimed at the military annihilation of the Communists' armies in Korea promised only to escalate the costs of stalemate further. Clark's intelligence was unjustifiably sanguine, underplaying Mao's capabilities by intentionally disregarding his intention not to lose in Korea.[18] The JCS, led by General Bradley, was un-enthusiastic, and their advice likely influenced Eisenhower to duck the issue while in Korea.[19]

Eisenhower's visit to Korea proved uneventful. During a two-day whirl-wind visit, Clark and Van Fleet accompanied the president-elect on a brief tour of the front, where he inspected US, Commonwealth, and ROK troops. However, the two generals were disappointed. Although they spent a lot of time with Eisenhower, the president-elect never paused long enough to give his former subordinates a chance to outline their victory plan. After a brief call on President Rhee (the president-elect, true to his modest form of leader-ship and not one given to lofty declamations, refused to appear with Rhee at a staged rally in Seoul), Eisenhower bundled himself in his plane and flew east.[20] With him went the conviction "we could not stand forever on a static front and continue to accept casualties without any visible result. Small at-tacks on small hills would not end the war."[21] It was this lesson that set the general's plans aside and determined that the United States would seek and agree to an honorable armistice.[22]

There was one general who likely did affect Eisenhower's views on the way forward for American strategy to end the war: Gen. Paik Sun-yup. Still a favorite of the Eighth Army's leadership (Van Fleet thought very highly of Paik's intellect, fighting spirit, and professionalism), Paik was now the ROK army's chief of staff and its first four-star general officer. In the presence of the American ground commanders and Eisenhower's military retinue, Paik presented a plan to expand the Korean army from twelve to twenty divi-sions. The fact that three Korean divisions cost less to man, equip, and main-tain than one American division could not have escaped notice. The fact that Korean divisions were at that time heavily engaged in battle, standing their ground, and killing Communists also could not have failed to affect the cal-culus. Clark appeared to offer to exchange dead Americans for sterile ground. Paik offered Koreans to fight the Chinese and North Korean armies with less American liability in exchange for continued military and political support.[23]

December was a relatively quiet month, with few attacks against Eighth Army patrols or positions. The number of Communist patrols remained stable, and incoming artillery declined to its lowest level since July. Reflecting Clark's reaction to Showdown and the JCS's cool reception to expanding offensive op-erations, Van Fleet directed Eighth Army commanders on December 12 "to make every effort to reduce combat losses to an absolute minimum consistent with the proper performance of the Army's current combat missions." Addi-tionally, Van Fleet reserved authority to approve all offensive actions larger than company-size. He continued to emphasize the value of patrolling and capturing prisoners. Should the Communists attack, Eighth Army needed to maintain the "necessary strength to throw back every offensive action against our presently held positions."[24] This guidance was barely changed since the advent of active defense, except that now, perhaps, Van Fleet really meant it.

A similar freeze persisted at Panmunjom. On December 30, KPA Col. Chu Yon replaced Col. Chang Chun-san as the senior Communist liaison officer. A day later, the Korean "battlefront was generally quiet." Fifth Air Force claimed its 500th MiG destroyed, FEAF medium bombers struck a four-target complex on the Yalu River, and the Americans switched out Col. Charles W. McCarthy with Col. Willard B. Carlock as the UNC liaison officer. Clark noted in the UNC's final command report of 1952 "there were no other noteworthy incidents connected with [the] armistice negotiations."[25]

Back in Washington, the new Eisenhower administration, inaugurated January 20, 1953, tackled the Korea problem but explored no new concrete initiatives. Eisenhower wondered aloud about flexing atomic muscle and other deeds "executed under circumstances of our choosing"—rhetoric that energized his hawkish secretary of state, John Foster Dulles, but failed to move the JCS, who preferred sticking to Truman's policy of finding a way to negotiate a settlement.[26]

When General Harrison suspended talks at Panmunjom in October 1952, the United Nations emerged as the new seat of the political fight for an armistice. Much to Acheson's chagrin, India's UN representative, Krishna V. K. Menon, circulated his own plan to settle the POW question. "Menon's cabal" (Acheson's term) proposed to repatriate immediately all willing POWs while turning over non-repatriates to third-nation custody. The fate of these POWs was left vague, and Acheson sensed that he was being manipulated by Great Britain and Canada into a settlement that appeared on paper to satisfy Truman's demands but lacked the enforcement mechanisms that would provoke Communist opposition. After significant arm twisting and maneuvering of his own, Acheson engineered two significant modifications to ensure an independent and autonomous repatriation commission and to guarantee that non-repatriate POWs would not be held indefinitely. Menon's modified proposal passed the UN General Assembly on December 3, over Soviet objections. Ten days later the Chinese rejected the proposal and the North Koreans shortly followed.[27]

Whatever trouble the Menon proposal caused the Americans in the last two months of 1952, the outcome was a significant moral victory. The UN stood behind Truman's voluntary repatriation policy, and Menon's plan, with some further modification, became the basis for the future resolution of the POW issue. The death of Josef Stalin on March 5, 1953, provided another shock to the diplomatic impasse and likely led to an extraordinary breakthrough. Zhou Enlai on March 28 agreed to Clark's proposal of February 22 to exchange sick and wounded prisoners. Zhou also indicated that the time was right to settle the "entire question" regarding POWs and "to insure the cessation of hostilities in Korea and to conclude the armistice agreement."[28] There was still much work to be done and plenty of fighting left in the most violent spring since 1951 before an armistice could be achieved, but the final pages had been written that would bring the destructive conflict finally to an end.

The Limited War Problem—Reassessed

Korea was the strangest war the United States had fought to this point in its history. Political goals and military strategy morphed no less than three times in the first twelve months of fighting. Between July and September 1950, American strategy aimed to stop and then repel North Korea's aggressive design on the South. The military strategy was familiar to veterans of World War II: generally unimpeded use of conventional military weaponry in all dimensions of conflict to defeat the KPA, but prior to MacArthur's attack at Inchon even that goal appeared to be problematic. Starting in October, policy flipped, as military success now ran ahead of its political purpose. Rather than restrain MacArthur's tactical momentum, Truman allowed for a more expansive objective, to destroy the KPA and the North Korean state. Peninsular unification under the ROK was the unstated consequential purpose of this new policy.

Mao's intervention changed everything. It was a new war for Korea. When Mao's volunteers failed to eject the UNC from Korea, both sides determined to prosecute their policy objectives in a different forum. CPVF and UNC strategies existed in parallel as both struggled to leverage their respective advantages into military gains sufficient to affect the strategic deadlock. The Chinese and American militaries had recent traditions of seeking decisive battle, but both ended up adapting their tactics and the scope of their operations in a similar fashion, seeking to limit their exposure in an extended contest of battlefield attrition. Both sides stressed the importance of patrolling, fortification, and firepower. Both realized the high stakes assigned to the loss of a hilltop or a battalion's worth of infantry, and both were stuck in the same limited war morass: too committed to back out but equally unable to grapple their way forward to impose a military settlement.[29]

Once truce talks began, Ridgway's broad attrition offensives were called off. However, when needed, Van Fleet turned the pressure on again, driving the Eighth Army forward several miles and killing thousands of communist troops. The result of this final limited offensive campaign (August–October 1951) was also politically rewarding. The Communists agreed to substantial concessions: to change venues for further talks and concede a demarcation line that followed the final line of military contact. But Eighth Army commanders were denied the chance to fight to a traditional victory and had to settle for ways to measure and report progress other than ground gained and enemy units destroyed. In practice though, these methods had little to do with winning a limited war: friendly and enemy casualties, ammunition expended or conserved, patrols conducted, prisoners taken, and outposts manned. Of course, platoon-, company-, and occasionally battalion-size raids and attacks did occur, but the art and skill of coordinating division and corps artillery, tank, and air support with a regiment-size infantry assault over difficult terrain against a skillful enemy had atrophied. But even if Eighth Army had maintained its fighting edge, it would not have mattered. It was a different kind of war, and Van Fleet missed the essential change to this war's character and conduct. Operation Showdown showed what many soldiers instinctively knew—it was not 1951 anymore. Van Fleet's vision for victory in Korea was a pipe dream.

Eighth Army leaders, under pressure to reduce casualties while inflicting them on the enemy, produced a mindset that encouraged micromanagement, a "chip[ping] away at the freedom of action . . . allow[ed] subordinate commanders."[30] When confidence in a quick armistice settlement was high, this attitude was understandable even if not professionally healthy. But once it became clear that the Communists would only make concessions under military duress, the prohibition of any offensive action by company-size and larger units without Eighth Army or FEC approval could only have one outcome. Reuben Jenkins (commanding IX Corps) concluded that this level of oversight on tactical initiative created "a varying degree of hesitancy on the part of commanders to take aggressive action without detailed instructions and approval from the next higher headquarters."[31] In other words, the Americans in particular were at a loss on how to respond to the CPVF's newly aggressive stance in the fall of 1952. The reaction was unimaginative and doomed to fail.

Away from the battlefield, the Americans labored under a significant handicap in negotiations. The evidence is clear that none of the senior UNC delegates considered their negotiation counterparts as true military equals. Admiral Joy never trusted their word, considering instead "they would rather lie than tell the truth even when the truth would make a better case for them. By whatever means are most effective, they assault Truth . . . they can do no other."[32] Some of this bias was racial and some a product of the Communist system that seemed to produce overideological confrontations by nature. The Communists could never consent to anything that struck at their image of legitimacy or appeared to undermine their military accomplishments, even if such compromise promised an end to the fighting, the ostensible goal of the negotiations. The Americans ignored the fact they (through their political masters) had accepted the task of treating as equals two revo-

lutionary regimes, who were militarily weak and forever fearful of exploitation or coercion by the free-world's preeminent military power. The maneuvering, dissembling, delaying tactics—attempts "to seize every advantage in a
largely disadvantageous situation" must be seen in this political context, and
the Americans should have been astute enough to recognize the situation for
what it was, even if they did not foresee it.[33]

The result was a structural inability to speak and be understood. Given
the UNC's own standards and expectations of negotiations, it appears they
paid the higher price in the process. The idea that the Communist soldier
only understood force led Van Fleet and Clark to endorse a coercive strategy
to bring about a settlement.[34] But the reality was that the Communists did
not remain unmoved at Panmunjom because insufficient force was being applied; exactly the opposite was true. Voluntary repatriation demanded the
Communists (in reality the Chinese) accept a significant loss of prestige, for
which their own battle sacrifices would have been in vain. No state would
willingly make terms under those conditions. The Americans were attempting to substitute military power (a means) for policy objectives (the ends),
a reversal of Clausewitz's dictum that the conduct of war is an extension or
continuation of policy.

Washington's political intervention to accept the immediate delineation of
a truce line that conformed to the battle line following the conclusion of the
battles for Heartbreak Ridge and the Jamestown Line "was the turning point
of the armistice conference. Thereafter, because the fighting slackened, we
lacked the essential military pressure with which to enforce a reasonable attitude toward negotiations."[35] Admiral Joy may have been correct, but he was
also out of bounds. The casualty list had been (too) long, and the Truman administration was eager to capitalize on the Communists' recent agreement to
resume talks at Panmunjom. Although it is impossible to know, a case can be
made that (absent Truman's late shift on POW repatriation) the mutual momentum of concessions could have produced an armistice agreement in the
early winter of 1952 that would have substantially satisfied all parties—the
ROK excepted, of course.

Was the delay in obtaining an armistice worth it? Shortly after Lt. Gen.
William Harrison delivered the UNC's final three-option package proposal
on September 28, 1952, Marine Corps commandant Gen. Lemuel C. Shepard
Jr. opined that he could see no honorable end to the Korean conflict "unless
we defeat the enemy," adding, "we've made every possible concession" at Panmunjom.[36] Negotiated deadlock convinced American commanders that only
on the battlefield could an armistice be obtained. American firepower doctrine and technique certainly proved its military value on the ground, and
the Chinese and North Koreans always paid a steep price for ground they

defended or seized from UNC troops. The Americans could call on nearly limitless destructive potential from the air, sea, and artillery. Sgt. Tony Espejo humanized the Americans' technical reliance on firepower, capturing the ebb and flow of adrenaline, and the thrill of massing artillery fire on time, on target, in response to a frantic call for help: "Then you'd hear, 'Fire for effect,' and they'd call the whole battery again . . . and fire for effect ten rounds [from each of six guns]. It went 'bang, bang, bang, bang!' But it was fun, I liked it, I enjoyed it. I didn't enjoy killing those people up there, because I knew we were killing people, and I always regretted it. I went up there on White Horse [Mountain], and you'd see all these men, these Chinese, who were dead . . . some with papers sticking out of their pockets and you'd pull them out and you'd see pictures of their babies and wives. It makes you feel bad that you killed these people.[37]

American airmen hoped that their efforts, as destructive as they were, would actually shorten the war by coercing the Communists to come to terms without the need for massive bloodletting on the ground. It was a misplaced hope and a disappointing coda for the obvious fact that airpower was indeed "indivisible," that its proper employment conferred real advantages and put at risk all important elements of an enemy's national structure, military power, and economic potential.[38] JCS chairman General Omar N. Bradley made a substantial admission shortly after Showdown's conclusion. Airpower, he said, "constitutes the most potent means at present available to the United Nations Command, of maintaining the degree of military pressure which might impel the Communists to agree, finally, to acceptable armistice terms."[39] Up until the end of 1952, however, airpower proved to be a weak panacea for real military pressure. UNC airmen subjected North Korea to massive devastation unheard of up to that time, but as one American veteran recognized, it was always difficult to evaluate from the air the full impact of the air campaign.[40] When the war entered its negotiations phase, hardly a structure of military value stood above ground between the MLR and the Yalu River that had not been thoroughly gutted, burned, and bombed out. The UNC air campaigns hampered communist logistics and reminded military and political leaders of the costs of continued conflict, but they did not threaten the military status quo.[41] Despite these benefits, airpower did not seize ground or force the Communists to lose face in the arena of negotiations. These were their true pressure points.

Airpower applied to the Communists' lines of supply, their logistical infrastructure, command and control, and rear areas beyond the reach of UNC artillery was at best a limited success. The various interdiction campaigns generated controversy mainly because airmen failed to justify interdiction in concrete terms affecting the ground battle. Despite the massive destruction of men, equipment, and material, the Communists were allowed to fight generally on their own terms, which negated many of the UNC's advantages in mobility and firepower. The Americans learned that a large portion of North Korea's rail network and transportation system had to be destroyed before Communist forces would feel its effect. FEAF never approached the 70 percent figure that estimates projected was necessary to really put the crimp on forward troops.[42] Fuel, munitions, manpower, and other supplies continued to flow in quantities sufficient to give the CPVF and KPA tactical options and autonomy to resist the UNC's attrition strategy. For all the bridges that were knocked down, repaired, and knocked down again, airmen could take cold comfort in the fact that they "won the battle to knock out the bridge, but lost the objective, which was to knock out the traffic."[43] While the claims of troops killed, trucks destroyed, roads and rail tracks cut, or bridges dropped might indicate aggregate success of the tactical missions flown by allied fighter-bombers, the strategic result of such success continued to elude the UNC.[44] Nam Il and his fellow negotiators were confident that without an expanded war, their forces would not be militarily defeated. However, the interdiction campaigns certainly affected the Communist field forces and denied their ability to apply their manpower advantage directly against the UNC to pressure a settlement to their liking, and Eighth Army never had to constrain operations due to the threat of enemy air attack—likely the most important contribution of allied airpower to the United Nations Command.[45]

The long-term continuation of the interdiction campaigns as a strategic lever actually hindered the UNC's military effort by mismatching means to ends. For a critical part of the conflict, the army and the navy were marginalized while the air force attempted to carry the greater part of the strategic burden to compel an armistice. Following the Chinese intervention, the number of tactical aircraft available to the UNC was never up to the challenge for air superiority, interdiction, and close air support. And the technology of the day simply was not up to the task that airpower theory demanded. The Communist armies on the ground could and did endure significant hardship and shortages caused by the UNC's nearly absolute control over the sky. After several months of strenuous effort, air interdiction inflicted horrendous casualties and destroyed significant amounts of material and infrastructure, but airmen had to admit that full interdiction was never achieved.[46]

After the war Van Fleet reflected, "If all arms—Ground, Sea, and Air—had struck together the pressure would have been too much for the enemy . . . the air effort could not win by itself."[47] Without a large-scale ground offensive, of the type envisioned by Van Fleet or Clark, which would have come at a too high cost for the Truman administration politically, airpower's coercive force was buffered to a degree that airmen had not anticipated. In other words, FEAF's attempts were doomed to fail by virtue of the American policy and strategy of limited war settled by negotiations.[48]

How did the Chinese army come out of the extended Korean War? Col. Lloyd Moses, the primary architect of Operation Showdown, gave Peng's veterans the credit they earned. "The enemy was resourceful and dangerous," he wrote several decades after the war, "becoming more skillful every week. Our only hope was to obtain an armistice and the Communists could delay the negotiations on any pretext as long as it was to their advantage to do so. They could show the world the US could be fought to a standstill."[49] Moses's praise, though, does not go far enough. Peng and his CPVF found a way to make attrition work for them as an operational method that supported their strategic approach to settle the war by negotiations.

Under Peng's leadership the PLA substantially attained Mao's political goals and learned to survive standing up to a better armed and resourced opponent. It is easy to dismiss casually Peng's achievement, chalking it up to "mass" or "subterfuge" or a willing prodigiousness with his men's lives. There is some merit in this criticism. However, the CPVF operated under significant handicaps during this stalemated phase: the linear warfare Ridgway imposed and Van Fleet upheld that forced the CPVF into a war of firepower attrition; daily and unremitting air attack that threatened supply lines and contributed greatly to Eighth Army's freedom of action; and, an ever-present maritime threat of amphibious attack. After the war, Peng reflected on the operational difficulties of supplying and sustaining large forces under an enemy air umbrella. It was not impossible to do, but with a touch of irony he allowed that the CPVF "gained a lot of experience in the War to Resist US Aggression and Aid Korea. Our success in moving supplies to the front without any air cover was likewise a valuable experience." One can sense the ruefulness of that observation.[50] The Chinese did not overcome all their operational handicaps, but they did adapt enough to endow their tactical actions with strategic significance.[51]

For their part, the Communists never could fully exploit their respective air arm for a variety of reasons. Political restrictions the Soviet leadership imposed limited strategic options for airpower to influence the ground battle. Marshals Peng Dehuai and Deng Hua had the unenviable task of fighting a strong enemy under modern conditions without all of the modern supporting arms necessary to assure success. Even under more liberal rules, it is doubtful Chinese or Soviet airpower would have had a more defining influence. Soviet doctrine had not yet prescribed an independent role for tactical airpower, and therefore their contribution remained defensive, protecting bridges, supply lines, and other strategic assets. Their focus was to shoot down as many bombers as possible. Although the Soviets, and later the Chinese, benefited from sanctuary close to the battle area, the Americans actually controlled the tempo of air engagement, choosing the time, place, and number of aircraft. Xiaoming Zhang has argued that despite the significant contribution of Soviet interceptor-fighters in Korea, the most valuable contribution to the CPVF's strategy of persistence was in supplying aircraft and trainers to create an active and formidable Chinese air force. If communist airpower could not affect the outcome of battles during the fall months when talks at Panmunjom were recessed, they could at least ensure that enough logistics support could successfully run the gauntlet from Sinuiju to Pyonggang and the Iron Triangle. This was probably the greatest threat and greatest frustration to the Americans throughout all of 1952.[52]

The armistice terms, concluded on July 27, 1953, were nearly identical to those Admiral Joy presented on April 28, 1952. Fifteen months of bitter fighting were required to convince both sides they were getting the best deal possible. The battles at Old Baldy, White Horse Mountain, Triangle Hill, and Sniper Ridge were part and parcel of the same strategic confrontation, the employment of ground-based military force to coerce the other side into making the key concession. That neither side succumbed to such crude pressure is indicative that both sides underestimated their opponents' resolve and were largely ignorant as to their actual strategic goals and the extent to which they would go to achieve them.

Whatever could be said of the armistice agreement, the process of negotiated settlement punctuated by spasms of violence on the ground, in the air, and at the conference table did prevent the outbreak of a third world war. Victory in its classical sense of dictating a peace to a vanquished enemy simply was not in the cards, and many American military leaders may have perceived the armistice "as a sorry substitute for American victory in Korea."[53] However, policy matters. Despite MacArthur's brief flirtation with decisive pursuit of the KPA in the fall of 1950, America's war in Korea was limited. Ultimately, the policy object was to turn back aggression, not defeat Asian communism. For all of Van Fleet's great qualities, this fact eluded his grasp. He did not understand the full import of Ridgway's strategic reflection—Active Defense—of political reality in Washington. His continued advocacy for some kind of tactically decisive maneuver, however packaged, simply placed him out of step with his military superiors and his political masters. Even Clark had a difficult time accepting something less than victory, but he was politically attuned enough to know when to back down and follow policy.

There is a direct linkage between political and strategic aspirations and the means devoted to back such aspirations with military force. Great risks result if the aspirations are greater than the means or resources made available to a commander, who is compelled then to fight a war that is unwinnable at an acceptable cost, measured in lives, time, and money. S. L. A. Marshall hit the issue squarely in his lecture to army majors at Fort Leavenworth: "National policy itself [has] to be based on what we could expect of the average American who was carrying a rifle on his shoulder."[54] Admiral Joy expanded Marshall's analysis: "We learned in Korea that crystallization of political objectives should precede initiation of armistice talks. All personnel in the United Nations Command delegation were aware of the chameleon-like character of American political objectives in Korea . . . the political objectives of the United States in Korea weather-vaned with the winds of combat, accommodating themselves to current military events rather than constituting the goal to be reached *through military operations* [emphasis added]."[55]

Note that Joy suggested that political objectives should have been determined prior to armistice talks and been independent of the vagaries of battle at any given time. The same advice would obtain for the war itself. Good strategy seeks to clarify political objectives before the shooting starts; if that is not possible, then political and military leaders must come together to reach that clarity before engaging in the endgame, whether that be militarily or diplomatically based. Of all the missteps made in the Korean War, the failure of this dialogue between civilian and military leadership (especially the field commanders) was the most egregious. The president determined policy and expected the military men to figure out how to achieve it. Perhaps Truman was too stung by MacArthur's performance to trust the military brass, but his decision over POW repatriation—as just one among many affecting the termination of the Korean War—was made without regard to the military consequences. It was this contingent process of policy and strategic decision-making, not the intransigence of North Korean and Chinese armistice delegates nor the respective fighting capabilities of American and communist soldiers, that produced the stalemate in Korea.

Maybe this was the lesson of Korea. If so, the United States paid a severe price for the schooling.

NOTES

Introduction

1. Yafeng Xia, *Negotiating with the Enemy* (Bloomington: Indiana University Press, 2006), 4.

2. A "time on target" was an artillery technique that allowed multiple units to fire volleys timed to land on target simultaneously. Anthony J. Sobieski, ed., *Fire Mission!* (Fairfield, CA: First Book Library, 2003), 7; Dan Raschen, *Send Port and Pyjamas!* (London: Buckland Publications, 1987), 156.

3. Walter G. Hermes, *Truce Tent and Fighting Front* (Washington, DC: US Government Printing Office, 1966), 184–85.

4. Raschen, *Send Port and Pyjamas!*, 162.

Chapter 1

1. Mark W. Clark, *From the Danube to the Yalu* (New York: Harper and Brothers, 1954), 1.

2. In December 1951, only 23 percent of voters approved of the president's job performance. Steven Casey, *Selling the Korean War: Propaganda, Politics, and Public Opinion in the United States, 1950–1953* (New York: Oxford University Press, 2008), 292.

3. Wayne Thompson, "Remarks on Planning and Operations in the Korean War," in *Coalition Air Warfare in the Korean War, 1950–1953: Proceedings of the Air Force Historical Foundation Symposium*, ed. Jacob Neufeld and George M. Watson Jr. (Washington, DC: US Air Force History and Museums Program, 2005), 6.

4. Truman fell for an old trick and allowed a reporter to put words in his mouth. "Police action" never escaped his lips, but the damage was done and the phrase would haunt American military policy in Korea until the end. Casey, *Selling the Korean War*, 28.

5. Harry S. Truman, *Memoirs*, vol. 2, *Years of Trial and Hope* (Garden City, NY: Doubleday, 1956), 459–64.

6. The fiction of employing Chinese "volunteers" rather than regular PLA units was devised to avoid the awkward diplomacy of an aspiring UN nation fighting against the will and forces of the United Nations. Anthony Farrar-Hockley, "A Remi-

niscence of the Chinese People's Volunteers in the Korean War," *China Quarterly* 98 (June 1984): 293.

7. Yafeng Xia, *Negotiating with the Enemy* (Bloomington: Indiana University Press, 2006), 43.

8. See Casey, *Selling the Korean War*, 286–89, 292–93, for a persuasive explanation of how the Truman administration attempted to convince the American public voluntary repatriation was a legitimate war aim.

9. William M. Donnelly, "A Damn Hard Job: James A. Van Fleet and the Combat Effectiveness of U.S. Army Infantry, July 1951–February 1953," *Journal of Military History* 82 (January 2018): 147–79.

10. Lloyd R. Moses, *Whatever It Takes: The Autobiography of General Lloyd R. Moses* (Vermillion, SD: Dakota Press, 1991), 189.

11. Chai Chengwen, "The Korean Truce Negotiations," in *Mao's Generals Remember Korea*, trans. and ed. Xiaobing Li, Allan R. Millett, and Bin Yu (Lawrence: University Press of Kansas, 2001), 188.

12. Jian Chen, "China's Changing Aims during the Korean War, 1950–1951," *Journal of American–East Asian Relations* 1, no. 1 (Spring 1992): 19, 26, 33.

13. Xiaobing Li, *China's Battle for Korea* (Bloomington: Indiana University Press, 2014).

14. Bin Yu, "What China Learned from Its 'Forgotten War' in Korea," in *Mao's Generals Remember Korea*, trans. and ed. Xiaobing Li, Allan R. Millett, and Bin Yu (Lawrence: University Press of Kansas, 2001), 9.

15. Yan Xu, "The Chinese Forces and Their Casualties in the Korean War: Facts and Statistics," *Chinese Historians* 6, no. 2 (Fall 1993): 45, 58.

16. As an indication of how important this phase of the war was to Mao, by 1952 CPVF troop strength reached 1.45 million men in fifty-nine infantry divisions and fifteen artillery divisions, along with an extensive logistics apparatus to keep nearly one-fourth of the PRC's active military strength to defend North Korea. See Xiaobing Li, *A History of the Modern Chinese Army* (Lexington: University Press of Kentucky, 2007), and Xu, "Chinese Forces and Their Casualties," 45–58.

17. Carter Malkasian, *A History of Modern Wars of Attrition* (Westport, CT: Praeger Publishers, 2002), 101.

18. John R. Bruning, *Crimson Sky: The Air Battle for Korea* (Dulles, VA: Brassy's, 1999), and Conrad C. Crane, *American Airpower Strategy in Korea, 1950–1953* (Lawrence: University Press of Kansas, 2000) remain the best comprehensive accounts in a very open field. The service's official history, Robert F. Futrell, *The United States Air Force in Korea* (Washington, DC: Office of the Air Force Historian, 1983), is badly in need of revision.

19. Yan Xu, *Mao Zedong yu kangmei yuanchao zhanzheng* [Mao Zedong and the war to resist the US and Aid Korea], 2nd ed. (Beijing: PLA Press, 2006), 222; Kechao Luan, *Xue ye huo de jiaoling: kangmei yuanchao jishi* [The contest: Blood v. fire; The records of resisting America and aiding Korea] (Beijing: China Literature Publishing House, 2008), 294–95. I am grateful to Professor Xiaobing Li for the translation of these sources and interpretation of Mao's military views.

Chapter 2

1. Allan R. Millett, *Their War for Korea* (Dulles, VA: Brassey's, 2002), xxi.

2. Proft served in Korea from 1951 to 1952. Quotation from Anthony J. Sobieski, ed., *Fire for Effect: Artillery Forward Observers in Korea* (Bloomington, IN: Author House, 2005), 65. See also Roy R. Jensen, *A War (Love) Story: One Marine's Korean War* (Sioux Falls, SD: Pine Hill Press, 2000), 461; Arthur L. Haarmeyer, *Into the Land of Darkness* (Self-published, Arthur L. Haarmeyer; prepared by the Donohue Group, 2013), xv–xix.

3. Rutherford M. Poats, *Decision in Korea* (New York: McBride 1954), 216.

4. Carl von Clausewitz, *On War*, ed. and trans. Michael Howard and Peter Paret (Princeton, NJ: Princeton University Press, 1976), 579.

5. The president's reasoning is found in Truman, *Years of Trial and Hope*, 337–48. Fortunately for him, "congressional leaders approved of my action." See also Sheila Miyoshi Jager, *Brothers at War: The Unending Conflict in Korea* (New York: W. W. Norton, 2013), 72–73.

6. See, for example, J. Lawton Collins, *War in Peacetime: The History and Lessons of Korea* (Boston: Houghton Mifflin, 1969), 32–35, for one perspective of how the American government determined its intervention objectives in Korea.

7. MacArthur designated his US Far East Command as the United Nations Command headquarters on July 10, 1950. Roy E. Appleman, *South to the Naktong, North to the Yalu* (Washington, DC: US Government Printing Office, 1961), 51.

8. For the military assessment, see Matthew B. Ridgway, *The Korean War* (Garden City, NY: Doubleday, 1967), 43–45; for a blended military-political assessment, see Collins, *War in Peacetime*, 143–49; for the political assessment, see Truman, *Years of Trial and Hope*, 360–62. For analysis of the complex interaction of international politics and military imperatives, see Dean Acheson, *Present at the Creation* (New York: W. W. Norton, 1969), 445–46, 451–55.

9. The quotation is from Dennis Bloodworth, *The Chinese Looking Glass* (New York: Farrar, Straus and Giroux, 1966), 51; Li, *History of the Modern Chinese Army*, 135.

10. Xu, "Chinese Forces and Their Casualties," 48.

11. Collins, *War in Peacetime*, 230–32, 245–46.

12. Burton I. Kaufman, *The Korean War: Challenges in Crisis, Credibility, and Command* (New York: Alfred A. Knopf, 1986), 117–19.

13. NSC 48/5 had been germinating for several months, but the controversy surrounding General MacArthur's insubordinate statements and his subsequent relief delayed its adoption as policy. Copies of both documents are in Spencer C. Tucker, ed., *Encyclopedia of the Korean War* (Santa Barbara, CA: ABC-CLIO, 2000), 3:970–72, 974–77.

14. Collins, *War in Peacetime*, 302.

15. I am indebted to Dr. Conrad Crane, Strategic Studies Institute, Carlisle, PA, for his advice to consider the conundrum American commanders faced in waging war while simultaneously attempting to strike a bargain for a cease-fire. Conrad C. Crane, "Measuring Gains on the Battle Field and the Peace Table: Shifting Assessments during the Korean War," unpublished, 5, author's copy.

16. Poats, *Decision in Korea*, 198.

17. For a theoretical construction of war's many interactions, see Clausewitz, *On War*, 75–89.

18. See William Stueck, *Rethinking the Korean War* (Princeton, NJ: Princeton University Press, 2002), 66–83, for analysis of the scale and scope of the Korean War.

19. For analysis of the South Korean army's early history (1946–49) and the initial attempts to undermine the American-sponsored system, see Bryan R. Gibby, *The Will to Win: American Military Advisors to Korea, 1946–1953* (Tuscaloosa: University of Alabama Press, 2012).

20. Gibby, *Will to Win*, 80–94, 122–30; transcript, "Stalin's Meeting with Kim Il-sung, Moscow, March 5, 1949," trans. Kathryn Weathersby, *Cold War International History Project Bulletin* 5 (Spring 1995): 1–6, 9.

21. Sung-hwan An, "Soviet Military Advisory Group Support to the NKPA, 1946–1953," in *New Research on Korean War History* (Seoul: Republic of Korea Ministry of National Defense Military History Compilation Committee, 2002), 2:345, 364–68, 371, 388. I appreciate Jiyul Kim providing an English translation of this source.

22. An, "Soviet Military Advisory Group," 386, 405–7, 412.

23. An, "Soviet Military Advisory Group," 432–37; Headquarters, Eighth United States Army Korea, Enemy Material, n.d., 12, USACMH; Millett, *Their War for Korea*, 42.

24. Sun-yup Paik, *Pusan to Panmunjom* (Dulles, VA: Brassey's, 1999), 7–8. See also Gibby, *Will to Win*, 82–94 and 126–36, for analysis of the ROK army's leadership, training, equipment, defensive plans, and resistance during the first week of the war.

25. Truman acknowledged the tension: "Every decision I made in connection with the Korean conflict had this one aim in mind: to prevent a third world war and the terrible destruction it would bring to the civilized world." Truman, *Years of Trial and Hope*, 345.

26. Acheson, *Present at the Creation*, 408–9.

27. On June 28, US air force planes bombed retreating ROK troops north of Seoul. Paik, *Pusan to Panmunjom*, 15; James T. Stewart, ed., *Airpower: The Decisive Force in Korea* (Princeton, NJ: D. Van Nostrand, 1957), 6, 272.

28. Thomas E. Hanson, *Combat Ready? The Eighth U.S. Army on the Eve of the Korean War* (College Station: Texas A&M University Press, 2010), 13–28.

29. Paik, *Pusan to Panmunjom*, 21; Soviet advisors were critical of the KPA's command relationships, use of artillery and armor, and poor communications and logistics. Transcript, "26 June 1950, Top Secret Report on Military Situation by Shtykov to Comrade Zhakarov," trans. Kathryn Weathersby, *Cold War International History Project Bulletin* 6/7 (Winter 1995/96): 40.

30. On August 2, 1950, the US marine corps's 1st Provisional Brigade, consisting of the Fifth Regimental Combat Team and Marine Air Group 33 arrived. Donald W. Boose, *US Army Forces in the Korean War, 1950–53* (Oxford: Osprey Publishing, 2005), 63–64.

31. American intelligence intercepts provided air commanders with persuasive insight that the attacks against KPA logistical targets were sapping front-line units of their combat strength. Matthew M. Aid, "American Comint in the Korean War: From

the Chinese Intervention to the Armistice," *Intelligence and National Security* 15, no. 1 (Spring 2000): 15.

32. Paik, *Pusan to Panmunjom*, 51–54.

33. Allan R. Millett, *The War for Korea, 1950–1951: They Came from the North* (Lawrence: University Press of Kansas, 2010), 282–91; Stewart, *Airpower*, 12; Omar N. Bradley and Clay Blair, *A General's Life* (New York: Simon and Schuster, 1983), 556–57.

34. David A. Graff and Robin Higham, eds., *A Military History of China* (Boulder, CO: Westview Press, 2002), 245, 250; Mark A. Ryan, David M. Finkelstein, and Michael A. McDevitt, eds., *Chinese Warfighting: The PLA Experience since 1949* (Armonk, NY: M. E. Sharpe, 2003), 91–92.

35. Transcript, Stalin to Zhou, July 5, 1950, telegram, in Kathryn Weathersby, "New Russian Documents on the Korean War," *Cold War International History Project Bulletin*, 6/7 (Winter 1995/96): 43.

36. Transcript, Stalin to Mao and Zhou, October 1, 1950, telegram, in Alexander Y. Mansourov, "Stalin, Mao, Kim, and China's Decision to Enter the Korean War, September 16–October 15, 1950: New Evidence from the Russian Archives," *Cold War International History Project Bulletin*, 6/7 (Winter 1995/96): 114; Xiaoming Zhang, *Red Wings over the Yalu: China, the Soviet Union, and the Air War in Korea* (College Station: Texas A&M University Press, 2002), 56–60, 64–67.

37. Peng Dehuai, "My Story of the Korean War," in *Mao's Generals Remember Korea*, trans. and ed. Xiaobing Li, Allan R. Millett, and Bin Yu (Lawrence: University Press of Kansas, 2001), 30; Peng Dehuai, *Memoirs of a Chinese Marshal*, trans. Zheng Longpu (Beijing: Foreign Language Press, 1984), 473–74.

38. Gerard H. Corr, *The Chinese Red Army* (New York: Schocken Books, 1974), 72–73; Jian Chen, "China's Changing Aims during the Korean War, 1950–1951," *Journal of American–East Asian Relations* 1, no. 1 (Spring 1992): 16.

39. Bradley and Blair, *A General's Life*, 557.

40. For explanation and analysis of what MacArthur and his intelligence staff knew, when they knew it, and what they thought it meant regarding Communist Chinese intervention in Korea, see Peter G. Knight, "MacArthur's Eyes: Reassessing Military Intelligence Operations in the Forgotten War, June 1950–April 1951" (PhD diss., Ohio State University, 2006), 199–206, 215–18, 230–43, 255–58.

41. Bradley and Blair noted, "Had a major at the Command and General Staff School [Fort Leavenworth, Kansas] turned in this solution to the problem [of conducting a pursuit], he would have been laughed out of the classroom." Bradley and Blair, *A General's Life*, 568. MacArthur's staff had no signals intelligence capability to assess Mao's intentions. The lack of Chinese linguists combined with the PLA's primitive radio communications meant that the Americans were stumbling blindly into North Korea's wasteland. Aid, "American Comint in the Korean War," 15–18.

42. Billy C. Mossman, *Ebb and Flow* (Washington, DC: US Government Printing Office, 1990), 53–55.

43. Mao Zedong, *Selected Military Writings of Mao Tse-tung* (Peking: Foreign Language Press, 1963), 217–18.

44. Transcript, Senior Officer Oral Interview of Matthew B. Ridgway, 1971–72, vol. 2, section 4, 11, Oral Histories, 1971–72, Ridgway Papers, USAHEC.

45. Hong Xuezhi, "The CPVF's Combat and Logistics," in *Mao's Generals Remember Korea*, trans. and ed. Xiaobing Li, Allan R. Millett, and Bin Yu (Lawrence: University Press of Kansas, 2001), 115–16; Zhang, *Red Wings*, 177–78.

46. Xu, "Chinese Forces and Their Casualties," 48–49; Headquarters, Eighth United States Army Korea, Enemy Material, 20, USACMH; Prisoner of War Preliminary Interrogation Report (Young Yin Yen), May 27, 1952, PW Interrogation Reports, Box 2, Ellis B. Richie Papers, USAHEC; Chen Li, "From Civil War Victor to Cold War Guard," *Journal of Strategic Studies* 38 (2015): 193.

47. Paik, *Pusan to Panmunjom*, 87, 91.

48. Headquarters, Eighth United States Army Korea, Enemy Tactics to Include Guerilla Methods and Activities, 69, USACMH; Anthony Farrar-Hockley, "A Reminiscence of the Chinese People's Volunteers in the Korean War," *China Quarterly* 98 (June 1984): 297–98.

49. Farrar-Hockley, "A Reminiscence of the Chinese People's Volunteers in the Korean War," 299.

50. Peng, *Memoirs of a Chinese Marshal*, 476; Yang Dezhi, *Weile Heping* [*For the sake of peace*] (Beijing: Long March Press, 1987); English language edition translated by Leo Kanner Associates (Dayton, OH: Defense Technical Information Center, Foreign Technology Division, 1989), 5–6; Chen, "China's Changing Aims during the Korean War," 15–17, 22.

51. Bradley and Blair, *A General's Life*, 581.

52. Xu, "Chinese Forces and Their Casualties," 49.

53. John R. Bruning, *Crimson Sky: The Air Battle for Korea* (Dulles, VA: Brassy's, 1999), 79.

54. Paik, *Pusan to Panmunjom*, 107–8.

55. Ridgway, *Korean War*, 77; Bradley and Blair, *A General's Life*, 603. Cf. Acheson, *Present at the Creation*, 469–77, where the secretary of state must have thought the collective military leadership had lost its nerve dealing with MacArthur and the Korean situation.

56. Millett, *The War for Korea, 1950–1951: They Came from the North*, 373; Ridgway, *Korean War*, 79–81. Paik Sun-yup, a loyal subordinate, praised Walker's generalship in his memoir: "General Walker's leadership was pivotal in shoring up our stubborn defense at the Naktong River line. The amphibious landing at Inchon that reversed the direction of the war could not have been launched had the Naktong River line collapsed. Indeed, the nation itself would have collapsed, and the Republic of Korea would not exist today." Paik, *Pusan to Panmunjom*, 114.

57. Mossman, *Ebb and Flow*, 177–80.

58. Ridgway, *Korean War*, 111.

59. Richard Peters and Xiaobing Li, eds., *Voices from the Korean War: Personal Stories of American, Korean, and Chinese Soldiers* (Lexington: University Press of Kentucky, 2004), 58–59; Bradley and Blair, *A General's Life*, 608; Millett, *The War for Korea, 1950–1951: They Came from the North*, 373, 377.

60. Collins, *War in Peacetime*, 255.

61. Ridgway, *Korean War*, 85–90. The quotation is from Clausewitz, *On War*, 189.

62. Carter Malkasian, "Toward a Better Understanding of Attrition: The Korean and Vietnam Wars," *Journal of Military History* 66 (July 2004): 924.

63. Col. Richard W. Jensen interview with Harold K. Johnson, Section III, 46, Senior Officer Debriefing Program, vol. 1, sections 3–6, Oral Histories 1971–74, Harold K. Johnson Papers, USAHEC.

64. Matthew B. Ridgway to Edward "Ned" Almond, January 2, 1951, Correspondence, Eighth Army-Almond, Box 9, Eighth US Army Dec 1950–April 1951 A-H, Ridgway Papers, USAHEC.

65. All quotations from Eighth Army Commander's Conference Notes, February 8, 1951, Correspondence, Eighth Army Corps Commanders, Eighth US Army Dec 1950–April 1951 A–H, Ridgway Papers, USAHEC.

66. The standard narrative is found in Mossman, *Ebb and Flow*, 237–65, 301–67. See also Ridgway, *Korean War*, 106–23.

67. Eighth Army Casualty Summary, 22 Jan 51–31 Mar 51, Official Correspondence (CinC Far East), A, Official Correspondence CinC Far East, Jan 1951–Jun 1952, Box 11, Ridgway Papers, USAHEC.

68. Acheson, *Present at the Creation*, 512; Mossman, *Ebb and Flow*, 300ff.

69. William Berebitsky, *A Very Long Weekend: The Army National Guard in Korea, 1950–1953* (Shippensburg, PA: White Mane Publishing, 1996), 102.

70. Jager, *Brothers at War*, 170.

71. William M. Donnelly, *Under Army Orders* (College Station: Texas A&M University Press, 2001), 22–24, 33, 63–64, 69, 72–75. The National Guard also contributed two antiaircraft battalions, six combat engineer battalions, three engineer bridge companies, six truck companies, three ordnance companies, one signal battalion, and headquarters for engineers, quartermaster, ordnance, and transportation units; Donnelly, *Under Army Orders*, 69; Berebitsky, *Very Long Weekend*, 40–41.

72. Mossman, *Ebb and Flow*, 329–33.

73. Matthew B. Ridgway to Stan Bayley, October 30, 1968, Korea, Box 38, Retirement, J–K, Ridgway Papers, USAHEC; Ridgway, *Korean War*, 112–14.

74. Walter Winton interview, May 9, 1984, Oral Histories, folder 16, box 88, Ridgway Papers, USAHEC.

75. Harold K. Johnson Senior Officer Oral History, 42, 46, Harold K. Johnson Papers, USAHEC.

76. Mossman, *Ebb and Flow*, 234–35.

77. Clay Blair, *The Forgotten War* (New York: Times Books, 1987), 614, 643–44. Ridgway agreed to "rotate out," rather than fire, these officers: David G. Barr, John H. Church, Hobart R. "Hap" Gay, William B. Kean, and John B. Coulter, who was "kicked upstairs" as Ridgway's deputy commander.

78. The newspapers dubbed this declaration as MacArthur's "Die-for-a-Tie" speech. If MacArthur hoped to galvanize pressure against the Truman administration, he failed, and his efforts merely disgusted fighting men who refused to believe their war did not have a positive objective. See Robert Leckie, *Conflict: The History of the Korean War* (New York: G. P. Putnam's Sons, 1962), 265–66.

79. Ridgway quotation in Leckie, *Conflict*, 266–67; the Ambassador in Korea to

the Secretary of State, March 17, 1951, *FRUS, 1951*, vol. 7, *Korea and China* (Washington, DC: US Government Printing Office, 1976), 244.

80. Paik, *Pusan to Panmunjom*, 136–38.

81. William T. Bowers and John T. Greenwood, *Passing the Test, April–June 1951* (Lexington: University Press of Kentucky, 2011), 5; Malkasian, "Toward a Better Understanding of Attrition," 922–23.

82. Poats, *Decision in Korea*, 181.

83. Poats, *Decision in Korea*, 182–83.

84. Poats, *Decision in Korea*, 182–83. The only complete biography of Van Fleet, unfortunately bordering on hagiography, is Paul F. Braim, *The Will to Win* (Annapolis, MD: Naval Institute Press, 2001). For a recent view that disputes Van Fleet's contribution to the Greek Civil War, see Christina J. M. Goulter, "The Greek Civil War: A National Army's Counter-Insurgency Triumph," *Journal of Military History* 78 (July 2014): 1017–55.

85. Commanding General, Eighth United States Army Korea to Corps Commanders, 23 April 1951, Van Fleet, James, Jan 1951–Jun 1952, Official Correspondence CinC Far East, N–Z, Jan 1951–Jun 1952, Box 13, Ridgway Papers, USAHEC.

86. Li, *China's Battle for Korea*, 54–55.

87. Korea Institute of Military History, *The Korean War* (Lincoln: University of Nebraska Press, 2000), 2:662–63.

88. James A. Van Fleet, "The Truth about Korea," *Life* 34, May 11, 1953, 132.

89. Headquarters, Eighth United States Army Korea, Memorandum for Record, 1 May 1951, Army Commanders' Conference (30 April 1951), 2–3, Van Fleet, James, Jan 1951–Jun 1952, Official Correspondence CinC Far East, N–Z, Jan 1951–Jun 1952, Box 13, Ridgway Papers, USAHEC.

90. Mossman, *Ebb and Flow*, 442n8.

91. Mossman, *Ebb and Flow*, 444–64; Poats, *Decision in Korea*, 192–94; Li, *China's Battle for Korea*, 212.

92. Van Fleet, "The Truth about Korea," 132. Peng later admitted the campaign was one of his four strategic mistakes. Li, *China's Battle for Korea*, 110.

93. Peng, *Memoirs of a Chinese Marshal*, 480.

94. Prior to the Fifth Campaign, the UNC had only three thousand Chinese POWs. Xu, "Chinese Forces and Their Casualties," 57.

95. Millett, *Their War for Korea*, 136. Peng acknowledged, "The losses in this campaign were the highest suffered by our forces in the War to Resist U.S. Aggression and Aid Korea." Peng, *Memoirs of a Chinese Marshal*, 480–81.

96. William Johnston, *A War of Patrols* (Vancouver: University of British Columbia Press, 2003), 118.

97. John Nolan, *Run-up to the Punchbowl: A Memoir of the Korean War, 1951* (Bloomington, IN: Xlibris, 2006), 43, 47.

98. Robert B. Bruce, "Tethered Eagle: Lt. Gen. James A. Van Fleet and the Quest for Military Victory in the Korean War, April–June 1951," *Army History* 82 (Winter 2012): 19; Van Fleet, "The Truth about Korea," 127.

99. Bowers and Greenwood, *Passing the Test*, 297–315; 328–29; Blair, *Forgotten War*, 888–97.

100. Blair, *Forgotten War*, 897–99; Bruce, "Tethered Eagle," 20.

101. Ridgway, *Korean War*, 155–57.

102. Commanding General, Far East Command to Commanding General, Eighth United States Army, Subject: Letter of Instructions, April 1951, 1–3, Letters of Instruction 1951, CinC Far East, 1951–52 Box 73, Series 3 Official Papers, Ridgway Papers, USAHEC.

103. Ridgway Senior Officer Oral Interview, vol. 2, section 4, USAHEC. Ridgway also openly admitted going around Van Fleet's back to form his own impressions of the battle by engaging corps and division commanders, "all of whom I knew intimately." This style of supervision and control was of course in his prerogative, but it was hardly conducive to generate the trust that Ridgway loudly proclaimed. Ridgway, *Korean War*, 162.

104. Message Commander in Chief, Far East, Tokyo, Japan, (Ridgway) to Joint Chiefs of Staff, 30 May 1951, Incoming Messages May 29, 1950–August 3, 1951, Box 1, Records of the Joint Chiefs of Staff, RG 218, NARA II.

105. Bruce, "Tethered Eagle," 22; Memorandum NSC48/5, May 17, 1951, United States Objectives, Policies, and Courses of Action in Asia; JCS Directive to CINCFE/CINCUNC, May 31, 1951, both found in Tucker, *Encyclopedia of the Korean War*, 3:970–72, 974–76.

106. Malkasian, "Toward a Better Understanding of Attrition," 922–23.

107. JCS Directive to CINCFE/CINCUNC, May 31, 1951. In late June, in response to the realization that any armistice agreement would likely require UN troops to withdraw a substantial distance from Line Kansas, Ridgway asked Van Fleet about the feasibility of restarting Eighth Army's attack to pick up cheap real estate. Van Fleet declined, citing sound reasons not to fight for a fictional line of contact farther north. Ridgway, and later Collins, disingenuously promoted this response as evidence that Van Fleet himself knew that a military victory was not in the cards. See Ridgway, *Korean War*, 181, and Collins, *War in Peacetime*, 306–7. Regarding Van Fleet's viewpoint of a lost opportunity to finish the war in Korea, see Bruce, "Tethered Eagle," 22–25.

108. Mossman, *Ebb and Flow*, 485–86.

109. Mossman, *Ebb and Flow*, 491–94.

110. James A. Van Fleet to Matthew B. Ridgway, 22 June 1951, Van Fleet, James, Jan 1951–Jun 1952, Official Correspondence CinC Far East, N–Z, Jan 1951–Jun 1952, Box 13, Ridgway Papers, USAHEC.

111. Peters and Li, *Voices from the Korean War*, 130.

112. Headquarters, Eighth United States Army Korea, Military History Section, Hills 717 and 682, 56, USACMH.

Chapter 3

1. Yafeng Xia, "The People's Republic of China," in *The Ashgate Research Companion to the Korean War*, ed. James I. Matray and Donald W. Boose Jr. (Burlington, VT: Ashgate, 2014), 64.

2. It is remarkable the level of continuity between Communist methods in Korea and those of the early Nationalist forces. Both armies fought under disadvan-

tageous conditions, and both found relatively similar methods to maximize their strengths while protecting their weaknesses in confrontations with more powerful opponents. See Peter Worthing, "Continuity and Change: Chinese Nationalist Army Tactics, 1925–1938," *Journal of Military History* 78 (July 2014): 995–1016.

3. Jian Chen, "China's Changing Aims during the Korean War, 1950–1951," *Journal of American–East Asian Relations* 1, no. 1 (Spring 1992): 38–39.

4. Peng, "My Story of the Korean War," 36.

5. Xiaoming Zhang, *Red Wings over the Yalu: China, the Soviet Union, and the Air War in Korea* (College Station: Texas A&M University Press, 2002), 182–83.

6. Omar N. Bradley and Clay Blair, *A General's Life* (New York: Simon and Schuster, 1983), 610–11.

7. Lt. Col. A. J. Kinney, USAF, Liaison Base, Far East Command, 9 July 1951, to CinC United Nations Command, Special File Diary, CinC Far East 1951–52, Box 72, Ridgway Papers, USAHEC.

8. See Matthew B. Ridgway, *The Korean War* (Garden City, NY: Doubleday, 1967), 182–83; C. Turner Joy, *How Communists Negotiate* (New York: Macmillan, 1955), xi–xii; J. Lawton Collins, *War in Peacetime: The History and Lessons of Korea* (Boston: Houghton Mifflin, 1969), 328–31; Sun-yup Paik, *Pusan to Panmunjom* (Dulles, VA: Brassey's, 1999), 168–70.

9. Joy, *How Communists Negotiate*, 1.

10. Li Kenong was a political operator with a wartime background in intelligence. Chai, "Korean Truce Negotiations," 186, 259n2; Allan R. Millett, *Their War for Korea* (Dulles, VA: Brassey's, 2002), 110; James L. Stokesbury, *A Short History of the Korean War* (New York: William Morrow, 1988), 143–53, 156–57. Deng's assessment of US and ROK fighting qualities is quoted in Paik, *Pusan to Panmunjom*, 97.

11. Rosemary Foot, *A Substitute for Victory* (Ithaca, NY: Cornell University Press, 1990), 15.

12. Joy, *How Communists Negotiate*, xi, 61.

13. Paik Sun-yup remembered some Americans predicting to "have the negotiations wrapped up in ten days or so." Paik, however, knew that speed would not favor the Communists' position, and therefore the talks were much more likely to be exceptionally difficult. "I noticed," Paik ruefully recalled, "however, that no one paid much attention to me [at the time]." Paik, *Pusan to Panmunjom*, 166.

14. Mark W. Clark, *From the Danube to the Yalu* (New York: Harper and Brothers, 1954), 105.

15. Quoted in Denis Stairs, *The Diplomacy of Constraint: Canada, the Korean War, and the United States* (Toronto: University of Toronto Press, 1974), 115.

16. Quoted in Sheila Miyoshi Jager, *Brothers at War: The Unending Conflict in Korea* (New York: W. W. Norton, 2013), 141.

17. Dean Rusk, Courses of Action in Korea, December 21, 1950, *FRUS*, vol. 7, *Korea 1950*, 1588; Memorandum of Conversation, December 27, 1950, *FRUS, 1950*, 7:1600.

18. Secretary of State Dean Acheson Draft Memorandum to President Harry Truman, February 23, 1951, *FRUS, 1951*, 201.

19. Ridgway, *Korean War*, 120–23.

20. Bradley and Blair, *A General's Life*, 558; Stairs, *Diplomacy of Constraint*, 220, 233; KIMH, *KW*, 3:32–33.

21. Transcript, Filippov (Stalin) to Soviet military advisor in Beijing Krasovsky, ciphered telegram 13 June 1951; Transcript, Filippov (Stalin) to Mao Zedong re meeting in Moscow with Gao Gang and Kim Il Sung, ciphered telegram, 13 June 1951, *Cold War International History Project Bulletin*, 6/7 (Winter 1995/96): 60–61.

22. Editorial Note, *FRUS, 1951*, 547; Collins, *War in Peacetime*, 327; KIMH, *KW*, 3:36.

23. Stairs, *Diplomacy of Constraint*, 237.

24. Collins, *War in Peacetime*, 328.

25. William Vatcher, *Panmunjom: The Story of the Korean Military Armistice Negotiations* (New York: Frederick A. Praeger, 1958), 206.

26. Rutherford M. Poats, *Decision in Korea* (New York: McBride 1954), 203.

27. Chai, "Korean Truce Negotiations," 188.

28. Stairs, *Diplomacy of Constraint*, 239.

29. Quoted in William Stueck, *The Korean War: An International History* (Princeton, NJ: Princeton University Press, 1995), 210.

30. Poats, *Decision in Korea*, 204. See also Austin Stevens, "Fighting for Several Weeks Is Foreseen by Washington; Observers Express Concern over Rising Optimism— Motives of Communists in Seeking Truce Talk Still Suspect," *New York Times*, July 8, 1951.

31. Handwritten letter from Gao Gang and Kim Il Sung to Stalin, 14 June 1951, with handwritten letter from Mao Zedong to Gao Gang and Kim Il Sung, 13 June 1951, *Cold War International History Project Bulletin*, 6/7 (Winter 1995/96): 61–62.

32. Jian Chen, *Mao's China and the Cold War* (Chapel Hill: University of North Carolina Press, 2001), 100.

33. Foot, *Substitute for Victory*, 11–12; Xia, *Negotiating with the Enemy*, 52–54. Both sides made changes to their respective delegations over the next two years.

34. Joy, *How Communists Negotiate*, 3.

35. KIMH, *KW*, 3:50–51; Collins, *War in Peacetime*, 328–29; Joy, *How Communists Negotiate*, 5–8.

36. Chai, "Korean Truce Negotiations," 187–88.

37. Dennis Bloodworth, *The Chinese Looking Glass* (New York: Farrar, Straus and Giroux, 1966), 399.

38. Quoted in Xia, *Negotiating with the Enemy*, 53.

39. Harry S. Truman, *Memoirs*, vol. 2, *Years of Trial and Hope* (Garden City, NY: Doubleday, 1956), 519–20.

40. JCS to Matthew Ridgway, June 30, 1951, *FRUS, 1951*, 7:598–600.

41. Burton I. Kaufman, *The Korean War: Challenges in Crisis, Credibility, and Command* (New York: Alfred A. Knopf, 1986), 193; Paik, *Pusan to Panmunjom*, 170.

42. Joy, *How Communists Negotiate*, 13; Paik, *Pusan to Panmunjom*, 167; KIMH, *KW*, 3:53–55.

43. Chai, "Korean Truce Negotiations," 192–93.

44. The Joint Chiefs of Staff to Matthew Ridgway, June 30, 1951, *FRUS, 1951*, 7:598–600.

45. Stueck, *Rethinking the Korean War*, 139. Mao had directed Peng to prepare for a "Sixth Offensive [campaign]" to take place in August or September to enforce his demands; Chen, *Mao's China and the Cold War*, 101. Nie Rongzhen, the PLA's acting chief of staff, demonstrated equal sensitivity to the issue of the 38th parallel, counseling "now that we have accomplished the political objective of driving the enemy out of North Korea, [we] should not cross the 38th parallel, [because] restoration of the status quo antebellum would be acceptable to all." Quoted in Xia, *Negotiating with the Enemy*, 48.

46. Joy, *How Communists Negotiate*, 18–19.

47. Collins, *War in Peacetime*, 330.

48. Joy, *How Communists Negotiate*, 22–23.

49. Joy, *How Communists Negotiate*, 19; KIMH, *KW*, 3:63–69; Collins, *War in Peacetime*, 330–31.

50. Joy, *How Communists Negotiate*, 28.

51. John Nolan, *Run-up to the Punchbowl: A Memoir of the Korean War, 1951* (Bloomington, IN: Xlibris, 2006), 95; Vatcher, *Panmunjom*, 83–84.

52. Doyle O. Hickey to Matthew B. Ridgway, 16 July 1951, Special File Apr–Dec '51, CinC Far East 1951–52, Box 72, Ridgway Papers, USAHEC.

53. Paik, *Pusan to Panmunjom*, 168.

54. Joy, *How Communists Negotiate*, 3–8.

55. KIMH, *KW*, 3:86–87.

56. Syngman Rhee to Matthew B. Ridgway, July 15, 1951, Special File Diary, Box 72 CINCFE 1951–52, Ridgway Papers, USAHEC. See also KIMH, *KW*, 3:70–77. Defense minister Lee Ki-pong informed General Paik that the South Koreans would "oppose any other formula." Paik, *Pusan to Panmunjom*, 171.

57. Allen E. Goodman, ed., *Negotiating While Fighting: The Diary of Admiral C. Turner Joy at the Korean Armistice Conference* (Stanford, CA: Hoover Institution Press, 1978), 22, 26–28.

58. Dean Acheson, *Present at the Creation* (New York: W. W. Norton, 1969), 536.

59. UN Secretary General Trygve Lie went so far as to say that a cease-fire agreement along the 38th parallel would fulfill "the main purpose of the Security Council resolutions of June 25 and 27 and July 7, 1950." Poats, *Decision in Korea*, 201; Stairs, *Diplomacy of Constraint*, 233–34; Vatcher, *Panmunjom*, 17–18.

60. Paik, *Pusan to Panmunjom*, 174; Joy, *How Communists Negotiate*, 24–26, 52; KIMH, *KW*, 3:87–93.

61. Nam Il was the thirty-seven-year-old chief of staff of the KPA's supreme headquarters. He spent the war years in the Soviet Union as a teacher. After returning to North Korea with the Red Army in 1945, he served in a succession of government education posts. His Chinese counterpart, Xie Fang, graduated from university in Moscow and was the chief of propaganda in Manchuria during the Chinese Civil War. Vatcher, *Panmunjom*, 30–31.

62. Quoted in Vatcher, *Panmunjom*, 49–50.

63. Gerard H. Corr, *The Chinese Red Army* (New York: Schocken Books, 1974), 20.

64. Foot, *Substitute for Victory*, 15–17.

65. Goodman, *Negotiating While Fighting*, 22–23; the Commander in Chief, United Nations Command to the Joint Chiefs of Staff, July 28, 1951, *FRUS, 1951*, 7:748–52.

66. Corr, *Chinese Red Army*, 48; transcript, Mao Zedong to Filippov (Stalin) conveying 12 August 1951 telegram from Li Kenong to Mao re armistice talks, ciphered telegram, August 13, 1951, *Cold War International History Project Bulletin*, 6/7 (Winter 1995/96): 67–68.

67. Doyle O. Hickey to Matthew B. Ridgway, July 16, 1952, Special File Apr–Dec '51 (Part 2 of 3), Box 72, CinC FE 1951–52, Ridgway Papers, USAHEC.

68. The Commander in Chief, Far East to the Joint Chiefs of Staff, August 7, 1951, *FRUS, 1951*, 7:787.

69. Chai, "Korean Truce Negotiations," 188–89.

70. Kaufman, *Korean War*, 204; KIMH, *KW*, 3:92–95, 100–108.

71. Joy, *How Communists Negotiate*, 30.

72. Joy, *How Communists Negotiate*, 26, 30–33.

73. Vatcher, *Panmunjom*, 60–66.

74. Joy, *How Communists Negotiate*, 33–38.

75. Dan Raschen, *Send Port and Pyjamas!* (London: Buckland Publications, 1987), 45.

76. Henry I. Hodes, Deputy Chief of Staff to Brig. Gen. Paul F. Yount, CG, 2nd Logistics Command, July 7, 1951, Adjutant General Section, Top Secret Correspondence, 1945–52, Eighth US Army, 1944–56, RG 338, NARA II.

77. Raschen, *Send Port and Pyjamas!*, 56; William J. White, *Triangle Hill* (Bloomington, IN: Xlibris, 2011), 52; Rudolph W. Stephens, *Old Ugly Hill: A GI's Fourteen Months in the Korean Trenches, 1952–1953* (Jefferson, NC: McFarland, 1995), 125.

78. Message CX 7022 KGO-O, July 18, 1952, CG Eighth Army to Corps Commanders, Command Report, July 1952, Army–Adjutant General, Command Reports, 1949–1954, RG 407, NARA II.

79. Raschen, *Send Port and Pyjamas!*, 53; "Faithful to Our Trust," *Army Combat Forces Journal* 5, no. 5 (December 1954): 19–20. The quotation is from Command Report, 40th Infantry Division, June 1952, RG 407, NARA II.

80. Joseph E. Gonsalves, *Battle at the 38th Parallel: Surviving the Peace Talks at Panmunjom* (Central Point, OR: Hellgate Press, 2001), 49–50.

81. William R. Richardson, Senior Officer Oral History Program, 62, William R. Richardson Papers, USAHEC.

82. Headquarters, 180th Infantry Regiment, Patrol Directive #8, May 24, 1952, Box 2, Ellis B. Richie Papers, USAHEC.

83. Quoted in William R. O'Connell, *Thunderbird: A History of the 45th Infantry Division in Korea* (Tokyo: Toppan Printing, n.d.), 12.

84. John A. Sullivan, *Toy Soldiers: A Memoir of a Combat Platoon Leader in Korea* (Jefferson, NC: McFarland, 1991), 97–98, 125–27; White, *Triangle Hill*, 106–7.

85. Millett, *Their War for Korea*, 104.

86. Kelly Jordan, "Right for the Wrong Reason: S. L. A. Marshall and the Ratio of Fire in Korea," *Journal of Military History* 66 (January 2002): 151.

87. Peters and Li, *Voices from the Korean War*, 41; Jensen, *A War (Love) Story*, 289; Sobieski, *Fire for Effect*, 71, 89.

88. Mark M. Boatner III, "Countering Communist Artillery," *Army Combat Forces Journal* 4 no. 2 (September 1953): 25.

89. Raschen, *Send Port and Pyjamas!*, 102–3.

90. Stephens, *Old Ugly Hill*, 49; E. F. Bullene, "It's Not New, but Napalm Is an All-Purpose Wonder Weapon," *United States Army Combat Forces Journal* 3, no. 4 (November 1952): 25.

91. S. L. A. Marshall, *Battlefield Analysis of Infantry Weapons* (Cornville, AZ: Desert Publications, 1984), 53, 55.

92. Headquarters, Eighth United States Army, Military History Section, Night Defense of Hill 200, n.d., 6. USACMH.

93. William M. Donnelly, "'The Best Army That Can Be Put into the Field in the Circumstances': The U.S. Army, July 1951–July 1953," *Journal of Military History* 71 (July 2007): 817–19. Gonsalves, *Battle at the 38th Parallel*, 65–66, describes the point rotation system and its influence on small unit tactics; Stephens, *Old Ugly Hill*, 87. FEC began to implement a theater rotation policy on September 1, 1951. Eighth Army Command Report, Narrative Section I, 8–9, August 1951, RG 407, NARA II.

94. Johnston, *War of Patrols*, 215. See also Headquarters, Eighth United States Army, Office of the Artillery Officer, A Study of the Employment and Effectiveness of the Artillery with the Eighth Army, October 1951–July 1953, 1954, 9, USAHEC; Sobieski, *Fire for Effect*, 93; Stephens, *Old Ugly Hill*, 59.

95. Headquarters, I Corps, Corps and Army Unit Commanders' Meeting June 9, 13 June 1952, Folder 3 US I Corps Commander's Notes, 1951–1952, Box 1 Correspondence 1943–1953: North Africa, Italy, Korea, Lt. Gen. John W. O'Daniel Papers, CAM; Gonsalves, *Battle at the 38th Parallel*, 38, 43.

96. Sobieski, *Fire for Effect*, 101.

97. Jensen, *A War (Love) Story*, 295–96.

98. Jiyul Kim, "United Nations Command and Korean Augmentation," in *The Ashgate Research Companion to the Korean War*, ed. James I. Matray and Donald W. Boose Jr. (Burlington, VT: Ashgate, 2014), 283, 291–93.

99. Millett, *Their War for Korea*, 219.

100. "*Yobo*" is a truncated form of a Korean greeting that means, "Hello." Nolan, *Run-up to the Punchbowl*, 57; Headquarters, US I Corps, Commanders' Conference, 30 October 1951, Folder 3, Box 1, O'Daniel Papers, CAM. Not all GIs had favorable impressions of the KSC. First Lt. Roy Conklin remembered the KSCs as lazy and slow moving and needing constant supervision. But he did acknowledge that it was "unbelievable how these KSC's, who were generally pretty frail, could carry such heavy loads." Roy W. Conklin, "Cease Fire: A Memoir of the Korean War," 50–51, USAHEC.

101. Moses, *Whatever It Takes*, 237; John G. Westover, ed., *Combat Support in Korea* (Washington, DC: US Government Printing Office, 1987), 168–69; Raschen, *Send Port and Pyjamas!*, 96–97; Sobieski, *Fire for Effect*, 89.

102. Department of the Army, Field Manual (FM) 7-40, *Infantry Regiment* (Washington, DC: US Government Printing Office, 1950), 253–80.

103. Corr, *Chinese Red Army*, 89.

104. Robert M. Neer, *Napalm: An American Biography* (Cambridge, MA: Belknap Press of Harvard University Press, 2013), 17, 92. Napalm (from *naph*thenate, and coconut *palm* oil) was a dry powder chemical compound mixed with gasoline. Continuous stirring and curing produced a smooth Jell-O-like substance that was stable until ignited. A stream of ignited gel apparently defied gravity, traveling a distance much greater than unignited fuel. It also tended to continue burning by flowing into enclosures still containing oxygen. Thus, it was often possible to wipe out an entire underground fortification complex by introducing napalm into a single dugout or fighting position.

105. Westover, *Combat Support in Korea*, 81–82.

106. Neer, *Napalm*, 93; Public Information Officer, United Nations Command, the Chronology of the Korean Campaign, 1 July–31 December 1952, 26, GEOG V Korea File 314.76, USACMH.

107. Bullene, "It's Not New," 25, 26.

108. Bowers and Greenwood, *Passing the Test*, 196, 207, and especially 230–33, for an account of a FO officer conducting a small unit engagement and being substantially responsible for up to eight hundred enemy soldiers killed and wounded; Sobieski, *Fire for Effect*, xi, 11.

109. Sobieski, *Fire for Effect*, 52, 54–55. Eighth Army, the Employment and Effectiveness of the Artillery, October 1951–July 1953, 1954, 9–10, 23–26, USAHEC.

110. Westover, *Combat Support in Korea*, 23–24, 29–32, 34; Nolan, *Run-up to the Punchbowl*, 167.

111. Sam Freedman, "Tankers at Heartbreak," *Armor* 61, no. 5 (September–October, 1952): 24.

112. Headquarters, Eighth United States Army Korea, Military History Section, Daylight Patrol North of Mago-ri (September 1951), 4, USACMH.

113. O'Connell, *Thunderbird*, 59.

114. Bowers and Greenwood, *Passing the Test*, 84–86. Each tank possessed in addition to its main gun (76 mm for the M4E3 Sherman and 90 mm for the M26 Pershing and M46 Patton variants), .50 cal. heavy and .30 cal. light machine guns. A single tank was equivalent to a platoon's heavy weapons' firepower potential. Headquarters, Eighth Army, Military History Section, Daylight Patrol, 5, USACMH.

115. Aid, "American COMINT in the Korean War," 19–20, 32. Aid points out that in August 1951, Eighth Army had three "communication reconnaissance battalions" deployed in Korea, one for each American corps zone. Further, by February 1952, each battalion was responsible for providing a liaison team to every American division headquarters (and to select ROK divisions, through their KMAG advisor teams). These measures helped get COMINT support into the hands of commanders while the information was fresh and useful.

116. Although both KPA and CPVF communicators tightened their procedures as the lines settled down, they never fully secured their messaging. This analysis of American COMINT is derived from David A. Hatch with Robert Louis Benson, *The Korean War: The SIGINT Background* (Center for Cryptologic History, National Secu-

rity Agency, January 2009). www.nsa.gov/about/cryptologic_heritage/center_crypt
_history/publications/koreanwar_sigint_bkg.shtml#13, accessed March 1, 2013.

117. Headquarters, X Corps Artillery, September 1951, 2, USAHEC.

118. David W. Hogan Jr., Arnold G. Fish Jr., and Robert K. White Jr., eds., *The Story of the Noncommissioned Officer Corps* (Washington, DC: Center of Military History, 2008), 156.

119. A US army's historical report indicated two to three months were required to train a man to be a competent photo interpreter who was familiar with the factors peculiar to the theater, such as the enemy's camouflage techniques and the unique Korean terrain. Headquarters, United States Army Forces and Eighth United States Army, Military History Section, Intelligence and Counterintelligence Problems during the Korean Conflict, 3, USACMH.

120. Samuel T. Dickens, "USAF Reconnaissance during the Korean War," in *Coalition Air Warfare in the Korean War, 1950–1953*, ed. Jacob Neufeld and George M. Watson (Washington, DC: US Air Force History and Museum Program, 2005), 244.

121. Headquarters, X Corps Artillery, May 1951, 2, and September 1951, 4, USAHEC.

122. Headquarters, Eighth Army, Military History Section, Intelligence and Counterintelligence Problems during the Korean Conflict, 3, 13–15, USACMH.

123. Stewart, *Airpower*, 95, 216–28.

124. Westover, *Combat Support in Korea*, 47–48.

125. Korean railroads moved upwards of 95 percent of bulk tonnages from ports of debarkation to the front. Westover, *Combat Support in Korea*, 65–66.

126. In June 1953, UNC and Korean troops fired off 2,746,000 shells, by far the highest total of the war. Eighth Army, the Employment and Effectiveness of the Artillery, 19, 43, USAHEC; Department of the Army, Historical Branch Programs Division, Historical Survey of Army Fire Support, March 18, 1963, 3–4, USACMH.

127. Westover, *Combat Support in Korea*, 150.

128. Bowers and Greenwood, *Passing the Test*, 287–88. Under the "Van Fleet rate of fire" a 105 mm howitzer received an allotment of 250 shells per day, a fivefold increase. Westover, *Combat Support in Korea*, 126.

129. Captain Lawrence Daly, commander Battery B, 15th Field Artillery Battalion, remembered that firing the Van Fleet load was only possible if every available soldier pitched in. Daly himself was at one point handed a shell and for the next five or so minutes, "I was there . . . passing ammo [sic] before I could get away." Bowers and Greenwood, *Passing the Test*, 241–42.

130. General Paik recalled when anticipating a Chinese attack, Van Fleet ordered him to shoot everything he had. "The quickest way to establish psychological mastery over the Chinese army, then, is by providing . . . sheer firepower." Paik, *Pusan to Panmunjom*, 200.

131. Hand grenades were also in high demand. Eighth Army used more than 400,000 in the same time period. Westover, *Combat Support in Korea*, 125.

132. Westover, *Combat Support Korea*, 150–51; Headquarters, X Corps Artillery, August 1951, 11, USAHEC.

133. O'Connell, *Thunderbird*, 43.

134. One American general who observed VT volleys in action against the Germans asserted the fuse was "the most important new development in the ammunition field since the introduction of high explosive projectiles." Rick Atkinson, *The Guns at Last Light* (New York: Henry Holt, 2013), 459.

135. Bryan R. Gibby, *The Will to Win: American Military Advisors to Korea, 1946–1953* (Tuscaloosa: University of Alabama Press, 2012), 210–13.

136. Eighth Army, The Employment and Effectiveness of the Artillery, 13–15, USAHEC; Headquarters, X Corps Artillery, July 1951, 3, USAHEC.

137. Sullivan, *Toy Soldiers*, 51–52; Headquarters, X Corps Artillery, September 1951, 5, USAHEC.

138. Eighth Army, The Employment and Effectiveness of the Artillery, 21, USAHEC.

139. Eighth Army, The Employment and Effectiveness of the Artillery, 2–3, USAHEC; Jensen, *A War (Love) Story*, 300–301; Sobieski, *Fire for Effect*, 108–9.

140. Peters and Li, *Voices from the Korean War*, 66.

141. Sobieski, *Fire for Effect*, 71–72, 103.

142. Westover, *Combat Support in Korea*, 73–75.

Chapter 4

1. Mark Clodfelter, *The Limits of Airpower* (New York: Free Press, 1989), 2–11.

2. Quoted in Gerald T. Cantwell, *Citizen Airman: A History of the Air Force Reserve, 1946–1994* (Dayton, OH: Air Force Museum Foundation, 1997), 90.

3. See Kenneth P. Werrell, "Airpower," in *The Ashgate Research Companion to the Korean War*, ed. James I. Matray and Donald W. Boose Jr. (Burlington, VT: Ashgate, 2014), 136–47; William M. Momyer, *Airpower in Three Wars* (Washington, DC: Office of Air Force History, 1978), 3.

4. Richard J. Blanchfield, "Weapons, Tactics, and Training," in *Coalition Air Warfare in the Korean War, 1950–1953*, ed. Jacob Neufeld and George M. Watson (Washington, DC: US Air Force History and Museum Program, 2005), 23.

5. Conrad C. Crane, *American Airpower Strategy in Korea, 1950–1953* (Lawrence: University Press of Kansas, 2000), 24–26.

6. Otto P. Weyland, "The Air Campaign in Korea," in *Airpower: The Decisive Force in Korea*, ed. James T. Stewart (Princeton, NJ: D. Van Nostrand, 1957), 16.

7. James T. Stewart, ed., *Airpower: The Decisive Force in Korea* (Princeton, NJ: D. Van Nostrand, 1957), 105.

8. Stewart, *Airpower*, 105, 107.

9. Pilots noted that jet aircraft did not produce the torque that made strafing attacks more accurate than from the F-51. George C. Loving, *Bully Able Leader: The Story of a Fighter-Bomber Pilot in the Korean War* (Mechanicsburg, PA: Stackpole Books, 2011), 78–80, 83, 95, 151. With two 265-gallon wingtip droppable fuel tanks, the F-80's range was more than 350 miles, enough to fly from Taegu to the Yalu River and back. Loving, *Bully Able Leader*, 59–60. William T. Y'Blood, ed., *The Three Wars of Lt. Gen. George E. Stratemeyer: His Korean War Diary* (Washington, DC: Air Force History and Museums Program, 1999), 101.

10. Loving, *Bully Able Leader*, 28, 34.

11. Gregory A. Carter, *Some Historical Notes on Air Interdiction in Korea* (Santa Monica, CA: Rand, 1966), 6; Y'Blood, *Three Wars*, 337, 362.

12. James A. Grahn and Thomas P. Himes Jr., "Air Power in the Korean War" Air Command and Staff College, 1998, 6–8; Eduard Mark, *Aerial Interdiction: Air Power and the Land Battle in Three American Wars* (Washington, DC, Center for Air Force History, 1994), 271–72. It turned out that marine F4U Corsairs and navy AD-4 Skyraiders proved to be the most suitable ground-attack platforms. Corsairs carried, in addition to one-thousand-pound bomb loads, up to eight High Velocity Aerial Rockets and four 20 mm wing-mounted cannon. Skyraiders packed an even greater wallop, eight thousand pounds of bombs and other ordnance, four times what a Shooting Star or Mustang typically carried. The Skyraider also sported four wing cannon, giving it a powerful close support punch. Blessed with physical toughness that could withstand tremendous punishment from ground fire and a flight endurance of ten hours, it is little wonder that American army units coveted Marine Corps forward air control teams who had such tremendous firepower at their call. Bruning, *Crimson Sky*, 39, 77, 87.

13. Y'Blood, *Three Wars*, 137, 141–43, 146–48, 179, 205, for examples of the bureaucratic turf battles the FEAF commander felt compelled to wage on behalf of the newly independent air force.

14. Quoted from Crane, *American Airpower Strategy in Korea*, 31.

15. Air Force Historical Division, US Air Force Operations in the Korean Conflict, 25 June–1 November 1950, US Air Force Historical Study 71 (Maxwell Air Force Base, 1955), 35.

16. Grahn and Himes, "Air Power in the Korean War," 9–10; Robert F. Futrell, *The United States Air Force in Korea* (Washington, DC: Office of the Air Force Historian, 1983), 186, 193.

17. Keith F. Kopets, "The Close Air Support Controversy in Korea," in Neufeld and Watson, *Coalition Air Warfare in the Korean War*, 123. Eduard Mark gives Weyland, then the vice commander for operations, credit for freeing FEAF "from what it had regarded as uninformed meddling" by MacArthur's admittedly inefficient General Headquarters Target Group, which was dominated by army officers not interested in airpower theories or targeting that did not contribute to the immediate ground battle. The US air force dates the beginning of their effective interdiction operations as August 3, 1950. Mark, *Aerial Interdiction*, 274–75.

18. Grahn and Himes, "Air Power in the Korean War," 11; Stokesbury, *Korean War*, 178; Weyland in all likelihood did not expect a general freeze in ground military activity. His proposal to "aerially envelope" the communist rear areas, when combined with destructive attacks at the enemy's front, offered the potential for substantial military effects, which could have been converted into negotiation capital at Kaesong. "But the tactics of the friendly army must be modified to capitalize fully upon the unique effects of air envelopment." Here is where Ridgway perhaps misjudged the military situation and assumed the Communists were on the ropes; airpower would easily put them on the mat. Weyland, "Air Campaign in Korea," 17–18.

19. Notes from Conference with Lt. Gen. Otto P. Weyland, August 30, 1951, Special File Part 2 of 4, Box 72 CINCFE 1951–52, Ridgway Papers, USAHEC.

20. The JCS thought the attack unnecessarily provocative. Ridgway was certain the Communists were building up supplies and reserves to renew hostilities, and the armistice talks were simply giving the enemy breathing space. He argued, "Withholding of this attack, an element in other planned operations may therefore result in serious and avoidable losses." The JCS eventually gave in to Ridgway's rhetoric; however, bad weather limited the results of the raid, which Ridgway reported as "profitable but not decisive." James F. Schnabel and Robert J. Watson, *The Joint Chiefs of Staff and National Policy*, vol. 3, part 2: *The Korean War* (Washington, DC: Office of Joint History, 1998), 24.

21. Futrell, *The United States Air Force in Korea*, 401–11, 433–35; Crane, *American Airpower Strategy in Korea*, 76–80.

22. Joint Chiefs of Staff, *Dictionary of United States Military Terms for Joint Usage*, JCS Publication 1, Washington, DC, December 1, 1964.

23. Mark, *Aerial Interdiction*, 1.

24. Christopher M. Rein, *The North African Air Campaign* (Lawrence: University Press of Kansas, 2012), 30.

25. Report, "Strategic Implications," February 3, 1947, quoted in John T. Greenwood, "The Emergence of the Postwar Strategic Air Force, 1945–1953," in *Air Power and Warfare: Proceedings of the Eighth Military History Symposium at the U.S. Air Force Academy*, ed. Alfred F. Hurley and Robert C. Ehrhart (Washington, DC: Office of Air Force History, 1979), 223.

26. See Mark, *Aerial Interdiction*, 281–83, for a partial analysis of interdiction's material effects on North Korean divisions fighting along the Naktong River, August–September 1950, which suggests a "typical" division receiving 206 tons of supplies in July was reduced to fighting on merely 22 tons by September. Food shortages became so acute as to be the determinative factor for the KPA's shattered morale.

27. Edward M. Almond to Mark W. Clark, January 23, 1951, Enclosure 1, Extract from News and Views X Corps, 19 January 1951, Folder 1 Jan–Aug 1951, Box 8 Correspondence 1951, Jan–1953, Jun, Mark W. Clark Papers, CAM; Momyer, *Airpower in Three Wars*, 5.

28. Weyland, "The Air Campaign in Korea," 20; Stewart, *Airpower*, 279.

29. Department of the Air Force, United States Air Force Statistical Digest–Fiscal Year 1953, Table 4, Tables 38–39.

30. Air force historian Eduard Mark developed a comprehensive taxonomy of aerial interdiction based on his study and analysis of American air force operations in three twentieth-century wars. Successful interdiction operations tended to enjoy sufficient—not necessarily superior—intelligence "about [the] enemies' lines of communication and tactical dispositions to identify targets the destruction of which would promote interdiction." A key prerequisite was air superiority or some other means of surveillance that could monitor and communicate changes in location, movement, or composition of targeted assets. Air superiority was also required to assure largely unimpeded access to the enemy's air space. Finally, sustained pressure had

to overcome the recuperative capability of the targeted system. Mark, *Aerial Interdiction*, 4.

31. Frank Merrill, "A Study of the Aerial Interdiction of Railways during the Korean War" (US Army Command and General Staff College, 1965), "Study of the Aerial Interdiction," 18, 20–21. Only five rail lines bridged the Yalu into Manchuria. One line connected North Korea with the Soviet Union.

32. Weyland, "Air Campaign in Korea," 22.

33. Loving, *Bully Able Leader*, 143.

34. Maj. Gen. Edward "Ned" Almond, no fan of the air force's interpretation of its ground support role, complained that armed reconnaissance admittedly resulted in a lot of destruction "beyond the bomb line," but not much reporting of intelligence value—the purpose of any "reconnaissance" mission—ever made it back to Eighth Army. Edward M. Almond to Matthew B. Ridgway, March 16, 1951, Correspondence, Eighth Army–Almond, Box 9, Eighth US Army Dec 1950–April 1951 A-H, Ridgway Papers, USAHEC.

35. Loving, *Bully Able Leader*, 99–100, describes such a mission in early 1951.

36. Stewart, *Airpower*, 83–84; Bruning, *Crimson Sky*, 86. As an example of the punishment dealt out by the Fifth Air Force against communist supply lines and logistics bases, the 49th Fighter-Bomber Squadron based out of Taegu in March 1951 mounted 615 missions with 2,167 sorties. These F-80 pilots expended more than 1,971,800 rounds of .50-caliber ammunition, fired 3,007 rockets, and dropped 80,100 gallons of napalm and 491,120 pounds of high-explosive bombs—all from just sixty aircraft (out of an authorized seventy-five). Loving, *Bully Able Leader*, 144.

37. Bruning, *Crimson Sky*, 90; Yang Dezhi, *Weile Heping* [*For the sake of peace*] (Beijing: Long March Press, 1987), 112–14.

38. The first Soviet MiGs to cross the Yalu River attacked a flight of F-80s on November 1, 1950. Zhang, *Red Wings*, 87.

39. Y'Blood, *Three Wars*, 471, 477.

40. Merrill, "Study of the Aerial Interdiction," 66, 68, 71–73, 76; Futrell, *Air Force in Korea*, 295. The loss rate was considered prohibitive, which caused the suspension of B-29 raids over MiG Alley. It also prompted a change in tactics. Whereas previous B-29 raids were conducted in 3–4 ship formations that were conducive to tight bomb concentrations on point targets, General Vandenberg directed a minimum of 12 ship formations, massed together for mutual protection and escorted by adequate fighter cover. One air force analyst concluded that "mass formations greatly restricted target selection . . . [depriving] them the flexibility of attacking four or five bridges or small marshalling yards in a given area . . . [to] stop the flow of traffic through that particular area for a few days at least." Merrill, "Study of the Aerial Interdiction," 77.

41. Mark, *Aerial Interdiction*, 298–99; Air Force Historical Division, US Air Force Operations in the Korean Conflict (1 November 1950–10 June 1952), US Air Force Historical Study 72, Maxwell Air Force Base, 1955, 84 (hereafter USAF Historical Study 72).

42. Mark, *Aerial Interdiction*, 295.

43. Y'Blood, *Three Wars*, 502.

44. James A. Van Fleet, *Rail Transport and the Winning of Wars* (Washington, DC: Association of American Railroads, 1956), 35.

45. Command Reference Book—General Headquarters, Far East Air Forces, 67, Annex 27, June 1951, FEC, GHQ, Annexes 27–30, FEAF June 1951, Record Group 407, NARA II.

46. Timberlake succeeded Lt. Gen. Earle E. Partridge as the Fifth Air Force commander in late May 1951. Partridge replaced General Stratemeyer as FEAF commander when Stratemeyer suffered a heart attack in May. These moves were temporary as both officers were designated to command in the United States. Lt. Gen. Otto P. Weyland took over FEAF and Maj. Gen. Frank P. Everest led the Fifth Air Force. Both appointments became effective in June.

47. Futrell, *Air Force in Korea*, 296; Merrill, "Study of the Aerial Interdiction," 81–82. Unfortunately, Timberlake's conception of historical analogy was flawed. The Korean theater differed from Italy in fundamental ways. The stalemate, such as it evolved, was not only permanent but also deliberate. There was no intent to march off to Pyongyang—no Rome attracted attention. Because the Manchurian sanctuary remained inviolate, air superiority was incomplete, and the battle to maintain that superiority would consume much of FEAF's resources. Mark, *Aerial Interdiction*, 289–90.

48. Carter, *Some Historical Notes on Air Interdiction in Korea*, 8.

49. Bruning, *Crimson Sky*, 106.

50. Y'Blood, *Three Wars*, 232, 416.

51. Grahn and Himes, "Air Power in the Korean War," 16.

52. Maj. Gen. Glenn O. Barcus assumed command of the Fifth Air Force in June 1952 and looked at these claims dubiously. "The current night intruder program is not effective in destroying enemy vehicles because of [the] inability to hit the targets." USAF Historical Study 72, 174–75.

53. Grahn and Himes, "Air Power in the Korean War," 16; USAF Historical Study 72, 153; Mark, *Aerial Interdiction*, 278, 304; Bruning, *Crimson Sky*, 108–11.

54. Far East Air Forces Command Report, vol. 1, 1–3, Annex 29, June 1951, FEC, GHQ, Annexes 27–30, FEAF June 1951, Record Group 407, NARA II.

55. USAF Historical Study 72, 68.

56. FEAF Command Report, vol. 1, 1–2, 5–6, Annex 28, July 1951, FEC, GHQ, FEAF, July 1951, Record Group 407, NARA II.

57. The suspension of talks following the aircraft incident further convinced intelligence analysts the Communists were preparing for a general offensive. Kaufman, *Korean War*, 199, 205.

58. Merrill, "Study of the Aerial Interdiction," 90; Carter, *Some Historical Notes on Air Interdiction in Korea*, 9.

59. Headquarters, Eighth Army, Supply and Transport: CCF-NKPA. Joint Study prepared by G-2 8th Army and A-2 5th AF, September 23, 1951, iv, 1, 104, Eighth Army Supporting Documents, Section II Book 3, Staff Section A/CoS G-2, RG 407, NARA II.

60. Carter, *Some Historical Notes on Air Interdiction in Korea*, 10.

61. Van Fleet, *Rail Transport*, 7.

62. FEAF Command Report, vol. 1, 1–2, Annex 29, September 1951, FEC, GHQ, FEAF, September 1951, Army–AG Command Reports, 1949–54, Record Group 407, NARA II.

63. USAF Historical Report 72, 149—as assessed by USAF intelligence analysts.

64. USAF Historical Study 72, 170. The B-26C allowed nighttime attacks to rely more on bombing than strafing, which required more precision, illumination, and nerve in Korea's treacherous terrain. Mark, *Aerial Interdiction*, 311.

65. Notes on Conference with Lt. Gen. Otto P. Weyland, August 30, 1951, Special File 2 of 4, Box 72 CINCFE 1951–52, Ridgway Papers, USAHEC.

66. Headquarters, X Corps Artillery, August, 1951, 3, 11, USAHEC.

67. Matthew B. Ridgway to Joint Chiefs of Staff (DRAFT), September 22, 1951, Special File Part 2 of 4, Box 72 CINCFE 1951–52, Ridgway Papers, USAHEC.

68. Note to Draft Msg, September 25, 1951, Special File Part 2 of 4, Box 72 CINCFE 1951–52, Ridgway Papers, USAHEC.

69. Zhang, *Red Wings*, 126–27, is a strong corrective to the US viewpoint. Cf. Futrell, *Air Force in Korea*, 402–5. F-86 numbers continued to rise modestly through the spring of 1952, when Fifth Air Force had 138 of the modern fighter-interceptors.

70. FEAF Command Report, vol. 1, 1, Annex 29, FEC, GHQ, FEAF, October 1951, Record Group 407, NARA II. The end of resistance at Heartbreak Ridge, the Punch-bowl area, and in the west along the Yokkok River coincided with the extreme difficulties Communist logisticians had to maintain even the most rudimentary and roundabout transportation network north of Line Kansas. USAF Historical Report 72, 149.

71. Loving, *Bully Able Leader*, 204; Zhang, *Red Wings*, 130–32; Bruning, *Crimson Sky*, 128–29.

72. Fifth Air Force had a false sense of the F-84's capabilities vis-à-vis the MiG-15. Black Tuesday confirmed that only a Sabrejet was a match for the MiG. Y'Blood, *Three Wars*, 401.

73. Bruning, *Crimson Sky*, 135–41, 152.

74. FEAF Command Report, vol. 1, 3–4, October 1951; Y'Blood, *Three Wars*, 363. The MiG-15 was designed as a bomber interceptor, which accounted for its slow firing but deadly armament. Its exploding shells caused gaping holes, which often severed fuel and hydraulic lines, making any "near-miss" a potentially fatal hit. Bruning, *Crimson Sky*, 160. See also Kenneth P. Werrell, "Aces and -86s: The Fight for Air Superiority during the Korean War," in Neufeld and Watson, *Coalition Air Warfare in the Korean War*, 54–56.

75. FEAF Command Report, vol. 1, 2, 23, Annex 29, Annex 29, FEC, GHQ, FEAF, November 1951, Record Group 407, NARA II.

76. Futrell, *Air Force in Korea*, 371–73; USAF Historical Report 72, 109.

77. Momyer, *Airpower in Three Wars*, 115.

78. Carter, *Some Historical Notes on Air Interdiction in Korea*, 10.

79. USAF Historical Study 72, 150–51.

80. Weyland, "Air Campaign in Korea," 23.

81. Headquarters, United Nations Command, Public Information Office, a Chronology of the Korean Campaign, 1 January–30 June 1952, 10, Folder 3 January–December 1952, Box 8 Correspondence, 1951, Jan.–1953, Jun., Clark Papers, CAM.

82. Chronology of the Korean Campaign, 1 January–30 June 1952, 10, Clark Papers, CAM.

83. USAF Historical Report 72, 151.

84. Crane, *American Airpower Strategy in Korea*, 80–81; Charles R. Schrader, *Communist Logistics in the Korean War* (Westport, CT: Greenwood Press, 1995), 25, 50.

85. Weyland, "The Air Campaign in Korea," 23. Bridge busting proved to be an inefficient method to interdict supplies. One steel cantilever bridge required daily attack for four weeks by eighty-six sorties (including B-29s) dropping 643 tons of bombs. Merrill, "Study of the Aerial Interdiction," 38–39. Rail attacks were not much more efficient. Air force analysis indicated that just less than 13 percent of bombs dropped on a railroad line resulted in some kind of track cut. USAF Historical Report 72, 150.

86. Merrill, "Study of the Aerial Interdiction," 94.

87. Merrill, "Study of the Aerial Interdiction," 137–42; Rein, *North African Air Campaign*, 182.

88. USAF Historical Report 72, 152, Kaufman, *Korean War*, 220–21.

89. Merrill, "Study of the Aerial Interdiction," 100–101; USAF Historical Report 72, 152.

90. USAF Historical Report 72, 153. The B-26s operated in pairs, one aircraft dropping flares or illuminating target areas with a powerful searchlight while a second plane conducted its attack with externally mounted 100 lb. bombs and its forward firing machine guns. Grahn and Himes, "Air Power in the Korean War," 16.

91. Futrell, *Air Force in Korea*, 417.

92. Chronology of the Korean Campaign, 1 January–30 June 1952, 12, Clark Papers, CAM.

93. KIMH, *KW*, 3:320–21; USAF Historical Report 72, 153.

94. Although not part of Saturate, close air support accounted for a reported 350 gun positions and 13 tanks destroyed and 1,140 enemy personnel killed. Chronology of the Korean Campaign, 1 January–30 June 1952, 14, Clark Papers, CAM.

95. USAF Historical Report 72, 154; Futrell, *Air Force in Korea*, 418.

96. FEAF Command Report, vol. 1, 1, Annex 29, FEC, GHQ, FEAF, February 1952, Record Group 407, NARA II.

97. Figures are from the US navy, "A Struggle to Strangle," quoted in Van Fleet, *Rail Transport*, 11.

98. USAF Historical Report 72, 158. US naval forces also played roles to interdict North Korean lines of communication, both by ship-to-shore bombardment and with naval aviation. The problem was the US navy refused to subordinate its air assets to US air force control, although navy planes often did collaborate to enhance the weight of particular attacks.

99. KIMH, *KW*, 3:322; USAF Historical Report 72, 156–58; Collins, *War in Peacetime*, 313.

Chapter 5

1. Headquarters, Eighth United States Army Korea, Enemy Tactics, 54, USACMH.

2. Col. John M. Blair, Senior Officer Oral Interview, 1971–72 v 2 section 4, Oral History Interview Transcript, 11, Box 89, Oral Histories, 1971–1972, Ridgway Papers, USAHEC.

3. Transcript, Fyn Si (Stalin) to Soviet Ambassador to the DPRK A. M. Razuvaev with message for Kim Il Sung, Ciphered telegram, January 30, 1951, trans. Kathryn Weathersby, *Cold War International History Project Bulletin* 6/7 (Winter 1995/96): 58.

4. Xu, "Chinese Forces and Their Casualties," 50; Yang, *For the Sake of Peace*, 173, 179.

5. Headquarters, X Corps Artillery, August 1951, 2, USAHEC.

6. Headquarters, Eighth United States Army Korea, Enemy Material, 30–32, USACMH; Headquarters, X Corps Artillery, September 1951, 4, USAHEC.

7. An, "Soviet Military Advisory Group," 459–60, 464. American "COMINT intercepts determined that enemy combat operations in Korea were being directed by General Peng's headquarters . . . not by a Combined Headquarters in Pyongyang headed by Kim Il Sung." Aid, "American COMINT in the Korean War," 34.

8. Headquarters, X Corps Artillery, September 1951, 3, USAHEC. During Operation Commando (October 1951), soldiers from the Fifteenth Infantry Regiment assessed Chinese bunkers as "extremely strong, often able to withstand a hit from 105 mm howitzers. Fighting positions like these effectively neutralized much of Eighth Army's firepower advantages. Headquarters, Eighth United States Army Korea, The Battle of Bloody Angle—September–October 1951, 5, USACMH.

9. Li, *China's Battle for Korea*, 92.

10. Academy of Military Science, *The Unforgotten Korean War* (Beijing: Military History Division of the PLA, 2006), 628.

11. Allan R. Millett, *Their War for Korea* (Dulles, VA: Brassey's, 2002), 110.

12. S. L. A. Marshall, *Infantry Operations and Weapons Usage in Korea* (London: Greenhill Books, 1988), 85–86.

13. Sobieski, *Fire for Effect*, 67.

14. Richards and Li, *Voices from the Korean War*, 41.

15. Headquarters, Eighth United States Army Korea, Military History Section, Daylight Patrol, 3, USACMH; Academy of Military Science, "Unforgotten Korean War," 629.

16. Johnston, *War of Patrols*, 132.

17. Bloodworth, *Chinese Looking Glass*, 329.

18. Corr, *Chinese Red Army*, 23–25, points out that the Chinese Communist soldier had a tradition of not shrinking from a fight. CPVF units possessed the discipline, motivation, and experience to adapt to the conditions of positional warfare, then emerge along the line of contact in the summer of 1951.

19. John A. English, *On Infantry* (New York: Praeger, 1984), 170–72; Stokesbury, *Short History of the Korean War*, 132–33; Allan R. Millett, *The War for Korea, 1950–1951: They Came from the North* (Lawrence: University Press of Kansas, 2010), 305–6.

20. Shu Guang Zhang, *Mao's Military Romanticism* (Lawrence: University Press of Kansas, 1995), 154–55, 232 (quotation).

21. Zhang, *Mao's Military Romanticism*, 155, 162 (quotation).

22. Mao, *Selected Military Writings*, 389.

23. Yang Dezhi, "Command Experience in Korea," in *Mao's Generals Remember Korea*, trans. and ed. Xiaobing Li, Allan R. Millett, and Bin Yu (Lawrence: University Press of Kansas, 2001), 155–56.

24. Zhang, *Mao's Military Romanticism*, 155–58; Ryan, Finkelstein, and McDevitt, *Chinese Warfighting*, 127, 136.

25. These were American terms, but they are adequately descriptive. Headquarters, Eighth United States Army Korea, Enemy Tactics, 29.

26. Bloodworth, *Chinese Looking Glass*, 260.

27. Corr, *Chinese Red Army*, 139.

28. Peng, *Memoirs of a Chinese Marshal*, 481.

29. Headquarters, Eighth United States Army Korea, Enemy Tactics, 47, USACMH.

30. Headquarters, X Corps Artillery, May 1951, 2, USAHEC.

31. See Schrader, *Communist Logistics in the Korean War*. Bowers and Greenwood, *Passing the Test*, 8; Millett, *Their War for Korea*, 134.

32. Raschen, *Send Port and Pyjamas!*, 204.

33. Headquarters, Eighth United States Army Korea, Enemy Tactics, 33, USACMH. CPVF penetration units were organized within individual infantry companies. Their mission was to assault and breach defensive obstacles and positions. The penetration unit was composed of an assault team, a demolition team, and a support team. The assault team carried two 60 mm mortars, two to three light machine guns, one to two heavy machine guns, and three to four submachine guns. The demolition team included antitank teams with a demolition squad equipped with bangalore torpedoes to clear wire entanglements, abatis, mines, and disable or destroy any armored vehicles or heavy weapons bunkers. Six to eight additional men made up the support team that carried ammunition and provided casualty evacuation for the other two teams. Significantly, the company commander was responsible for leading the penetration unit.

34. Zhang, *Mao's Military Romanticism*, 162–64.

35. Peng, *Memoirs of a Chinese Marshal*, 482.

36. Zhang, *Mao's Military Romanticism*, 162–64.

37. It is significant that this defensive conception was not doctrinal but imposed by the conditions of terrain and policy objectives in Korea. Department of the Army, Field Manual (FM) 100-5, Operations (Washington, DC: US Government Printing Office, 1949), para. 526–27; Eighth Army Command Report, Narrative Section I, 1–2, August 1951, Army—AG Command Reports, 1949–54, RG 407, NARA II. See also CG, EUSAK to Corps Commanders, GX 984 TAC, July 30, 1951, Adjutant General Section, Top Secret Correspondence, 1945–52, Eighth U.S. Army, 1944–56, RG 338 Records of U.S. Army Operational, Tactical, and Support Organizations, NARA II.

38. The Research Institute of Military History, Academy of Military Science, eds.,

CPVF's War History of Resist America and Assist Korea (Beijing: Military Science Publishing, 1988), quoted in KIMH, *KW*, 3:110–11.

39. Headquarters, X Corps Artillery, July 1951, 2, USAHEC.

40. Eighth Army Command Report, Section I, 5, August 1951, RG 407, NARA II.

41. See for example, Estimate of the Situation, IX Corps Sector, September 10, 1951, 4–6, Memoranda and Communiques 1950–1952, CinC Far East 1951–52 Box 73, Series 3 Official Papers, Ridgway Papers, USAHEC.

42. Headquarters, X Corps Artillery, July 1951, 2, USAHEC.

43. KIMH, *KW*, 3:112–13.

44. Collins, *War in Peacetime*, 309.

45. Walter G. Hermes, *Truce Tent and Fighting Front* (Washington, DC: US Government Printing Office, 1966), 83–84.

46. Paik, *Pusan to Panmunjom*, 176–77; Headquarters, X Corps Artillery, August 1951, 6–7, USAHEC.

47. Eighth Army Command Report, Section I, 60, August 1951, RG 407, NARA II.

48. Second Infantry Division Command Report, Section I, 11, August 1951, RG 407, NARA II.

49. Haydon Boatner, Notes on Bloody Ridge-Heartbreak Ridge-Mundung-ni, n.d., Boatner Report and Maps Concerning the Battles of Bloody Ridge, Heartbreak Ridge, and Mundung-ni Valley, Korea, 1951, Box 1, The Haydon Boatner Papers, USAHEC; Nolan, *Run-up to the Punchbowl*, 102–3.

50. Headquarters, Eighth United States Army Korea, Enemy Tactics, 64–66, USACMH.

51. For his leadership at the Soyang River, May 16–24, 1951, Gen. Ruffner was awarded the Distinguished Service Cross, the nation's second-highest recognition for battlefield valor. The division as a whole received the Presidential Distinguished Unit Citation, which is the highest decoration awarded to a unit. General Officer Biography, Gen. Clark Louis Ruffner, USACMH.

52. Division intelligence estimated that the North Koreans had divined the signs of an attack and had rushed additional troops onto the ridge. Second Infantry Division Command Report, Section I, 10–12, 15, August 1951, RG 407, NARA II.

53. Peters and Li, *Voices from the Korean War*, 160.

54. KIMH, *KW*, 3:140.

55. Headquarters, Eighth United States Army Korea, Enemy Tactics, 47, USACMH.

56. Won-moo Hurh, *I Will Shoot Them from My Loving Heart* (Jefferson, NC: McFarland, 2012), 6, 56; Peters and Li, *Voices from the Korean War*, 159–60.

57. Eighth Army Command Report, Section I, 73, August 1951, RG 407, NARA II.

58. Second Infantry Division Command Report, Section I, 22, August 1951, RG 407, NARA II.

59. Haydon L. Boatner, Comments on "Truce Tent and Fighting Front," OCMH, 1966, January 31, 1967, Encl A, 1, unmarked folder, Box 1, Haydon L. Boatner Papers, USAHEC. Van Fleet admitted that too much attrition among the ROK junior officers and noncoms amplified losses in equipment and weaponry that made a successful at-

tack problematic. From 17–27 August, the Thirty-Fifth and Thirty-Sixth Regiments lost 132 KIA, 824 WIA, receiving as replacements only 181 soldiers and 4 officers. Eighth Army Command Report, Section I, 79, August 1951, RG 407, NARA II.

60. I appreciate Dr. William M. Donnelly pointing out that the troop rotation policy did not originate with FEC headquarters, but was a Department of the Army solution to the severe manpower crisis that affected all of the army's worldwide commitments. See Donnelly, "Best Army That Can Be Put into the Field," 809–47.

61. Boatner, Comments on Truce Tent and Fighting Front, Encl A, 2–3. Boatner also noted the particularly poor performance of the Third Battalion, an all "Negro" outfit. The following month, all African American soldiers—524 in all—from the battalion were transferred to other division units. It was the last unit in Korea to be forcibly integrated.

62. Headquarters, X Corps Artillery, August 1951, 11, USAHEC.

63. Second Infantry Division Command Report, Section I, 25, August 1951, RG 407, NARA II.

64. Peters and Li, *Voices from the Korean War*, 159–60; 163–72; KIMH, *KW*, 3:143–46; John Miller and Owen J. Carroll, *Korea: 1951–1953* (Washington, DC: US Government Printing Office, 1959), 116; William Russell, *Stalemate and Standoff: The Bloody Outpost* War (DeLeon, FL: E. O. Painter Printing, 1993), 7–11. Brig. Gen. Thomas E. DeShazo assumed command, according to the division's command report, on September 1, 1951. Second Infantry Division Command Report, Section I, 1, September 1951, RG 407, NARA II.

65. Boatner, "Comments on Truce Tent and Fighting Front," OCMH, 1966, 1, Boatner Papers, USAHEC.

66. Headquarters, X Corps Artillery, September 1951, 2, USAHEC; Headquarters, Eighth United States Army Korea, Enemy Tactics, 79–80, USACMH.

67. KIMH, *KW*, 3:147–48.

68. Headquarters, X Corps Artillery, August 1951, 4, USAHEC.

69. Miller and Carroll, *Korea: 1951–1953*, 116–17; Nolan, *Run-up to the Punchbowl*, 158–63.

70. Collins, *War in Peacetime*, 309–11.

71. Hermes, *Truce Tent and Fighting Front*, 88; Miller and Carroll, *Korea: 1951–1953*, 117.

72. Miller and Carroll, *Korea: 1951–1953*, 117; Hermes, *Truce Tent and Fighting Front*, 88–89.

73. General Officer Biography, Maj. Gen. Thomas Edward DeShazo, USACMH.

74. Quoted in Arned L. Hinshaw, *Heartbreak Ridge* (Westport, CT: Praeger, 1989), 11.

75. Second Infantry Division Command Report, Section I, 1, September 1951, RG 407, NARA II.

76. Quoted in Johnston, *A War of Patrols*, 186–87.

77. Jordan, "Right for the Wrong Reason," 153. See also Marshall's own observation on this central figure of the infantry squad. Marshall, *Battlefield Analysis of Infantry Weapons*, 53.

78. Donald Knox and Alfred Coppel, *The Korean War: Uncertain Victory* (New York: Harcourt Brace Jovanovich, 1988), 383.

79. Russell, *Stalemate and Standoff*, 14–15.

80. General Hong Nim, NKPA Sixth Division commander, was able to exchange the tired First Regiment for the fresh Thirteenth Regiment without any loss in the defenders' strength or capability. Hermes, *Truce Tent and Fighting Front*, 90.

81. Hermes, *Truce Tent and Fighting Front*, 91.

82. Although reinforcements arrived during the night, a strong counterattack overwhelmed and drove the Americans back. Russell, *Stalemate and Standoff*, 18.

83. Hinshaw, *Heartbreak Ridge*, 61–62.

84. General Officer Biography, Lt. Gen. Robert Nichols Young, USACMH.

85. Virgil E. Craven, "Operation Touchdown Won Heartbreak Ridge," *Army Combat Forces Journal* 4, no. 5 (December 1953): 25.

86. After Action Interview with Robert N. Young, Commanding General, 2nd Infantry Division, Headquarters, Eighth United States Army Korea, Historical Section, "Heartbreak Ridge, September–October, 1951, 2nd Infantry Division, n.d., 140–43, USACMH.

87. "Ralph Monclar" was the nom de guerre of Raoul Charles Magrin-Vernerey, a French Foreign Legion lieutenant general and veteran of both world wars. He reportedly accepted, or demanded, a reduction in grade to be eligible to fight in Korea and lead France's battalion assigned to the UNC. Ridgway, Van Fleet, and the other senior American commanders greatly admired his courage, calmness, and experience. Ridgway, *Korean War*, 107, and Hinshaw, *Heartbreak Ridge*, 83–84. See also Matthew B. Ridgway to James A. Van Fleet, October 22, 1951, Official Correspondence, CinC Far East, N–Z, Jan 51–Jun 52, Folder 8, Van Fleet, James, Jan 51–Jun 52, Ridgway Papers, USAHEC.

88. Craven, "Operation Touchdown," 26.

89. Hinshaw, *Heartbreak Ridge*, 84–88; Headquarters, Eighth United States Army Korea, Historical Section, "Action on Heartbreak Ridge," n.d., 20–21, USACMH.

90. Craven, "Operation Touchdown," 27–28.

91. Craven, "Operation Touchdown," 28–29.

92. Freedman, "Tankers at Heartbreak," 26–27.

93. The North Koreans also suffered supply difficulties due (likely) to Operation Strangle. Although they possessed an estimated 187 pieces of calibers from 76 mm to 150 mm, the sharp decrease in shelling compared to the previous month aggravated the effects of the already steep losses in infantry. Headquarters, X Corps Artillery, September 1951, 3, USAEHC.

94. Boatner, Bloody Ridge-Heart Break Ridge-Mundung-ni, Boatner Papers, USAEHC.

95. Maj. Gen. Robert N. Young to Gen. James A. Van Fleet, 26 October 1951, 3, Van Fleet, James, Jan 1951–Jun 1952, Official Correspondence CinC Far East, N–Z, Jan 1951–Jun 1952, Ridgway Papers, USAHEC; Russell, *Stalemate and Standoff*, 12, 20–22; Hinshaw, *Heartbreak Ridge*, 123.

96. Headquarters, X Corps Artillery, September 1951, 3–4, USAHEC.

97. Maj. Gen. Robert N. Young to Gen. James A. Van Fleet, 26 October 1951, 1–2, Van Fleet, James, Jan 1951–Jun 1952, Official Correspondence CinC Far East, N–Z, Jan 1951–Jun 1952, Ridgway Papers, USAHEC; Knox and Coppel, *Korean War: Uncertain Victory*, 385.

98. Eighth Army Command Report, G-3 Book 4, September 1951, 5–6, Eighth Army Command Report, Section II, Sep 51, RG 407, NARA II; Van Fleet, *Rail Transport*, 4, 12.

99. Eighth Army Command Report, October 1951, 1–2; 29, RG 407, NARA II.

100. Van Fleet, *Rail Transport*, 4, 12; Eighth Army Command Report, G-3 Book 4, September 1951, 5–6, Eighth Army Command Report, Section II, Sep 51, RG 407, NARA II.

101. Headquarters, US I Corps, Minutes of Commanders' Meeting, 4 September 1951, Folder 3, Box 1, O'Daniel Papers, CAM.

102. Headquarters, US I Corps, Minutes of Commanders' Meeting, 4 September 1951, Folder 3, Box 1, O'Daniel Papers, CAM.

103. Headquarters, Eighth United States Army Korea, Military History Section, The Battle of Bloody Angle—September–October 1951, 1, USACMH.

104. Headquarters, Eighth United States Army Korea, Military History Section, Bloody Angle, 4, 7, USACMH.

105. Yang, "Command Experience in Korea," 149, 151; Eighth Army Command Report, October 1951, 7, RG 407, NARA II; Marshall, *Battlefield Analysis of Infantry Weapons*, 62.

106. KIMH, *KW*, 3:214–15; Raschen, *Send Port and Pyjamas!*, 89.

107. Headquarters, I Corps, Operation Commando, 25, Typescript After Action Report, USAHEC.

108. I Corps Command Report, October 1951, 9–27, RG 407, NARA II; Knox and Coppel, *Korean War: Uncertain Victory*, 316–17.

109. I Corps Command Report, October 1951, 28, RG 407, NARA II; Marshall, *Battlefield Analysis of Infantry Weapons*, 62.

110. Headquarters, I Corps, Operation Commando, 33, Annex C, 1, USAHEC; Hermes, *Truce Tent and Fighting Front*, 99–102; Van Fleet, *Rail Transport*, 23.

111. Capt. Harry E. Trigg, a battalion staff officer, spoke of the infantrymen's frustration when he stated in an after action report, "The atomic artillery shell is, of course, the obvious solution if and when it becomes available." Headquarters, Eighth United States Army Korea, Battle of Bloody Angle, Memorandum for Record, Observations Attack—Hill 477, 3, USACMH.

112. Headquarters, I Corps, Operation Commando, 32, USAHEC; I Corps Command Report, October 1951, 64, RG 407, NARA II. The First Commonwealth Division lost 505 killed, wounded, and missing while the ROK First Division suffered only 147 casualties in the same time period.

113. Eighth Army Command Report, October 1951, 45, RG 407, NARA II; Headquarters, I Corps Operation Commando, Annex K, "Enemy Casualties," USAHEC. The Eighth Army G-2 reported 25,500 confirmed and estimated casualties: 2,500 counted killed; 3,000 estimated killed; 20,000 estimated wounded. The I Corps

G-2's figures were slightly more modest, claiming 22,520 enemy killed and wounded and 550 prisoners taken. Chinese sources acknowledged 7,000 soldiers lost from the Forty-Seventh Army. Academy of Military Science, "Unforgotten Korean War," 561–63.

114. IX Corps Command Report, October 1951, 10, Command Report Bk I–II, Oct 51, RG 407, NARA II; Estimate of the Situation, IX Corps Sector, September 10, 1951, 2–3, Ridgway Papers, USAHEC.

115. IX Corps Command Report, October 1951, 11, 18–21, RG 407, NARA II; Bradley Lynn Coleman, "The Colombian Battalion in Korea, 1950–1954," *Journal of Military History* 69 (October 2005): 1158–59.

116. IX Corps Command Report, November 1951, 11, RG 407, NARA II.

117. Academy of Military Science, "Unforgotten Korean War," 567–68.

118. The Eighth Army reporting breaks down Chinese casualties as follows:

> 12,711 known enemy killed
> 16,818 estimated enemy killed
> 1,022 enemy prisoners

US, ROK, and Colombian losses were significantly less:

> 710 killed
> 3,714 wounded
> 70 missing in action

Eighth Army Command Report, October 1951, 61–62, RG 407, NARA II.

119. IX Corps Command Report, October 1951, 22, 25, RG 407, NARA II; Eighth Army Command Report, October 1951, 62, RG 407, NARA II.

120. The IX Corps G-2 (Intelligence officer) reported that the Sixty-Seventh Army appeared to have lost its strength as a fighting unit under the relentless advance of the US Twenty-Fourth Infantry and ROK Sixth Divisions. The Sixty-Eighth Army elements thrown in to blunt the attack were likewise mauled and failed to stop the IX Corps advance. IX Corps Command Report, November 1952, 1, Command Report Bk I–II, Nov 51, RG 407, NARA II.

121. Yang, "Command Experience in Korea," 151–52.

122. Maj. Gen. Milburn to Ridgway, 29 September 1951, Special File April– December 1951, CinC Far East 1951–52 Box 72, Ridgway Papers; General Headquarters, Far East Command, Office of the G-1, Subject: Casualties, 16 October 1951, Memoranda and Communiques 1950–52, CinC Far East 1951–52, Box 73, Ridgway Papers, USAHEC. When US marine casualties are included (213 KIA, 1,691 WIA), September becomes the deadlier month; however, the *daily* average of casualties in the first two weeks of October remained nearly twice that of the entire month of September.

123. Eighth Army Command Report, October 1951, 69, RG 407, NARA II.

124. Joy, *How Communists Negotiate*, 139–40.

125. Paik, *Pusan to Panmunjom*, 178; Kaufman, *Korean War*, 208–9; Russell, *Stalemate and Standoff*, 24; Bradley and Blair, *General's Life*, 649.

Chapter 6

1. William Johnston, *A War of Patrols* (Vancouver: University of British Columbia Press, 2003), 202–3.

2. Van Fleet to CincFE, Subj: Outline Plan Cudgel, Sept 19, 1951; Van Fleet to CincFE, Subj: Outline Plan Wrangler, September 25, 1951; CINCFE to CG EUSAK ADV October 9, 1951, Adjutant General Section, Top Secret Correspondence, 1945–52, Eighth US Army, 1944–56, RG 338, NARA II.

3. Memorandum for Diary, 5 September 1951, Special File Apr–Dec '51, CinC Far East 1951–52, Box 72, Ridgway Papers, USAHEC.

4. James F. Schnabel and Robert J. Watson, *The Joint Chiefs of Staff and National Policy*, vol. 3, part 2, *The Korean War* (Washington, DC: Office of Joint History, 1998), 17.

5. Schnabel and Watson, *Joint Chiefs of Staff and National Policy*, vol. 3, part 2, *The Korean War*, 18.

6. Schnabel and Watson, *Joint Chiefs of Staff and National Policy*, vol. 3, part 2, *The Korean War*, 19, 21.

7. J. Lawton Collins to Matthew B. Ridgway, September 8, 1951, Official Correspondence (CINCFE) Collins, J. Lawton, EUSA-CinCFE Jan '51–Jun '52 A–H, Box 11, Ridgway Papers, USAHEC.

8. Matthew B. Ridgway to J. Lawton Collins, "Eyes Only" TEW 166, 26 September 1951, Special File Apr–Dec 51, CinC Far East 1951–52, Box 72, Ridgway Papers, USAHEC.

9. Schnabel and Watson, *Joint Chiefs of Staff and National Policy*, vol. 3, part 2, *The Korean War*, 20–21.

10. Vatcher, *Panmunjom*, 66, 70, 72–73.

11. Joy, *How Communists Negotiate*, 37; Kaufman, *Korean War*, 209.

12. Johnston, *War of Patrols*, 182.

13. Bloodworth, *Chinese Looking Glass*, 261; Raschen, *Send Port and Pyjamas!*, 124–28, 133. The Colombian Battalion was awarded the US Presidential Unit Citation for its action on the Kumsong front, October–November. Coleman, "Colombian Battalion in Korea," 1159–60.

14. James A. Van Fleet to Matthew B. Ridgway, November 5, 1951; Matthew B. Ridgway Diary Memo, November 8, 10, 1951, Special File Part 3 of 4, Box 72 CINCFE 1951–52, Ridgway Papers, USAHEC.

15. JCS 86804 DA to CINCFE, November 15, 1951; CX 57332 CINCFE to DA, November 15, 1951, July 1951–September 1952, Adjutant General Section, Top Secret Correspondence, 1945–52, Eighth U.S. Army, 1944–56, RG 338, NARA II.

16. Department of Defense Office of Public Information, Report of US Casualties, Summary No. 65, November 21, 1951, HRC GEOG V Korea File, 704 Casualties, Korean War, USACMH.

17. American Institute of Public Opinion, *The Gallup Poll: Public Opinion, 1935–1971*, vol. 2, *1949–1958* (New York: Random House, 1972), 1019, 1027. The president's job approval rating during the same time period (published December 31, 1951), was 23 percent favorable against 58 percent unfavorable with 19 percent expressing no opinion.

18. Assistant Secretary to the General Staff to Matthew B. Ridgway, October 13,1951, Special File Part 3 of 4, Box 72 CINCFE 1951–52, Ridgway Papers, USAHEC.

19. For their part, the Canadians felt particularly vulnerable to American decisions in Asia. They had drastically reduced their own ground force capabilities, intending to rely on American airpower to fight World War III, should it ever come to that. Denis Stairs, *The Diplomacy of Constraint: Canada, the Korean War, and the United States* (Toronto: University of Toronto Press, 1974), 71–76.

20. Stueck, *Rethinking the Korean War*, 157.

21. Chai, "Korean Truce Negotiations," 203–4.

22. Chai, "Korean Truce Negotiations," 204.

23. Kaufman, *Korean War*, 211–12; Collins, *War in Peacetime*, 334; Raschen, *Send Port and Pyjamas!*, 141.

24. Joy, *How Communists Negotiate*, 131. Chai Chengwen was an experienced political and liaison officer. He was the deputy director of the intelligence section for the Eighth Route Army during the anti-Japanese war. He spoke fluent English and often butted heads with his UNC counterparts on the sensitive issues regarding POWs and the demarcation line. See Chai Chengwen, "The Korean Truce Negotiations," in *Mao's Generals Remember Korea*, trans. and ed. Xiaobing Li, Allan R. Millett, and Bin Yu (Lawrence: University Press of Kansas, 2001), 184.

25. Headquarters, EUSAK, Letter of Instructions, November 12, 1951, Official Correspondence (CINCFE) N–Z, Van Fleet, Box 13 EUSA, CinCFE Jan '51–Jun '52, Ridgway Papers, USAHEC.

26. CINCFE to CG Eighth Army (Advanced HQ) Korea, 12 November 1951, Special File April–December 1951, CinC Far East 1951–52 Box 72, Ridgway Papers, USAHEC; CX 57143 CINCFE to CG EUSAK ADV, November 12, 1951, July 1951–September 1952, Adjutant General Section, Top Secret Correspondence, 1945–52, Eighth U.S. Army, 1944–56, RG 338, NARA II.

27. Collins, *War in Peacetime*, 311–12. Ridgway had unfortunately handicapped Van Fleet by prohibiting him from divulging to his staff and subordinate commanders the text and intent of Ridgway's November 12 directive for active defense. CINCFE to CG Eighth Army (Advanced HQ) Korea, 12 November 1951, Ridgway Papers, USAHEC.

28. Eighth Army Command Report, Section I, 43, November 1951, RG 407, NARA II.

29. Russell, *Stalemate and Standoff*, vi.

30. The relationship between war and battle is best analyzed by Clausewitz, *On War*, 253–62, which I have followed.

31. Personal for General Van Fleet from Ridgway, 29 November 1951, Van Fleet, James, Official Correspondence, CinC Far East, N–Z, Jan 1951–Jun 1952, Box 13, Ridgway Papers, USAHEC.

32. Collins, *War in Peacetime*, 312.

33. O'Daniel called "touch-base" raids the sharp attacks by Chinese troops that overran an objective and then withdrew before artillery and air strikes could in-

flict serious damage. What O'Daniel was actually observing was the practice of Mao's *niupitang* strategy of exhaustion. Headquarters, US I Corps, Commanders' Meeting, 20 November 1951, Folder 3, Box 1, O'Daniel Papers, CAM.

34. Joy, *How Communists Negotiate*, 173–74. The Clausewitzian model is summed up: "War in general, and the commander in any specific instance, is entitled to require that the trend and designs of policy shall not be inconsistent with the means [provided]." Clausewitz, *On War*, 87.

35. Eighth Army Command Report, Section I, 32–33, 36, November 1951, RG 407, NARA II.

36. Moses, *Whatever It Takes*, 190–91; Stephens, *Old Ugly Hill*, 66–67.

37. Johnston, *War of Patrols*, 239–40.

38. The author, a veteran of World War II and Korea, requested anonymity. "Faithful to Our Trust," *Army Combat Journal* 5, no. 5 (December 1954): 21.

39. Headquarters, Eighth United States Army Korea, Military History Section, Operation Clam Up, 1–4, USACMH.

40. One of the few prisoners taken during this period claimed his unit's mission was "to hold at all costs against an anticipated attack on their positions." Eighth Army, Operation Clam Up, 20, USACMH.

41. Quoted in Johnston, *War of Patrols*, 245–46.

42. Eighth Army, Operation Clam Up, 26–29, USACMH.

43. Eighth Army, Operation Clam Up, 16, USACMH.

44. Paik, *Pusan to Panmunjom*, 179–80.

45. Paik, *Pusan to Panmunjom*, 183; Memorandum for Record, Coordination Conference on Anti-Guerrilla Activities, 14 November 1951, Correspondence-Memoranda, October 1951–December 1952, Box 82/1, Van Fleet Papers, GCMLA. Van Fleet was also under considerable political pressure from President Rhee, who was increasingly embarrassed by the strong show of communist power within the confines of the ROK; Van Fleet to Ridgway, 15 November 1951, T–Z Correspondence, Ridgway Papers.

46. KMAG Command Report, January 1952, Weekly Intelligence Summary #33, G-2 Annex, 4, RG 407, NARA II; Harold G. Clode, Historical Report, Conduct of Anti-Guerrilla Operations in Southwest Korea by Task Force Paik, 2 December 1951–8 February 1952, 14, USAHEC.

47. Paik, *Pusan to Panmunjom*, 188; Clode, Historical Report, 7–8, USAHEC. Paik's operation displayed all the hallmarks of modern counterinsurgency methods to clear, hold, and build in areas formerly controlled by insurgent forces.

48. Paik, *Pusan to Panmunjom*, 188; KIMH, *KW*, 3:311–19; Clode, Historical Report, 8, USAHEC; KMAG Command Report, January 1952, G-3 Narrative, 1–2, RG 407, NARA II.

49. A KMAG analysis of the discrepancy between preoperation intelligence estimates and postoperation claims suggested that the much larger number of killed and captured was due to civilians impressed against their will to side with the Communists, indigenous bandits who also hid in the rugged Chiri mountains, and family members of local guerrillas swept up in the dragnet. Clode, Historical Report, 5–6, USAHEC.

50. Paik, *Pusan to Panmunjom*, 188.

51. G-2 Intelligence Estimate, December 27, 1951, 4–5, Intelligence Estimates, Jan 51–Dec 51, Assistant Chief of Staff, G-2, Eighth US Army, 1946–56, RG 338, NARA II.

52. Yang, *For the Sake of Peace*, 91.

Chapter 7

1. Poats, *Decision in Korea*, 216.

2. Collins, *War in Peacetime*, 339.

3. Joy, *How Communists Negotiate*, 135–36.

4. Anthony J. Sobieski, ed., *Fire Mission!* (Fairfield, CA: First Book Library, 2003), 7; Kaufman, *The Korean War*, 220–21.

5. Joy, *How Communists Negotiate*, 103.

6. Vatcher, *Panmunjom*, 89–90.

7. Poats, *Decision in Korea*, 213–14.

8. Collins, *War in Peacetime*, 334–35.

9. Joy, *How Communists Negotiate*, 66–67.

10. Goodman, *Negotiating While Fighting*, 255. The Americans eventually agreed to Poland and Czechoslovakia as sufficiently neutral parties to the Korean War.

11. Joy, *How Communists Negotiate*, 74–75; Kaufman, *Korean War*, 223–24. Nam Il was consistent, telling Joy, "We do not make any such demand [to employ observer teams in South Korea or conduct overhead reconnaissance flights] and we are not accustomed to doing so." In fact, Nam Il very well knew the Communists did not have the ability as the Americans did to maintain intrusive surveillance for the purpose of monitoring the status of military equilibrium south of the future Demilitarized Zone. Joy, *How Communists Negotiate*, 68–71.

12. Collins, *War in Peacetime*, 336–38; Kaufman, *Korean War*, 224–25. Joy called the Communist argument of "interference in internal affairs" weak and worried that Washington's directive was watering down the meaning of an armistice, which would only encourage further adventurism at Panmunjom. Joy, *How Communists Negotiate*, 72–73.

13. Chai, "Korean Truce Negotiations," 205.

14. Goodman, *Negotiating While Fighting*, 115–16.

15. Chai, "Korean Truce Negotiations," 215–16; Poats, *Decision in Korea*, 215.

16. Headquarters, United States Army Pacific, Office of the G3, Military History Office, the Handling of Prisoners of War during the Korean Conflict, June 1960, 5, USACMH.

17. Stueck, *Rethinking the Korean War*, 94.

18. Memorandum by the Acting Secretary of State, October 29, 1951, *FRUS, 1951*, 7:1073.

19. Eighth Army Command Report, Narrative Section I, 19–20, November 1951, RG 407, NARA II.

20. Collins, *War in Peacetime*, 340–41.

21. Headquarters, United States Army Pacific, Handling of Prisoners of War, 5–6,

8–9, USACMH. So rapid was the physical collapse of the KPA that UNC forces had to establish temporary holding facilities at Inchon and Pyongyang that quickly overwhelmed the units assigned as guards. A FEC Inspector General (IG) report determined, "The implied belief in early cessation of hostilities was mirrored in the 'attitude of complacency in regard to the docility of prisoners of war,'" and appeared to justify the lax security measures taken. As representative examples, the IG recorded incidents where a handful of military police escorted hundreds of North Korean prisoners "without incident." United States Army Pacific, Handling of Prisoners of War, 7–8, USACMH.

22. United States Army Pacific, Handling of Prisoners of War, 13–14, USACMH. POW holding areas were broken down into camps, enclosures, compounds, and subcompounds.

23. KIMH, *KW*, 3:363; Collins, *War in Peacetime*, 343–44; Chronology of the Korean Campaign, 1 January–30 June 1952, 7, Clark Papers, CAM.

24. United States Army Pacific, Handling of Prisoners of War, 10, USACMH.

25. Kaufman, *Korean War*, 237.

26. Collins, *War in Peacetime*, 340–41.

27. Memorandum by the Assistant Secretary of State for United Nations Affairs, February 4, 1952, *FRUS, 1952–1954*, vol. 15, *Korea* (Washington, DC: US Government Printing Office, 1984), 15:38–39.

28. Kaufman, *Korean War*, 237–38. Throughout January 1952 several meetings took place as the president's principal advisors grappled with various schemes "so as to face the Communists with a *fait accompli*." The fate of UNC and ROK prisoners and the likelihood of an armistice agreement should the Communists face such a fait accompli remained open to question. Memorandum for the Record, by the Deputy Assistant Secretary of State for Far Eastern Affairs, February 4, 1952, *FRUS, 1952–1954*, 15:32–34.

29. Excluded from this count, though they remained under UNC military control, were 37,000 recently reclassified CI, Koreans who had been detained but were later determined not to have been actual combatants. A Chronology of the Korean Campaign, 1 January–30 June 1952, 4, Clark Papers, CAM; Joy, *How Communists Negotiate*, 148–49; Hermes, *Truce Tent and Fighting Front*, 141.

30. Poats, *Decision in Korea*, 219; Xu, "Chinese Forces and Their Casualties," 56–57.

31. Millett, *Their War for Korea*, 227–28.

32. Chief of Staff United States Army (Collins) to CinC FE Tokyo (Ridgway), November 16, 1951; CinC FE to Chief of Staff, November 16, 1951, Memoranda and Communiques, Box 73, CinCFE 1951–52, Ridgway Papers, USAHEC.

33. Millett, *Their War for Korea*, 229.

34. Joy, *How Communists Negotiate*, 150–52.

35. Lee Sang-cho informed the UNC delegates that they had released 53,000 ROK and UNC soldiers, which accounted for the discrepancy between propaganda and the list presented at Panmunjom. Joy, *How Communists Negotiate*, 104–7, 150; Vatcher, *Panmunjom*, 129–30, provides Lee's extensive explanation of his side's version of "voluntary repatriation."

36. Stueck, *Rethinking the Korean War*, 162.

37. The Secretary of State to the Secretary of Defense, August 27, 1951, *FRUS, 1951*, 7:857–59, quotation on 857. Cf. with Acheson, *Present at the Creation*, 652–54, which compresses the debate timeline and frames the secretary's position as more in line with the president's view much earlier in the process.

38. Goodman, *Negotiating While Fighting*, 178–79; Chronology of the Korean Campaign, 1 January–30 June 1952, 1, Clark Papers, CAM; Poats, *Decision in Korea*, 221–22.

39. Goodman, *Negotiating While Fighting*, 175–77, 181, 184, 199.

40. Poats, *Decision in Korea*, 223.

41. Chai, "Korean Truce Negotiations," 216.

42. Truman, *Years of Trial and Hope*, 460–61.

43. Memorandum by the Secretary of State to the President, February 8, 1952, *FRUS, 1952–1954*, 15:44–45.

44. Collins, *War in Peacetime*, 341; Memorandum for the Record, February 19, 1952, *FRUS, 1952–1954*, 15:56–57. The UNC delegates argued that the Communists had already endorsed voluntary repatriation by "allowing" South Korean soldiers to join the KPA during the summer of 1950. They did not, however, realize at this time the different views the Chinese would maintain on the issue of POWs. Memorandum for Record, February 19, 1952, Special File Jan–Apr 52, CinC Far East 1951–52, Box 72, Ridgway Papers, USAHEC.

45. Memorandum of Conversation, February 25, 1952, *FRUS, 1952–1954*, 15:58–59.

46. Stueck, *Rethinking the Korean War*, 164–65; Dairy entry, January 27, 1952, President's Secretary Files, Harry S. Truman Papers, Harry S. Truman Library and Museum, Independence, Missouri.

47. Joy, *How Communists Negotiate*, 151–52.

48. In November 1951, Mao asserted his intent to reject a "principle of one for one" and to propose instead "exchange according to the principle of return of all prisoners of war by both sides." He then expressed his confidence, "I think it will not be difficult to reach agreement on this question." Transcript Mao Zedong to Filippov (Stalin), Ciphered telegram, November 14, 1951, *Cold War International History Project Bulletin* 6/7 (Winter/Spring 1995), 71.

49. Chai, "Korean Truce Negotiations," 218; Goodman, *Negotiating While Fighting*, 291–92.

50. Chai, "Korean Truce Negotiations," 221; Goodman, *Negotiating while Fighting*, 328–31.

51. Goodman, *Negotiating While Fighting*, 331.

52. Memorandum of Conversation, February 25, 1952, *FRUS, 1952–1954*, 15:59.

53. Sheila Miyoshi Jager, *Brothers at War: The Unending Conflict in Korea* (New York: W. W. Norton, 2013), 206.

54. By February 1952 all of the POW compounds were overcrowded and generally mixed both officers and enlisted men. This oversight allowed the Communists to maintain a chain of command and for their leaders to exercise control over their soldiers. Headquarters, Eighth United States Army Korea, Military History Sec-

tion, Intelligence and Counterintelligence Problems during the Korea Conflict, 32, USACMH.

55. Construction of Koje-do's compounds began on February 1, 1951. By the end of the month, 53,588 POWs had been transferred from Pusan's enclosures. The population doubled to 98,799 a month later. By the end of June, Koje-do's enclosures held just over 140,000 POWs. United States Army Pacific, Handling of Prisoners of War, 12–14, USACMH.

56. Ridgway, *Korean War*, 206; Headquarters, Eighth United States Army Korea, Intelligence and Counterintelligence Problems during the Korea Conflict, 31, USACMH. Intelligence officials found prisoner identification to be problematic as each unit used their own numbering system to identify POWs. Add to this confusion the high frequency of some Korean and Chinese family names, and it was common for intelligence personnel to have to screen "ten to fifteen POWs . . . to determine the one being sought." Later in the war Eighth Army corrected the problem by assigning blocks of numbers to each corps, which in turn assigned number blocks to its subordinate units. The capturing unit then assigned one of these numbers to the POW, and this number was used by all higher echelons to identify the POW "from the time of his capture until release from Army control." Headquarters, Eighth United States Army Korea, Intelligence and Counterintelligence Problems during the Korea Conflict, 6, 31, USACMH.

57. Joy, *How Communists Negotiate*, 153; William C. Latham Jr., "Kaesong and Panmunjom," in *The Ashgate Research Companion to the Korean War*, ed. James I. Matray and Donald W. Boose Jr. (Burlington, VT: Ashgate, 2014), 398.

58. Poats, *Decision in Korea*, 227.

59. Stueck, *Rethinking the Korean War*, 166.

60. Kaufman, *Korean War*, 246; GHQ, UNC, Public Information Office, Essential Elements of the Armistice Negotiations on Agenda Item 4, April 25, 1952, Folder 3 Jan–Dec 1952, Box 8 Correspondence 1951, Jan.–1953, Jun., Clark Papers, CAM.

61. Essential Elements of the Armistice Negotiations on Agenda Item 4, April 25, 1952, Clark Papers, CAM.

62. Acheson, *Present at the Creation*, 653; Xiaoming Zhang and Zhihua Shen, "Ending the Korean Conflict: The Communist Perspective," *New England Journal of History* 60 (Fall 2003–Spring 2004): 254–55; Gideon Rose, *How Wars End* (New York: Simon and Schuster, 2010), 132; Clark, *From the Danube to the Yalu*, 37.

63. Joy, *How Communists Negotiate*, 132–33.

64. Collins, *War in Peacetime*, 341–42; Commander in Chief, Far East (Ridgway) to the Joint Chiefs of Staff, CX-5593, October 27, 1951, *FRUS, 1951*, 7:1068–70; Rose, *How Wars End*, 139–40.

65. April 18, 1952, Battle Report to Washington, April 20, 1952, Folder 4 of 4, Apr–May 1952, Box 71 CINCFE, 1950–52, Ridgway Papers, USAHEC.

66. Goodman, *Negotiating While Fighting*, 367–68.

67. Chronology of the Korean Conflict, 1 January–30 June 1952, 17–18, Clark Papers, CAM.

68. Chronology of the Korean Conflict, 1 January–30 June 1952, 19, Clark Papers,

CAM; Headquarters, Far East Command, Public Information Officer, May 7, 1952, Folder 4 of 4, Apr–May 1952, Box 71 CINCFE, 1950–52, Ridgway Papers, USAHEC.

69. Goodman, *Negotiating While Fighting*, 406, 437. Admiral Joy may have felt he failed as the chief UNC delegate, but Ridgway had only praise for him as a sailor and diplomat. In an annual evaluation report, the UNC commander opined, "[Joy] has displayed in high degree those qualities of integrity, loyalty, balanced judgment, patience, fearlessness of expression, and readiness to assume responsibility, which have contributed vitally to the results achieved by the Unified Command in the Far East . . . distinctly *superior* [original emphasis]." Efficiency Report, Vice Admiral C. Turner Joy, September 10, 1951, Special File 2 of 4, Box 72 CINCFE 1951–52, Ridgway Papers, USAHEC.

70. Clark, *From the Danube to the Yalu*, 79–80.

Chapter 8

1. Zhihua Shen, trans. and ed., *Chaoxian zhanzheng: Eguo dang'anguan de jiemi wenjian* [The Korean War: Declassified documents from Russian archives] (Taipei, Taiwan: Central Research Printing Office, 2003), 2: sections 5–7. See also Contemporary China Editorial Department, *Xu Xiangqian zhuan* [Biography of Xu Xiangqian] (Beijing: Contemporary China Press, 1991). Translations provided by Xiaobing Li.

2. In September, the Twenty-Third Army Group brought four divisions devoted to airfield construction and the logistics battle. Xu, "Chinese Forces and Their Casualties," 50–51.

3. Transcript VKP(b) CC Politburo decision with approved message Filippov (Stalin) to Mao Zedong, November 19, 1951, *Cold War International History Project Bulletin* 6/7 (Winter 1995/96): 72.

4. Du Ping, "Political Mobilization and Control," in *Mao's Generals Remember Korea*, trans. and ed. Xiaobing Li, Allan R. Millett, and Bin Yu (Lawrence: University Press of Kansas, 2001), 63, 89–94.

5. The condition remained even in the summer of 1952. See Prisoner of War Preliminary Interrogation Reports for May 1952, PW Interrogation Reports, 180th Infantry Regiment, Ellis B. Richie Papers, USAHEC.

6. Headquarters, Eighth United States Army Korea, Enemy Material, 12, 15, USACMH; Xu Xiangqian, "The Purchase of Arms from Moscow," in *Mao's Generals Remember Korea*, trans and ed. Xiaobing Li, Allan R. Millett, and Bin Yu (Lawrence: University Press of Kansas, 2001), 141–42.

7. Transcript, Mao Zedong to Filippov (Stalin), Ciphered telegram, November 14, 1951, *Cold War International History Project Bulletin* 6/7 (Winter 1995/96): 71.

8. Quotation from Zhang, *Mao's Military Romanticism*, 162.

9. Headquarters, I Corps, Operation Commando, Annex C, 1, USAHEC; Conklin, "Cease Fire," 19, USAHEC.

10. I am indebted to Professor Xiaobing Li, University of Central Oklahoma, for this understanding of the CPVF's adaptation to modern positional warfare in Korea.

11. China National Military Museum, ed., *Kangmei yuanchao zhanzheng jishi* [A

chronological record of the war to resist the U.S. and aid Korea] (Beijing: PLA Press, 2008), 166–67. Translation provided by Xiaobing Li.

12. Raschen, *Send Port and Pyjamas!*, 90.

13. Headquarters, Eighth United States Army Korea, Enemy Tactics, 66–67, USAHEC.

14. Yang Dezhi, *Weile Heping* [*For the sake of peace*] (Beijing: Long March Press, 1987), 128–36, explains the origins of the "Underground Great Wall" and its evolution from "anti-artillery holes" to interconnected trench lines with thick overhead cover to elaborate tunnel-bunkers in mutually supporting arrays capable of withstanding the heaviest bombardments; Yang, "Command Experience in Korea," 154.

15. Academy of Military Science, "Unforgotten Korean War," 592–93.

16. Yu, "The Chinese People's Volunteers Force," in Matray and Boose, *Ashgate Research Companion to the Korean War*, 278.

17. Boatner, "Countering Communist Artillery," 24.

18. Peng, *Memoirs of a Chinese Marshal*, 482–83.

19. Jensen, *A War (Love) Story*, 301–2.

20. Corr, *Chinese Red Army*, 26.

21. Raschen, *Send Port and Pyjamas!*, 65; Bloodworth, *Chinese Looking Glass*, 329.

22. Rudolph W. Stephens, *Old Ugly Hill: A GI's Fourteen Months in the Korean Trenches, 1952–1953* (Jefferson, NC: McFarland, 1995), 77–78.

23. Boatner, "Countering Communist Artillery," 24.

24. Johnston, *War of Patrols*, 286–87.

25. Eighth Army, The Employment and Effectiveness of the Artillery, 39, 42, USAHEC.

26. Eighth Army Intelligence Estimate #5, September 22, 1952, 3, Intelligence Estimates, Apr 52–Jul 53, Assistant Chief of Staff, G-2, Eighth US Army, 1946–56, RG 338, NARA II.

27. William G. Robertson, "The Korean War: The United Nations' Response to Heavy Bombardment," in *Tactical Responses to Concentrated Artillery*, CSI Report 13 (Fort Leavenworth, KS: Combat Studies Institute, n.d.), 109.

28. Stueck, *Rethinking the Korean War*, 137; Mark, *Aerial Interdiction*, 290.

29. Zhang, *Red Wings*, 60–64.

30. Zhang, *Red Wings*, 91. George G. Loving recalled the shock of tangling with MiGs while flying the slower and less maneuverable F-80 Shooting Star. However, after a few indecisive close encounters, Loving concluded, "They turned out to be paper tigers. Flying a superior airplane in an aerial encounter doesn't guarantee success, nor does having an inferior airplane mean failure. A well-trained, experienced pilot with a cool head can carry the day." Loving, *Bully Able Leader*, 169.

31. Zhang, *Red Wings*, 98; Millett, *The War for Korea, 1950–1951: They Came from the North*, 388–90; Ridgway, *Korean War*, 101–11; Stewart, *Airpower*, 13.

32. Quoted in Zhang, *Red Wings*, 114.

33. Millett, *Their War for Korea*, 60; Zhang, *Red Wings*, 117–20.

34. Kathryn Weathersby, "The Soviet Union," in *The Ashgate Research Compan-*

ion to the Korean War, ed. James I. Matray and Donald W. Boose Jr. (Burlington, VT: Ashgate, 2014), 92.

35. Stewart, *Airpower*, 58; Zhang, *Red Wings*, 112.

36. The PLAAF's first jet ace, Zhao Baoong, flew with the Third Division. He finished the war with a score of seven kills. Zhang, *Red Wings*, 146–53.

37. Zhang, *Red Wings*, 155.

38. Zhang, *Red Wings*, 155.

39. North Korea's reconstituted air force, though much smaller, also joined the air war with Soviet-supplied MiGs. These planes also flew from Manchuria bases. Millett, *Their War for Korea*, 61.

40. Zhang, *Red Wings*, 168–69.

41. Headquarters, Eighth United States Army Korea, Enemy Material, 10, USACMH.

42. Merrill, "Study of the Aerial Interdiction," 112–13; Gonsalves, *Battle at the 38th Parallel*, 107.

43. Air Force Historical Division, US Air Force Operations in the Korean Conflict (1 July 1952–27 July 1953), US Air Force Historical Study 127, Maxwell Air Force Base, July 1, 1956, 152 (hereafter USAF Historical Study 127).

44. Kenneth P. Werrell, *Archie, Flak, AAA, and SAM: A Short Operational History of Ground-Based Air Defense* (Maxwell Air Force Base, AL: Air University Press, 1988), 74–76.

45. Xu, "Chinese Forces and Their Casualties," 54.

46. USAF Historical Study 72, 156.

47. Headquarters, Eighth United States Army Korea, Enemy Tactics, 70; Van Fleet, *Rail Transport*, 35.

48. Van Fleet, *Rail Transport*, 49.

49. Quoted in Carter, *Some Historical Notes on Air Interdiction in Korea*, 13.

50. Van Fleet, *Rail Transport*, 1, 31.

51. S. C. M. Paine, *The Sino-Japanese War of 1894–1895* (Cambridge: Cambridge University Press, 2003), 142–45, 177–78, 363.

52. Bloodworth, *Chinese Looking Glass*, 313.

53. Xuezhi, "The CPVF's Combat and Logistics," 106–38.

54. Bin Yu asserts the emergence of positional warfare was a surprise and not necessarily welcomed by Chinese commanders. This may be true, but it is also clear that positional warfare saved Peng's veterans from being annihilated as a field force in the summer and fall of 1951. Yu, "The Chinese People's Volunteers Force," in Matray and Boose, *Ashgate Research Companion to the Korean War*, 275, 277.

55. Commander Hong complained of one particularly effective strike on April 8 against a logistics depot at Samdung. American fighter-bombers, using napalm mixed with high-explosive bombs, destroyed eighty-four rail cars packed with more than 140 tons of grain and enough clothing and shoes to outfit nearly two hundred thousand soldiers. Chinese estimates were 30–40 percent of all supplies were lost between the Yalu River and the fighting front. Hong, "CPVF's Combat and Logistics," 124–26. For the effect of AA artillery on road interdiction, see Eighth Army G-2 and Fifth Air Force A-2 Study, Supply and Transport: CCF-NKPA, September 1951, 82, Eighth

Army Supporting Documents, Section II Book 3, Staff Section A/CoS G-2, September 1951, RG 407, NARA II.

56. Academy of Military Science, "Unforgotten Korean War," 552–53, 556.

57. Hong, "CPVF's Combat and Logistics," 128, 134–35; Loving, *Bully Able Leader*, 159, 163.

58. Academy of Military Science, "Unforgotten Korean War," 585; Peng, *Memoirs of a Chinese Marshal*, 480; Hong, "CPVF's Combat and Logistics," 130, 136–38. American COMINT analysis confirmed that tens of thousands of CPVF soldiers were kept behind the front to fight the battle of the rear area. During the ending days of Peng's Fifth Campaign, food shortages reduced the CPVF's momentum and significantly hindered the establishment of a solid line of resistance that summer. Aid, "American COMINT in the Korean War," 26.

59. Academy of Military Science, "Unforgotten Korean War," 586.

60. Academy of Military Science, "Unforgotten Korean War," 593, 632–33.

61. Sullivan, *Toy Soldiers*, 105.

62. Stueck, *Rethinking the Korean War*, 167–68.

Chapter 9

1. Roger J. Spiller, ed., *S. L. A. Marshall at Leavenworth: Five Lectures at the U.S. Army Command and General Staff College* (Fort Leavenworth, KS: Combined Arms Center, 1980), 1:1, 3. Marshall was something of a professional icon among American army officers at the time, being the author of the influential *Men against Fire* (1947), among other works. Although not a formal historian, he possessed a keen eye and could spin a good story. Much of what he said about infantry combat rang true to those who had led soldiers in battle. In later years, Marshall's work and methods became objects of intense scrutiny and occasional scorn. For an analysis of Marshall's influence generally, and on his theories related to infantry fire combat, see Jordan, "Right for the Wrong Reason," 135–47.

2. A Chronology of the Korean Campaign, 1 January–30 June 1952, 17, Clark Papers, CAM.

3. Rick Atkinson, *The Day of Battle: The War in Sicily and Italy, 1943–1944* (New York: Henry Holt, 2007), 263.

4. Maj. Gen. Fred Walker, Clark's subordinate as the commander of the US Thirty-Sixth Infantry Division in Italy, quoted in Atkinson, *Day of Battle*, 331. In an example of wartime fate, Walker was older than Clark, his former War College instructor, and senior in grade prior to World War II. Martin Blumenson, *Mark Clark* (New York: Congdon and Weed, 1984), 125.

5. *Time*, May 19, 1952, 36; Telegram, Eyes Only Eisenhower, 1946, Folder 1 Correspondence 1946, Box 9 Rapido River Controversy, 1946, Clark Papers, CAM. See also in the same location a copy of Frank Aston's Scripps-Howard article, January 21, 1946, publicizing details of the battle at the Rapido River at the behest of the 36th Infantry Division Association. Aston made much of the casualty figures (136 KIA, 932 WIA, 908 MIA), the enemy and environmental conditions that appeared to stack the odds against the assaulting Americans, and the division commander's objection to

the location that Clark allegedly insisted on. See also House Committee on Military Affairs hearing, March 18, 1946, 5, where spokesmen for the association petitioned Congress to block Clark's nomination to permanent major general rank to prevent "future soldiers being sacrificed wastefully and uselessly." For Clark's time as an army commander and then army group commander, see the excellent analysis by Stephen R. Taffe, *Marshall and His Generals* (Lawrence: University Press of Kansas, 2011), 94–133.

6. Samuel M. Meyers and Albert D. Biderman, eds., *Mass Behavior in Battle and Captivity: The Communist Soldier in the Korean War* (Chicago: University of Chicago Press, 1968).

7. Ridgway, *Korean War*, 210.

8. See Peters and Li, *Voices from the Korean War*, 242–58, for a comprehensive view of camp life at the time of the Koje-do incidents. In January 1953, the Far East Command released an intelligence report detailing the events surrounding the Koje-do riots. Among the conclusions was the assertion that the Communist negotiators themselves directed the collection of intelligence information for use at Panmunjom. Clark, *From the Danube to the Yalu*, 50–55.

9. Korean sources identify Senior Col. Lee Hak-ku as the North Koreans' lead prisoner on Koje-do. Lee was allegedly intentionally captured to organize prisoner resistance against voluntary repatriation; KIMH, *KW*, 3:365. The timing of Lee's capture (he was the chief of staff of the KPA's Thirteenth Division), during the Battle of the Pusan Perimeter, however, suggests his story is a post hoc rationale, but it is likely that Lee understood his role to organize POWs and make mischief for the UNC. See also Paik, *Pusan to Panmunjom*, 53; Peters and Li, *Voices from the Korean War*, 243–44.

10. ROK sources indicate that discipline on the island was so poor that prisoners maintained a brisk black market trading system, selling or trading American provided amenities (mandated by the Geneva Conventions) in exchange for money or materials to make weapons; KIMH, *KW*, 3:364–65. An American officer, Lt. Norman Isler, Company B, 430th Engineer Construction Battalion, recalled that prisoners from Compound 76 had nearly tunneled their way to freedom. Following the POW relocation, Isler examined the tunnel system and estimated the POWs were about a week away from a mass escape. Norman Isler to the author, Personal Correspondence, November 4, 2018.

11. Headquarters, United States Army Pacific, Handling of Prisoners of War, 15, USACMH.

12. Peters and Li, *Voices from the Korean War*, 245, 249–50.

13. Headquarters, United States Army Pacific, Handling of Prisoners of War, 25, USACMH; Ridgway, *Korean War*, 208–9.

14. Clark, *From the Danube to the Yalu*, 36, 39; Collins, *War in Peacetime*, 344; Chronology of the Korean Campaign, 1 January–30 June 1952, 7, Clark Papers, CAM.

15. United States Army Pacific, Handling of Prisoners of War, 26, USACMH.

16. Collins, *War in Peacetime*, 344. Prisoners at Koje Island also received mail

"from the Reds." On March 5, 1952, the eighth and largest batch, containing 1,038 pieces of mail, was delivered. By this time, communist leaders would have clearly identified measures to retaliate against the UNC's POW stance and could have transmitted coded instructions through the UNC's own mail system. Chronology of the Korean Campaign, 1 January–30 June 1952, 10, 21, Clark Papers, CAM.

17. Memorandum by P. W. Manhard of the Political Section of the Embassy to the Ambassador in Korea, March 14, 1952, *FRUS, 1952–1954*, 15:98–99. These observations were passed to General Yount at the same time they were communicated to the State Department.

18. United Nations Commission Report, March 27, 1952, quoted in Jager, *Brothers at War*, 260–61.

19. United States Army Pacific, Handling of Prisoners of War, 27, USACMH. Following the main riot on Koje-do, Ambassador Muccio cabled Washington his own findings and criticism of Operation Scatter. He noted, based on eyewitness testimony from an American Chinese linguist, that Scatter's implementation and security protocols were deficient and had likely resulted in false screening results that probably hindered a fair settlement. Muccio was dismayed by the military's apparent lack of concern over the integrity of screening, noting American army G-1 (Personnel) and G-2 (Intelligence) staff officers were aware of pro-Nationalist violence aimed at coercing additional non-repatriates, but "showed disinclination [to] treat or discuss it as possibly [a] decisive factor." The Ambassador in Korea to the Department of State, May 12, 1952, *FRUS, 1952–1954*, 15:192.

20. The Commander in Chief, United Nations Command to the Joint Chiefs of Staff, April 29, 1952, *FRUS, 1952–1954*, 15:184–85. Ironically, the JCS the same day agreed with Ridgway's plan to omit screening the remaining POWs on Koje-do.

21. Chronology of the Korean Campaign, 1 January–30 June 1952, 16, Clark Papers, CAM.

22. Peters and Li, *Voices from the Korean War*, 254.

23. Ridgway, *Korean War*, 211–12; Clark, *From the Danube to the Yalu*, 38.

24. Peters and Li, *Voices from the Korean War*, 255–56.

25. Clark, *From the Danube to the Yalu*, 39–41; Collins, *War in Peacetime*, 345.

26. Ridgway, *Korean War*, 214. General Yount convened a board of inquiry that cleared both Dodd and Colson. Van Fleet disagreed, as did Clark. Clark, who knew that allied intelligence had uncovered orders to prisoners to capture American officers, recommended reduction in grade for both officers to colonel, which Secretary of the Army Frank Pace approved. Yount also received an administrative reprimand, effectively ending his career, for his errors (or neglect) in dealing with the Koje-do crisis. Collins, *War in Peacetime*, 346.

27. Mark W. Clark, Commander in Chief, United Nations Command, May 15, 1952, Folder 1 Official Statements, May 1952–September 1953, Box 54 Korean War: UN Command Reports, 1952–1953, Clark Papers, CAM.

28. Clark, CINCUNC, May 17, 1952, Official Statements, Clark Papers, CAM.

29. Boatner, Comments on "Truce Tent and Fighting Front," Encl B, 1, Boatner

Papers, USAHEC. Boatner's testimony conflicts with the official history that suggests
Van Fleet appointed Boatner as Colson's replacement. Cf. Hermes, *Truce Tent and
Fighting Front*, 259.

30. KIMH, *KW*, 3:371.

31. The Senior Delegate, United Nations Command Delegation to the Commander in Chief, Far East, May 12, 1952, *FRUS, 1952–1954*, 15:193–94.

32. Eighth Army Command Report, June 1952, Narrative Section I, 7, Record
Group 407, NARA II; Boatner, Comments on "Truce Tent and Fighting Front," Encl
B, 2, Boatner Papers, USAHEC. General Dodd never had more than one thousand
mixed US and ROK troops. Boatner culled out four hundred of these soldiers as being "sub-standard" and sent them back to the mainland. He also immediately relieved
one US colonel, two lieutenant colonels, and one major.

33. General Officer Biography, Haydon N. Boatner, USACMH.

34. Lieutenant Isler speculated the directive was designed to prevent an accidental discharge that the Communists might use as evidence of POW mistreatment. Isler,
Personal Correspondence, November 4, 2018.

35. Headquarters, 430th Engineer Construction Battalion, Commander's Report
Prepared in Support of Request for Class "B" Time for Military Operations on Koje-do,
Korea, September 18, 1952, 1. Author's possession, courtesy of Norman Isler.

36. Boatner, Comments on "Truce Tent and Fighting Front," Encl B, 1–2, 5,
Boatner Papers, USAHEC.

37. Boatner, Comments on "Truce Tent and Fighting Front," Encl B, 7, Boatner
Papers, USAHEC.

38. United States Army Pacific, Handling of Prisoners of War, 34, USACMH.

39. Clark, *From the Danube to the Yalu*, 63; Isler remembered, "I think these
POWs were a different breed than those from previous wars . . . did not act like
POWs from previous wars." Isler, personal correspondence November 4, 2018.

40. Chronology of the Korean Conflict, 1 January–30 June 1952, 22–23, Clark Papers, CAM.

41. United States Army Pacific, Handling of Prisoners of War, 34, USACMH.

42. Collins, *War in Peacetime*, 346–47; Chronology of the Korean Conflict, 1 January–30 June 1952, 24, Clark Papers, CAM. Once the communist-controlled compounds were cleared out, US troops discovered caches of arms that included 3,000
spears fashioned from tent poles, 1,000 gasoline grenades, 4,500 knives, and an un-
counted number of clubs, hammers, and barbed wire flails. Documents indicated
battle plans to resist that nearly guaranteed prisoner causalities in any confrontation
with soldiers. Clark, *From the Danube to the Yalu*, 64–65.

43. Ridgway, *Korean War*, 213.

44. Memorandum by the Deputy Assistant Secretary of State for Far Eastern Affairs to the Deputy Under Secretary of State, May 22, 1952, *FRUS, 1952–1954*, 15:222;
Peters and Li, *Voices from the Korean War*, 258. The North Koreans were less invested
in the question of voluntary repatriation as Kim Il-sung's regime had little intention
to account for South Korean prisoners. His desire to end the war (aerial bombardment was the most pressing issue) as soon as possible also muted North Korean ob-

jections to the repatriation question. See Zhang and Shen, "Ending the Korean Conflict," 254–58.

45. Ambassador Muccio was another skeptic of the administration's voluntary repatriation policy. His own independent fact finding developed several areas of concern regarding Operation Scatter's accuracy and objectivity. He reported to Washington results of post-Koje-do interviews with Chinese Communist POW leaders. They claimed between 2,800 and 3,200 Chinese pro-repatriation prisoners had been tattooed against their will with Nationalist slogans. The presence of organized Nationalist Chinese prisoners tended to have significant influence over undetermined POWs as camp guards rarely felt their duty to exert discipline within the compounds. POW trustees routinely abused their position to continue "political civil war" in the camps, "replete with kangaroo courts, polit[ical] murders, beatings, [and] torture." The UNC failure to maintain discipline and exercise restraint were among the chief catalysts of the disturbances. Muccio was careful to point out that his view was not necessarily that of the POWs, but that the number of Chinese non-repatriates was probably suspect. The Ambassador in Korea to the Department of State, June 28, 1952, and July 2, 1952, *FRUS, 1952–1954*, 15:360–61, 369–70.

46. Kaufman, *Korean War*, 269–70; Won-moo Hurh, *I Will Shoot Them from My Loving Heart* (Jefferson, NC: McFarland, 2012), 41–54.

47. Clark, *From the Danube to the Yalu*, 142–43.

48. The Chargé in Korea to the Department of State, June 3, 1952, *FRUS, 1952–1954*, 15:290. During the constitutional crisis Secretary of State Dean Acheson instructed Muccio to remind Rhee of American foreign policy objectives and norms, and that it was "impossible to expect that [the] US can remain indifferent to an internal situation in a country which owes the very fact of its existence to the still continuing loss of life and sacrifices of hundreds of thousands of Amer[ican] men, as well as to the sacrifices of all the Amer[ican] people." The Secretary of State to the Embassy in Korea, June 4, 1952, *FRUS, 1952–1954*, 15:303.

49. Paik, *Pusan to Panmunjom*, 197.

50. Memorandum by the Assistant Secretary of State for United Nations Affairs to the Deputy Under Secretary of State, June 13, 1952, *FRUS, 1952–1954*, 15:334; Stueck, *Rethinking the Korean War*, 196–97.

51. UNC Command Report No. 46, 11, Clark Papers, CAM.

52. Editorial Note, *FRUS, 1952–1954*, 15:242; Clark, *From the Danube to the Yalu*, 151–52.

53. The Commander in Chief, United Nations Command to the Chief of Staff, United States Army, May 31, 1952, *FRUS, 1952–1954*, 15:274–76; Memorandum by the Deputy Assistant Secretary of State for Far Eastern Affairs to the Secretary of State, June 2, 1952, *FRUS, 1952–1954*, 15:281–85.

54. Clark served as the US High Commissioner for Austria, and later as deputy to Secretary of State Marshall, on the negotiations for an Austrian peace treaty. Mark W. Clark, *Calculated Risk* (New York: Harper and Brothers, 1950), 452–94.

55. President Truman to the President of the Republic of Korea, June 2, 1951, *FRUS, 1952–1954*, 15:285–86.

56. Paik, *Pusan to Panmunjom*, 201.

57. The Chargé in Korea to the Department of State, June 3, 1952, *FRUS, 1952–1954*, 15:291; the Ambassador in Korea to the Department of State, June 12, 1952, *FRUS, 1952–1954*, 15:325; UNC Command Report No. 47, 10, Clark Papers, CAM.

58. The Ambassador in Korea to the Department of State, June 12, 1952, *FRUS, 1952–1954*, 15:324–26.

59. The Chargé in Korea to the Director of the Office of Northeast Asian Affairs, June 5, 1952, *FRUS, 1952–1954*, 15:307–8; the Chargé in Korea to the Department of State, June 3, 1952, *FRUS, 1952–1954*, 15:287–88.

60. E. Allan Lightner Oral History, October 26, 1973, 114–18, transcript by Richard D. McKinzie, Harry S. Truman Library and Museum.

61. Memorandum by the Assistant Secretary of State for United Nations Affairs to the Deputy Under Secretary of State, June 13, 1952, *FRUS, 1952–1954*, 15:336.

62. The Commander in Chief, United Nations Command to the Joint Chiefs of Staff, July 5, 1952, *FRUS, 1952–1954*, 15:377–78.

63. Headquarters, United Nations Command, Public Information Officer, A Chronology of the Korean Campaign, 1 July–31 December 1952, 1, GEOG V Korea, 314.76, USACMH; the Secretary of Defense to the Commander in Chief, United Nations Command, June 4, 1952, *FRUS, 1952–1954*, 15:301; Clark, *From the Danube to the Yalu*, 152; Kaufman, *Korean War*, 273–74. Van Fleet had briefed Ridgway in March 1952 on his plan to replace dissident political or military leaders with those of demonstrated loyalty who were also competent. The UNC commander concurred with Van Fleet's planning progress and advised "the utmost secrecy in the development and handling of [these] plans." This was Operation Everready that Clark revised and presented to the JCS. Ridgway to Van Fleet, March 9, 1952, Operation Plan Everready, Official Correspondence (CINCFE) N–Z, Van Fleet, Box 13 EUSA, CinCFE Jan '51–Jun '52, Ridgway Papers, USAHEC.

64. Stairs, *Diplomacy of Constraint*, 239; KIMH, *KW*, 3:371–72.

65. Yang, "Command Experience in Korea," 159–60; Vatcher, *Panmunjom*, 156–57.

66. William C. Latham Jr., "Kaesong and Panmunjom," in *The Ashgate Research Companion to the Korean War*, ed. James I. Matray and Donald W. Boose Jr. (Burlington, VT: Ashgate, 2014), 416; Millett, *Their War for Korea*, 251; Clark, *From the Danube to the Yalu*, 213–19.

67. Yang, "Command Experience in Korea," 157. The accusations generated intensive controversy with Western scientific groups carefully vetted going to China "to investigate" and substantiate the Communists' claims. Jager, *Brothers at War*, 242–57, narrates and analyzes the Communists' effort to use germ warfare propaganda to attack the UNC's prestige while shoring up Mao's domestic revolutionary agenda with linkages between the war against germs at home and the war against Western capitalist imperialism in Korea.

68. Headquarters, Eighth United States Army, Intelligence and Counterintelligence Problems during the Korea Conflict, 45, USACMH.

69. Clark, *From the Danube to the Yalu*, 214–15.

70. The only biography of Harrison is D. Bruce Lockerbie, *A Man under Orders* (San Francisco: Harper and Row, 1979).

71. William K. Harrison to Sis and Tad, February 24, 1952, 8th Army HQ, Dep Army Commander, Box 3 Oral History and 9th Inf Div Annual Report, William K. Harrison Papers, USAHEC; Vatcher, *Panmunjom*, 148–50, 153.

72. Chai, "Korean Truce Negotiations," 222.

73. Vatcher, *Panmunjom*, 228.

74. William K. Harrison, Senior Officer Oral History, vol. 2, 469, 470–71, 472, Harrison Papers, USAHEC.

75. William K. Harrison to Sis and Tad, May 31, 1952, 8th Army HQ, Dep Army Commander, Box 3 Oral History and 9th Inf Div Annual Report, Harrison Papers, USAHEC.

76. Memorandum of the Substance of Discussion at a Department of State–Joint Chiefs of Staff Meeting, May 14, 1952, *FRUS, 1952–1954*, 15:197–99.

77. The Senior Delegate, United Nations Command Delegation to the Commander in Chief, United Nations Command, May 19, 1952, *FRUS, 1952–1954*, 15:209.

78. The Commander in Chief, United Nations Command to the Joint Chiefs of Staff, May 31, 1952, *FRUS, 1952–1954*, 15:270–73.

79. Chronology of the Korean Conflict, 1 January–30 June 1952, 23, Clark Papers, CAM.

80. The Joint Chiefs of Staff to the Commander in Chief, Far East, June 5, 1952, *FRUS, 1952–1954*, 15:311, 314.

81. UNC Command Report No. 47, 1–15 June 1952, 1, Clark Papers, CAM.

82. Chronology of the Korean War, 1 January–30 June 1952, 23, Clark Papers, CAM; Chai, "Korean Truce Negotiations," 224. Vatcher, *Panmunjom*, 161–64, provides another firsthand account of this episode, which thoroughly surprised the Communist team as another method to maintain the principle of voluntary repatriation.

83. Chai, "Korean Truce Negotiations," 225.

84. Eighth Army Command Report, June 1952, Narrative Section I, 93, Record Group 407, NARA II; UNC Command Report No. 48, 16–30 June 1952, 6, Clark Papers, CAM; the Commander in Chief, United Nations Command to the Joint Chiefs of Staff, July 2, 1952 and July 3, 1952; Memorandum by the Assistant Secretary of State for Far Eastern Affairs to the Secretary of State, July 9, 1952, *FRUS, 1952–1954*, 15:372–74, 396.

85. UNC Command Report No. 50, 16–31 July 1952, 1–3, Clark Papers, CAM.

86. Chai, "Korean Truce Negotiations," 225.

87. A Chronology of the Korean Campaign, 1 July–31 December 1952, 7–10, GEOG V Korea, USACMH (Van Fleet quotation, 9–10).

88. USAF Historical Study 72, 159.

89. Stewart, *Airpower*, 279–80.

90. Poats, *Decision in Korea*, 233; Stewart, *Airpower*, 152–53.

91. USAF Historical Study 72, 159.

92. Mark Clodfelter, *The Limits of Airpower* (New York: Free Press, 1989), 17.

93. FEAF statistics from the initiation of Saturate to the beginning of the Air Pressure Campaign tell the story of reduced emphasis on rail interdiction:

	February	March	April	May	June
Locomotives destroyed/ damaged	55	55	21	44	10
Rail cars destroyed	700	595	325	527	195
Trucks destroyed	2,365	1,765	1,835	2,690	1,990
Bridges destroyed	80	90	63	72	15
Rail cuts reported	2,470	2,700	2,320	2,577	***

Chronology of the Korean War, 1 January–30 June 1952, 10, 14, 18, 22, 28, Clark Papers, CAM.

94. USAF Historical Study 127, 108–9.

95. Clodfelter, *Limits of Airpower*, 16; Eighth Army Command Report, July 1952, Narrative Section I, 159–61, Record Group 407, NARA II.

96. Merrill, "Study of the Aerial Interdiction," 108, 110. The last major effort against transportation infrastructure was on January 9, 1953, when around-the-clock bombing was ordered to destroy eleven bridges between Sinanju and Yongmedong, a natural chokepoint for three of five routes from Manchuria. Fifth Air Force fighter-bombers and Bomber Command B-29s flew 2,292 sorties over a five-day period to damage these bridges so thoroughly that rail traffic was blocked for sixteen days. The target area was wrecked sufficiently that the Communists opted to build a 70-mile bypass rather than repair the damage. Six months later, only three bridges were operational. The cost was seven fighter-bombers and one B-29—the sortie count represented 54 percent of FEAF's total activity for the week. It is a wonder that after nine months of intensive interdiction a target as fruitful as this was not identified and attacked much sooner. Stewart, *Airpower*, 156–62.

97. Crane, *American Airpower Strategy in Korea*, 118–19; Stewart, *Airpower*, 120–21, 126–32; Mark W. Clark to Field Marshal Earl Alexander, July 8, 1952, Folder 3 Jan–Dec 1952, Box 8 Correspondence 1951, Jan 1953, Jun., Clark Papers, CAM.

98. FEAF Command Report, vol. 1, 2, Annex 29, FEC, GHQ, FEAF, June 1952, Record Group 407, NARA II.

99. Futrell, *Air Force in Korea*, 483–85; Crane, *American Airpower Strategy in Korea*, 119; Stewart, *Airpower*, 132–33; Clark, CINCUNC, June 24, 1952, Official Statements, Clark Papers, CAM; Stokesbury, *Korean War*, 177–78.

100. Stewart, *Airpower*, 136–37. FEAF placed the hydroelectric plants on the enduring target list, much like North Korean airfields. As repairs advanced, tactical aircraft returned to foil all attempts to restore even partial operations. Suiho came under assault two more times, on September 12, 1952, and finally on February 15, 1953. It remained unusable to the end of the war.

101. FEAF Command Report, vol. 1, 4, Annex 29, FEC, GHQ, FEAF, June 1952, Record Group 407, NARA II.

102. Zhang, *Red Wings*, 186–87; Transcript Mao to Kim, telegram, July 18, 1952, "New Russian Documents," *Cold War International History Project Bulletin* 6/7 (Winter 1995/96): 78.

103. By war's end, aerial bombardment would completely destroy 8,700 factories and 80 percent of the mining industry's potential. Destruction was almost complete in the fields of pig iron, copper, aluminum, alkali, and fertilizer production. Other significant economic sectors such as metal, chemical, electrical, fishing, and construction goods dropped between 60 percent and 93 percent of prewar totals. Soon Sung Cho, "The Politics of North Korea's Unification Policies, 1950–1965," *World Politics* 19, no. 2 (January 1967): 222.

104. Eight hundred and thirty air force and navy planes participated in the strike, dropping 425 tons of bombs and 23,000 gallons of napalm. One only F-84 failed to return, downed by ground fire. FEAF Command Report, vol. 1, 1, Annex 29, FEC, GHQ, FEAF, July 1952, Record Group 407, NARA II; Chronology of the Korean Campaign, 1 July–31 December 1952, 3, 5, GEOG V Korea, USACMH.

105. UNC Command Report No. 49, 1–15 July 1952, 6 and UNC Command Report No. 50, 16–31 July 1952, 6, Clark Papers, CAM; Stewart, *Airpower*, 95–96. See also Futrell, *Air Force in Korea*, 516–17. The quotation is from Yang, *For the Sake of Peace*, 158.

106. Raschen, *Send Port and Pyjamas!*, 203.

107. The Acting Secretary of State to the Embassy in the United Kingdom, June 24, 1952, *FRUS, 1953–1954*, 15:353; Crane, *American Airpower Strategy in Korea*, 120–22. A reporter asked Secretary of Defense Robert Lovett if the attack had been ordered in response to Senator Robert A. Taft's (a Republican presidential aspirant) allegation the US had lost control of the air over Korea. General Bradley's comment, "It is amazing how people read political implications into everything," highlights by what degree the entire war's process had been politicized by the summer of 1952. *FRUS, 1952–1954*, 15:357.

108. Mark W. Clark to Field Marshal Earl Alexander, July 8, 1952, Clark Papers, CAM. Clark had hosted Alexander in Japan as the planning for these strikes was developing. The British press implied that Clark had deliberately snubbed Alexander and disparaged British support to the UNC by failing to inform Alexander about the ongoing escalation in the air war. Clark assured Alexander (who had been Clark's immediate military superior in Italy) that political consultation with allies was ongoing and that the JCS approval to bomb Suiho had arrived after Alexander's departure from Clark's headquarters.

109. FEAF Command Report, vol. 1, 1, Annex 29, FEC, GHQ, FEAF, August 1952, Record Group 407, NARA II.

110. UNC Command Report No. 51, 1–15 August 1952, 7 and UNC Command Report No. 52, 16–31 August 1952, 7–8, Clark Papers, CAM.

111. Transcript Kim to Mao, telegram, July 15, 1952, "New Russian Documents," *Cold War International History Project Bulletin* 6/7 (Winter 1995/96): 79; Zhang, *Red Wings*, 188–89.

112. "Asians in UN Fear Raids Harm Truce," *New York Times*, July 12, 1952, 2.

113. I owe the idea of the linkage between the air pressure campaign and its unintended strategic and political consequences to Conrad Crane, "Measuring Gains on the Battle Field," 25–26.

Chapter 10

1. Gibby, *Will to Win*, 230ff.

2. GHQ UNC, Public Information Officer, UP Correspondent's Written Questions to CinCUNC, June 1952, Folder 3 Jan–Dec 1952, Box 8 Correspondence 1951, Jan.–1953, Jun., Clark Papers, CAM.

3. See Gibby, *Will to Win*, 165–69, 205–9, for analysis of the ROK army expansion debates and issues surrounding military effectiveness of South Korean divisions.

4. Ridgway, *Korean War*, 194.

5. Formation of ROK 155 mm Howitzer Battalions, ROK Correspondence, 1951–1953 #15–19, Box 86/6 Van Fleet Papers, GCMLA; Eighth Army, The Employment and Effectiveness of the Artillery, 37–38, USAHEC.

6. Won-moo Hurh, *I Will Shoot Them from My Loving Heart* (Jefferson, NC: McFarland, 2012), 113.

7. Formation of ROK 155 mm Howitzer Battalions, Van Fleet Papers, GCMLA; Kenneth W. Myers, KMAG's Wartime Experiences, 11 July 1951–27 July 1953, Office of the Military History Officer, 1958, 90–93, USCMH. See also Robert K. Sawyer, *Military Advisors in Korea: KMAG in Peace and War*, ed. Walter G. Hermes (Washington, DC: Office of the Chief of Military History, 1962), 183–84.

8. Eighth Army, The Employment and Effectiveness of the Artillery, 38; Hurh, *I Will Shoot Them from My Loving Heart*, 116–17.

9. James A. Van Fleet Oral History, vol. 2, tape 4, 53, Senior Officer Oral History Program, USAHEC; James A. Van Fleet to J. Lawton Collins, 13 June 1951, Correspondence—Alphabetical, Collins, J. Lawton, Box 68/17, Van Fleet Papers, GCMLA.

10. See Gibby, *Will to Win*, chapter 7.

11. Headquarters, Korean Army, Training Memorandum 75, August 7, 1951, Annexes 2–6, Box 4, Daniel Doyle Papers, USAHEC.

12. Paik, *Pusan to Panmunjom*, 162.

13. Mark W. Clark, "The Truth about Korea," *Collier's*, February 1954, 34–39.

14. For example, see Yang, "Command Experience in Korea," 166–70, and Transcript, Mao to Stalin, Ciphered Telegram, July 18, 1952, *Cold War International History Project Bulletin*, 6/7 (Winter 1995/96): 78. Although the North Koreans and Chinese presented a unified view to Stalin, in reality Kim Il-sung was eager to end the

war as soon as possible. Peng Dehuai generally agreed, but only under the right military conditions. Shen Zhihua, "Sino-North Korean Conflict," *Cold War International History Project Bulletin* 14/15 (Winter/Spring 2003/4): 21.

15. Hermes, *Truce Tent and Fighting Front*, 187–88; UNC Command Report No. 45, 1–15 May 1952, 6, Clark Papers, CAM.

16. Bradley and Blair, *A General's Life*, 546. For background on the Forty-Fifth Infantry Division's experience and status as of 1950, see William M. Donnelly, *Under Army Orders* (College Station: Texas A&M University Press, 2001), 89–92, and William Berebitsky, *A Very Long Weekend: The Army National Guard in Korea, 1950–1953* (Shippensburg, PA: White Mane Publishing, 1996), 112.

17. Donnelly, *Under Army Orders*, 101–2.

18. William R. O'Connell, *Thunderbird: A History of the 45th Infantry Division in Korea* (Tokyo: Toppan Printing, n.d.), 11.

19. Donnelly, *Under Army Orders*, 105–6.

20. Hermes, *Truce Tent and Fighting Front*, 183; Donnelly, *Under Army Orders*, 108.

21. Sobieski, *Fire for Effect*, 97.

22. O'Connell, *Thunderbird*, 12–13, 15; Berebitsky, *A Very Long Weekend*, 114.

23. Donnelly, *Under Army Orders*, 110–13, 115–18; Headquarters, Eighth United States Army, Military History Section, Night Defense of Hill 200, 26 May 1952, 179th Infantry, 45th Division, 1–3, USACMH.

24. Eighth Army, Night Defense of Hill 200, 10, USACMH.

25. Eighth Army, Night Defense of Hill 200, 17–22, USACMH.

26. O'Connell, *Thunderbird*, 18.

27. General Officer Biography, Maj. Gen. David L. Ruffner, USACMH.

28. Likely due to poor maintenance standards or dust and debris blown about by the Chinese shelling, each of the platoon's machine guns had to be disassembled, cleaned, and reassembled before they could be used. In either case, the soldiers' leaders failed to protect their most important weapons. Had the outpost been farther away from the MLR, or not situated within the right angle of the MLR, it likely would have been overrun. Eighth Army, Night Defense of Hill 200, 11–12, 18, USACMH.

29. Headquarters, 180th Infantry Regiment, Annex 1 (Intel) to Opn 043, Summary of Enemy Situation, 1, May 28, 1952, Box 2, Richie Papers, USAHEC.

30. Donnelly, *Under Army Orders*, 115–18; O'Connell, *Thunderbird*, 18–19.

31. O'Connell, *Thunderbird*, 19.

32. Hermes, *Truce Tent and Fighting Front*, 287; Russell, *Stalemate and Standoff*, 33–34. On June 12, the division executed phase II of Counter to seize and occupy Hill 191 and Outpost Eerie, which the division had lost in March 1952. O'Connell, *Thunderbird*, 19–20.

33. The practice of constructing bunkers to protect UNC troops from their own artillery was already common. At the I Corps commanders' conference in March 1952, General O'Daniel advocated the construction of more bunkers and the preplanned use of VT artillery on friendly positions as an acceptable tactic. He highlighted the experience of one company using VT shelling from the Forty-Fifth Infantry Division that resulted in thirty-one confirmed enemy dead on their own hilltop

position. Headquarters, US I Corps Commanders' Meeting, 30 March 1952, 8, Folder 3, Box 1, O'Daniel Papers, CAM.

34. Hermes, *Truce Tent and Fighting Front*, 287–88.

35. Sobieski, *Fire for Effect*, 97.

36. UNC Command Report No. 47, 1–15 June 1952, 5–6, Clark Papers, CAM; Chronology of the Korean Campaign, 1 January–30 June 1952, 24–25, Clark Papers, CAM.

37. The 145th Anti-Aircraft Artillery Battalion's motto thereafter became "Running Water." O'Connell, *Thunderbird*, 54–55.

38. O'Connell, *Thunderbird*, 20.

39. Eighth Army Command Report, June 1952, Narrative Section I, 31, Record Group 407, NARA II; UNC Command Report No. 48, 16–30 June 1952, 7–8, Clark Papers, CAM; Russell, *Stalemate and Standoff*, 34.

40. Lloyd R. Moses, *Whatever It Takes: The Autobiography of General Lloyd R. Moses* (Vermillion, SD: Dakota Press, 1991), 193–94.

41. Chronology of the Korean Campaign, 1 January–30 June 1952, 25–26, Clark Papers, CAM; Moses, *Whatever It Takes*, 202–3, 206.

42. Hermes, *Truce Tent and Fighting Front*, 292.

43. Clark, *From the Danube to the Yalu*, 79.

44. James A. Van Fleet Oral History, Tape Four, March 4, 1973, 38–40, 50, USAHEC; Hermes, *Truce Tent and Fighting Front*, 292–93.

45. Quoted in Johnston, *War of Patrols*, 268.

46. A sharp clash over Old Baldy on June 27, 1952, only reinforced Clark's view of the UNC's tactical posture: approximately one thousand Chinese stormed over the Second Infantry Division's position. At the end of the night's fight, more than two hundred confirmed and estimated dead were reported to Eighth Army. Chronology of the Korean Campaign, 1 January–30 June 1952, 27, Clark Papers, CAM.

47. Maj. Gen. Michael M. Alston-Roberts-West, commanding the Commonwealth Division, quoted in Johnston, *War of Patrols*, 283.

48. Eighth Army Command Report, July 1952, Section I, 75–78, RG407, NARA II.

49. O'Connell, *Thunderbird*, 20–21; UNC Command Report No. 49, 1–15 July 1952, 3, Clark Papers, CAM.

50. General Fry assumed command of the division in May 1952. Maj. Gen. James Clyde Fry, General Officer Biography, USACMH; Hermes, *Truce Tent and Fighting Front*, 293.

51. Stephens, *Old Ugly Hill*, 109–11.

52. Yang Dezhi, *Weile Heping* [*For the sake of peace*] (Beijing: Long March Press, 1987), 169–70, 172–73.

53. Headquarters, 23rd Infantry Regiment, Command Report, July 1952, 9, RG 407, NARA II.

54. Stephens, *Old Ugly Hill*, 112–15.

55. 23rd Infantry Regiment Command Report, July 1952, RG 407, NARA II, 12; Affidavit of Lt. Col. Ralph D. Burns, Appendix E, 23rd Infantry Regiment Command Report, July 1952, RG 407, NARA II.

56. 23rd Infantry Regiment Command Report, 13; Division Chief of Staff Journal, July 18, 2nd Infantry Division Journals, June–July 1952, RG 338, NARA II.

57. Burns Affidavit, 2. Elements of Company B had actually made two attempts to capture the hill but were thrown back twice. The twenty survivors withdrew from the hilltop at the company commander's initiative just before midnight 18/19 July. 23rd Infantry Regiment Command Report, July 1952, 13–14, RG 407, NARA II.

58. Division Chief of Staff Journal, July 18, 2nd Infantry Division Command Report, July 1952, RG 407, NARA II.

59. Fry ordered his assistant division commander, Brig. Gen. Lionel C. McGarr, to put Lt. Col. Garrett in charge of the attack and to tell Mergens to go to sleep. McGarr concurred, simply stating, "We need leaders." Division Chief of Staff Journal, July 18, 2nd Infantry Division Command Report, July 1952, RG 407, NARA II. Lt. Gen. Paul W. Kendall commanded the Eighty-Eighth Infantry Division in Italy from September 1944 to June 1945. He was awarded the Distinguished Service Cross and three Silver Stars for gallantry. Lt. Gen. Paul W. Kendall, General Officer Biography, USACMH.

60. Stephens, *Old Ugly Hill*, 119–20.

61. Division Chief of Staff Journal, July 19, 2nd Infantry Division Command Report, July 1952, RG 407, NARA II.

62. Second Infantry Division Command Report, Narrative Section I, 7, July 1952, Record Group 407, NARA II.

63. Division Chief of Staff Journal, July 20, 2nd Infantry Division Command Report, July 1952, RG 407, NARA II.

64. Division Chief of Staff Journal, July 20, 2nd Infantry Division Command Report, July 1952, RG 407, NARA II.

65. Eighth Army Command Report, July 1952, Narrative Section I, 73, Record Group 407, NARA II.

66. 23rd Infantry Regiment Command Report, July 1952, 15–16, RG 407, NARA II; Division Chief of Staff Journal, July 21, 2nd Infantry Division Command Report, July 1952, RG 407, NARA II.

67. Division Chief of Staff Journal, July 22, 2nd Infantry Division Command Report, July 1952, RG 407, NARA II.

68. Burns affidavit, 3; 23rd Infantry Regiment Command Report, July 1952, 18, RG 407, NARA II. Even though Garrett had been de facto in control of the battle, Mergens had retained both his position as commander and a place at the regimental command post. A day after the incident of the combat refusal, however, Fry ordered Mergens out of the regiment's area and sent both him and Burns to Eighth Army headquarters. Division Chief of Staff Journal, July 23, 2nd Infantry Division Command Report, July 1952, RG 407, NARA II.

69. Division Chief of Staff Journal, July 22, 2nd Infantry Division Command Report, July 1952, RG 407, NARA II.

70. Division Chief of Staff Journal, July 23, 2nd Infantry Division Command Report, July 1952, RG 407, NARA II.

71. UNC Command Report No. 50, 16–31 July 1952, 3, Clark Papers, CAM;

2nd Infantry Division Command Report, July 1952, 8, RG 407, NARA II. The summer monsoon began on July 25 and dumped more than two feet of rain over the
next three days. Small runoff streams soon became raging torrents that washed away
supply routes, flooded fighting positions, and caused bunker cave-ins. The destruction
wrought by Mother Nature was almost as devastating as that caused by the Chinese.
Gonsalves, *Battle at the 38th Parallel*, 42–43. The monsoon also put a cap on what was
going to be a significantly high level of incoming artillery fire. Eighth Army reported
169,271 shells landing on or around the OPLR and MLR during the first three weeks
of July before heavy rains so reduced visibility and ground action that the communist gunners virtually ceased firing. By comparison, communist artillery fired 110,595
rounds in May and 205,300 in June. Eighth Army Command Report, July 1952, Section I, 40, 43, RG 407, NARA II.

72. 23rd Infantry Regiment Command Report, July 1952, 20, RG 407, NARA II.

73. Stephens, *Old Ugly Hill*, 116–18. General Fry jubilantly reported to Kendall that the Chinese were "pretty well licked." Division Chief of Staff Journal, July 1
(actual date is August 1, but record is mislabeled and filed with the July journal), 2nd
Infantry Division Command Report, July 1952, RG 407, NARA II.

74. 2nd Infantry Division Command Report, July 1952, 9, RG 407, NARA II;
UNC Command Report No. 51, 3, Clark Papers, CAM; Stephens, *Old Ugly Hill*, 152.

75. See Eighth Army Command Report, July 1952, 79–81, RG 407, NARA II, for
description of these raids, their composition, action, and results.

76. Yang, "Command Experience in Korea," 162.

77. Jensen, *A War (Love) Story*, 407, 412–21; Pat Meid and James M. Yingling, *US
Marine Operations in Korea, 1950–1953*, vol. 5, *Operations in West Korea* (Washington, DC: US Government Printing Office, 1972), 111–38.

78. Johnston, *War of Patrols*, 291.

79. UNC Command Report No. 53, 1–15 September 1952, 3, Clark Papers, CAM.

80. Hermes, *Truce Tent and Fighting Front*, 296.

Chapter 11

1. UNC Command Report No. 54, 16–30 September 1952, 8, Clark Papers, CAM.

2. Yang, "Command Experience in Korea," 166–67; Academy of Military Science,
"Unforgotten Korean War," 593–96.

3. Yang, "Command Experience in Korea," 168; Academy of Military Science,
"Unforgotten Korean War," 597–98.

4. Paik, *Pusan to Panmunjom*, 207; KIMH, *KW*, 3:476–80; Academy of Military
Science, "Unforgotten Korean War," 599; Russell, *Stalemate and Standoff*, 69–72.

5. Academy of Military Science, "Unforgotten Korean War," 603.

6. Academy of Military Science, "Unforgotten Korean War," 604.

7. Russell, *Stalemate and Standoff*, 74–75; Academy of Military Science, "Unforgotten Korean War," 604; Headquarters, IX Corps, Special After Action Report, Hill
395 (White Horse Mountain) 6-15, October 1952, 3–4, Ninth Corps, Book IV, Parts
1–3, October 1952, RG 407, NARA II. Hereafter referred to as IX Corps Special AAR.

8. KIMH, *KW*, 3:458–64, summarizes the Korean action on White Horse Mountain. Scarce mention, though, is given to the invaluable US support (material and psychological), and there is little analysis as to why the ROK Ninth Division fought as well as it did against overwhelming Chinese numbers.

9. David A. Hatch with Robert Louis Benson, *The Korean War: The SIGINT Background* (Center for Cryptologic History, National Security Agency, January 2009). By October 1952 fifteen LLI teams were in operation.

10. IX Corps Special AAR, 6.

11. KMAG Command Report, October 1952, Annex F-50, ROK 9th Division, 6, 87, RG 407, NARA II. The officer was Lt. Paul F. Braner, a FO in the 213th FA Battalion, stationed on OP Roger (Hill 284). Anthony J. Sobieski, ed., *Fire Mission!* (Fairfield, CA: First Book Library, 2003), 75.

12. KIMH, *KW*, 3:458–60; KMAG Command Report, October 1952, Annex F-50, ROK 9th Division, 88, RG 407, NARA II.

13. Anthony Sobieski, *A Hill Called White Horse* (Bloomington, IN: Author House, 2009), 2, 7, 17–18.

14. Sobieski, *A Hill Called White Horse*, 10–11.

15. IX Corps Special AAR, 4–5, 29–30; Sobieski, *A Hill Called White Horse*, 29–30, 74; Russell, *Stalemate and Standoff*, 78.

16. Sobieski, *A Hill Called White Horse*, 35–40, 42–44, 54.

17. IX Corps Special AAR, 8.

18. IX Corps Special AAR, 40.

19. KMAG Command Report, October 1952, Annex F-50, ROK 9th Division, 10–11, RG 407, NARA II. For the period of October 3–4, ROK troops counted 117 rounds landing on Hill 395; on October 5 the daily average doubled to 132, and in only six and one-half hours on October 6 (0600–1230) the total spiked by almost ten times, to 1,291 rounds. Six hours later, just as the Chinese infantry began their attack, more than 3,300 rounds had hit the Koreans' positions. KMAG Command Report, October 1952, Annex F-50, ROK 9th Division, 7, 8–10, 89, RG 407, NARA II.

20. Academy of Military Science, "Unforgotten Korean War," 605; KIMH, *KW*, 3:460; IX Corps Special AAR, 9. The French Battalion defended Hill 281 for four days, which prevented the Chinese from enveloping White Horse from the west. Mark M. Boatner, "The French Battalion at Arrowhead, Korea—October 1952," GEOG V Korea 370.22 Hill 281, USACMH.

21. Boatner, "French Battalion," 148.

22. KIMH, *KW*, 3:460; Academy of Military Science, "Unforgotten Korean War," 605; Sobieski, *A Hill Called White Horse*, 93–95.

23. Lt. Adams's brush with the Chinese comes from Sobieski, *A Hill Called White Horse*, 102–18.

24. Sobieski, *A Hill Called White Horse*, 119–31. Adams was evacuated immediately after his ordeal, but Callaway stayed on OP Roger for several more days. It was not until after the battle was over that the two lieutenants enjoyed an emotional reunion.

25. Sobieski, *A Hill Called White Horse*, 138–47; KIMH, *KW*, 3:460–62.

26. KMAG Command Report, October 1952, Annex F-50, ROK 9th Division, 15, RG 407, NARA II.

27. KMAG Command Report, October 1952, Annex F-50, ROK 9th Division, 91, RG 407, NARA II; Academy of Military Science, "Unforgotten Korean War," 605; KIMH, *KW*, 3:462–63.

28. KMAG Command Report, October 1952, Annex F-50, ROK 9th Division, 22, RG 407, NARA II.

29. KMAG Command Report, October 1952, Annex F-50, ROK 9th Division, 29, RG 407, NARA II. KMAG officers reported that from 0001 to 0400 on the ninth, 2,149 shells fell on the hill and were the primary reason for the Korean withdrawal. KMAG Command Report, October 1952, Annex F-50, ROK 9th Division, 92–93, RG 407, NARA II.

30. Russell, *Stalemate and Standoff*, 84–85; Academy of Military Science, "Unforgotten Korean War," 605; KIMH, *KW*, 3:463; KMAG Command Report, October 1952, Annex F-50, ROK 9th Division, 94, RG 407, NARA II; IX Corps Special AAR, 34.

31. The 140th Tank Battalion was organic (assigned) to the Fortieth Infantry Division, which was in corps reserve. It was customary for divisions in reserve to place their artillery, tank, and engineer assets at the corps's disposal.

32. KMAG Command Report, October 1952, Annex F-50, ROK 9th Division, 94, RG 407, NARA II; Russell, *Stalemate and Standoff*, 91–93.

33. KMAG Command Report, October 1952, Annex F-50, ROK 9th Division, 96, RG 407, NARA II.

34. KIMH, *KW*, 3:463; Associated Press, "Allies Recapture 'Triangle' Summit," *New York Times*, October 15, 1952; KMAG Command Report, October 1952, Annex F-50, ROK 9th Division, 98, RG 407, NARA II.

35. KMAG Command Report, October 1952, Annex F-50, ROK 9th Division, 59, RG 407, NARA II.

36. IX Corps Special AAR, 20.

37. Academy of Military Science, "Unforgotten Korean War," 605.

38. Maj. Mark Boatner, the Twenty-Third Infantry Regiment operations officer, recognized "we could not hold Whitehorse without also holding Arrowhead." Boatner, "French Battalion," 142–43.

39. Academy of Military Science, "Unforgotten Korean War," 605.

40. KMAG Command Report, October 1952, Annex F-50, ROK 9th Division, 59, 104, 106–7, RG 407, NARA II.

41. IX Corps Special AAR, 6–7, 29, 31–32.

42. IX Corps Special AAR, 32, 36.

43. KMAG Command Report, October 1952, Annex F-50, ROK 9th Division, 61, 109, RG 407, NARA II; KIMH, *KW*, 3:464.

44. Academy of Military Science, "Unforgotten Korean War," 606.

45. Academy of Military Science, "Unforgotten Korean War," 606–7.

46. Academy of Military Science, "Unforgotten Korean War," 607.

47. IX Corps Special AAR, 24. The average number of Chinese artillery shells (not mortars) in the previous thirty days was 244 per twenty-four-hour period.

48. Johnston, *War of Patrols*, 330.

49. Yang, "Command Experience in Korea," 151–52.

50. UNC Command Report No. 55, 1–15 October 1952, 8, Clark Papers, CAM.

51. James A. Van Fleet to J. Lawton Collins, September 26, 1952, Folder 3 Jan–Dec 1952, Box 8 Correspondence 1951, Jan–1953, Jun., Clark Papers, CAM.

52. The Commander in Chief, United Nations Command to the Joint Chiefs of Staff, September 29, 1952, *FRUS, 1952–1954*, 15:548–49.

53. Clark, *From the Danube to the Yalu*, 117.

54. Headquarters, United Nations Command, Public Information Officer, October 8, 1952, Press Release Statement, Folder 3 Jan–Dec 1952, Box 8 Correspondence 1951, Jan–1953, Jun., Clark Papers, CAM; Collins, *War in Peacetime*, 348–50.

55. The Chronology of the Korean Campaign, 1 July–31 December 1952, 18, GEOG V Korea, USACMH. Although the UNC delegate left Panmunjom, liaison officers remained in place for the duration of the recess. The President to the Commander in Chief, Far East, September 26, 1952, and the Commander in Chief, United Nations Command to the Joint Chiefs of Staff, September 28, October 8, 1952, *FRUS, 1952–1954*, 15:544–57.

56. US Department of State *Bulletin*, October 20, 1952, 600.

57. Rosemary Foot, *A Substitute for Victory* (Ithaca, NY: Cornell University Press, 1990), 150.

58. Vatcher, *Panmunjom*, 167; Collins, *War in Peacetime*, 323–24.

Chapter 12

1. A version of this chapter was previously published as "The Battle of Shangganling, Korea, October–November 1952," *Journal of Chinese Military History* 6, no. 1 (2017): 53–89. https://brill.com/page/RightsPermissions/rights-and-permissions.

2. Lloyd R. Moses Daily Journal, 213, Journal-Correspondence/Memorabilia, Lloyd R. Moses Papers, USAHEC; Moses, *Whatever It Takes*, 206.

3. Malkasian, "Toward a Better Understanding of Attrition," 925.

4. Maj. Gen. Lyman L. Lemnitzer, commanding the Seventh Infantry Division during the summer of 1952, had disapproved a plan to attack Hill 598, believing the likely US casualties were a poor exchange for a vulnerable outpost. Donnelly, "A Damn Hard Job," 173–74, 174n72.

5. KIMH, *KW*, 3:416–18; Clark, *From the Danube to the Yalu*, 78.

6. Eighth Army, The Employment and Effectiveness of the Artillery, 39, 43, USAHEC.

7. Clark, *From the Danube to the Yalu*, 100–101.

8. Clark, *From the Danube to the Yalu*, 78–79.

9. Academy of Military Science, "Unforgotten Korean War," 596

10. Academy of Military Science, "Unforgotten Korean War," 609; Yang, "Command Experience in Korea," 171–72.

11. Stephens, *Old Ugly Hill*, 70–71; Sobieski, *Fire Mission!*, 42.

12. Richard Ecker, *Friendly Fire* (Clarendon Hills, IL: Omega Communications, 1996), 4–5.

13. Russell, *Stalemate and Standoff*, 37.

14. KIMH, *KW*, 3:466.

15. Academy of Military Science, "Unforgotten Korean War," 612, 627. Captain Zheng Yanman, a company commander in the 134th Regiment, had a map depicting three tree-shaped tunnel systems, twenty to thirty feet below ground level. Each tunnel connected to eight side tunnels, like tree branches. From these tunnels the Chinese soldiers stockpiled supplies, cared for their wounded, and staged for attacks. Peters and Li, *Voices from the Korean War*, 174.

16. Academy of Military Science, "Unforgotten Korean War," 613; Yang, "Command Experience in Korea," 172.

17. Zhang Songshan, *Tanpai: Zhengduo Shangganling jishi* [The showdown: The true story of the Battle of Shangganling] (Nanjing: Jiangsu renmin chubanshe, 1998), 86–94; China National Defense University, *Zhongguo renmin zhiyuanjun zhanshi jianbian* [A concise history of the CPVF warfighting] (Beijing: Jiefangjun chubanshe, 1992), 128–30.

18. Moses Daily Journal, 202, Moses Papers, USAHEC.

19. Moses, *Whatever It Takes*, 208, 213.

20. James A. Van Fleet to Mark W. Clark, October 5, 1952, Box 87, Folder 36, Van Fleet Papers, GCMLA.

21. Headquarters, IX US Corps, October 9, 1952, Operation Plan 32 (OPLAN 32), Ninth Corps G-3, Book V, October 1952, RG 409, NARA II. Hereafter referred to as OPLAN 32.

22. OPLAN 32, KIMH, *KW*, 3:466.

23. Van Fleet to Clark, October 5, 1952, Van Fleet Papers, GCMLA.

24. Annex 2 (Artillery and Air) to OPLAN 32; KIMH, *KW* 3:467.

25. Werrell, *Archie, Flak, AAA, and SAM*, 80.

26. Reuben E. Jenkins to James A. Van Fleet, 2nd Indorsement, Deviation from Corps Directive in the Execution of Operation Showdown, October 24, 1952, Box 87, Folder 36, Van Fleet Papers, GCMLA.

27. UNC Command Report No. 55, 1–15 October 1952, 10, Clark Papers, CAM.

28. Headquarters, 7th Infantry Division Command Report, October 1952, Annex 2 "Close Air Support for 'Operation Showdown,'" 64–65, RG 407, NARA II; Stewart, *Airpower*, 96.

29. 7th Infantry Division Command Report, October 1952, 1, RG 407, NARA II.

30. Donnelly, "The Best Army That Can Be Put into the Field," 825.

31. Clark, *From the Danube to the Yalu*, 192.

32. Moses, *Whatever It Takes*, 222–24.

33. 7th Infantry Division Command Report, October 1952, 3, RG 407, NARA II.

34. Moses, *Whatever It Takes*, 215–18.

35. Headquarters, 7th Infantry Division, Command Report, October 1952, Annex 2 "Operation Showdown," 33–33c, RG 409, NARA II; Moses, *Whatever It Takes*, 219.

36. Van Fleet to Clark, October 5, 1952, Van Fleet Papers, GCMLA.

37. KIMH, *KW*, 3:466–69; Headquarters, KMAG (2nd ROK Division), Command Report, 1–31 October 1952, Enclosure 2 (Extract G2/G3 Journal), Annex F-44 to KMAG Command Report, October 1952, RG 407, NARA II.

38. 7th Infantry Division Command Report, October 1952, "Operation Showdown," 34–35, RG 407, NARA II.

39. *Direct lay* refers to the artillery technique to sight a gun visually rather than relying on a separate forward observer. The advantage of greater accuracy and precision is compensated by a reduction in rate of fire and concentration of multiple guns on a single target.

40. Ecker, *Friendly Fire*, 63, 75.

41. Peter R. Johnston, "Attack on Triangle Hill," *Military History* 22, no. 10 (January/February 2006): 57.

42. Moses, *Whatever It Takes*, 221.

43. Public Information Officer, *Bayonet: The History of the 7th Infantry Division in Korea* (Dai Nippon Printing, 1953). Hereafter, PIO, 7ID, *Bayonet*. White, *Triangle Hill*, 121, 123.

44. Colonel Isbell was detailed to the Quartermaster Corps for seven years, 1939 to 1946. During World War II he commanded the Twenty-Seventh Quartermaster Truck Regiment in England, followed by duty as Assistant Chief of Transportation, European Theater of Operations from 1944 to 1946. In Korea, he served as the Seventh Infantry Division's Inspector General from April 1952 to September 1952, when he finally got back to his artillery roots. Association of Graduates United States Military Academy, Obituary—William Harris Isbell Jr., *Assembly* (January/February 1996): 156.

45. PIO, 7ID, *Bayonet*; Entry for William H. Isbell, Find-a-Grave.com, www.findagrave.com/cgi-bin/fg.cgi?page=gr&GRid=49263945. Accessed January 24, 2015. A native of Maryland, Colonel Isbell was posthumously awarded the Distinguished Service Cross for his gallantry on Triangle Hill.

46. Richard Ecker, "Showdown on Triangle Hill," *Veterans of Foreign Wars* (September 2002): 2. Johnston, "Attack on Triangle Hill," 58.

47. Yang, "Command Experience in Korea," 171, 173; Academy of Military Science, "Unforgotten Korean War," 613.

48. Moses, *Whatever It Takes*, 222.

49. 7th Infantry Division Command Report, October 1952, "Operation Showdown," 35, RG 407, NARA II. Although American sources refer to artillery, the Chinese sources suggest that CPVF artillery had not yet entered the battle: "The two battalions of the 135th Regiment had to rely on pure infantry weapons and equipment." Academy of Military Science, "Unforgotten Korean War," 614.

50. Moses, *Whatever It Takes*, 223; 7th Infantry Division Command Report, October 1952, "Operation Showdown," 36, RG 407, NARA II. Lieutenant Schowalter was awarded the Medal of Honor for his actions on Triangle Hill. He spent the remainder of the war recuperating from his wounds.

51. Moses, *Whatever It Takes*, 224; IX Corps Command Report, October 1952, 23, RG 407, NARA II; 7th Infantry Division Command Report, October 1952, "Opera-

tion Showdown," 36, RG 407, NARA II; Academy of Military Science, "Unforgotten Korean War," 616.

52. KMAG (2nd ROK Division), Command Report, G2/G3 Journal Extract, 14 October, RG 407, NARA II.

53. White, *Triangle Hill*, 184–85, 188.

54. Russell, *Stalemate and Standoff*, 102; Academy of Military Science, "Unforgotten Korean War," 616; KIMH, *KW*, 3:467–69; IX Corps Command Report, October 1952, 24, RG 407, NARA II. The ROK Second Division's senior advisor noted that over one thousand artillery and mortar rounds were used to support the Chinese counterattack—ten times the daily enemy average for indirect fire support. KMAG (2nd ROK Division), Command Report, G2/G3 Journal Extract, 14 October, RG 407, NARA II.

55. "You know I have felt for sometime [*sic*] the inadvisability of offensive action even of a limited nature unless the plans for the forces involved were in sufficient force to ensure success." Clark to Van Fleet, TEK 88, October 15, 1952, Subject Files, Operations and Personnel, Box 84, Folder 30, Van Fleet Papers, GCMLA.

56. Van Fleet to Clark re TEK 88, 2, October 15, 1951, Van Fleet Papers, GCMLA.

57. Wayne C. Smith to Reuben E. Jenkins, 1st Indorsement, Deviation from Corps Directive in Execution of Operation "Showdown," October 22, 1952, Box 87, Folder 36, Van Fleet Papers, GCMLA.

58. 7th Infantry Division Command Report, October 1952, 6–7, 10, RG 407, NARA II; Van Fleet to Clark re TEK 88, 3, October 15, 1951, Van Fleet Papers, GCMLA; Moses, *Whatever It Takes*, 224–25.

59. Academy of Military Science, "Unforgotten Korean War," 616.

60. Yang, "Command Experience in Korea," 173.

61. Moses, *Whatever It Takes*, 224–25.

62. Moses, *Whatever It Takes*, 225.

63. Thomas Martin, Oral History, September 13, 2001, National Guard Militia Museum of New Jersey, Department of Military and Veterans Affairs.

64. Johnston, "Attack on Triangle Hill," 59.

65. Moses, *Whatever It Takes*, 226–28.

66. White, *Triangle Hill*, 123.

67. 7th Infantry Division Command Report, October 1952, "Operation Showdown," 39–41, RG 407, NARA II. Colonel Moses was awarded a Silver Star (later upgraded to a Distinguished Service Cross) for his direction of the battle from October 14 to 16, when the regiment was relieved by the Thirty-Second Infantry. Moses, *Whatever It Takes*, 245.

68. Associated Press, "Allies Recapture 'Triangle' Summit," *New York Times*, October 15, 1952; Peters and Li, *Voices from the Korean War*, 175.

69. Guadalupe A. Martinez, "The Colombians' Role in the Battle for Triangle Hill (Hill 598)," *Graybeards* 23, no. 1 (January–February 2009): 30–31.

70. Yang, *For the Sake of Peace*, 190–92.

71. White, *Triangle Hill*, 123.

72. White, *Triangle Hill*, 123–24; IX Corps Command Report, October 1952, 25, RG 407, NARA II; PIO, 7ID, *Bayonet*; 7th Infantry Division Command Report, October 1952, "Operation Showdown," 42–43, 48, RG 407, NARA II.

73. Bloodworth, *Chinese Looking Glass*, 326.

74. Peters and Li, *Voices from the Korean War*, 173; Gonsalves, *Battle at the 38th Parallel*, 79.

75. IX Corps Command Report, October 1952, 25, RG 407, NARA II; 7th Infantry Division Command Report, October 1952, "Operation Showdown," 43–45, 48, RG 407, NARA II; Martin Oral History.

76. A smaller force also attacked Company G of the Seventeenth Infantry defending Jane Russell Hill. Although the Chinese managed to occupy the easternmost knoll, an American counterattack supported with artillery drove the Chinese back by dawn on October 20. Headquarters, Eighth United States Army, Military History Detachment, Chinese Counterattack on Hill Jane Russell, 1953, USACMH.

77. Millett, *Their War for Korea*, 239–41.

78. Johnston, "Attack on Triangle Hill," 60.

79. Yang, "Command Experience in Korea," 175.

80. 7th Infantry Division Command Report, October 1952, 10, RG 407, NARA II.

81. Yang, *For the Sake of Peace*, 195–96.

82. Entry October 15, 1952, James A. Van Fleet Journal, Commanding General, Eighth Army, Van Fleet Papers, GCMLA.

83. IX Corps Command Report, October 1952, 24, RG 407, NARA II; KIMH, *KW*, 3:469; KMAG (2nd ROK Division), Command Report, G2/G3 Journal Extract, 15–16 October, RG 407, NARA II.

84. KMAG (2nd ROK Division), Command Report, G2/G3 Journal Extract, 17–18 October, RG 407, NARA II.

85. KMAG (2nd ROK Division), Command Report, G1/4 Journal Extract, 18 October, RG 407, NARA II.

86. KMAG (2nd ROK Division), Command Report, G2/G3 Journal Extract, 19 October, RG 407, NARA II.

87. Academy of Military Science, "Unforgotten Korean War," 617.

88. UNC Command Report No. 56, 16–31 October 1952, Clark Papers, CAM.

89. Peters and Li, *Voices from the Korean War*, 179–81. Chinese troops concealed in bunkers and tunnels continued to harass the Americans with long-range machine gun fire and occasional sorties. Headquarters Eighth Army, Military History Detachment, Chinese Counterattack on Hill Jane Russell, 1953, Tab B Interview with Captain Howard A. Smith, S-3, 2nd Battalion, 17th Infantry Regiment, 1 and Tab C Interview with Lt. Thomas H. Maddox, Company Commander, 3, USACMH.

90. Yang, "Command Experience in Korea," 177.

91. Zhang, *Mao's Military Romanticism*, 230. Deng Hua also dispatched the 610th Anti-Aircraft Artillery Regiment and one engineer battalion to the Fifteenth Army. Academy of Military Science, "Unforgotten Korean War," 618–19.

92. White, *Triangle Hill*, 161.

93. 7th Infantry Division Command Report, October 1952, "Operation Show-down," 60, 62, RG 407, NARA II; IX Corps Command Report, October 1952, 26, RG 407, NARA II.

94. Clark, *From the Danube to the Yalu*, 79.

95. IX Corps Command Report, October 1952, 26–27, RG 407, NARA II; KIMH, *KW*, 3:470. KMAG reported on October 25 that the Chinese fired 26,429 artillery rounds in the fighting for Sniper Ridge, a sixfold increase over the previous week's daily average. KMAG (2nd ROK Division), Command Report, G2/G3 Journal Extract, 25 October, RG 407, NARA II.

96. Yang, "Command Experience in Korea," 177–78.

97. Academy of Military Science, "Unforgotten Korean War," 620; Yang, "Command Experience in Korea," 179; PIO UNC, The Chronology of the Korean Campaign, 1 July–31 December 1952, 24, USACMH.

98. Associated Press, "Reds Seize Triangle Hill and Cut Off One UN Unit," *Washington Post*, October 31, 1952.

99. IX Corps Command Report, October 1952, 27, 65, RG 407, NARA II; KMAG (2nd ROK Division), Command Report, G2/G3 Journal Extract, 26–31 October, RG 407, NARA II.

100. Lt. William J. White claimed to be the last American soldier to leave Triangle Hill after a hasty orientation to the Korean troops that relieved him and his company. The battle handover was apparently not well coordinated below the division level, with the expected consequences that the Koreans did not gain the necessary appreciation for the terrain or the enemy's tactical techniques employed in the Seventh Division's zone. If White's account is accurate, it represents gross negligence of American leadership on Triangle Hill. White, *Triangle Hill*, 122, 168–69, 172.

101. Lindsey Parrott, "Allies Pull Back in 'Triangle' Fight for Korean Hilltop," *New York Times*, November 1, 1952.

102. IX Corps Command Report, October 1952, 26, RG 407, NARA II; KIMH, *KW*, 3:470.

103. Associated Press, "Reds Seize Triangle Hill and Cut Off One UN Unit," *Washington Post*, October 31, 1952.

104. Yang, "Command Experience in Korea," 179.

105. Lindsey Parrott, "Red Shells Repel 3 Korean Attacks up 'Triangle Hill,'" *New York Times*, November 4, 1952.

106. Academy of Military Science, "Unforgotten Korean War," 620–21; Van Fleet also wanted to guard Chung's reputation by promoting him to the corps level while the ROKs could claim some success in Showdown. Most importantly, though, for Van Fleet was his intention that Chung take command of the ROK II Corps in the spring of 1953. In this capacity Chung was responsible for confronting the largest and last Chinese offensives just before the armistice ended the conflict.

107. Yang, "Command Experience in Korea," 180.

108. Headquarters, IX Corps Command Report, November 1952, 13–14, RG 409, NARA II; KIMH, *KW*, 3:470. Ironically, William White found himself as a liaison officer to the ROK Thirtieth Regiment. White learned to appreciate the ROK soldiers'

fighting qualities, noting their attention to mimic US practices and their superior skills at night fighting, outpost operations, and prisoner snatching. White, *Triangle Hill*, 187–88.

109. "Destruction" is a task rarely assigned because of the inordinate amount of ammunition required. Van Fleet also began recasting his objective from the seizure of key terrain to "chewing up" Chinese infantry. "We occupy all the territory we want to occupy," he told his subordinates as he noted that Chinese casualties for the month of October were assessed as greater than any month since November 1951, and as he planned to shift offensive efforts from infantry assaults to artillery strikes. Parrott, "Red Shells Repel 3 Korean Attacks."

110. James A. Van Fleet to Mark W. Clark, November 3, 1952, Subject Files Operations and Planning, Box 84, Folder 30, Van Fleet Papers, GCMLA; Sobieski, *Fire for Effect*, 158.

111. David W. Gray to James A. Van Fleet, Operations Report G31040, November 12, 1952, and Special Operations Report #5, November 26, 1952, Subject Files, Special Operations Reports and Training #1–6, 1953, Box 87, Folder 10, Van Fleet Papers, GCMLA.

112. Academy of Military Science, "Unforgotten Korean War," 621; Yang, "Command Experience in Korea," 181.

113. Headquarters, KMAG (2nd ROK Division), Command Report, 1–30 November 1952, Enclosure 2 (Extract G2/G3 Journal), 11–17 November, Annex F-44 to KMAG Command Report, November 1952, RG 407, NARA II; KIMH, *KW*, 3:471–72.

114. UNC Command Report No. 58, 16–30 November 1952, 2, Clark Papers, CAM. The daily average of Chinese artillery fell to 9,000 rounds, 2,000 fewer than in the first half of the month, and the trend continued to decline as the month ended.

115. KIMH, *KW*, 3:506.

116. Stephens, *Old Ugly Hill*, 94.

117. KMAG (2nd ROK Division), Command Report, G2/G3 Journal Extract, 18–25 November, RG 407, NARA II; IX Corps Command Report, November 1952, 12, RG 407, NARA II; Academy of Military Science, "The Unforgotten Korean War," 622–25; UNC Command Report No. 59, 1–15 December 1952, 2, Clark Papers, CAM.

118. Clark, *From the Danube to the Yalu*, 79.

119. Ecker, *Friendly Fire*, 129.

120. As with all battles, casualty reports are inconsistent and there are discrepancies in accounting for killed and wounded in the reports of the various echelons. The Korean official history records 1,096 killed, 3,496 wounded, and 97 missing while the KMAG senior advisor reported 1,483 killed, 4,681 wounded, and 228 missing. On the US side, the corps G-1 reported 187 killed, 1,413 wounded, and 67 missing. Soldiers finally accounted as missing in action were most likely killed and never recovered. Nonbattle losses added another two thousand soldiers to the casualty rolls. KIMH, *KW*, 3:472; IX Corps Command Report, October 1952, 87; KMAG (2nd ROK Division), Command Reports, October–November 1952.

121. Gonsalves, *Battle at the 38th Parallel*, 137.

122. Johnston, "Attack on Triangle Hill," 60.

123. Academy of Military Science, "Unforgotten Korean War," 626. Another Chinese participant assessed the Fifteenth Army lost 11,400 soldiers on Triangle Hill alone. Peters and Li, *Voices from the Korean War*, 184.

124. KIMH, *KW*, 3:472–73.

125. KMAG (2nd ROK Division), Command Report, October–November 1952. The ROK Second Division received 2,282 new soldiers between October 14 and the end of the month; 3,600 were received in November.

126. IX Corps Command Report, October 1952, 85; KMAG (2nd ROK Division), Command Report, October 1952.

127. 7th Infantry Division Command Report, October 1952, "Operation Showdown," 33c, RG 407, NARA II.

128. Ecker, *Friendly Fire*, 227; UNC Command Report No. 56, 16–31 October 1952, 5, Clark Papers, CAM.

129. Yang, "Command Experience in Korea," 182.

130. Academy of Military Science, "Unforgotten Korean War," 626–27.

131. Quoted in Zhang, *Mao's Military Romanticism*, 232.

132. Ecker, *Friendly Fire*, 228–29.

133. KIMH, *KW*, 3:473; Ecker, "Showdown on Triangle Hill," 3.

134. Moses, *Whatever It Takes*, 237.

135. Russell, *Stalemate and Standoff*, 103.

Chapter 13

1. Clark, *From the Danube to the Yalu*, 69.

2. Letter, September 27, 1952, Commanding General X Corps, "Observations Made by an Experienced Division Commander," X Corps AG Section, General Correspondence, RG 338, NARA II; Clark, *From the Danube to the Yalu*, 190–92; Sullivan, *Toy Soldiers*, 61–63.

3. 7th Infantry Command Report, October 1952, 71–77, RG 407, NARA II.

4. Stephens, *Old Ugly Hill*, 94.

5. Enlisted men appreciated this kind of caution, which was born of the belief that stalemate did not deserve another dead American soldier. Stephens, *Old Ugly Hill*, 128.

6. James A. Van Fleet to Willis D. Crittenberger, September 28, 1952, File 22, Box 68, Van Fleet Papers, GCMLA.

7. James A. Van Fleet to Lyman L. Lemnitzer, January 17, 1953, File 26, Box 70, Van Fleet Papers, GCMLA.

8. Kaufman, *Korean War*, 303.

9. General Bradley was "stunned" when he heard of Eisenhower's pronouncement, as "Ike was well informed on all aspects of the Korean War and the delicacy of the armistice negotiations. He knew very well that he could achieve nothing by going to Korea." Bradley also worried that the president-elect's presence in Korea could undermine the UNC's position at Panmunjom. "It was pure show biz," he judged. Bradley and Blair, *General's Life*, 656. For an analysis of the 1952 US presidential campaign and Korea's place in it, see Steven Casey, *Selling the Korean War: Propaganda,*

Politics, and Public Opinion in the United States, 1950–1953 (New York: Oxford University Press, 2008), 325–36.

10. Schnabel and Watson, *Korean War*, 191–92.

11. Collins, *War in Peacetime*, 323–24.

12. United Nations Command, OPLAN 8-52, Annex C, 1–3, Entry P155 United Nations Command, J-3 Section, Formerly Top Secret Operations Plan 8-52, 1952, GHQ Far East Command, Supreme Commander Allied Powers and UN Command, RG 554, NARA II.

13. Collins, *War in Peacetime*, 324; Bradley and Blair, *General's Life*, 658. For the contemplated use of atomic weapons throughout the war, see Conrad C. Crane, "To Avert Impending Disaster: American Plans to Use Atomic Weapons during the Korean War," *Journal of Strategic Studies* 23, no. 2 (2000): 72–88.

14. The Commander in Chief, United Nations Command to the Joint Chiefs of Staff, September 29, 1952, *FRUS, 1952–1954*, 15:549.

15. United Nations Command, OPLAN 8-52, 1–5, Annex A, 4, Annex B, 1, 3–4, 6–7, Entry P155 United Nations Command, J-3 Section, Formerly Top Secret Operations Plan 8-52, 1952, RG 554, NARA II.

16. My critical analysis of OPLAN 8-52 derives from Clausewitz, *On War*, 71, 197, 204.

17. UNC OPLAN 8-52, Annex B, 1–2, RG 554, NARA II.

18. The intelligence estimate admitted that the Chinese expected and had prepared for a general UNC offensive, but they feared "a possible serious defeat." Therefore, the Americans expected the Communists to sue for the best negotiation terms they could get to avoid the "obviously" greater loss of face that battlefield defeat would inflict. Naturally, that would mean giving in on the voluntary repatriation principle. See UNC OPLAN 8-52, Annex B, 1–2, 6, 10–11, RG 554, NARA II.

19. Schnabel and Watson, *Korean War*, 193–94, 330 n49.

20. President Rhee personally extended the invitation to attend a "U.S. President-elect Eisenhower Welcome Rally" while Eisenhower was touring the Capital Division's front. According to Paik Sun-yup, Rhee refused to accept the rejection and waited for the Americans to change their minds. Putting the best face on a political disaster, Rhee went forward with his staged rally, without the Americans. Perhaps there was some symbolic message there. Paik, *Pusan to Panmunjom*, 215–16.

21. Dwight D. Eisenhower, *Mandate for Change, 1953–1956* (New York: Doubleday, 1963), 59.

22. Collins, *War in Peacetime*, 324; Kaufman, *Korean War*, 300–301. Eisenhower penned a letter to President Rhee expressing his appreciation and "genuine pleasure" at their meeting. Eisenhower was impressed by the ROK army and its pride, determination, and fighting skills. But, the president-elect gave no hint as to where future policy may lead. In fact, the obvious absence of commitment to expand the war or to overturn Truman's policy of negotiated settlement must have been a bitter pill for Rhee to swallow. Dwight D. Eisenhower to President Syngman Rhee, December 5, 1952 (copy), Folder 3 Jan–Dec 1952, Box 8 Correspondence 1951, Jan.–1953, Jun., Clark Papers, CAM.

23. Paik, *Pusan to Panmunjom*, 215; Schnabel and Watson, *Korean War*, 193, 197. After his retirement in February 1953, General Van Fleet never tired promoting the virtues of the Korean soldier and the ROK army that he had birthed between 1951 and 1953. See James A. Van Fleet, "25 Divisions for the Cost of One," *Reader's Digest*, February 1954, 3–7.

24. Memorandum, December 12, 1952, Eighth US Army Korea to Corps Commanders, Subject: Conduct of Operations, Folder 370, Headquarters Eighth Army Security Classified Correspondence, 1952, Records of the Eighth United States Army, RG 500, NARA II.

25. The Chronology of the Korean Campaign, 1 July–31 December 1952, 39, USACMH; UNC Command Report No. 60, 16–31 December 1952, 1–2, Clark Papers, CAM.

26. Dean Acheson, *The Korean War* (New York: W. W. Norton, 1971), 149; Schnabel and Watson, *Korean War*, 200–7.

27. Acheson, *Korean War*, 137–48.

28. Clark, *From the Danube to the Yalu*, 240–41; Bradley and Blair, *General's Life*, 661.

29. Li, "From Civil War Victory to Cold War Guard," 208; Xiaobing Li, "Military Stalemate," in *The Ashgate Research Companion to the Korean War*, ed. James I. Matray and Donald W. Boose Jr. (Burlington, VT: Ashgate, 2014), 390.

30. Donnelly, "The Best Army That Can Be Put into the Field," 844.

31. Lt. Gen. Reuben E. Jenkins, "Comments on Operations in Korea," October 6, 1953, Box 292, IX Corps General Correspondence, 1942–1954, RG 338, NARA II.

32. Joy, *How Communists Negotiate*, 118.

33. Stueck, *Rethinking the Korean War*, 152.

34. Joy, *How Communists Negotiate*, 128.

35. Joy, *How Communists Negotiate*, 128–29.

36. The Chronology of the Korean Campaign, 1 July–31 December 1952, 17, GEOG V Korea, USACMH.

37. Sobieski, *Fire Mission!*, 50.

38. Weyland, "Air Campaign in Korea," 30.

39. USAF Historical Study 127, 9.

40. Loving, *Bully Able Leader*, x.

41. Stueck, *Rethinking the Korean War*, 168.

42. Chinese records counted over 190,000 bombs dropped on North Korean railroads—one bomb for every seven meters of track. After White Horse Mountain, the CPVF kept a low strategic profile until June 1953, when it launched its last multiarmy offensives aimed at the ROK army. Zhang, *Red Wings*, 204.

43. Van Fleet, *Rail Transport*, 35.

44. See the very competent memoir of an American fighter-bomber pilot flying close support and interdiction missions during the war's first year: George C. Loving, *Bully Able Leader: The Story of a Fighter-Bomber Pilot in the Korean War* (Mechanicsburg, PA: Stackpole Books, 2011).

45. Carter, *Some Historical Notes on Air Interdiction in Korea*, 2; Loving, *Bully Able Leader*, 212.

46. Interdiction and armed reconnaissance missions accounted for 47.7 percent of the combat sorties flown by FEAF during the war. The remaining sorties were devoted to counter-air, close-support, reconnaissance, and strategic bombing missions. Carter, *Some Historical Notes on Air Interdiction in Korea*, 6.

47. Van Fleet, *Rail Transport*, 3.

48. Mark, *Aerial Interdiction*, 262; cf. Stewart, *Airpower*, iii, 30, and Momyer, *Airpower in Three Wars*, 172. Momyer asserts that "this freedom to target and to use airpower brought the war to an acceptable conclusion. Interdiction was the fundamental mission that pressured a settlement." A Rand analysis commissioned in 1966, at the height of interdiction in Vietnam, came to the same conclusion, but went even further. "To be effective, interdiction must be carried out against an enemy who is using his supplies at a high rate, i.e., an enemy continually fighting. In Korea, the enemy was allowed, in most cases, to initiate or break off contact at his option, so he could fight when he had supplies and rest when his supplies were low. Under conditions such as this, it would be virtually impossible to successfully interdict, i.e., to isolate the battlefield to the extent that the enemy is incapable of sustained offensive action." Carter, *Some Historical Notes on Air Interdiction in Korea*, 16–17.

49. Moses, *Whatever It Takes*, 189.

50. Peng, *Memoirs of a Chinese Marshal*, 484.

51. Corr, *Chinese Red Army*, 85–88.

52. Zhang, *Red Wings*, 139, 142.

53. Joy, *How Communists Negotiate*, 163.

54. Roger J. Spiller, ed., *S. L. A. Marshall at Leavenworth: Five Lectures at the U.S. Army Command and General Staff College* (Fort Leavenworth, KS: Combined Arms Center, 1980), 1:9.

55. Joy, *How Communists Negotiate*, 173.

BIBLIOGRAPHY

Archival and Manuscript Sources

The Citadel Archives and Museum, Charleston, South Carolina
Clark, Mark W. Papers.
O'Daniel, John W. Papers.

George C. Marshall Library and Archives, Lexington, Virginia
Van Fleet, James A. Papers.

Harry S. Truman Presidential Library and Museum, Independence, Missouri
E. Allan Lightner Oral History.
Truman, Harry S. Papers.

National Archives and Records Administration, College Park, Maryland
Record Group 218 Records of the Joint Chiefs of Staff.
Record Group 338 Records of US Army Operational, Tactical, and Support Organizations.
Record Group 407 Army–Adjutant General, Command Reports, 1949–54.
Record Group 500 Records of the Eighth United States Army.
Record Group 554 General Headquarters, Far East Command, Supreme Commander Allied Powers and UN Command.

United States Army Center of Military History, Fort Lesley J. McNair, Washington, DC
Boatner, Mark M. "The French Battalion at Arrowhead, Korea—October 1952," GEOG V Korea 370.22 Hill 281.
Department of the Army, Historical Branch Programs Division, Historical Survey of Army Fire Support, March 18, 1963.
Eighth United States Army in Korea After Action Reviews and Summaries.
General Officer Biographies.
Headquarters, Eighth United States Army Korea, Enemy Material, n.d.
Headquarters, Eighth United States Army Korea, Enemy Tactics to Include Guerrilla Methods and Activities, December 26, 1951.

Headquarters, Eighth United States Army Korea, Historical Section, "Heartbreak Ridge, September–October 1951, 2nd Division," n.d.

Headquarters, United States Army Pacific, Office of the G-3, Military History Office, The Handling of Prisoners of War during the Korean Conflict, June 1960.

Public Information Officer, United Nations Command, The Chronology of the Korean Campaign, 1 July–31 December 1952, GEOG V Korea File 314.76.

United States Army Heritage and Education Center, Carlisle, Pennsylvania

Boatner, Haydon L. Papers.

Command Report, Headquarters X Corps Artillery, December 1950–September 1951.

Conklin, Roy W. "Cease Fire: A Memoir of the Korean War."

Doyle, Daniel Papers.

Harrison, William K. Papers.

Headquarters, Eighth United States Army, Office of the Artillery Officer, A Study of the Employment and Effectiveness of the Artillery with the Eighth Army, October 1951–July 1953, 1954.

Headquarters, I Corps, Operation Commando.

Johnson, Harold K. Papers.

Moses, Lloyd R. Papers.

Richardson, William R. Papers.

Richie, Ellis B. Papers.

Ridgway, Matthew B. Papers.

Van Fleet, James A. Oral History.

Primary Sources

Acheson, Dean. *The Korean War*. New York: W. W. Norton, 1971.

———. *Present at the Creation*. New York: W. W. Norton, 1969.

Boatner, Mark M., III, "Countering Communist Artillery." *Army Combat Forces Journal* 4, no. 2 (September 1953): 25–27.

Bradley, Omar N., and Clay Blair. *A General's Life*. New York: Simon and Schuster, 1983.

Clark, Mark W. *Calculated Risk*. New York: Harper and Brothers, 1950.

———. *From the Danube to the Yalu*. New York: Harper and Brothers, 1954.

———. "The Truth about Korea." *Colliers* 133 (February 5, 1954): 34–39.

Collins, J. Lawton. *War in Peacetime: The History and Lessons of Korea*. Boston: Houghton Mifflin, 1969.

Craven, Virgil E. "Operation Touchdown Won Heartbreak Ridge." *Army Combat Forces Journal* 4, no. 5 (December 1953): 24–29.

Ecker, Richard. *Friendly Fire*. Clarendon Hills, IL: Omega Communications, 1996.

———. "Showdown on Triangle Hill." *Veterans of Foreign Wars* (September 2002): 34–35.

Eisenhower, Dwight D. *Mandate for Change, 1953–1956*. New York: Doubleday, 1963.

"Faithful to Our Trust." *Army Combat Forces Journal* 5, no. 5 (December 1954): 18–21.

Freedman, Sam. "Tankers at Heartbreak." *Armor* 61, no. 5 (September–October, 1952): 24–27.

Gonsalves, Joseph E. *Battle at the 38th Parallel: Surviving the Peace Talks at Panmunjom*. Central Point, OR: Hellgate Press, 2001.

Goodman, Allen, E., ed. *Negotiating While Fighting: The Diary of Admiral C. Turner Joy at the Korean Armistice Conference*. Stanford, CA: Hoover Institution Press, 1978.

Haarmeyer, Arthur L. *Into the Land of Darkness*. Self-published. Arthur L. Haarmeyer; prepared by the Donohue Group, 2013.

Hurh, Won-moo. *I Will Shoot Them from My Loving Heart*. Jefferson, NC: McFarland, 2012.

Jensen, Roy R. *A War (Love) Story: One Marine's Korean War*. Sioux Falls, SD: Pine Hill Press, 2000.

Johnston, Peter R. "Attack on Triangle Hill." *Military History* 22, no. 10 (January/February 2006): 54–60.

Joy, C. Turner. *How Communists Negotiate*. New York: Macmillan, 1955.

Li, Xiaobing, Allan R. Millett, and Bin Yu, trans. and eds. *Mao's Generals Remember Korea*. Lawrence: University Press of Kansas, 2001.

Loving, George C. *Bully Able Leader: The Story of a Fighter-Bomber Pilot in the Korean War*. Mechanicsburg, PA: Stackpole Books, 2011.

Mao Zedong, *Selected Military Writings of Mao Tse-tung*. Peking: Foreign Language Press, 1963.

Martin, Thomas. Oral History, September 13, 2001, National Guard Militia Museum of New Jersey, Department of Military and Veterans Affairs.

Moses, Lloyd R. *Whatever It Takes: The Autobiography of General Lloyd R. Moses*. Vermillion, SD: Dakota Press, 1991.

Nolan, John. *The Run-up to the Punchbowl: A Memoir of the Korean War, 1951*. Bloomington, IN: Xlibris, 2006.

Paik, Sun-yup. *From Pusan to Panmunjom*. Dulles, VA.: Brassey's, 1999.

Peng, Dehuai. *Memoirs of a Chinese Marshal*. Translated by Zheng Longpu. Beijing: Foreign Language Press, 1984. Reprint; Honolulu: University Press of the Pacific, 2005.

Peters, Richard, and Xiaobing Li, eds. *Voices from the Korean War*. Lexington: University Press of Kentucky, 2004.

Raschen, Dan. *Send Port and Pyjamas!* London: Buckland Publications, 1987.

Ridgway, Matthew B. *The Korean War*. Garden City, NY: Doubleday, 1967.

Stephens, Rudolph W. *Old Ugly Hill: A G.I.'s Fourteen Months in the Korean Trenches, 1952–1953*. Jefferson, NC: McFarland, 1995.

Sobieski, Anthony J., ed. *Fire for Effect: Artillery Forward Observers in Korea* Bloomington, IN: Author House, 2005.

———. *Fire Mission!* Fairfield, CA: First Book Publishing, 2003.

Sullivan, John A. *Toy Soldiers: Memoir of a Combat Platoon Leader in Korea*. Jefferson, NC: McFarland, 1991.

Truman, Harry S. *Memoirs*. Vol. 2, *Years of Trial and Hope*. Garden City, NY: Doubleday, 1956.

Van Fleet, James A. "The Truth about Korea: From a Man Now Free to Speak." *Life* 34, part 3, May 11, 1953, 127–42.

——. "25 Divisions for the Cost of One." *Reader's Digest* 64, no. 382, February 1954, 3–7.

Vatcher, William H. *Panmunjom: The Story of the Korean Military Armistice Negotiations.* New York: Frederick A. Praeger, 1958.

White, William J. *Triangle Hill.* Bloomington, IN: Xlibris, 2011.

Yang Dezhi, *Weile Heping [For the Sake of Peace].* Beijing: Long March Press, 1987. English language edition translated by Leo Kanner Associates, Dayton, OH: Defense Technical Information Center, Foreign Technology Division, 1989.

Y'Blood, William T., ed. *The Three Wars of Lt. Gen. George E. Stratemeyer: His Korean War Diary.* Washington, DC: Air Force History and Museums Program, 1999.

Zhang, Songshan. *Tanpai: Zhengduo Shangganling jishi* [The showdown: The true story of the Battle of Shangganling]. Nanjing: Jiangsu renmin chubanshe, 1998.

Official Publications and Collected Documents

Department of the Air Force. United States Air Force Statistical Digest—Fiscal Year 1953.

Department of the Army. Field Manual (FM) 7-40, *Infantry Regiment.* Washington, DC: US Government Printing Office, 1950.

Department of the Army. Field Manual (FM) 100-5, *Operations.* Washington, DC: US Government Printing Office, 1949.

Department of State Bulletin 27 (1952).

Department of State. *Foreign Relations of the United States, 1950.* Vol. 7, *Korea.* Washington, DC: US Government Printing Office, 1976.

——. *Foreign Relations of the United States, 1951.* Vol. 7, *Korea and China.* Washington, DC: US Government Printing Office, 1976.

——. *Foreign Relations of the United States, 1952–1954.* Vol. 15, *Korea.* Washington, DC: US Government Printing Office, 1984.

Joint Chiefs of Staff. *Dictionary of United States Military Terms for Joint Usage.* JCS Publication 1, Washington, DC, December 1, 1964.

Shen, Zhihua, trans. and ed. *Chaoxian zhanzheng: Eguo dang'anguan de jiemi wenjian* [The Korean War: Declassified documents from Russian archives]. Taipei, Taiwan: Central Research Institute Printing Office, 2003.

Tucker, Spencer C., ed. *Encyclopedia of the Korean War.* Vol. 3, *Documents.* Santa Barbara, CA: ABC-CLIO, 2000.

Woodrow Wilson International Center for Scholars. *Cold War International History Project Bulletins.* Washington, DC.

Secondary Literature

Official Histories

Appelman, Roy E. *South to the Naktong, North to the Yalu.* Washington, DC: US Government Printing Office, 1961.

Futrell, Robert F. *The United States Air Force in Korea*. Washington, DC: Office of the Air Force Historian, 1983.

Hermes, Walter G. *Truce Tent and Fighting Front*. Washington, DC: US Government Printing Office, 1966.

Hogan, David W., Jr., Arnold G. Fish Jr., and Robert K. White Jr., eds. *The Story of the Noncommissioned Officer Corps*. Washington, DC: US Army Center of Military History, 2008.

Korea Institute of Military History. *The Korean War*. 3 vols. Lincoln: University of Nebraska Press, 2000.

Meid, Pat, and James M. Yingling. *US Marine Operations in Korea, 1950–1953*. Vol. 5, *Operations in West Korea*. Washington, DC: US Government Printing Office, 1972.

Miller, John, Owen J. Carroll, and Margaret E. Tackley. *Korea: 1951–1953*. Washington, DC: US Army Center of Military History, 1956.

Mossman, Billy C. *Ebb and Flow*. Washington, DC: US Government Printing Office, 1990.

Myers, Kenneth W. *KMAG's Wartime Experiences, 11 July 1951–27 July 1953*. Camp Zama, Japan: Office of the Military History Officer, 1958. Manuscript copy at the US Army Center for Military History, Fort McNair, Washington, DC.

O'Connell, William R. *Thunderbird: A History of the 45th Infantry Division in Korea*. Tokyo: Toppan Printing, n.d.

Public Information Officer. *Bayonet: The History of the 7th Infantry Division in Korea*. Dai Nippon Printing, 1953.

Sawyer, Robert K. *Military Advisors in Korea: KMAG in Peace and War*. Edited by Walter G. Hermes. Washington, DC: Office of the Chief of Military History, 1962.

Schnabel, James F., and Robert J. Watson. *The Joint Chiefs of Staff and National Policy*. Vol. 3, part 2, *The Korean War*. Washington, DC: Office of Joint History, 1998.

Official Studies

Academy of Military Science. "The Unforgotten Korean War." Beijing: Military History Division of the PLA, 2006. Produced and translated by the US Department of Defense, Office of Net Assessments. Author's copy provided by Dr. Allan R. Millett.

Air Force Historical Division. The Employment of Strategic Bombers in a Tactical Role, 1941–1951. US Air Force Historical Study 88, Maxwell Air Force Base, 1954.

Air Force Historical Division. US Air Force Operations in the Korean Conflict (25 June–1 November 1950), US Air Force Historical Study 71. Maxwell Air Force Base, 1955.

Air Force Historical Division. US Air Force Operations in the Korean Conflict (1 November 1950–10 June 1952), US Air Force Historical Study 72. Maxwell Air Force Base, 1955.

Air Force Historical Division. US Air Force Operations in the Korean Conflict (1 July 1952–27 July 1953), US Air Force Historical Study 127, Maxwell Air Force Base, 1956.

An, Sung-hwan. "Soviet Military Advisory Group Support to the NKPA, 1946–1953."

In *New Research on Korean War History*, vol. 2. Seoul: Republic of Korea Ministry of National Defense Military History Compilation Committee, 2002.

Carter, Gregory A. *Some Historical Notes on Air Interdiction in Korea*. Santa Monica, CA: Rand, 1966.

Marshall, S. L. A. *Battlefield Analysis of Infantry Weapons*. Cornville, AZ: Desert Publications, 1984.

Momyer, William M. *Airpower in Three Wars*. Washington, DC: Office of Air Force History, 1978.

United States Air Force. *USAF Tactical Operations World War II and Korean War with Statistical Tables*. Historical Division Liaison Office, 1962.

Westover, John G., ed. *Combat Support in Korea*. Washington, DC: US Government Printing Office, 1987.

Books

American Institute of Public Opinion. *The Gallup Poll: Public Opinion, 1935–1971*. Vol. 2, *1949–1958*. New York: Random House, 1972.

Atkinson, Rick. *The Day of Battle: The War in Sicily and Italy, 1943–1944*. New York: Henry Holt, 2007.

———. *The Guns at Last Light: The War in Western Europe, 1944–1945*. New York: Henry Holt, 2013.

Berebitsky, William. *A Very Long Weekend: The Army National Guard in Korea, 1950–1953*. Shippensburg, PA: White Mane Publishing, 1996.

Blair, Clay. *The Forgotten War*. New York: Times Books, 1987.

Bloodworth, Dennis. *The Chinese Looking Glass*. New York: Farrar, Straus and Giroux, 1966.

Blumenson, Martin. *Mark Clark*. New York: Congdon and Weed, 1984.

Boose, Donald W. *US Army Forces in the Korean War, 1950–1953*. Oxford: Osprey Publishing, 2005.

Bowers, William T., and John T. Greenwood, eds. *Passing the Test, April–June 1951*. Lexington: University Press of Kentucky, 2011.

Braim, Paul F. *The Will to Win*. Annapolis, MD: Naval Institute Press, 2001.

Bruning, John R. *Crimson Sky: The Air Battle for Korea*. Dulles, VA: Brassy's, 1999.

Cantwell, Gerald T. *Citizen Airman: A History of the Air Force Reserve, 1946–1994*. Dayton, OH: Air Force Museum Foundation, 1997.

Casey, Steven. *Selling the Korean War: Propaganda, Politics, and Public Opinion in the United States, 1950–1953*. New York: Oxford University Press, 2008.

Chen, Jian. *Mao's China and the Cold War*. Chapel Hill: University of North Carolina Press, 2001.

China National Defense University. *Zhongguo renmin zhiyuanjun zhanshi jianbian* [A concise history of the CPVF warfighting]. Beijing: Jiefangjun chubanshe, 1992.

China National Military Museum, ed. *Kangmei yuanchao zhanzheng jishi* [A chronological record of the war to resist the US and Aid Korea]. Beijing: PLA Press, 2008.

Clausewitz, Carl von. *On War*. Edited and translated by Michael Howard and Peter Paret. Princeton, NJ: Princeton University Press, 1976.

Clodfelter, Mark. *The Limits of Airpower*. New York: Free Press, 1989.

Contemporary China Editorial Department. *Xu Xiangqian zhuan* [Biography of Xu Xiangqian]. Beijing: Contemporary China Press, 1991.

Corr, Gerard H. *The Chinese Red Army*. New York: Schocken Books, 1974.

Crane, Conrad C. *American Airpower Strategy in Korea, 1950–1953*. Lawrence: University Press of Kansas, 2000.

Donnelly, William M. *Under Army Orders*. College Station: Texas A&M University Press, 2001.

English, John A. *On Infantry*. New York: Praeger, 1984.

Foot, Rosemary. *A Substitute for Victory: The Politics of Peacemaking at the Korean Armistice Talks*. Ithaca, NY: Cornell University Press, 1990.

Graff, David A., and Robin Higham, eds. *A Military History of China*. Boulder, CO: Westview Press, 2002.

Gibby, Bryan R. *The Will to Win: American Military Advisors to Korea, 1946–1953*. Tuscaloosa: University of Alabama Press, 2012.

Hanson, Thomas E. *Combat Ready? The Eighth US Army on the Eve of the Korean War*. College Station: Texas A&M University Press, 2010.

Hatch, David A., and Robert Louis Benson. *The Korean War: The SIGINT Background*. Center for Cryptologic History, National Security Agency, January 2009. www.nsa.gov/about/cryptologic_heritage/center_crypt_history/publications /koreanwar_sigint_bkg.shtml#13.

Hinshaw, Arned L. *Heartbreak Ridge*. Westport, CT: Praeger, 1989.

Hurley, Alfred F., and Robert C. Ehrhart, eds. *Air Power and Warfare: Proceedings of the Eighth Military History Symposium at the US Air Force Academy*. Washington, DC: Office of Air Force History, 1979.

Jager, Sheila Miyoshi. *Brothers at War: The Unending Conflict in Korea*. New York: W. W. Norton, 2013.

Johnston, William. *A War of Patrols: Canadian Army Operations in Korea*. Vancouver: University of British Columbia Press, 2003.

Kaufman, Burton I. *The Korean War: Challenges in Crisis, Credibility, and Command*. New York: Alfred A. Knopf, 1986.

Knox, Donald, and Alfred Coppel. *The Korean War: Uncertain Victory*. New York: Harcourt Brace Jovanovich, 1988.

Leckie, Robert. *Conflict: The History of the Korean War*. New York: G. P. Putnam's Sons, 1962.

Li, Xiaobing. *China's Battle for Korea: The 1951 Spring Offensive*. Bloomington: Indiana University Press, 2014.

———. *A History of the Modern Chinese Army*. Lexington: University Press of Kentucky, 2007.

Lockerbie, D. Bruce. *A Man under Orders*. New York: Harper and Row, 1979.

Luan, Kechao. *Xue ye huo de jiaoling: Kangmei yuanchao jishi* [The contest: Blood v. fire; The records of resisting America and aiding Korea]. Beijing: China Literature Publishing House, 2008.

Malkasian, Carter. *A History of Modern Wars of Attrition*. Westport, CT: Praeger Publishers, 2002.

Mark, Eduard. *Aerial Interdiction: Air Power and the Land Battle in Three American Wars*. Washington, DC: Center for Air Force History, 1994.

Marshall, S. L. A. *Infantry Operations and Weapons Usage in Korea*. London: Greenhill Books, 1988.

Matray, James I., and Donald W. Boose Jr., eds. *The Ashgate Research Companion to the Korean War*. Burlington, VT: Ashgate Publishing, 2014.

Meyers, Samuel M., and Albert D. Biderman, eds. *Mass Behavior in Battle and Captivity*. Chicago: University of Chicago Press, 1968.

Millett, Allan R. *Their War for Korea*. Dulles, VA: Brassey's, 2002.

———. *The War for Korea, 1950–1951: They Came from the North*. Lawrence: University Press of Kansas, 2010.

Neer, Robert M. *Napalm: An American Biography*. Cambridge, MA: Belknap Press of Harvard University Press, 2013.

Neufeld, Jacob, and George M. Watson, eds. *Coalition Air Warfare in the Korean War, 1950–1953: Proceedings of the Air Force Historical Foundation Symposium*. Washington, DC: US Air Force History and Museum Program, 2005.

Paine, S. C. M. *The Sino-Japanese War of 1894–1895*. Cambridge: Cambridge University Press, 2003.

Poats, Rutherford M. *Decision in Korea*. New York: McBride, 1954.

Rein, Christopher M. *The North African Air Campaign*. Lawrence: University Press of Kansas, 2012.

Robertson, William G. "The Korean War: The United Nations' Response to Heavy Bombardment." In *Tactical Responses to Concentrated Artillery*. CSI Report 13. Fort Leavenworth, KS: Combat Studies Institute, n.d.

Rose, Gideon. *How Wars End*. New York: Simon and Shuster, 2010.

Russell, William. *Stalemate and Standoff: The Bloody Outpost War*. DeLeon, FL: E. O. Painter Printing, 1993.

Ryan, Mark A., David M. Finkelstein, and Michael A. McDevitt, eds. *Chinese Warfighting: The PLA Experience since 1949*. Armonk, NY: M. E. Sharpe, 2003.

Schrader, Charles R. *Communist Logistics in the Korean War*. Westport, CT: Greenwood Press, 1995.

Sobieski, Anthony. *A Hill Called White Horse*. Bloomington, IN: Author House, 2009.

Spiller, Roger J., ed., *S.L.A. Marshall at Leavenworth: Five Lectures at the US Army Command and General Staff College*. Fort Leavenworth, KS: Combined Arms Center, 1980.

Stairs, Denis. *The Diplomacy of Constraint: Canada, the Korean War, and the United States*. Toronto: University of Toronto Press, 1974.

Stewart, James T., ed. *Airpower: The Decisive Force in Korea*. Princeton, NJ: D. Van Nostrand, 1957.

Stokesbury, James L. *A Short History of The Korean War*. New York: William Morrow, 1988.

Stueck, William. *The Korean War: An International History*. Princeton, NJ: Princeton University Press, 1995.

———. *Rethinking the Korean War*. Princeton, NJ: Princeton University Press, 2002.

Taffe, Stephen R. *Marshall and His Generals.* Lawrence: University Press of Kansas, 2011.

Van Fleet, James A. *Rail Transport and the Winning of Wars.* Washington, DC: Association of American Railroads, 1956.

Werrell, Kenneth P. *Archie, Flak, AAA, and SAM: A Short Operational History of Ground-Based Air Defense.* Maxwell Air Force Base, AL: Air University Press, 1988.

Xia, Yafeng. *Negotiating with the Enemy.* Bloomington: Indiana University Press, 2006.

Xu, Yan. *Mao Zedong yu kangmei yuanchao zhanzheng* [Mao Zedong and the war to resist the US and aid Korea], 2nd ed. Beijing: PLA Press, 2006.

Zhang, Shu Guang. *Mao's Military Romanticism.* Lawrence: University Press of Kansas, 1995.

Zhang, Xiaoming. *Red Wings over the Yalu: China, the Soviet Union, and the Air War in Korea.* College Station: Texas A&M University Press, 2002.

Journals, Newspapers, and Periodicals

Aid, Matthew M. "American COMINT in the Korean War (Part II): From the Chinese Intervention to the Armistice." *Intelligence and National Security* 15, no. 1 (Spring 2000): 14–49.

Bruce, Robert B. "Tethered Eagle: Lt. Gen. James A. Van Fleet and the Quest for Military Victory in the Korean War, April–June 1951." *Army History* 82 (Winter 2012): 6–29.

Bullene, E. F. "It's Not New but Napalm Is an All-Purpose Wonder Weapon." *Army Combat Forces Journal* 3, no. 4 (November 1952): 25–28.

Chen, Jian. "China's Changing Aims during the Korean War, 1950–1951." *Journal of American–East Asian Relations* 1, no. 1 (Spring 1992): 8–41.

Cho, Soon Sung. "The Politics of North Korea's Unification Policies, 1950–1965." *World Politics* 19, no. 2 (January 1967): 218–41.

Coleman, Bradley Lynn. "The Colombian Army in Korea, 1950–1954." *Journal of Military History* 69 (October 2005): 1137–77.

Crane, Conrad C. "To Avert Impending Disaster: American Plans to Use Atomic Weapons during the Korean War." *Journal of Strategic Studies* 23, no. 2 (2000): 72–88.

Donnelly, William M. "A Damn Hard Job: James A. Van Fleet and the Combat Effectiveness of U.S. Army Infantry, July 1951–February 1953." *Journal of Military History* 82 (January 2018): 147–79.

———. "'The Best Army That Can Be Put in the Field in the Circumstances': The US Army, July 1951–July 1953." *Journal of Military History* 71 (July 2007): 809–47.

Farrar-Hockley, Anthony. "A Reminiscence of the Chinese People's Volunteers in the Korean War." *China Quarterly* 98 (June 1984): 287–304.

Jordan, Kelly C. "Right for the Wrong Reasons: S. L. A. Marshall and the Ratio of Fire in Korea." *Journal of Military History* 66 (January 2002): 135–62.

Li, Chen. "From Civil War Victor to Cold War Guard." *Journal of Strategic Studies* 38 (2015): 183–214.

Malkasian, Carter. "Toward a Better Understanding of Attrition: The Korean and Vietnam Wars." *Journal of Military History* 68 (July 2004): 911–42.

Martinez, Guadalupe A. "The Colombians' Role in the Battle for Triangle Hill (Hill 598)," *Graybeards* 23, no. 1 (January–February 2009): 30–31.

New York Times

Time

Washington Post

Worthing, Peter. "Continuity and Change: Chinese Nationalist Army Tactics, 1925–1938." *Journal of Military History* 78 (July 2014): 995–1016.

Xu, Yan. "Chinese Forces and Their Casualties in the Korean War: Facts and Statistics." *Chinese Historians* vol. 6, no. 2 (1993): 45–58.

Zhang, Xiaoming, and Zhihua Shen. "Ending the Korean Conflict: The Communist Perspective." *New England Journal of History* 60 (Fall 2003–Spring 2004): 253–79.

Unpublished Materials

Crane, Conrad C. "Measuring Gains on the Battle Field and the Peace Table: Shifting Assessments during the Korean War." Copy furnished to author.

Grahn, James A., and Thomas P. Himes Jr., "Air Power in the Korean War." Air Command and Staff College, 1998.

Knight, Peter G. "MacArthur's Eyes: Reassessing Military Intelligence Operations in the Forgotten War, June 1950–April 1951." PhD diss., Ohio State University, 2006.

Merrill, Frank. "A Study of the Aerial Interdiction of Railways during the Korean War." US Army Command and General Staff College, 1965.

INDEX

Page numbers in italics refer to illustrations.

Ridge, 116; ineffectiveness due to Chinese tunnel complexes, 101; and Old Baldy, 212; and Operation Showdown, 249; technique, 69–70; and White Horse Mountain, 230
Craigie, Maj. Gen. Laurence C., 44

Dally, Capt. Lawrence, 67
demarcation line, issue of. *See* military demarcation line (MDL)
demilitarized zone (DMZ), 44, 240
Deng Hua, CPVF deputy commander, 244, 287; and armistice talks, 38, 44; assessment of autumn counterattack operations, 237–38; assessment of tunnel system in fighting for Osongsan, 264; handling of Operation Showdown battle, 272, 351n91; "Tactical Counterattacks," 225–27, 244
DeShazo, Brig. Gen. Thomas, 113, 115–17, 317n64
Dodd, Brig. Gen. Francis T., 181–84, 186, 333n26, 334n32
Dodds, Lt. Col. William A., 142
Dulles, John Foster, 281

Ecker, Lt. Richard, 244–45
Eighth United States Army Korea (EUSAK) (Eighth Army)
— 1950–1951: advance toward Iron Triangle, 27–30; arrival of artillery battalions, 25–26; and battle for Pusan Perimeter, 15; communications reconnaissance battalions, 305n115; forced to fight for political, tactical, and psychological reasons, 4, 293n15; hand grenade usage, 306n131; January 1, 1951 Time on Target (TOT), xviii; on Main Line of Resistance (MLR), July 1951, 4, 35; move toward Yalu River and collapse under CPVF Second Campaign, 18, 21; Operation Piledriver (May 10-June 7, 1951), 33–35, 43, 67, 85, 245; regain of 38th parallel

and recapture of Seoul, March 1951, 26–27, 32, 41; revival of under Ridgway, 23–27
— summer 1951–spring 1952: decreasing morale during "active defense" situation, 140–41, 165, 275; fatality rate, September–October, 126–27, 320n122; limited-objective operations, 3, 106–7, 113–27, 283; Operation Commando, 120–25; Operation Nomadic, 125–26; "peace at hand" tactical posture, 137–40; Punchbowl, 107–20, 168 (*See also* Bloody Ridge; Heartbreak Ridge). *See also* outpost war (war of posts)
— summer–fall 1952, 201–24; Air Pressure Strategy (APS), 199–203; casualties per week by November 1952, 276; Chink Baldy, 217–20; field artillery, 68–69; movement of MLR closer to Iron Triangle, 225; Old Baldy (Hill 266), 210, 217–23, 343n57 (*See also* Old Baldy (Hill 266)); Operation Counter, 5, 212–15, *213*; Operation Creeper and new outpost line, 215; Operation Showdown, 5, 7, 241, 242–73, 275 (*See also* Operation Showdown, October–November 1952); and Outpost Eerie, 214; and thrusts into Chorwon, 208; weakened by troop rotation and inactivity, 247, 250, 274–75, 304n93; White Horse Mountain, 227–40 (*See also* White Horse Mountain [Hill 395])
Eisenhower, Gen. Dwight D., 177; and Korea problem, 281; visit to Korea following presidential election in November 1952, 179, 276, 280, 354n9, 355n22
Espejo, Sgt. Tony, 285
Everest, Maj. Gen. Frank P., 311n46

Far East Air Forces (FEAF): attacks against KPA logistical targets, 15,